D0408571

After Emily

AFTER EMILY

TWO REMARKABLE WOMEN
AND THE LEGACY OF AMERICA'S
GREATEST POET

JULIE DOBROW

W. W. NORTON & COMPANY

Independent Publishers Since 1923

New York · London

For information about permission to reproduce selections from this book, write to
Permissions, W. W. Norton & Company, Inc., 500 Fifth Avenue, New York, NY 10110

For information about special discounts for bulk purchases, please contact
W. W. Norton Special Sales at specialsales@wwnorton.com or 800-233-4830

Manufacturing by LSC Communications Harrisonburg
Book design by Chris Welch
Production manager: Lauren Abbate

Library of Congress Cataloging-in-Publication Data

Names: Dobrow, Julie, author.
Title: After Emily : two remarkable women and the legacy of
    America's greatest poet / Julie Dobrow.
Description: First edition. | New York : W.W. Norton & Company, [2018] |
    Includes bibliographical references and index.
Identifiers: LCCN 2018016671 | ISBN 9780393249262 (hardcover)
Subjects: LCSH: Dickinson, Emily, 1830–1886—Friends and associates. |
    Todd, Mabel Loomis, 1856–1932. | Bingham, Millicent Todd, 1880–1968.
Classification: LCC PS1541.Z5 D56 2018 | DDC 811/.4 [B] —dc23
LC record available at https://lccn.loc.gov/2018016671

W. W. Norton & Company, Inc., 500 Fifth Avenue, New York, N.Y. 10110
www.wwnorton.com

W. W. Norton & Company Ltd., 15 Carlisle Street, London W1D 3BS

1 2 3 4 5 6 7 8 9 0

For my parents and my grandmother, who first taught me to believe that

"There is no frigate like a book

To take us lands away"

Biography first convinces us of the fleeing of the biographied

EMILY DICKINSON

CONTENTS

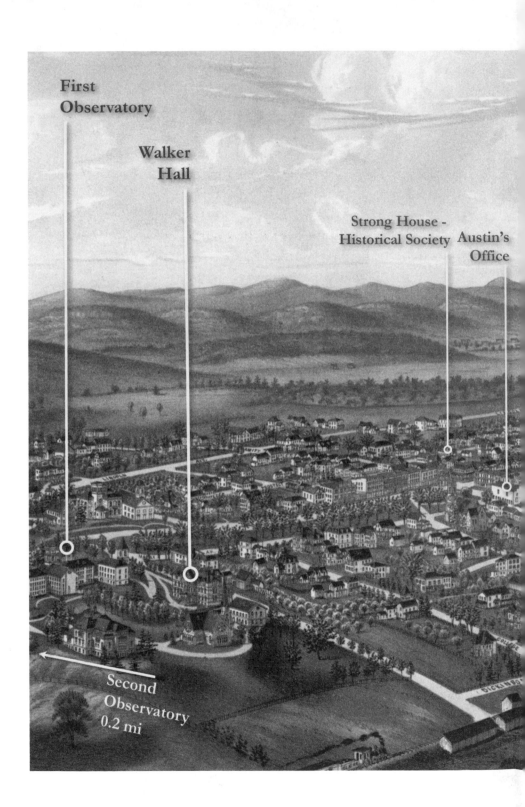

First
Observatory

Walker
Hall

Strong House -
Historical Society

Austin's
Office

Second
Observatory
0.2 mi

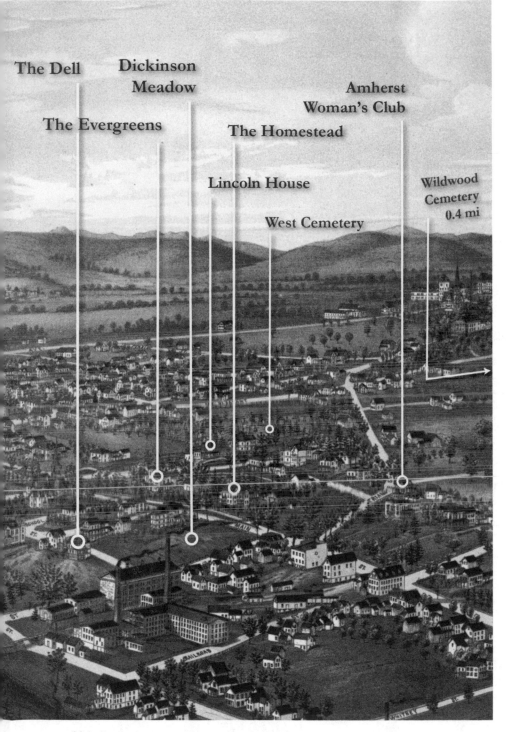

The Dell Dickinson Meadow Amherst Woman's Club

The Evergreens The Homestead

Lincoln House Wildwood Cemetery 0.4 mi

West Cemetery

1886 MAP OF AMHERST WITH ANNOTATIONS

⁓

"The most positively brilliant life"

Emily Dickinson is perhaps the most beloved and the most puzzling of all American poets. Just as she held the world at arm's length during her life, so has she revealed little of her true self since her death in 1886—despite the devotion of countless biographical and literary detectives. As her words once prophesied:

So we must keep apart,
You there, I here,
With just the door ajar
That oceans are,
And prayer,
And that pale sustenance,
Despair![1]

The outlines of the poet's life are fairly well-known. Emily Elizabeth Dickinson, born in 1830 in Amherst, Massachusetts, came into life as the second child of Edward Dickinson and his wife, Emily Norcross. The Dickinson family had deep roots in Amherst, their forebears having been among the original settlers in neighboring Hadley. The Dickinsons were intensively engaged in local civic affairs; Edward even became immersed in state and national politics, elected to terms in the Massachusetts House of Representatives and later in the U.S. Congress as a member of the Whig Party. Affluent (though they had endured a period of economic instability), integrally tied to Amherst College (which Emily's grandfather, Samuel Fowler Dickinson, helped to found) and heavily invested in the cultural capital of the day, the Dickinson family commanded respect and admiration.

Bookended by brother William Austin (known as Austin), older by a year, and sister Lavinia (Vinnie), three years younger, Emily grew up in a household that valued independence, literature and the natural world. Biographer Richard Sewall suggests that while Emily was reared within a family and a community still clenched by their Puritan roots, Emily, herself, broke from its grip. Her "sense of the past . . . could hardly be called vivid," he writes. Emily rejected the orthodoxy of the many religious revivals sweeping the region. She developed a caustic wit that often led her to question authority. And yet, as Sewall points out, young Emily linked a sense of wonder with the Puritan value of intellectual rigor. She embraced the Puritan tenets of hard work, practicality and intensity of purpose. "She was prepared to accept the loneliness of such a course, a loneliness endemic in the New England Puritan way and intensified by her own peculiar defections."[2]

Emily's immediate family bounded and defined her world. Her relationship with her father was complicated: when she was a child, Edward's strict, sometimes authoritarian manner led Emily to fear his reproach, but as a young woman, to rebel from or even to poke fun at his Puritan-derived ways. Yet she also deeply respected her father's dedication to family, community and country, as well as his intellect. As Sewall writes, Emily's nuanced understanding of Edward was perhaps never more poignantly expressed than in a letter to family friend Joseph Bardwell Lyman, in which she explained her father as "the oldest and the oddest sort of a foreigner," someone caught between his work and his family though fully in touch with neither, a man whose life had "passed in a wilderness or on an island."[3]

Her relationship with her mother and siblings was perhaps more clear-cut and less conflicted. By most accounts, Emily Norcross Dickinson's life centered on her home and her gardens, and she had little interest in discussing politics, philosophy or literature of the day. Indeed, her namesake daughter once wrote that her mother "does not care for thought." Both girls were committed to Emily Norcross, nonetheless, caring for her in sickness and never leaving her.

Emily's relationship with Austin was extremely close when the two were young; they shared a consciousness of kind. Many of their early letters show the pair exchanged thoughts about their parents and sister, their community, ideas about philosophy and nature. After Austin married his relationship with Emily changed, but she remained dedicated to enabling his happiness in the ways she could. While no less deep than her relationship with Austin, Emily's relationship with her sister differed in significant ways. Despite the dissimilarities in personality (Vinnie was ebullient, highly social and, as Sewall notes, "never noted for her profundity") and interests (Vinnie was neither a serious student nor a writer), Emily's connection with her sister was constant, loyal and dependent. She once described the bond between them as "indissoluble." Lavinia both revered and respected her older sister and would remain faithfully devoted to her.

Emily received formal education at the Amherst Academy from 1840 to 1847. She then joined the ranks of middle-class nineteenth-century women who went on to college and spent a year studying at the Mount Holyoke Female Seminary when she was seventeen. She left for unknown reasons (thought having to do either with her physical or emotional health), but Emily's informal education continued at home. Emily Dickinson—voracious reader, precise recorder of nature, enthusiastic cultivator of flowers and herbs, stalwart baker of breads and cakes—observed the world around her with unusual acuity and insight.

Though Emily's life centered on her family, she maintained a circle of friends close by and correspondents, afar. Her circle enlarged with trips to Washington, D.C., and Philadelphia in 1855, and to Boston in 1864 and 1865. Emily's friends and acquaintances were both women and men: some of the most meaningful relationships included Susan Huntington Gilbert, who would become Emily's sister-in-law when she married Austin in 1856; the *Springfield Republican* editor and Dickinson family friend Samuel Bowles; the Reverend Charles Wadsworth, with whom Emily corresponded though she met him on only a couple of occasions; and Judge Otis Phillips Lord, her father's closest friend who developed an independent relationship with Emily late in his life. It's not clear whether any of these relationships also involved romantic attachment, though numerous sources indicate that some of Emily's letters, as well as references from family members in their correspondence, strongly suggest the relationship with Judge Lord had a romantic element to it. What is clear is that by the late 1860s, Emily Dickinson's contacts with people other than her immediate family occurred more through the written word than through the spoken one. She began the reclusion that would characterize the rest of her life.

By the end of that decade she barely left the confines of her own home. Neither she nor Lavinia ever married. After both of their parents died, the sisters spent the remainder of their lives living together in their cavernous family home. During the final years of her life the number of people Emily actually saw in person further dwindled, and yet she maintained significant connection to those with whom she did engage. The intensity of emotion expressed in many of Emily's letters, including the so-called Master letters, reveal other sides of a woman whose outwardly simple and reclusive life belied the complexities that lay within. Scholars have long debated whether these three passionate and highly stylized missives to an unnamed recipient addressed only as "dear Master," were written to a particular person and if so, what his or her identity was. It's believed that these letters were written between 1858 and 1861. It is not known whether versions of them were ever sent. Some scholars and literary analysts insist that the intended recipient was, in fact, Judge Lord. But others suggest it was Reverend Charles Wadsworth, while some name Samuel Bowles. Still others believe that "Master" was scientist William Smith Clark, or Dr. George Gould, a minister and Amherst classmate of Austin's. And some posit that Susan Dickinson was actually the intended recipient of the "Master letters."[4]

The mysteries surrounding "Master's" identity and whether he or she ever knew the intensity of Emily's feelings remain unresolved. But these letters, along with the extent of the poet's correspondence with others outside her immediate family, and her avid reading of local and national events in contemporary newspapers and journals as evidenced by references in her letters, demonstrate that it would be incorrect to think of Emily Dickinson as someone completely isolated. The limits to Emily's world were largely self-imposed, the edges ones she defined. She navigated through her choices in life in ways few of us are able to control so pristinely. Even though her life is well documented by biographies and literary analyses, the impetus behind Emily's reclusion remains elusive.

Emily began writing poetry as a teenager. Though she didn't date her poems, many scholars believe that she began writing serious and highly stylized poetry in the late 1850s. Sometime around 1858, she began collecting her poems and sewing them into small packets. In all, she wrote nearly eighteeen hundred poems. It's believed that few people were aware of her prodigious poetic production, much less its genius. Her sister-in-law, Sue, certainly knew of Emily's talent, as Emily shared with her more than two hundred poems. Another person who knew of Emily's poetic gifts was Colonel Thomas Wentworth Higginson. Higginson, whose importance in late nineteenth-century America emanated from his work as a Unitarian minister, his leadership of a regiment composed of freed African American soldiers during the Civil War and his advocacy of abolition and women's rights, was also a leading literary figure. Emily reached out to him in 1862, sending him a letter and several poems. This led to two visits and a correspondence that lasted until the end of her life.

During her lifetime a dozen of Emily's poems appeared in print in various newspapers and collections of poetry. None of the poems were published under her name; in fact, many scholars do not believe that Emily was aware of their publication. It wasn't until after the poet's death at the age of fifty-five that Lavinia discovered the huge cache of poems and became determined to share them all with the world.

These are the outlines of the poet's life. But a biographical entry in one of the many publications recounting great poets or classic American writers, or a Wikipedia post, tell only so much. We have been puzzling over Emily Dickinson—her being, her secrets, her essence—ever since the publication of the initial book of her poems in 1890 first jolted us into awareness. The layering of a life quietly lived, the motivations inspiring a sparkling brilliance, remain mysterious, shadowed, occasionally illuminating from behind her door. We wonder what happened, after Emily.

Who was Emily Dickinson? A shape-shifter confronts us as scholars and acolytes, though we continue to seek answers: How much of the poet's life can we discern from her poetry? Which of the many word and phrasing possibilities she offered did she truly intend in her poems? Why did she partially secede from the world? Did she really wear only white? Can anyone ever truly know Emily Dickinson?

Perhaps two women came closest to understanding the enigmatic poet: Mabel Loomis Todd and her daughter Millicent Todd Bingham, the women arguably most responsible for bringing Emily Dickinson to the world through their editing and publishing of her poems and letters, as well as their scholarly analysis of her work. As of this writing, neither Mabel nor Millicent has before been the subject of a full-length biography, and each of them led fascinating lives. By elucidating Mabel's and Millicent's stories, I hope also to shed new light on how Dickinson's work was presented to the public and the effect their efforts had on Emily's enduring legacies. Understanding their own stories and influences, as well as their complicated mother/daughter relationship, helps push Emily's door ajar a bit farther.

Mabel's and Millicent's considerable work on Emily Dickinson began to shape both the image of the poet and the contours of her poetry as we know it today. Mabel edited and published three volumes of Emily

Dickinson's poetry, and two volumes of her letters, as well as a reissue of the letters at the centennial of the poet's birth. Millicent was responsible for editing and publishing one additional volume of poetry, and wrote three other books about the poet's craft and life. During her lifetime, Mabel worked tirelessly to promote Emily's poetry, which included carefully honed marketing campaigns and innumerable public talks about the poet intended to build intrigue and promote sales. Millicent, as heir to her mother's unfinished Dickinson business and all of the original Dickinson manuscripts in her possession, found herself in the improbable position of navigating between high-powered forces fueled by long-simmering internecine tensions; her tortured decisions ultimately meant that Emily's papers reside in different repositories across the Commonwealth of Massachusetts.

That Emily Dickinson's poetry first came to be published in 1890 in a volume coedited by Mabel Loomis Todd and Thomas Wentworth Higginson is relatively well known; the stories behind it are not. And these stories help to broaden the world of Emily Dickinson by illuminating the lives of others central to her universe. Mabel's work editing and promoting Emily's poetry not only cast her public image but also figured into a complicated web of relationships between members of the Dickinson family and the Todds whose animosities have lasted for generations. And importantly, the narrative of "Emily Dickinson's literary debut" (as Millicent would later refer to it) is inextricably linked to the narratives of Mabel and Millicent, themselves. Mabel's and Millicent's Dickinson work became a driving and significant force for each of them, so central that it irrevocably recast their professional directions, so powerful that it irreversibly altered their personal lives.

By seeing events through the minds of Mabel and Millicent as revealed in their own words, a new context for the life and times of Emily Dickinson emerges. Mabel first learned of Emily Dickinson when she arrived in Amherst in the early 1880s. She later came to know the woman known as "the Amherst myth" through her close associations with the Dickinson family, including her life-altering relationship with Austin, which roiled everyone in both families. We better understand, in light of this, how Emily's sister, Lavinia, came to entrust the publication of her poems to Mabel—then later betrayed this trust and launched a lawsuit that became a much gossiped-about scandal. We see how Millicent was shaped by her mother's affair and larger-than-life persona, and how they ultimately hewed the path not only to Millicent's work on Dickinson but also to her inability to find true love and career clarity. We realize in turn how Millicent's own discontents influenced her readings of Emily. We learn how the personal relationships each woman had affected her outlook on life—and her understanding of Dickinson. We comprehend that other aspects of Mabel's and Millicent's lives—Mabel's passion for music and writing, Millicent's precision and scientific rigor, the world travels each undertook—not only enriched their own lives and made them rare among female peers of their respective eras but also inspired their crafting of Emily Dickinson.

But perhaps most importantly, by more fully articulating these women's inner lives, we can see various ways their worldviews affected their editing and interpretations of Dickinson's work. The resonances Mabel and Millicent felt with Emily—all outsiders, all obsessed with writing about the meaning of nature and human experience, all women pushing up against the boundaries of their times—suggest new insights into why Emily's work was important to them and how they portrayed both the poet and her poems.

Mabel Loomis Todd's revising, ordering and titling of Dickinson's poems and her regularizing of Dickinson's punctuation in her poetry have long been contested among literary scholars and Dickinson fans. The ways in which Mabel altered spellings, gave some poems names, grouped them thematically rather than chronologically and at times even changed words to make lines that might have scanned or rhymed better but which possibly altered their meaning, have been the subject of many an academic debate. But the clever and cutting-edge ways in which Mabel designed and marketed the early volumes of Dickinson's poetry—ensuring that these brilliant works that defied most conventions of nineteenth-century verse actually sold out in their first editions and went through several printings—have almost never been recognized or discussed.

These new perspectives are possible only because of the enormous reservoir of previously unmined and unpublished papers that both Mabel and Millicent left behind. Neither woman ever threw out a single scrap of paper; indeed, one of the major ongoing themes of the final three decades of Millicent's life was her tormented quest to figure out what to do with all the STUFF—the hundreds upon hundreds of boxes of saved letters, diaries, journals, scrapbooks and photographs that had scrupulously recorded the lives of her grandparents, her parents and herself.

Eventually Millicent donated the great majority of these papers to Yale University. I have spent several years slowly making my way through the seven hundred-plus boxes of primary source materials that live at Yale's Sterling Library, as well as uncovering materials that reside in libraries in Amherst, at Harvard, at Brown, and other repositories— even in the attic of an old house. Systematically reading Mabel's and Millicent's diaries and journals (each woman religiously kept both for many decades—Mabel for sixty-six years and Millicent for close to eighty) has given me insights into the lives, hopes and dreams of these women who so obsessively documented their lives. Sometimes I even had the great advantage of reading about the same event in each of their private writings, through each of their eyes and individual perspectives.

In their other extensive papers, I have unearthed some astonishing materials: among them, Millicent's revealing notes from her psychiatric sessions that divulge why she felt compelled to take on her mother's Dickinson work despite her own very considerable ambivalence, and Mabel's lecture notes from the talks she gave on Emily Dickinson that helped craft a certain image of the poet and her work. I had the unique opportunity to read internal documents from Amherst College that shed new light on the battles over where Emily Dickinson's papers would ultimately reside. None of these materials have ever been extensively cited in any published work. And the plethora of additional materials has yielded many other telling discoveries about these fascinating women.

These primary sources illuminate a set of captivating and intricately interconnected lives. This is ultimately a story about sorting through Mabel's and Millicent's papers to tell the full narrative of their lives, uncover their secrets, and see how they created mythologies and defined identities for themselves as well as for Emily Dickinson.

Mabel, who often reflected that hers was "the most positively brilliant life I know of," came to believe that Emily Dickinson, too, lived a life with moments of dazzling vividness. It was a life she felt she understood, a torch whose shine she had seen. And yet for Mabel and for Millicent, the light of Emily's life was still glimpsed only from a distance, shadows that emerged sporadically from her partly opened door.

—

ONE FINE DAY IN MAY (1886)

Mabel Loomis Todd stared unhappily out the window, her eyes filled with tears. The beauty of the May afternoon was heart-stopping. Though the morning had been hazy, by midday the sun had broken through, brokering a quintessential New England spring day. Newly opened lilac and crabapple blossoms filled the air with their scents. "The most deliciously brilliant sunny afternoon,"[1] she noted. Yet how, Mabel wondered, could such beauty exist on this day?

She dressed with care, knowing that soon she would be among the Dickinson family and other neighbors, and that she would see the woman whom she often referred to in her diaries and journals as "my dear friend, Miss Emily Dickinson." Rather than one of the elaborate dresses on which she'd carefully hand-painted orange lilies or purple irises, on this day Mabel chose something simple. She peered at her reflection in the gilt-framed oval mirror, carefully styling her light brown hair into a series of upsweeps secured by an intricate system of combs and pins and scrutinized the small worry lines that marked her otherwise smooth porcelain skin. Five years had passed since she'd met the Dickinsons, whose wealth, many civic and artistic activities and long-standing ties to Amherst College made them one of the most influential families in town. Time had taken its toll. So much had happened, so many complications: the drama with Ned, the Dickinsons' eldest son; the unexpected death of little Gib, youngest of the three Dickinson children. And then there was her relationship with Emily's brother, Austin. The gathering at the Dickinsons' was bound to be fraught with unspoken tensions.

Walking carefully down the stairs in a pair of the high-heeled shoes she insisted upon wearing each day no matter what the occasion, Mabel joined her husband, David Peck Todd. David, too, looked as if he'd aged during their time in Amherst: his blond hair was already thinning on top, though his beard and mustache were thick and bushy. The early promise of his career had yet to be realized, as both he and Mabel were all too aware.

They had arrived in the small Massachusetts college town in 1881, both in their midtwenties, filled with the dreams and determination of a young couple to succeed. They aspired to move beyond the modest circumstances in which each of them had grown up. But here they were, still renting rooms in the Lincoln family's large, white house on Lessey Street. In many ways it hadn't been quite the life that Mabel envisioned when she married the brilliant and dashing astronomer in 1879. She was keenly aware of the compromises.

They left the house and walked without saying a word. And yet their silence was companionable. Mabel was cognizant of her husband's potential and his limitations; David knew all the reasons his wife was feeling so unsettled.

For Mabel the silence was also filled with bittersweet uncertainty and anticipation. They slowly made their way to the end of Lessey Street and turned left onto Main Street, which, despite being the central thoroughfare, still looked very much like a country road, narrow and unpaved. The canopies of trees planted in rows in front of the white picket fences met over the road, shielding Mabel and David from the sunshine as they walked toward the imposing mustard-colored house that was the Dickinson family home. Mabel carried with her a small bouquet of flowers—wildflowers—some of Emily Dickinson's favorites. She had painted a

VIEW OF THE TWO DICKINSON HOMES ON MAIN STREET IN THE LATE NINETEENTH CENTURY.

panel of Indian pipe wildflowers for Emily several years before. "That without suspecting it you should send me the preferred flower of life seems almost supernatural," Emily had written, "and the sweet glee that I felt at meeting it, I could confide to none."[2] Mabel copied the note in its entirety into her journal, noting that it "made me happier than almost any other I have ever received."[3]

As the Todds strode purposively on this short walk they had taken dozens of times, Mabel thought about other notes and gifts she'd received from Emily, their shared love of nature, and above all their love of words. She thought of the many hours that she had happily spent at The Homestead playing the piano and singing for Emily, her sister, Lavinia, and their invalid mother, Emily Norcross Dickinson, before her death four years ago, in 1882. Emily always rewarded Mabel's music with small offerings: a glass of wine on a silver salver, a flower from her conservatory, a piece of cake. And sometimes, there was a poem, "usually impromptu, evidently written on the spot."[4]

Brought up to appreciate great literature, a careful and voracious reader who kept lists of all the books she'd read, Mabel knew that Emily's poetry was unique. She was keenly aware that while Emily's style and punctuation was nothing like that of the well-known poets of the day— Tennyson or John Greenleaf Whittier or William Ellery Channing— her verse was nevertheless strangely evocative and "full of power."[5] More than anything else, Mabel desired to make her own mark on the world as a writer. She had an inkling of Emily's brilliance the very first time she read one of her poems in 1882. The deep affinity Mabel felt for Emily came from her respect for Emily's gift with words, most of all.

But despite these feelings of connection and friendship over the past four years—despite the frequently exchanged notes and gifts, despite living in homes separated by less than half a mile and despite the many connections between their two families—in fact, Mabel and Emily had never actually spoken. During all of the many times that Mabel had come to The Homestead to play music, Emily had listened, hidden from view. She was always sequestered behind the partially opened door of the drawing room or beyond the door of her upstairs bedroom. Once or twice Mabel thought she had caught a fleeting glimpse of the mysterious Emily, flitting down the hall in ethereal white.

This fine day in May might have been the only time that Mabel was truly ever to see Emily. When she did see her that day, it would also be for the last time. For inside The Homestead, surrounded by family, Emily Dickinson lay dead in her white coffin, a little bunch of violets along with one pink cypripedium around her neck.

——

Emily Dickinson's funeral was as sparse and as lovely as one of her poems. She was clothed in one of her trademark white dresses. Her sister, Lavinia, placed two heliotropes in Emily's hand. Colonel Thomas Wentworth Higginson, the noted writer, literary critic and abolitionist who traveled across the state from Cambridge to attend the funeral, read Emily Brontë's poem on immortality, "Last Lines," and the Dickinson family's former pastor, Reverend Jonathan Jenkins, came almost fifty miles from Pittsfield to lead the prayer service. Higginson wrote in his diary, "The country exquisite, day perfect, & an atmosphere of its own, fine & strange about the whole house and grounds . . . E. D.'s face a wondrous restoration of youth—she is 54 . . . & looked 30, not a gray hair or wrinkle, & perfect peace on the beautiful brow."[6]

Mrs. John Jameson, a neighbor of the Dickinsons', later commented, "Nothing could have been lovelier than . . . the day of Miss Emily's funeral—The service was suited to her—unlike any other I ever attended and very beautiful. . . . It was a never to be forgotten burial and seemed singularly fitting to the departed one."[7]

After a brief service in The Homestead, the mourners walked across the fields filled with innocents and buttercups. In a letter to her mother, Mabel described the cortege, including the president of Amherst College, professors and neighbors who served as honorary pallbearers and brought Emily's casket out the rear door of her home. Then, Mabel recorded, the "stout arms of six or eight Irish workmen, all of whom have worked about the place or been servants in the family for years, & all of whom Emily saw & talked with" carried her casket to West Cemetery, and "the friends who chose followed on irregularly through the ferny footpaths to the little cemetery." Mabel told her parents that despite Emily's "patrician" roots, she seemed to notice and respect the working people who surrounded her, just as she appreciated the small scenes of backyard nature so many take for granted. "The funeral—if so ghastly a name could apply to anything so poetical . . . was the most beautiful thing I ever saw,"[8] Mabel wrote.

For Mabel, the beauty of the event paled in comparison to the loss she felt. She solemnly followed a small knot of the bereaved to the cemetery. Emily's older brother, Austin, walked alone in silence, just behind the pallbearers. With his striking auburn hair and tall stature, held erect, cloaked in elegant mourning attire, Austin's austere appearance and aloof demeanor set him apart from other funeral-goers.

When the procession reached the small Dickinson family plot where Emily would join her parents, Mabel and Austin exchanged a knowing glance, an unspoken acknowledgment of shared and private grief. But if they thought that the blaze of light in their eyes when they looked at each other went unnoticed, they were mistaken.

Mrs. Todd "was at Emily's funeral dressed in black, looking haggard as if she had lost a dear friend," puzzled Mrs. John Jameson. "I hear much gossip, and that many people are leaving Mrs. T 'alone.' It does seem a pity her fair name should be so tarnished, and such mean things said."[9]

—

"And in the spring, also rare Emily Dickinson died & went back into a little deeper mystery than that she has always lived in. The sweet spring days have something in all their tender beauty when she was carried through the daisies and buttercups across the summer fields to be in her flowered couch," Mabel later reflected in her journal. "It was a very great sorrow to Austin, but I have lived through greater with him, when little Gib died. He and I are so one that we comfort each other for everything, perfectly."[10]

Mabel knew and felt this because she and Austin Dickinson were in love. They had admitted their feelings to each other in the fall of 1882, and with this admission, their lives changed forever. So did the lives of their respective spouses, David and Susan, along with everyone else in their families. Theirs was the dirty little secret that everyone in Amherst seemed to know. This was the subject of the gossip Mrs. Jameson had heard. This was the reason that some in Amherst would question Mabel's friendship with Austin's sister, Emily. This was why some would whisper about Mabel's attendance at her funeral and the extreme grief she so publicly displayed for a woman she had never met face-to-face.

Mabel and Austin's relationship is certainly what first brought Mabel into Emily's house and to Emily's door. It may also have been why initially Mabel felt a deeper connection to Emily than their actual interactions might have suggested. Mabel's relationship with Austin was undoubtedly the lever that catapulted Mabel, and later her daughter, Millicent Todd Bingham, into becoming the two women who would introduce Emily Dickinson and her poetry to the world.

On May 16, the day after Emily's death, Mabel wrote in her diary, "I went to church. It was very hard for me to get through the service. I wore all black and felt that way."[11] She told her parents, "all spirit in anything is for the time lost to me, for Emily Dickinson died . . . & everything is grey & ashen this morning."[12]

Four days later, phoenixlike, the ashen haze on the morning of Emily's funeral turned to an afternoon blaze of color that is springtime in New England. Mabel was keenly aware of the contrasts.

But what Mabel couldn't have known on that fine day in May was that Emily Dickinson's death would be a defining moment in her own life. Though Mabel did not realize it at the time, Emily's death would soon yield the discovery of a treasure trove of poems no one knew existed. In odd ways, her death would ultimately mean that Mabel and Millicent would each develop a kinship with the poet through her writings that neither of them had known with her during her life. Her death began to stir simmering tensions between the Dickinson and Todd families. And it would heighten both the connections and the strains between Mabel and her daughter in ways that would irreversibly and permanently dominate their lives. Emily Dickinson's death was just the beginning: it launched Mabel and Millicent's efforts for the next three-quarters of a century to produce and cultivate her legacy.

⸺

CHAPTER I

ARRIVING IN AMHERST
(1856–1881)

"All my radiant wishes and beliefs"

To truly understand Mabel Loomis Todd and her daughter, Millicent Todd Bingham—to understand why it was that they would each become entranced by the life and poetry of Emily Dickinson, and to understand why each would wish to take on Emily's work as part of her own life's mission—you have to go back. You have to know what it meant to be a woman born into the Wilder family.

The Wilder family's matrilineal heritage could be traced straight to John and Priscilla Alden. This direct line to the *Mayflower* was something that all the Wilder women told their daughters they should feel proud of: it carried with it an authenticity, a connection to Puritan values and a heritage that gave them both gentility and social standing regardless of economic circumstance. Part of the narrative passed along generationally, the vaunted Alden connection provided a sense of entitlement, a surety that bloodlines meant distinction. For the Wilder women, who often seemed to marry men unable to provide a lifestyle that would match their sense of what it should be, the arts—music, painting and literature—which in the nineteenth century were thought of as acceptable ways for women to demonstrate their position in society, took on special prominence. The

THE "WILDER WOMEN," 1884: FROM LEFT, MARY (MOLLY) ALDEN WILDER LOOMIS, MILLICENT TODD, MARY WALES FOBES WILDER ("GRANDMA WILDER"), MABEL LOOMIS TODD.

Wilder women aspired to excel in artistic expression, or to champion and link themselves with those who did.

Mabel's grandmother, Mary Wales Fobes Jones, married John Wilder II, the Trinitarian minister of Concord, Massachusetts, in the 1830s. This was when Ralph Waldo Emerson, Bronson Alcott and Henry David Thoreau were making Concord the epicenter of American transcendentalism. John and Mary were deeply connected with these artists and philosophers and valued the craft of writing; they were also active in the growing abolition movement based in Concord. John invited abolitionists to speak from his pulpit, and Mary served as first president of the Concord Female Anti-Slavery Society. Of their three children only the middle daughter, Mary, known as Molly, survived to carry the Wilder line forward.

Mary Alden Wilder inherited the high moral and intellectual standards by which to judge everyone and everything else. She lauded her vaunted connection to Concord and its famous residents for her entire life. She believed, and told her daughter and granddaughter, that they came from a procession of thoughtful, intellectual, artistic and refined individuals, who were among the most important thinkers of their respective eras. Embodying this, Molly once wrote Mabel that her husband, Eben Jenks Loomis, told a visitor, "the Wilders were a race of old school scholars and gentlemen."[1] In a letter written to her granddaughter Millicent in 1897, Molly emphasized the Wilder/Concord connections and explained their significance: "The Alcotts and Hawthornes led a pathetic life quite like our own; and they loved each other in a spiritual way, very much as we do—And had to make constant sacrificing to carry out their plans . . . as we do."[2]

It was into this family that connected cultural affinity and artistic excellence with social standing that Mabel was born in 1856. From the start, she was imbued with the Wilder women's ethos. There is a story, perhaps apocryphal, that on a visit back to Concord, Molly and Eben put their infant daughter into the arms of Henry David Thoreau. Thoreau "did not know which end was which! . . . After one agonized moment the bewildered man, with a groan of relief, relinquished me to the giver. Apparently babies bore no large part in Henry's scheme of life."[3] It may be that Henry wanted little to do with the infant Mabel, but Mabel would continue to link her own story with his, and to connect her family to the important writers and thinkers of the transcendentalist movement. She would always seek out those whom she considered to be great artists, ally herself with them, and most of all, aspire to be remembered as a great writer, herself.

Up until the time of her marriage to David, Mabel's life was almost entirely focused on herself. When later in life Mabel wrote a series of memories of her earliest years, she recalled that "my childhood was a rather lonely one, and the trees and sky were to me quite the same as playmates."[4] Mabel was home schooled; she noted that her parents limited her playfellows to those who were the children of Harvard professors or others whose parents were deemed by her own parents to be "refined."

Although she was young and living a fairly sheltered life, Mabel was nonetheless deeply affected by the Civil War, as were almost all Americans of the era. She recalled her uncle John Wilder writing letters home to his mother before his death, and how anxious her grandmother was to receive them. And though she was but nine years old, Mabel retained a strong memory of the time in 1865 when President Lincoln was assassinated: "to all of us in the north, the tragedy pre-eminent. All I can recall of this nationwide sorrow is the somber decorations in Harvard Square when I went there hand in hand with my father."[5]

After the conclusion of the Civil War, Eben set off for Florida, where he had invested his meager savings in a cotton plantation partnership. The enterprise failed within a year, perhaps not surprisingly since it was an odd investment to have made given the labor implications of the war. To make ends meet, Molly sold the Wilder family home and moved herself, her mother and her daughter into a boardinghouse in Cambridge. Eben then moved to Washington, D.C., where he worked as a clerk at the Nautical Almanac Office, bringing in little but at least some income. Molly refused to join him until 1868, wanting him to be more solvent and not wishing to leave her native New England. But when she eventually conceded and the three generations of Wilder women arrived in D.C., Molly found that her family still had to live in boardinghouses to get by.

Mabel's family led a peripatetic existence, moving from one boardinghouse to the next. This was not uncommon: as American cities grew in the nineteenth century, between a third to half of urban residents were either boarders themselves, or took boarders into their homes, according to some contemporary social historians.[6] But for Mabel, however common it was, living in a boardinghouse would become something she associated with her parents' inability to ascend into a solidly middle-class existence.

There was also another consequence of such an upbringing. As an only child living in these conditions, Mabel spent an inordinate amount of time around adults. She passed the winter and spring seasons in Washington, and then went with her mother and grandmother for several months back to New England. Historian Polly Longsworth observes that this effectively put Molly "in authority" half the year and Eben in charge the other half, setting up a loose structure of parental supervision that the strong-willed young Mabel quickly learned to subvert. Molly and Eben couldn't have been more different: she, practical, frugal, obsessively doing what she could to economize all the while touting the importance of her Wilder family heritage; he, a dreamer, an intellectual who "had the manner of a gentleman scholar [who] read and studied and observed acutely throughout his life, but never acquired academic training nor achieved professional standing in any of the several vocations he admired and emulated."[7]

Mabel adored her father. Despite his insolvency and his lack of formal education, in Mabel's eyes Eben was a brilliant, thoughtful man who supported his daughter at every turn and whose nature was in sync with her own. Mabel always thought of him as "a lovely, saintly character" with whom she had an exceptionally close relationship.

But her relationship with her mother was more complex. Though they were in some ways extremely close and she was quite dependent upon her mother, Mabel also grew to believe that Molly's values did not align with her own. For example, although Mabel left behind approximately a thousand letters she'd written to her mother between 1879 and 1910, many of these letters better document what Mabel was *doing* rather than what she was *feeling*. Mabel often complained in her journal that while she loved her mother, Molly fundamentally did not understand her and that it was easier to keep their relationship on an even keel if Mabel didn't reveal her mind and heart.

In a reflection on her childhood written in 1933, Millicent expounded upon the relationship between her mother and grandmother: "Though my mother was her only and adored child, my grandmother never quite understood her. Her gaiety was not the trouble, not even her love of dress. . . . With temperaments strangely similar, a different slant on the Eternal Values forever kept them apart."[8]

Despite the differences in her relationships with her parents, Mabel knew that they were very supportive and protective of her. They tried to provide her with the best education that they could afford, and they were extremely nurturing of her growing love and incipient talent for art, music and writing.

As a young child, Mabel's parents encouraged her aptitude for drawing. Eben hoped his daughter would someday become a well-known artist.[9] Though Mabel often recorded in her journals the praise others heaped on her paintings ("I am painting a great deal and everybody is ecstatic over my pictures"), she also frequently posted blistering critiques on the back of her sketches ("Failure! An attempt at something I cannot at present do, an example of perspective.")[10]

Mabel wrote that as a child "my delight was in picking out not only tunes and melodies played by ear on my mother's sweet old piano, but in dissecting as it were the keyboard, and finding out the connections of the different keys, one to the other, and the relation of their minors to each major." Somehow, even as a child without any conventional instruction, Mabel formed a fairly sophisticated understanding of the principles of harmony and chord formation, an understanding so nuanced it surprised her music theory teachers years later.[11] Recognizing her daughter's inherent musical talents, Molly struggled to find ways to provide formal training. In 1873 she managed to scrape together enough savings to pay for Mabel to have several weeks of piano lessons at the New England Conservatory of Music in Boston.

Because literature was highly valued in the Loomis household, it's little surprise that Mabel began to write essays early in life. An avid reader, Mabel often tried to emulate the styles of many of the authors she most admired. Around the age of fifteen, Mabel began maintaining both diaries and journals, a practice she would follow throughout her life. The diaries tended to record the day-to-day details of her life, while the journals often recorded what her daughter Millicent later referred to as "what lay beneath the surface." Mabel often embellished her diaries and journals with sketches, fragments of music she wrote out on tablature in the margins, and flowers gathered and flattened. Superstitious throughout her life, Mabel also dried and pressed lucky four-leafed clovers into the pages she penned, saving them and placing them on days of particular importance to her.

As a girl Mabel tried her hand at writing stories, extended letters and essays. Her first published piece, an essay entitled "My Summer at Lake Champlain," appeared in a magazine called *Our Young Folks* in 1871. A few years later, Mabel published a number of pieces about time spent in Maine, and later shared these with Louisa May Alcott. "She said they were unusually well written and showed two of the great characteristics of a successful writer, viz: observation and the power of description." This praise, Mabel reported to her parents in 1875, "formed very bright epochs in my already bright life."[12] It also served to heighten her ambition to become a recognized writer. Of all her many and considerable talents, it was Mabel's writing in which she was most invested. Her early determination to be known as a great writer haunted her throughout her life; she always believed her "brilliance" should be focused in her writing and that this would be her historic legacy. No doubt this desire would later draw her to recognize the brilliance of Emily Dickinson's writing and intensified a desire to connect herself to it.

Mabel's polymath interests manifested themselves in her formal schooling. From 1869 to 1874 Mabel attended the Georgetown Female Seminary, studying literature, writing, "mental arithmetic," grammar, history and botany. Mabel delighted in attending school after years of home schooling and did well in all her subjects. Her omnivorous appetite for learning was characterized in a letter she wrote to David a year before their marriage: "Do you suppose I shall be satisfied with myself when I am an extraordinary musician, & a fine artist, & a noble French, German, Latin & Greek student, & an accomplished astronomer, botanist, ornithologist and mythologist, & a thorough mistress of literature in general?"[13]

Not only was young Mabel Loomis bright and artistically gifted, she was also charming. Her parents' moves to many different boardinghouses helped her to make her own mark wherever she went. Writes Longsworth, "for Mabel a public parlor or dining room comprised a small stage which she learned to dominate with her conversational and artistic gifts. . . . Adulation from adults was a sustaining element of her life."[14]

In her early twenties, Mabel was well aware of her charms and their effects on people. In one typical journal entry she wrote, "If I may say so, it assumed an all-embracing genius which took entire possession of me—not a genius for painting nor for music nor for writing alone—but as if I could do any of these things with perfect sense of glorious success if I but gave myself to any one of them . . . this grand sense of power [has] pervaded every act and thought of my life."[15]

Nor did it take long before Mabel realized the effect that she seemed to have on men. Her early journals are peppered with the names of various young men who walked her to and fro, were "madly in love with me" or who flattered her by saying things such as "I could do any and everything." Mabel often recorded such sentiments as "I have had such an exuberance of spirits . . . for so many nights in succession, that I greatly fear a reaction will come, and then the 'blues' will keep me company for a while. But I won't distress myself about that until they really arrive and meantime get so much out of life as possible!"[16] She grew increasingly confident of her charms and her abilities to attract eligible men and seemed to revel in their attentions to her. "I . . . can't see why I should have a power over men, but I do. I'm sure of that."[17]

When Molly and Eben managed to save enough money for Mabel to return to the New England Conservatory for an extended period of study, her time in Boston served to throw open the window of her aspirations more widely. "My life is nothing but beginnings," she wrote to her parents. In clear opposition to the traditions of the day she added, "There is no earthly reason (or heavenly either) why I should give my music up even if I should get married." She concluded defiantly, "No man can make a drudge out of me."[18]

Mabel remained in Boston until 1876, when she moved back to Washington and rejoined her parents. She never completed the coursework necessary to obtain a degree. There doesn't appear to be any precipitating incident or any obvious reason why Mabel decided that she'd learned enough for the moment to leave the conservatory. She'd gotten what she wanted: she had won the battle of wills with her parents and established that she would pursue her own path, regardless of convention, no matter what others might think.

Twenty-year-old Mabel engaged in a torrent of social activities back in Washington. "I am very busy all the time; we have a great many callers," she noted in her journal.[19] Though she had attracted the attention of many men whom she mentioned in her private writings, none of them captured her attention fully until she met David Peck Todd. He seemed to fit all the Wilder woman criteria. Handsome, charming and articulate, David was working with noted astronomer Simon Newcomb. Newcomb served as the director of the same office in which Eben Jenks Loomis worked. David was also living with Newcomb and his family in a home that, as fate would have it, was just across the street from the Loomises' boardinghouse.

MABEL AND DAVID TODD IN THE EARLY 1880S.

When David first paid a call on Mabel in November of 1877, she observed in her journal that he was charming and "very good looking, a blond with magnificent teeth, pleasant manners, and immense, though innocent enough, powers of flirting. Well, so have I."[20] Mabel was drawn to him at once. David was bright (he had gone to Columbia University on a scholarship at age fifteen and then transferred to Amherst College because unlike Columbia, it had both an observatory and a program in astronomy), he was musical (a gifted organist) and he was smooth and sophisticated. At just twenty-two he had already had a fair amount of experience with women. More than Mabel knew.

Throughout the winter and spring of 1878 their relationship deepened during long walks and while attending concerts. Mabel clearly believed that in David, she had met a man who matched her interests, intelligence and passion. "I love him so! Not merely in an intellectual way—but every way you can mention—mentally, spiritually, morally & physically" she wrote. And David wrote to her, "Ah! My darling little woman, how perfectly I love you," observing their harmonious interests in music, nature and astronomy, their paired sense of ambition and their growing physical attraction. Without doubt, David's adulation fed Mabel's image of herself: "Every charm, every fascination which I possess, he notes and loves, and he thinks more of than most girls' ardent admirers in their first stage of attraction," she noted.[21]

Despite David's charisma, he had a darker side. He confided to Mabel "things I wouldn't have known," she wrote. He hinted at sexual indiscretions and told her of times his moods were inexplicably clouded by depressive thoughts. He referred to Mabel, by contrast, as "perpetual blue sky."

When Mabel left for the yearly pilgrimage to New England with her mother and grandmother, she and David exchanged almost a hundred letters that continued to deepen their relationship. It was clearly important to Mabel that David not only understand but also endorse her own ambitions and that their relationship must allow her latitude to pursue her goals. Mabel confided to her journal, "There are capabilities in me, I know, which I've not yet begun to feel, & they shall be developed & filled, & he [David] shall help me. He is so tender & gentle that I shall have full sway—when I wish to be let alone to carry out an idea, I may be, or I can confidently count on his loving help to aid me when needed."[22] Mabel's surety of David's support was consistent with late nineteenth-century practice: as increasing numbers of middle-class women attained higher amounts of education, expectations within marriages about traditional divisions of labor also began to shift.[23] Her attraction for David, his vow that he had "shut the door on his past," along with her belief in his unyielding support and love for her, convinced Mabel that the relationship should go forward. She allowed herself to believe that the sunny side of David would prevail.

The couple seemed headed toward commitment, though Molly and Eben Loomis were not as enthusiastic as one might have expected, especially since they had thwarted at least one of Mabel's previous relationships with a suitor they deemed less appropriate. But David's family did not come from the sort of "significant" background that the Loomises hoped for, even though his forebears included the noted theologian Jonathan Edwards. Though he made more money than Eben, David's financial future was uncertain, having failed the mathematics examination that was a prerequisite for promotion at the U.S. Naval Observatory. And there was both marital strife (his parents had separated) and mental illness in David's close family, both relatively taboo topics in the late nineteenth century. However, Molly and Eben did not give voice to these concerns until years later, and by November of 1878, Mabel and David were formally engaged.

Two months before they married on March 5, 1879, Mabel confided in her diary, "Have only come to a knowledge—this very day—of the wonderful depth & strength of my love for him. I know myself now and what it is to love him . . . and the happiest afternoon of all our love."[24] And for the first time, she used a symbol she'd deploy many times in her private notations, a record for all times that marked when she had sex.

There are many things that become clear about Mabel Loomis Todd from reading her journals and diaries. She held strong opinions about most things that she did not hesitate to articulate. She exuberantly expressed her love of life. She wrote rapturous entries about her passion for nature and her joy at music, art and literature. She was supremely confident of herself and never shy about touting her own abilities. Mabel also wrote of her sensual nature and the delight she took in love's physical expressions, frequently and explicitly.

During the early months of her marriage to David, Mabel's diaries and journals are filled with entries such as "David and I very happy together for an hour this morning" or "the most rapturous & sacred night of all our love." She recorded in her journal that David's "love for me is so passionate, and yet so pure, he tries to make it just what I desire in every respect that I frequently find myself singing aloud, out of the music in my heart which is felt in emotion and dearest utterances by our deepest love for each other."[25] Mabel refined her system of symbols for recording both intercourse and orgasm in her diaries. She also meticulously recorded her monthly "time of sickness."

Neither Mabel nor David wanted to have a child right away. On the anniversary of Millicent's conception years later, David wrote to Mabel that neither of them had wanted children from their union for at least the first five years of their marriage.[26] In letters to her mother during the summer of 1879, Mabel continued to insist that she had never thought about the idea of becoming pregnant. However, neither Mabel nor David had a very good understanding of when ovulation actually occurs in a woman's cycle. Mabel also believed that conception could only occur "at the climax moment of my sursation—that once passed, I believed the womb would close, and no fluid could reach the fruitful point."[27]

Just a few months after they were married, Mabel began to record in her diary that she was "not feeling at all well—something the matter with my stomach." She did not have her usual level of energy. She noted that when it came time for her to be "ill" she was not, but that because there were other things going on in her life at the time, she assumed that there was no problem. Then she started to get headaches, feel anxious and moody. She had a little "brown flow" that quickly stopped, and she went to a doctor to give her something to bring the flow on again—claiming she never suspected that "it could be anything other than a temporary suspension." The doctor told her to take long walks, hot sitz baths and to insert belladonna and morphine vaginally to "induce distension and local looseness."[28] Mabel did this, and yet still did not get her period.

In the weeks that followed, Mabel traveled to upstate New York to spend time with David's family while he was away on an astronomical project in Texas. There, she felt worse, unable to eat, nauseated, highly emotional. "Could this be the thing I never believed would happen just yet?" she pondered. She went to another doctor, who prescribed a preparation of quinine, believing that she was suffering from malaria. Or at least this is what she chose to record; quinine was also a commonly prescribed mode of inducing abortion in the late nineteenth century.

Finally, in August, at the beginning of her second trimester, Mabel wrote in her journal that she felt for the first time "a little protuberance below my stomach . . . quite noticeable . . . it flashed upon me the startling conviction that I had a little child within me. It came like an unchangeable surety."[29] It's a little hard to believe that this conviction could have been "startling" to Mabel, since she had clearly suspected a pregnancy weeks earlier. But Mabel always maintained an ability to convince herself of whatever was the most expedient belief of the moment.

Mabel wrote to tell David of her suspicion, and, much to her great relief, he was delighted. David knew just what to say to console his young wife. He responded, "Oh! How I love the spotless purity and wonderful perfection of your womanhood," and went on to say how he knew that with her broad hips and "all those parts for never having been distorted by tight-lacing," her body was built for having a baby—and more importantly, that he continued to desire her and would, always.[30]

David's letters to Mabel from this period reveal that he understood and sought to assuage her fears. His effusive declarations of love and passion allayed her worries that he would no longer find her attractive. His proclamations that he would provide adequate funding for child care so that Mabel could continue with all of the activities in which she was so deeply involved, or that their baby when born would be cared for by her grandmother and her great-grandmother, addressed Mabel's concerns about having her activities curtailed by motherhood. David promised Mabel that she would "not be bound down by the low drudgery of a purely mother's cares" and that her life would have "all of those pretty, simple, fascinating charms that it has always known before."[31] In other words, David stated, Mabel's life would essentially not change. And she chose to believe this.

After the first trimester, Mabel had an easy and uneventful pregnancy. Mabel was mostly relieved that her pregnancy did not prevent her from doing the things she wanted to do, that she and David could still have sex and that pregnancy did not diminish the things she felt. "My life has been so healthful and natural that this beautiful and natural function can be exercised without any general disturbance of the system or strangeness," she wrote.[32] Mabel was convinced that her child would be a girl, based on her (probably incorrect) idea of when conception had occurred. David was also convinced that they would have a daughter, though his reasoning had to do with listening to fetal heartbeats, which he counted at 146 per minute ("far above the average for a boy," Mabel noted in her journal).[33]

In one diary entry, Mabel wrote, "Odd that for nearly four months I should have kept this little life within me without being conscious of it, or hardly even suspecting it. And my perfectly exuberant health and spirits! Well, it shall be loved and welcomed. . . . I do not show this new development yet, except in a generally stouter appearance, which is very becoming. . . . I was made for a wife—for a mother, truly, no. . . . My life is in my husband—a child or children will be merely incidentals yet know I shall love this little one, yet not with the strength in that sort of love which I put in my wife love."[34]

Several months after Millicent was born on February 5, 1880, Mabel began a new journal she entitled "Millicent's Life," ostensibly focusing on her new daughter. In this journal she wrote about her theories of when conception could occur and what could be done to prevent it. She also chronicled her efforts throughout pregnancy to remain attractive and

unchanged: "I have taken considerable pleasure in being...winsome
& a bit coquettish, and in cultivating those attitudes of mind & heart
which my dear husband best loves."[35]
Mabel reported that although Millicent weighed ten pounds at birth,
she'd had an easy labor and delivery.
Mabel wrote that immediately after
her birth, "Millicent received her
first loving touch from her youthful
grandma."[36]

Very shortly after Millicent's
birth, Mabel was back to her usual
variety of artistic and social endeavors. In fact, so that there would be
no real cessation in the recording
of her daily life, Mabel actually had

MABEL WITH MILLICENT, 1880.

David write a few rudimentary things in her diary for a period of a cou-
ple of weeks right after Millicent's birth until she felt ready to resume.
When she did, at the end of February, Mabel wrote triumphantly, "Here
I come—back again!... Thank God for my perfect restoration."[37]

In the second part of "Millicent's Life," written when the baby was
a few months old, Mabel joyfully recorded some of Millicent's milestones: her measurements, beginning smiles and laughs and babbling,
her first tooth. Mabel wrote a poem to Millicent in which she celebrated
the pleasure that this baby brought to her, and in one verse noted, as
so many parents have done from time immemorial, how quickly time
seems to pass through childhood:

Sweet babyhood is far too fleeting,
For even now I see you meeting
A little girl with happy greeting,
Millicent.[38]

She wrote of the time in October of 1880 when for a month she "left my little sweet child at home with her three ancestors" because she thought that it would be less painful to wean her this way. She observed gleefully that Millicent's first word was "mamma" and her second word was "book." Mabel expressed a hope that Millicent would become involved in the world of literature. "Simply turning the leaves of a book without pictures gives her untold delight. I hope the prophecy this expresses of her early taste, may find a notable and magnificent fulfillment in her after life." Mabel also recorded in detail Millicent's early love of music, how she attended to it from the start, how she began to sing back tunes and even compose them at an early age, commenting on her certainty that Millicent had "a most remarkable gift in music. I predict an exceptional career in that."[39]

Mabel also recorded some of her ambivalence and anxiety about her daughter. She was quick to note the beauty of Millicent's eyes but her concern that the baby did not have a "handsome nose." Mabel wrote often of how fat or how chunky Millicent was. When Millicent was still a toddler, Mabel worried that her daughter was not going to be as outgoing as herself: "It worries me so, that she is so solemn before strangers. I shall be indeed distressed if she is going to be a shy child."[40] On another occasion she wrote, "Although I passionately love Millicent, I do not in general care for children, & I do not want another."[41]

A year of motherhood did little to reconcile Mabel's complicated feelings. At the end of 1880, Mabel penned, "With the snowy departure of 1880—the kind of year which gave me my precious little treasure—I can only hope fervently that all my radiant wishes and beliefs for her very future may be more than realized. May she always be my joy and delight."[42]

As Millicent's first birthday approached, Mabel wrote, "It is most astonishing to me to remember that my sweet Millicent is nearly a year old. A year means so much to her, and it is a mere drop in the bucket to me. A year has changed her from a red, soft, helpless baby into a brilliant little girl, strong, self-reliant, beautiful and fascinating. A year has not changed me, except in additional experiences and more things accomplished.["43] Perhaps without realizing it at the time, Mabel encapsulated what would become some of the dominant themes in her relationship with her daughter: implicit contrasts of personality that each of them would make explicit, a tension between two different outlooks on the world that would widen the gulf between them, and a bond that endured, in spite of it all. Mabel's ambivalence about motherhood marked her relationship with Millicent from the start; its legacy colored it throughout her life and lived beyond her own death. And the complex push/pull in Mabel and Millicent's relationship in many ways set the stage for arguably the most significant professional work in each of their lives, the editing of Emily Dickinson's letters and poetry.

"Amherst! Washington is in the past!["44] twenty-four-year-old Mabel announced in her journal in September of 1881, trying to convince herself that her charmed life would continue. She wasn't at all sure that this was true. And little did she realize that here would begin the story that would forever change her identity and her life's path.

When David received an offer to teach astronomy and become director of the observatory at Amherst College, his alma mater, he was thrilled. Mabel was not. They moved to the small New England college town from the nation's capital, where they'd lived since they married, leaving behind David's career at the U.S. Naval Observatory and the U.S. Nautical Almanac offices, and Mabel's richly active social and cultural life. They also left Millicent in the care of her grandparents.

Though she wished to be supportive of her ambitious husband, Mabel had her own aspirations, and the opportunities for her in Amherst were none too clear. "I can hardly breathe, and I am so sad!" she wrote. She mused that the offer from Amherst "and one other thing have almost broken my heart . . . [can] this crooked matter ever . . . be straightened out? All but this untellable thing is perfect in my life, and I am otherwise so joyful that I must think it a bad dream.["45]

Mabel's fears about Amherst, her concerns about the unnamed "other thing" (which had nothing to do with the move but with David's state of mind and his honesty about sexual indiscretions Mabel thought had ended when she married him), and disquiet about leaving their baby girl, gave her pause. But determined to plow ahead, Mabel believed—as she always would—that somehow her life would work out for the best. It always had.

Though retaining more than a few doubts, Mabel came to Amherst with her characteristic "zest," (the word she used more than any other to characterize herself). An accomplished musician and a skillful painter, Mabel was used to a thriving arts environment and she feared that Amherst would be too small and provincial to offer these opportunities. In Washington, Mabel's social calendar was always filled. Petite, with dark liquid eyes, soft light brown hair that elegantly framed her fine features, the combination of Mabel's beauty, her talents and her vivacious personality had made heads turn her entire life—especially male heads—and she was used to commanding significant attention wherever she went. She wasn't so sure that the same would be true in Amherst.

And at first, Mabel was also second-guessing her decision to leave Millicent behind. "What have I done?" she berated herself in her journal. But just one month later Mabel wrote in her diary: "Do you know, I think Amherst in many respects quite ideal. I always did like a college town, with its air of quiet cultivation, and by living in such a one it is possible to continue two things which are otherwise generally not found together—I mean the possibility of living in the country, amid the luxuriance of nature, and yet of having refined and educated society at the same time."[46]

In this stunningly short time, Mabel seems to have stabilized and actively engaged in Amherst's artistic and social possibilities. Where she had expressed both sadness and disbelief at the prospect of leaving Millicent behind, within a month there were only occasional mentions in her journal or diary of missing her child, of things her mother reported that Millicent had learned to say or do, or of the sheets and pillowcases that Mabel was embroidering for Millicent (all the while complaining how much she hated to sew). The "crooked matter" of David's sexual indiscretion she alluded to in a journal entry shortly before coming to Amherst "straightened itself out very very nicely," as David's attentions now focused on her, alone.

And although the reception by some of the Amherst faculty and their wives had initially been a bit cool, within weeks Mabel was involved in a whirlwind of social activities. Her diary records her attending lectures and concerts and resuming her painting. She began practicing piano and singing and quickly gained a reputation as the finest pianist in Amherst and was a much called-upon vocal soloist. Busy and happy, Mabel once again felt the world was her domain.

The key to Mabel's quick entry into Amherst society was making the acquaintance of Susan and Austin Dickinson, whom she met in late September 1881. In her diary is the brief notation that she was called upon by "Mr. and Mrs. Dickinson. They are charming. He is Treasurer of the College."[47]

Austin was scion of the venerable Dickinson family, a leading and important member of the Amherst community. He had a thriving legal practice and was involved with myriad civic endeavors. His wife, Susan Gilbert Dickinson, widely known as a prominent member of the Amherst arts and literary community, routinely entertained and tried to establish a salon in her home of the most interesting guests. The Dickinsons lived with their three children—Edward ("Ned"), Martha ("Mattie") and Gilbert ("Gib") in a fine, Italianate home on the main street of town that had been built for them by Austin's father, Edward. "The Evergreens" was right next door to Austin's family home, "The Homestead," in which his widowed mother still lived with his two sisters, Emily and Lavinia.

Mabel was instantly drawn to the Dickinsons. She wrote to her mother that Sue was "the most of a real society person here." Sue's dark hair was parted in the middle and worn up off her neck. Though not conventionally beautiful, her strong features certainly rendered her attractive. Mabel was equally impressed by "Squire" Dickinson, whom she found to be "fine (& very remarkable) looking—& very dignified

& strong. . . ."[48] With a full head of auburn-colored hair and intense blue eyes, Austin's high cheekbones and cleft chin gave him a dignified patrician look.

Mabel's letters home and her journals each record how she was instantly enraptured by both Sue and Austin Dickinson. "I told you I admired Mrs. Dickinson at first, but I am thoroughly captivated with her now," she told her parents, adding that upon finding Mabel so good a musician and so congenial a companion, Sue had quickly invited her to many events she was holding at her home.[49] Mabel was instantly—and irrevocably—drawn in.

CHAPTER 2

MEETING AND COURTING THE DICKINSONS (1881–1882)

"Rubicon"

By midfall of 1881, Mabel was well on her way to being accepted as part of Amherst's elite society. Her diaries record an almost continuous procession of social engagements, lectures, dinners, musicales, carriage rides and games of whist. Many of these activities revolved around invitations from Susan Dickinson and her children. Mabel noted in her diary early in October 1881, "I just spent the evening in Mrs. Dickinson's elegant home . . . I like her so much." Just a week later she was writing, "I spent the morning with Mrs. Dickinson and played and sang three hours for her," and then days later, "Mrs. Dickinson came for and brought me to the church for me to sing."[1] It was clear that Sue Dickinson had made a big impression on Mabel and that Mabel had made enough of an impression on Sue that she took the younger woman under her wing. Neither Sue nor Mabel could have predicted what consequences would grow from those early halcyon days, nor how Sue and Austin's imperfect marriage and Mabel's complicated interactions with members of the Dickinson family would end up shaping both her personal and professional life.

AUSTIN AND SUSAN DICKINSON.

Mabel and Sue had much in common. Both were from modest circumstances, each was eager to ascend socially through the nineteenth-century women's sphere of the arts. They had similar predilections for literature and, as it would turn out, similar preferences in male companionship. Each recognized Emily Dickinson's genius, but it was strangely because of the feud that would erupt between the two of them that Dickinson's poetry became Mabel's to edit and interpret.

Sue did not seem inherently destined to become the leading lady of Amherst arts and society. Susan Huntington Gilbert, born in 1830 to a working-class family in Deerfield, Massachusetts, was the youngest of six children. Orphaned by the time she was only eleven years old, she spent the rest of her girlhood rotating among relatives in upstate New York, Michigan and on and off, in Amherst. It was there that she met both Austin Dickinson, whom she would marry in 1856 after a drawn-out six-year courtship, and his sisters, Emily and Lavinia. Sue and Emily formed a particularly close friendship (some scholars have attributed varying levels of intimacy to it)[2] that lasted until the poet's death in 1886. Like most intense friendships, Sue and Emily's had moments of greater and lesser closeness: the Emily Dickinson Museum's website suggests that their relationship was "interrupted by periods of seeming estrangement." The two exchanged hundreds of letters over many years. It is clear that Emily respected Sue's opinion on literature and the two traded books and their thoughts about them. Emily sent more of her poetry in more forms to Sue than to anyone else during her lifetime; indeed, some scholars suggest that knowing the layers of this friendship is critical to a "profound significance for understanding Dickinson's poetic project." Others acknowledge that Emily's loyalties to her brother and her sister-in-law were "intricate and complex," and that Emily's resulting independence created problems between herself and the woman she had referred to as "Sister Sue."[3]

When Sue married Austin, the two considered moving west either to Chicago or Michigan. But Austin's father, Edward, enticed them to stay in Amherst by making Austin a partner in his law firm and by building the couple an elegant home on a plot of land next door to his own. The house, designed by the well-known architect from nearby Northampton, William Fenno Pratt, was "unlike any other house in Amherst," writes Polly Longsworth. "Its flat, projecting roofs, arched windows, wide verandas, and central tower stood out like a foreign accent among the Greek Revival facades and plain, pitched-roof farmhouses of the village."[4]

Ensconced in The Evergreens, as she chose to name the house, and now part of what was arguably Amherst's leading family, Sue sought to cement her position by decorating her home with fine artwork and installing all the latest fashions in interior home architecture and technology. These included a green marble fireplace, a mechanical call bell system and an early centralized heating system from the coal-fired furnace. Innovative home trends continued to be important to Sue: by the mid-1890s she owned one of the first indoor ice chests in town.

THE TWO DICKINSON FAMILY HOUSES: THE HOMESTEAD, HOME OF EMILY AND
LAVINIA DICKINSON (*TOP*), AND THE EVERGREENS, HOME OF AUSTIN AND SUSAN
DICKINSON (*BOTTOM*).

Sue also made her home the center of Amherst social and artistic activity, inviting Amherst College faculty members and luminaries who came to visit the town into her home. Among the guests who graced Sue's dining table were philosopher and lecturer Ralph Waldo Emerson, celebrated children's author Frances Hodgson Burnett, editor Samuel Bowles, writer Harriet Beecher Stowe, celebrity firebrand minister Henry Ward Beecher and writer/poet Helen Hunt Jackson. Years later, in her obituary in the *Springfield Republican*, Sue was heralded as "a woman of rare quality and truly a distinguished citizen of the town, who had made her home for many years one of the notable features of the community. She had undoubtedly entertained at her board more men and women of distinction in the world of literature and affairs than any other householder in the place."[5]

Mabel was awestruck. "I have been entertained with a great deal of quiet elegance here, and I have had a really very brilliant experience," she recorded. "I was 'taken in' at once, and I have been constantly invited, for weeks." She later suggested that Sue "took an immediate fancy to me and to my experiences of life, and she followed me up with invitations until life began to take on a glamorous tint and to glow with colours beyond this existence."[6] To her mother Mabel wrote of her first impressions of Sue: "her presence filled the room with an ineffable grace and elegance," and of her lifestyle, with a lovely home, a "handsome double carriage & pair, and coloured driver" and a "beautiful new upright piano."[7]

It was not only Sue Dickinson, who at age fifty one was actually one year older than Mabel's mother, who befriended Mabel. Her two older children, Ned (age twenty) and Mattie (age fifteen), seemed equally entranced. "Spent the morning with Mattie Dickinson" or "Ned Dickinson came in for a moment" or "went out in the carriage with Mattie," Mabel wrote in her diary. By mid-October through the time she left for Washington in mid-December, Mabel spent at least part of three or four days of each week doing something with some member of the Dickinson family, sometimes more than once a day.

During the fall of 1881, Mabel spent the most time with Sue and with Mattie. But toward the end of the fall she began to spend more time with

Ned. This was something his mother encouraged, believing that the charming Mrs. Todd would exert a positive influence on her shy young son. And although Mabel noticed and admired the elder Mr. Dickinson greatly, in those first few months it was mostly from a distance. While Austin was certainly present at some of the events that took place in his home, he participated little in the increasing social exchanges between Mabel and the rest of his family.

Despite all of her social engagements, as well as numbers of musical commitments to play or sing around town, Mabel maintained a close, loving and supportive relationship with David. In her journals she wrote of how David babied her and took care of her. In tender detail, she described how each night he would undress her before the fire in their room, warm their bed with hot bricks, and then hold her close and kiss her, and how each morning he would warm her clothes and bring her figs and grapes and feed them to her.

However, Mabel also continued to have some concerns about her husband. They were living in rented rooms, with no real prospect for owning their own house. Like her mother and her grandmother before her, Mabel often worried that her husband was not making enough money to support her in the style to which she greatly wanted to become accustomed. Quite soon after their arrival in Amherst, Mabel began to write in her journal with growing urgency about how the college needed to procure a bequest to build and support a new observatory that David could direct. Mabel desperately wished for David to be successful. Perhaps given the contrast between the Dickinsons' lifestyle and her own, she saw that unless David ascended in his profession, their lives would suffer the same kind of constant economizing and scrambling for funds that her parents—and her grandparents—had endured.

Mabel and David returned to visit Washington just ahead of Christmas 1881. Her reunion with Millicent, whom she'd not seen for months, at first merited surprisingly little discussion in her journal or diary. Mabel marginally remarked on how much her daughter had grown: "her teeth are pretty, even and white but she shows them very little," and her concern that Millicent seemed to be a "very cautious child." She wrote glowingly about Millicent's incipient musicality, even transcribing in her journal musical notation of the tunes her daughter made up. "It is certainly remarkable that a little child . . . should have so accurate an idea of pitch and time. Of course I am delighted."[8]

While in Washington, Mabel resumed writing in "Millicent's Life" in mid-January of 1882. She recorded breaking Millicent of her habit of sucking her thumb, giving Millicent baths, counting her new teeth, singing her to sleep. She wrote at length about her daughter's initial efforts to walk, about her first words, about her continuing interest in books and singing, and also about her own artistic and social activities during her time in D.C.

Marriage and motherhood had not at all changed Mabel's joy in her ability to attract men. In one journal entry she wrote of a New Year's Eve party she attended, at which "I have flirted outrageously with every man I have seen—but in a way which David likes to share me, too. I have simply felt as if I could attract any man to any amount."[9]

Historian Peter Gay, who extensively studied "bourgeois sexuality" in Victorian America, argued that although the prevailing twentieth-century view of the period was one of a strict and repressive moral code, in fact nineteenth-century documents demonstrate that the reality of middle-class female sexuality was often far from the stereotype. One of the chapters in Gay's *Education of the Senses* focuses on Mabel Loomis Todd's discussions of sexuality. Gay notes that Mabel's "blessed precision, engaging garrulity and never-flagging interest in herself are not Mabel Todd's only charms for the student of nineteenth-century middle-class culture," but in fact, "the stream of her autobiographical musings and . . . their introspective candor and their fine lucidity set her apart, memorably." Gay speculates that Mabel's open flirtations with many men were in some way sanctioned by the middle-class bourgeois society in which a public standard of repressed sexuality found relief in such "safe" expressions as explicit flirtation by a married woman.[10]

But perhaps another explanation for David's seeming benevolence (if not actual encouragement) of his wife's flirtations is that they provided an opening and an excuse for his own ongoing dalliances. David's premarital promises about putting his past behind him were not borne out. In an unpublished dissertation, historian Sharon Nancy White speculates that Mabel was all too well aware of her young husband's past history of sexual involvements, and indeed, that at least some of these continued even shortly after their marriage. White cites Mabel's complicated system of recording sexual activity in her diaries and journals that seemed to mark whether it was "full intercourse" ("f.m.") coitus interruptus ("o"), sexual activity of another kind ("#") and her own orgasms ("—"), but she also seems to have used these notations to record some of David's sexual activities outside of their relationship. For example, on January 11, 1882, when he had returned to Amherst ahead of Mabel, David wrote her, "you must mark another # (no. 2) for January 10, but I shall do my best that there may be as few as possible." White postulates that some of the alluded-to but not fully discussed "issues" in Mabel's journals and diaries, as well as these symbolic notations, refer to David's past history, masturbation and affairs with women, including some "lower class liaisons." These would have particularly distressed Mabel, given her beliefs about the importance of associating only with those of social standing.[11]

Perhaps for David, Mabel's flirtations with men seemed harmless within the overall context of Victorian society and he quite possibly found Mabel's flirtations to be affirmations of his wife's attractiveness to others. Mabel's easy ability to attract and charm successful men was also something David viewed as potentially advantageous as he began to build a career that would require contacts who could invest large sums to support his acquisitions of expensive astronomical and photographic equipment and his travels around the world to document eclipses. But he would not always find other men's romantic behavior toward his wife as acceptable as he did in the waning days of 1881.

Mabel was back in Amherst by January 26, 1882. Her social activities picked up right where they had left off, and continued to revolve mostly around spending time with members of the Dickinson family. Her diaries depict many days of going over to The Evergreens for piano practice (often for hours at a time), and also for social outings. Mabel wrote, "I have been at Mrs. Dickinson's a great deal since my return, and she admires me extravagantly and praises me to Ned and Mattie as a sort of model for them. She appreciates me completely, and I love and admire her equally. She is a rare woman, and her home is my haven of pleasure in Amherst."[12]

Within the next couple of months two events would prove to be significant turning points in Mabel's relationship with the Dickinson family, and ultimately, in her life.

The first came on February 8, 1882. A brief entry in Mabel's diary read, "went in the afternoon to Mrs. Dickinson's. She read me some strange poems by Emily Dickinson. They are full of power."[13]

It is the first mention of Emily or her poetry in any of Mabel's writings. At the time, fifty-two-year-old Emily Dickinson had already written the majority of her eighteen hundred or so poems; contemporary analysts believe that many of the poems she wrote during this period of her life were less "finished" than earlier ones. Yet despite the prodigious output of poetry, few people were aware of its existence. Mabel became one of the few people outside of Emily's family and some of her friends who knew that Emily wrote poetry. Sue Dickinson was also aware of her sister-in-law's talents. During her lifetime, Emily shared at least 250 of her poems with Sue, and Sue offered Emily her comments and editorial suggestions on some of them. It might have been Sue who submitted a number of Emily's poems to newspapers; between 1850 and 1866, ten of her poems were published anonymously. Three of Emily's poems were published in 1864 in a short-lived publication called *The Drum Beat*, edited by Amherst College alumnus Richard S. Storrs, and another appeared in *The Round Table*, edited by fellow Amherst graduate Charles Sweetser. It is unclear exactly through what networks the poems were contributed and whether Emily knew that they had been published.[14]

Author and poet Helen Hunt Jackson, who grew up in Amherst and was a childhood acquaintance of Emily's, was another in the small circle of people who knew that she was a poet. Helen got Emily to agree to contribute one of her poems to a volume of edited but unattributed poetry entitled *A Masque of Poets* (1876), and subsequently wrote to Emily in a letter that it was wrong for her not to share her great talent with the world. Thomas Niles, who had published the book, attempted to convince Emily to allow him to bring out a collection of her poems but she demurred. And in 1880 some representative of a charity in Amherst, possibly tipped off by Sue Dickinson, tried to persuade Emily to donate some of her poetry to a book whose profits would "aid unfortunate Children"; apparently Emily did submit several poems for consideration but it is not certain whether they were published.[15]

Mabel's instant recognition that Emily's odd poems that defied contemporary poetic conventions were "full of power," would become a key to one of the most significant endeavors and accomplishments of her own life, as well as the basis for the complex relationships that she—and Millicent—would have with the Dickinson family.

Throughout February into March, Mabel's diaries continued to note the many times that she spent at the Dickinsons' home, or went out for moonlit sleigh rides with Ned, or danced with him, or times he came to call on her. She often noted that "we had a jolly time" or "Ned is very lovely to me" or "excellent waltz with Ned." In mid-March, Mabel was invited to a grand event at the home of Amherst College president Julius Seelye, at which she had been asked to play several piano pieces. Mabel wrote that the prospect of playing in front of a significant audience of "the most important people" made her somewhat nervous and that "I wore Ned's Alpha Delta pin."[16] For Mabel, Ned became a companion, or as she sometimes referred to him in her diaries, a "knight errant," who could escort her to social events "whenever David could not attend me."

But for Ned, it appeared to have meant much more. At twenty years old, he led a somewhat sheltered existence. He was not as quick-witted as either of his parents or his siblings. Yet as scholar Barton Levi St. Armand points out, Ned was nonetheless clever in his use of language, and absolutely dedicated to his family, especially his beloved mother, two siblings and his aunt Emily.[17] Though a sophomore at Amherst College, Ned had a kind of "special student" status in which he did not take a full course of study and received no grades.

THOUGHT TO BE NED
DICKINSON, CIRCLED, IN
A PHOTO WITH AMHERST
COLLEGE CLASSMATES, 1884
(DETAIL).

Ned also had epilepsy. The disease's onset came when he was fifteen, and both Sue and Austin sought to shield him from it. In the nineteenth century, epilepsy was not well understood and heavily stigmatized. Those with epilepsy were marginalized and feared. Marriage was discouraged for fear of passing the disease along to offspring. The shame associated with epilepsy often caused people with the malady—or their family members—to hide it. (Emily Dickinson biographer Lyndall Gordon asserts that Emily, herself, also suffered from epilepsy. Though it is true that a tendency for epilepsy can be genetically linked and run in families, Gordon's hypothesis, based both on historical records of doctors' visits, medications and symptoms, as well as interpretations from Emily's poetry, is highly controversial among Dickinson scholars. Unlike her nephew, Ned, whose parents left detailed accounts in their diaries delineating his epileptic seizures, there is no similar record for Emily.)[18]

It was Austin who cared for Ned during his "fits," which tended to occur at night, and his diaries note the many times he would go to his son's room after a terrifying scream alerted his parents to another seizure. In Millicent's readings of Austin's diaries, entrusted to Mabel and saved after his death, she noted Austin's descriptions of Ned's "fits," how they were often so violent that he described them as "an earthquake that shook the house."[19] Sue, too frightened to be helpful, left Austin to deal with their son. This clearly became a source of tension in the marriage. Neither Austin nor Sue ever told Ned about what occurred, though it is difficult to believe that Ned never realized the issue, himself. Austin believed that his son's illness emanated from Sue's several attempts to abort him when she was pregnant—at least, according to what he later told Mabel, who passed this theory along to Millicent, who dutifully recorded it in the notes she took for Mabel.

Perhaps out of guilt or perhaps out of a sense that she needed to over-compensate for her eldest child who wasn't quite on par with his peers, Sue Dickinson did all she could to arrange Ned's social engagements. Part of this included encouraging him to escort Mabel about town. She certainly never imagined that this relationship would be anything other than instructive and convenient for her beloved son.

But Ned fell in love with Mabel. Undeterred by the five-year age difference, unconcerned about the impropriety of it all and indifferent to the fact that she was married and had a young child—to say nothing of the fact that he spent time with and respected David—Ned was soon head over heels. "Dear Madame Valentine," he wrote her on February 14, 1882, "Would you do me the great honor to drive a little while *avec moi* this afternoon at half past four. With hope, Sam Weller. p.s.—Never sign a valentine with your own name!"[20] (The name Ned penned, in fact, belongs to a character from Charles Dickens's *The Pickwick Papers*, who sends a valentine to a woman with whom he fell in love at first sight.)

And Ned's passion for Mabel seemed only to intensify. "My dear Desdemona," he wrote her two months later. "Now you are gone & Amherst has fallen and great was the fall thereof. No longer shall the sweet tones of your voice be heard in the land; the piano keys are still in mute appeal for the hand that wrought such marvelous melody from them. The sprite has sailed away to warmer climes but she has left something which can never part—abundant food for thought, sweet, sweet thought. . . . Give my love and missing to Mr. Todd . . . I can't send it to you for you have it all."[21]

"Indeed, I think it will not hurt Ned . . . that he worships the very ground I walk on," Mabel suggested in her journal. "He is only a boy—only 20—but he is the most graceful host in his own home that I have ever seen. And he is so very manly and careful of his sister, and he is simply devoted to his mother. . . . He looks so helplessly at me and said he never experienced any such feeling before that he does not know how to regard it, and he knows he is unsettled and inattentive to his studies and thinking of me every moment. . . . I could twist him around my little finger, that he would go off and kill somebody if I bade him," she gleefully concluded.[22] For Mabel, Ned's attentions were likely an affirmation not only of her own allure and magnetism but also of her ability to attract a man who was a member of the kind of aristocratic, educated, artistic and wealthy family she most coveted.

"I have nothing but romances to write of myself," she reflected in her journal. "As soon as I put distance between myself and one romance, another one comes to me. It's odd, but I do like it intensely."[23]

—

In April of 1882, as Mabel prepared to depart for two months in Washington to see Millicent and study painting, she reflected on her relationship with Ned in her journal entries, revealing the depth of Ned's feelings for her and acknowledging that they might create problems. "What is there in me which attracts men to me, young and old? I am deeply grateful for the power, and hope I may use it for the good of those who succumb to it; but really do believe in my heart that it will be years before Ned gets entirely over it . . . I think it is well that I am soon going away. But I am really very fond of him and I shall miss him very much and he does not begin to realize how much he will miss me."[24]

Once back in Washington, Mabel alternated between continuing to revel in her power over Ned and finding it troubling. She noted Ned was so smitten with her that he convinced Sue to delay the date of the gala party for his twenty-first birthday until Mabel returned to Amherst so that he could have the first dance with her. (Surprisingly, Sue appeared to find nothing amiss in this request.) Mabel commented on a letter Ned had written in which he told her that he wore in his buttonhole a pussy willow she had given him for an entire week, until the fluffy white blossoms dried and dropped off. "It would be mean and underhand to write down the tender and loving things he says to me for they are only for me, and no one else ought to hear them," she reflected. "Of course I tell David in general about it, but my darling husband has perfect trust and confidence in me and tells me to act my own pleasure about these things." She added, Ned "is in character a very determined and steadfast person, and I mistake him very much if his feelings will have changed at all toward me by June. . . . Well, time alone can extricate him—if he is to be extricated."[25]

But Mabel clearly was coming to realize that Ned's feelings for her were so intense that it could be inextricable—and problematic. In her journal she continued to insist that the situation had spun out of control more from Ned's feelings than from any particular action or inaction on her part: "What can I do? He had plunged in irrevocably before I suspected it, and every time he sees me gay and brilliant in society, or sweet and tender to his mother, or tired after dancing, or kind to him, or in fact however he sees here, it adds to his love for me, and I cannot help it. . . . Of course I have told him he ought to get over it, but he cannot see that it is wrong, and I certainly shall not open the knowledge of good and evil to him."

And Mabel also began to realize that Ned's feelings for her could affect her relationship with Sue. She added, "His mother does not know it or of it all, of course, and she thinks it such a fine thing for her young son to have a brilliant and accomplished married lady for his friend & likes to have him pay me attention. She worships Ned, and I don't know what she would do, if she knew just how far he appreciates having me for his friend."[26] Indeed, though she had some suspicions, Mabel had no idea of just what Sue's wrath might mean.

During the two months in D.C. Mabel spent with Millicent in the spring of 1882, she was starting to grapple with the realization that she might need to deal with Ned Dickinson differently. But she invested much of her time in pursuit of her ongoing desire to be well-known as an artist of some kind.

In Washington her diaries record the many hours each day she spent practicing piano, the difficulty of some of the new pieces she was learning to play, and on the number of hours she spent painting. She was excited by the opportunity to study with Martin Johnson Heade. After all, Heade (though probably better known today than he was in his own era and considered by some contemporary art historians to be a preeminent member of the Hudson River School of landscape painters) had a reputation for painting extraordinary landscapes that featured the interplay between light and shadow. His paintings of tropical flowers and of hummingbirds, in particular, were quite in vogue in late nineteenth-century America. Mabel knew she had a lot to learn from him. She was thrilled when Heade told her that her painting of an iris "is the very best of everything I have done."[27] She recorded Heade's suggestion that the small details of nature in art were the most revealing; this would also be something Mabel later realized was a key feature of Emily Dickinson's poetry.

Although David's work with Simon Newcomb would keep him in Washington well into the summer, Mabel made plans to return to Amherst. Ned Dickinson was delighted; the time apart seemed only to increase his ardor. "My little girl, your dear little note has settled all my plans for the summer," he wrote Mabel. "But I must confess that the dark thought had occurred to me that you would fly away with the end of the festivities to some seaside resort and bask upon the sand surrounded by the usual crowd of admirers. But it seems that I am really going to have you for the summer. Oh! What a summer it will be for me. I think of the drives we can have by sunshine and shadow and perhaps an occasional one by moonlight." He asked Mabel to bring a riding habit with her so that he could teach her to ride—"Think of me as being the one to teach you with all new things." He concluded, "I am so intoxicated with joy that I have written a very disconnected note . . . you see although out of sight it's not out of mind one moment with me."[28]

As wisteria and lupines bloomed at June's start, Mabel returned to Amherst, along with Millicent and Grandma Wilder. In her diary Mabel recorded that the first thing she did after dinner on her first day back was to bring Millicent over to the Dickinsons'. Mabel was particularly keen to introduce her daughter to Gilbert Dickinson. Gib was seven years old at the time, and hardly a well-matched playmate for two-year-old Millicent. But Mabel remained determined to make a connection between the two children.

Days after her arrival in Amherst, Millicent got sick. A stomach virus combined with being in new surroundings and out of her usual routine made the toddler clingy. She would cry ceaselessly anytime Mabel attempted to leave her. Mabel recorded in her diary each day how she found this "fearfully disheartening and lonesome," forcing her to cancel out of picnics and whist parties to which she had been invited. "I can't so much as go down to a meal without a shriek and five minutes of hard crying," Mabel complained. She quickly wrote to Molly and Eben, begging for help.

Grandma Wilder could not handle the situation. Neither could Mabel. Less than a week after her return, Mabel wrote in her diary: "A perfect day. But Millicent would not leave me for half a minute. I am as blue as an indigo bag. All my happiness is trembling in the balance. And there is utter silence from the home people as to whether they will come & help me."[29] Her parents and David ultimately urged Mabel to engage a nurse to help spell herself and Grandma Wilder.

And as soon as Lizzie, a young nursemaid, came aboard to help, Mabel resumed her activities. Just days after she'd written so despondently of being stuck with the crying Millicent, Mabel recorded: "This is Ned's birthday. The party was very brilliant—I danced continually all night, I sang and played and had a glorious time. Ned looked splendidly and we were all at our best."[30] In the days that followed came the whirlwind of social activities that attended Amherst College's commencement; Mabel was concerned that she'd twisted her ankle and wouldn't be able to dance but "Dr. Cooper came after tea and put on a bandage so I could dance . . . I did not think of my foot at all. It was a very brilliant ball."[31] She went riding with Ned on many occasions in those weeks and reveled in reporting how everyone thought her such a natural equestrian. She seemed to put aside, for the moment, any concerns about Ned's feelings for her, or any guilt over leaving Millicent in the care of a fifteen-year-old nursemaid and an eighty-five-year-old great-grandmother.

In Mabel's rendering of this time a few weeks later in "Millicent's Life" she cast it slightly differently: "I struggled along, & when she was physically well, & more happy, I went for my long deferred visit at the Dickinsons. . . . I see now that it was a mistake to bring her before Commencement, for my mind was constantly pre-occupied, & she did not fall in the new place and ways as much, or as soon as she would if I had not had other things to distract me." These thoughts caused her to muse further: "It is a great & most stupendous question with me—this matter of children. A mother should give herself up to her children, & let nothing come between, and yet even then she cannot be with them every moment. She must sometimes be away, even if she does not go into society, nor do anything frivolous. It is a subject constantly before me, and it seems very weighty. I have not the quality of motherhood sufficiently developed."[32]

Though such moments of introspection are rare among discussions of Mabel's daily life in this time period, they give insight into her growing recognition of herself as an individual with needs, hopes and dreams that perhaps differed from those dictated by society. Such entries also tell us about Mabel's belief that she thought of herself as an unusual woman in late nineteenth-century America, a woman who would not be content to live her life within the conventionally prescribed boundaries of mother or wife.

After the frenzied social calendar surrounding commencement had passed, Amherst settled into the somewhat slower pace of summer. Mabel's almost daily interactions with the Dickinsons began to change. She wrote of Ned, "Of course I am a woman, and I am older than he, and I know more of life than he. I can help somewhat against himself and will try. But that is all I can do. Of course I do care for him—the wonderfully chivalrous devotion he showed me could not fail to affect me. . . . When a young man of his age comes to love any woman with the intensity with which he loves me, it cannot fail to affect his whole life."[33]

At the same time, Mabel's diaries and journals begin to record more time she spent with Austin. She noted the times when "Mr. Dickinson brought me home," or times throughout the summer when Austin attended gatherings such as a party in nearby Shutesbury, or the times she stopped by his law office. As the summer wore on, the mentions of contact with Austin became more frequent. On September 6 she wrote: "I went to the Dickinsons in the evening and sat on the veranda alone with Mr. Dickinson senior about an hour discussing religion, thoughts and so forth. I admire him."[34]

While Austin was indeed beginning to spend more time with Mabel, he was also spending more time with both Mabel and David. Throughout the summer and into the fall of 1882, there were multiple occasions on which both Mabel and David joined members of the Dickinson family for outings, dinners or other events. David, as well as Mabel, began to know and to respect Austin greatly.

Though the entries in Mabel's journals occasionally still contained phrases such as "my darling husband" and chronicled David's comings and goings, increasing numbers of her writings focused on Austin. In one entry in September she wrote: "Everything is so joyous and my circumstances are so pleasant. Dear Mr. Dickinson—Ned's father—is so very fond of me. It was one of the proudest moments of my life when he told me that I had more ideas which are of consequence to him than any other person he ever met. For I most extravagantly admire him. . . . He is almost in every particular my ideal man. He is true—so true—that one look into his blue eyes when I first met him caused me to think involuntarily, 'he could be forever trusted.' I did not really know until lately that he is a very sensitive man, for he has a very strong, almost brusk way with his business relations. But he says he has suffered more than he can ever tell from sensitiveness." This remarkable journal entry not only clearly shows that Mabel was falling in love with Austin, but also shows why. "All his life he has passionately loved all nature. The autumn chirp of crickets thrills him most pressibly, and the misty hills and the first red leaves. The first thing which made me sure he was a true, if silent, poet, was his saying one day up in Sunderland Park that when he died he wanted to be buried where the crickets could constantly chirp around him." Mabel continued that day's entry commenting, "He and I are the fastest friends. To think that out of all the splendid and noble women he has known, he should pick me out—only half his age—as the most truly congenial friend he ever had! There is no one in Amherst, or any where else, to compare with him."[35]

———

In some ways it was surprising that Austin should have found himself on the cusp of a deep connection with Mabel Loomis Todd. William Austin Dickinson, the eldest child of Edward and Emily Norcross Dickinson, was twenty-seven years older than Mabel—and just one year younger than her father, Eben. A graduate of Amherst College and Harvard Law School, Austin maintained a robust legal practice in town and was active in Amherst's civic affairs, serving as town moderator for fourteen years, as a founder of Wildwood Cemetery, and succeeding his father as treasurer of Amherst College in 1873. Austin was passionate about landscape design; as president of the Amherst Village Improvement Society one of his major coups was to get Frederick Law Olmsted to design a new plan for the town common. Millicent once reflected that "shrubs seemed as important as people" to Austin.[36]

Austin's character was in many ways formed both because of and in opposition to his parents. By all accounts his father was an austere man not given to overt displays of love or emotion. Edward's own father, Samuel Fowler Dickinson, had been one of the founders of Amherst College, and his personal financial overinvestment in it plummeted the family fortunes to such an extent that Edward was forced to sell the family home for a time. Determined to rebuild, Edward developed his law practice and became solvent enough to repurchase and remodel The Homestead. He was twice elected to the state legislature, and served as well in the Massachusetts Senate and Governor's Council. As a devoted member of the Whig Party and elected to Congress, he instilled in Austin a sense of civic duty. Edward was responsible for the railway service that in 1853 would connect Amherst with other parts of the state and he served as Amherst College's treasurer for thirty-seven years before Austin took the reins. He imparted to his son the responsibility that came with the name "Dickinson" in the town of Amherst.

When Edward died in 1874, Austin became responsible for the law practice, the finances of Amherst College, the care of his mother and two sisters, as well as his own family and the two family homes. Emily Norcross Dickinson, his mother, was a bright woman whose life was completely circumscribed by the time in which she lived. Emily spent a good part of her adult life suffering from one malady or another. The Dickinson children did not see in their mother a model for anything other than a woman who conformed to prescribed roles, though surely they knew she was capable of more. In fact, some scholars have suggested that her few surviving letters and other records show she possessed a keen intelligence, particularly in the area of sciences, though this rarely found expression in her life.[37] Emily was completely subservient to Edward. She never worked outside the family home, nor did she participate in any of her husband's civic endeavors. Indeed, she appeared to her children to be so dominated by her husband that whatever sense of purpose in life she had vanished once Edward was gone. She had a stroke that paralyzed her almost a year later, leaving daughters Emily and Lavinia largely tasked with her care until her death in 1882.

Austin's marriage was no happier than his parents' union had been. From a careful reading of the written record of their relationship, historian Polly Longsworth concludes that from the start, the relationship had its strains and conflicts. As an orphaned girl, the youngest of her siblings, Sue had to take much responsibility for her own education and livelihood. Longsworth suggests that Sue learned to withhold her true feelings as a defense mechanism, that this grew "out of her need to protect herself against fears of weakness."[38] Sue had a habitual distrust of people other than her own family members. Of necessity she became more independent than many women of her era tended to be, though she found in her marriage to Austin a kind of financial (if not emotional) security that eluded her up until that point. "The pattern of Sue's behavior . . . indicates she made strenuous efforts to erase the past and its humiliations," writes Longsworth.[39] Sue clearly hoped to find a kind of stability in her life with Austin that she never experienced as a child.

Sue's close relationship with Austin's sister Emily, and his father's approval of Sue as a potential match, no doubt encouraged Austin in his courtship. There are some suggestions in Austin's letters that his earlier affections lay with one of Sue's older sisters, Mattie, but he clearly ended up selecting the younger sister, even though Sue did not match his own emotional intensity. Austin later found out that Sue had a morbid fear of childbirth (one of her sisters died shortly after giving birth). This might have prevented her from wishing to have much of an intimate relationship with her husband, something Mabel alluded to in her journal. Austin also realized later in his marriage that Sue was socially ambitious in ways he found distasteful, shallow and vacuous. His own diaries often use phrases such as "Sue and her crowd" or "Sue and her co-spreers." Austin increasingly found the social activities going on in his home to be objectionable disruptions to his life, referring to Sue's parties and those of Mattie and Ned as "riots" that went on too late in the evening; he once referred to The Evergreens as "my wife's tavern."[40]

Austin, Millicent noted years later, "was oppressed by his family's lack of serious interests." He wrote of how Sue, Ned and Mattie were trying to find "something to interest them," how Ned wasn't thoughtful enough about his studies at Amherst College, how he was "sick to death" of his family's pursuit of pleasure and their efforts to amuse themselves in ways he considered superficial. And Mabel once recalled Austin telling her that Ned and Mattie "never were my children," and he feared that even little Gilbert, whom he loved dearly, was becoming more like his mother and siblings: "When he turned up his nose at his small friends Austin said, 'Don't talk like that, Gilbert,' and he replied, 'But that is what mamma says.'"[41]

Mabel was a woman who was bright, vivacious, beautiful and physically affectionate, in sharp contrast to Austin's mother and his wife, and she shared his passions for nature and ideas. He was instantly attracted. He viewed Mabel as intellectually and artistically ambitious; he recognized that Mabel's boundless spirit and aspirations set her apart as a woman who could be independent, even as her growing devotion meant she would also need him.

Mabel found in Austin some of the same qualities—a love for nature and a poetic soul—she so revered in her father. But Austin was highly educated, successful and socially prominent. As she wrote many years after his death in her introduction to the second edition of Emily Dickinson's letters, Austin "was a poet too, only the poetry of his temperament did not flower in verse or rhyme, but in an intense and cultivated knowledge of nature, in a passionate joy in the land-scapes seen from Amherst hill-tops."[42] She began to feel that Austin understood her true nature as no one else ever had and that she, in turn, understood his. They were powerfully and irrevocably pulled into each other's orbits.

As the leaves began to turn and display their brilliant fall colors, Mabel's relationship with Austin also deepened. Meanwhile, Ned openly declared his love for her in mid-September, and she knew that she needed to try to defuse his ardor. But rather than confront this directly with Ned, she chose, instead, to spend more time with his father.

Austin began to bring Mabel about town and out for drives in his fine carriage. (Millicent quipped, years later, "he lived in his buggy as much as modern people live in their automobiles.")[43] His diary from the time made more frequent mention of Mabel's appearances at his home and at events around town.

Austin also began to bring Mabel more frequently to The Home-stead. Mabel was pleased to go there and to play piano, though old Mrs. Dickinson was too ill to come downstairs and Austin's mysterious sister Emily never appeared beyond her door, either. "It was odd to think, as my voice rang out through the big silent house that Miss Emily in her weird white dress was outside in the shadow hearing every word." Mabel wrote several days after Austin first brought her there.[44]

Later Mabel wrote in her journal that Emily "is called in Amherst 'the myth.' She has not been out of her house for fifteen years. One inevitably thinks of Miss Havisham in speaking of her. She writes the strangest poems, and very remarkable ones. She is in many respects a genius. . . . She has frequently sent me flowers & poems, & we have a very pleasant friendship in that way."[45] Though Mabel's writing is often filled with hyperbole, and although some biographers and scholars have suggested that in her later attempts to market Emily's poetry Mabel might have purposively added to what might be called "the legend of Emily Dickinson" by suggesting that she had withdrawn from the world, most sources do, in fact, concur that starting in midlife, Emily lived a life of seclusion within the walls of The Homestead, only occasionally venturing outdoors or next door to The Evergreens.[46]

In early October, Mabel brought with her a painting of Indian pipe wildflowers, and had it dispatched upstairs to Emily. "I had pondered for a long time to send her a painting of something," Mabel wrote in her journal, "but when I came back I looked over my studies and by a sudden inspiration I determined to paint the Indian pipes on a black panel for her." Emily thanked her with a letter about which Mabel wrote, with a rare moment of thoughtful introspection, "It fairly thrilled me—which shows that my susceptibility to magnetic friendships is not entirely confined to men, as I have occasionally thought myself." Though they'd still never met, Mabel suggested, "I may call her my dear friend, Miss Emily Dickinson."[47] Mabel was so thrilled by Emily's letter that she rewrote it in its entirety into her journal:

Dear friend,

That without suspecting it you should send me the preferred flower of life, seems almost supernatural, and the sweet glee that I felt at meeting it, I could confide to none. I still cherish the clutch with which I bore it from the ground when a wandering child, an unearthly booty, and maturity only enhances mystery, never decreases it. To duplicate the vision is almost more amazing, for God's unique capacity is too surprising to surprise. I know not how to thank you—We do not thank the rainbow, although its twoplay is a snare.

To give delight is hallowed—perhaps the toil of angels whose avocations are concealed.

I trust that you are well, and the quaint little girl with the deep eyes, every day more fathomless.

With joy, E. Dickinson[48]

Mabel felt her bond with Emily increase each time Austin brought her to The Homestead. Emily's thanks in the form of a glass of wine or a flower or a poem were signs, Mabel believed, of her growing connection to Austin's sister. Since Austin and Emily had a close relationship, Mabel no doubt believed that Austin would approve of her making a deeper connection to his sister. And clearly this all was taking on increasing importance to her as her relationship with Austin continued to develop and intensify.

On September 11, 1882, Austin came to fetch Mabel to another social gathering at The Evergreens. But before they went into the house, they walked out into the meadow past it. Austin's diary on that date simply lists what he did during the day, with the word "Rubicon" inexplicably written alongside. Mabel's diary from that day also mostly focuses on the weather and what she did during the day. That same word, "Rubicon," appears at the bottom of the page. Mabel would write Austin more than twenty letters about this shared moment.

"And we walked toward the sunset—and leaning on an old fence, began to reach each other a very, very little—It was very peaceful, and very bright—but it was the beginning, unmistakably. . . . You reached out your hand without knowing it, almost . . . and you met another—warm and tender. You clasped it, knowing it was your fate, and it staid with you. It will never be withdrawn."[49]

CHAPTER 3

Soaring Love and Seething Tensions (1883–1894)

"Where is the wrong in preferring sunshine to shadow!"

In the early 1880s, Amherst was still a town dominated by Calvinism, steeped in traditional values derived from a Puritan past. As historian Joseph Conforti suggests, the Puritan emphasis on literacy and on the importance of history, as well as the "sense of moral and intellectual superiority," permeated different regions well into the nineteenth century. Religious revivals "seemed to reanimate the spirit of the Puritans."[1] This legacy of strict morality maintained a foothold in small-town Amherst life, Millicent noted. "In 1850 two centuries of Puritanism still shaped their behavior, their mode of living and their entire outlook."[2]

And it was within this climate that Mabel and Austin began, developed and maintained their relationship. For the first time in her life, Mabel came to know a darkness of the soul spawned by both the real and perceived shaming she received for cultivating a love outside of her marriage. It was a turning point that deepened her insights, making her a woman who could understand and interpret both the light and darkness of Emily Dickinson's poetry, and setting up a toxic dynamic between the two families, the reverberations of which are arguably still felt today.

THE "RUBICON" MOMENT, A DAY OF NOTE INDICATED IN MABEL'S (*LEFT*) AND AUSTIN'S (*RIGHT*) DIARIES.

Shortly after the Rubicon moment, Mabel took a short trip to Washington. In a letter she thanked Austin for "what you did at the Trustee meeting." Stating that she was "very, very grateful," Mabel added, "I must write and thank you myself, although I think Mr. Todd is also writing you today."[3] Austin, it seemed, had used his political sway to help David's career. Though it was customary at the time for a faculty member to remain at the instructor rank for a number of years before moving up the academic totem pole, after just one year at Amherst College, David was promoted to associate professor and given a significant salary increase. Austin's ability to influence David and Mabel's economic well-being was already obvious.

The brief interlude in D.C. was to resettle Grandma Wilder and Millicent back into life with Molly and Eben. As Mabel suggested in her diary entries, their several-month sojourn in Amherst had proven inconvenient for Mabel, and it was clear to the whole family that it might be better for all concerned if Grandma Wilder and Millicent were to return to Washington. In "Millicent's Life," Mabel noted that her daughter was "saying many quaint & brilliant things all the time—I wish I could record even half of them," but she devoted more of her entries to discussing how she tried to prepare Millicent for the eventuality of leaving her behind. When it came time to say good-bye, Mabel wrote that the little girl waved and, "she called out 'Mabel!' in her strong clear voice."[4]

In the weeks after her return to Amherst, Mabel's diaries were filled with entries about her time spent with "dear Mr. Dickinson." In one such typically rapturous entry she wrote, "What a soul-stirring morning this was! . . . Mr. D. and I had a long, long ride in the buggy, to Pelham, thence across to Shutesbury, and to home," and in another, "I went for a drive with dear Mr. Dickinson senior. We did not come back until six o'clock. Among other lovely places we went to visit a little old house that stands high on the Pelham hills. We stopped beside it for ten or fifteen minutes for the wonderful views—the kingdoms of the earth and their glory lay spread out below."[5]

This time must have felt relatively unencumbered for Mabel and Austin. On October 19, 1882, Sue and Mattie departed Amherst to attend the wedding of a relative in Grand Rapids, Michigan, and were gone three weeks. Shortly after that, David departed for San Jose, California, where he'd agreed to be the primary photographer at the Lick Observatory on Mt. Hamilton for the upcoming Transit of Venus, an extremely rare astronomical occurrence that happens only twice each century. This was David's chance to see and photograph the event during his lifetime, and he left Amherst for two months in its pursuit.[6] Mabel and Austin took advantage of their respective spouses' absence and spent as much time together as possible. "It feels very odd and very much like my early girlish days to be all alone so much, with time to write in a journal during the day," Mabel reflected. "I rather enjoy the freedom, and I am going to make the most of it for a while. To be sure, I am not alone very much, for everyone is very kind to me, especially the Dickinsons, and of them especially Mr. Dickinson."[7]

During this time the relationship between Mabel and Austin deepened significantly. "Mr. Dickinson is the most true and satisfying friend I ever had," she mused. "I respect and admire him boundlessly. I wish I could write of it, but it is beyond writing. I say little about it, but it is the rarest and truest friendship I have ever had."[8]

Mabel's claim that what was developing with Austin was "beyond writing" is found throughout their many letters, journal and diary entries. They believed what they felt about each other was unique, so great and so powerful that it could never adequately be captured in words—and yet they generated thousands of words to define, articulate and preserve a record of their love. So it is relatively easy to chart the trajectories of their relationship, even though they made some efforts to disguise and conceal it as their situation became increasingly complicated.

Once Mabel began spending time with Austin, the presence of Ned Dickinson meant little to her: "I really did care for him a great deal, in one way, some time ago, but have not a particle of that romantic interest in him left. . . . I am delighted to see how so entirely he has passed out of my life," she wrote. She went on to discuss how when she "put him out . . . his father and I began to discover that we had a great many things in common and from that began a friendship which is the most true and satisfying I ever had."[9]

In addition to spending time together carriage riding throughout the Pelham hills, Austin and Mabel explored their emerging feelings through a series of written exchanges. Historian Polly Longsworth notes, "Austin and Mabel at first destroyed all tangible evidence of their liaison, burning many, many notes and letters soon after receiving them, until Austin began copying Mabel's precious messages in his own hand before disposing of the originals, and slipped the copies into an outsize envelope that he gave to Lavinia. Across the envelope was scrawled this directive: "Vin—if anything happens to me, Burn this package at once—without opening. Do this as you love me." Mabel, for her part, also copied many passages of his early letters.

However, as the relationship wore on, neither Austin nor Mabel could bear to destroy each other's letters and they each lovingly retained them, so that a considerable written record of more than a thousand letters exchanged over the duration of their relationship exists. Austin kept his letters from Mabel in his law office; when a fire destroyed some of his papers he gave the rest of Mabel's letters back to her to hold. And as Longsworth points out, Austin apparently urged Mabel to preserve their letters in the belief that should he die, they would in some way "protect her."[10] These are probably the only reasons that they still exist.

Among the fragments of early notes that Mabel and Austin recopied were indications of the recognition that their feelings for each other ran deep and permeated their everyday lives. "I am glad beyond expression to see you. I have an accumulation of things in my mind for you," wrote Mabel to Austin. "Just a word my beloved before I harness to work, to tell you that my love is only stronger & richer this morning than ever," Austin responded. "Is this not a royal morning! I recognize you in the beautiful day somehow."

Even at this early point in their relationship, Austin and Mabel were finding ways to justify and rationalize it. "Why should I! and why shouldn't I! Who made & who rules the human heart! Where is the wrong in preferring sunshine to shadow! Does not the unconscious plant lean toward light?" Austin wrote passionately. Mabel responded in kind: "I am not sorry—or otherwise—but it is all very strange. You too may be sure of me, of just what & how I am thinking of you and how infinitely I am trusting you. Through and above every other feeling, is this wonderful restfulness, expressed by nothing so nearly as complete trust. And I love you—I cannot say how much."[11]

Even after the beginning of Mabel's and Austin's admission of love for each other, Mabel continued to be an extremely frequent guest at The Evergreens. For a time, while their budding relationship remained secret, she seemed an erstwhile member of the family. Mabel's diaries from late fall 1882 contain almost daily mentions of horseback rides with Ned, Mattie stopping by her rooms, dinners and musical soirees or going places with some combination of Dickinsons. Eventually, she'd become such a fixture at the Dickinson household that on the rare occasion she was not there, it was noticed. Mattie and Ned reportedly recounted to Mabel, who went on to tell David, "at supper Mr. Dickinson looked around & said 'Where's Mrs. Todd?' & they said I had gone home. 'Well,' said he, 'it's very empty and unnatural without her. I don't like it at all.'"[12] Between the private joy of her mutual discovery with Austin and her more public acceptance at a seemingly endless merry-go-round of social activities at The Evergreens, Mabel's life could not have been more full.

"My life is positively the most brilliant one I know of," Mabel noted in her journal in early December in her characteristically self-congratulatory and overly effusive fashion. "I mean in its continual succession of delightful things, with almost never a second to dim the brightness of my sun. I am a great favorite here in Amherst. I have many callers every day. I have many letters every day. I practice and paint a great deal. . . . Millicent is superbly well and radiantly happy. David has had exceptional success . . . and my admirable, noble, strong, true Mr. Dickinson is entirely devoted to me."[13]

In the early days of December 1882, Mabel and Austin were all but consumed by the ecstasy of a new and profound love. For the moment, their secret was intact. But the notes and letters they exchanged, sometimes handed to each other inside of folded newspapers on the street or written alongside a "cover" letter about some innocuous issue or often revealing a pin mark suggesting Mabel wore them inside her dress until they could be exchanged or read privately, tell a story of increasing pent-up passion.

"Dearer, nearer, sweeter every time," wrote Austin in late 1882. "Those forty minutes last night, the happiest fullest most joyous yet. It seemed to me we touched bottom in that walk and talk so far as words can do it. I have been happier in the hours since than ever before. I do believe you, my darling, and believe you love me as I love you." And Mabel reported to Austin when he went on a brief excursion to Boston that "the town is empty and desolate & cold & dreary to me, & why? I walk the streets apparently as usual, but the spirit & joy of my life are gone. . . . It seems as if I cannot possibly bear it until you come. . . . I want you—I long for you—I need you in every way, at this moment."[14]

Discreet as Mabel and Austin thought they were being, there was at least one person who noted their growing closeness. "Ned got a little jealous because I seemed to prefer his father," wrote Mabel to David. "[He] went to his mother & told her I was an awful coquette, and that I had allowed him [Ned] to fall in love with me, and now I had left him, & was doing the same thing with his father. . . . I suppose Ned told her all sorts of things about me, with embellishments, so she began to watch me a little and I felt it and was very uncomfortable." However, she continued, "I heartily admire Mr. D & had never for a moment tried to flirt with him. He likes me very much, & likes to go out with me & do things for me, & it makes him very angry that such a construction should be put on it. But of course I do not give any cause for watching. My demeanor is perfect. . . . I hope when you come back, & every thing settles into its old routine, that this nonsense will be forgotten."[15]

While Mabel's attempt to throw David off track might have temporarily succeeded, Ned's warning aroused Sue's suspicions. Where she had previously dismissed her husband's attentions to young Mrs. Todd, she now looked at their relationship in a new light. The long carriage rides Austin took no longer seemed innocuous. Quite suddenly, it seemed to Mabel, Sue's attitude toward her shifted. Mabel's notes to Austin began to query him about how the "Home atmosphere" was, and then, more directly, she wrote him that his wife's coldness to her "was dreadful, but I should not have cared so much if I could have thought it accidental, or natural. Of that I am not in the least certain."

Days after that, Mabel began referring to Sue (and later to other members of her family) as "the Powers": "the 'Powers' did not give us [the chance for a sleigh ride] together." Notes replaced rides, and then as they tried to defuse the situation, even the notes became scarcer. "Do you know, I have come to look for your daily note as for the bread of life," wrote Mabel. "I do not know what I should do if it failed me."[16] It seemed that old routines would not be resumed and "this nonsense" would not soon be forgotten.

Mabel returned to Washington to spend Christmas with Millicent, her parents and her grandmother, borrowing money from Austin to get there. Her time in D.C. was filled with her usual flurry of social doings. But any holiday joy was tempered by a feeling of anxiety as Mabel worried about what was going on back in Amherst. Her diary records that she had sent notes to Sue and to Mattie, perhaps in an effort to defuse tensions and normalize relations. She wrote a single lengthy letter to Austin over the course of a week in which she alternately told him of her hesitancy in writing to him and her great desire to communicate her love: "I do not know whether or not I shall dare to send these words to you. One moment I think I will, and the next it seems impossible. You will understand why, I am sure.... The thought of you is joy always. And yet I am very much troubled ... I only know I love you & that any kind of note in your writing is joy. I love you. I *love* you."[17]

Austin was more circumspect in his communications. Though he'd sent her two notes that Mabel received in places she'd stayed along the way, he did not write her at the boardinghouse where the Loomises were living until the end of December. At that point he addressed a very formal note to "My dear Mrs. Todd," in which he told her of his family's comings and goings and concluded with the elliptical line, "Hope you are having the most delightful time and that your health is better, and to be better." In a postscript he gave her Lavinia's address, which she presumably already knew, a clear though coded suggestion that she should send any letters to him care of his sister.[18]

When David notified Mabel about his travel plans for returning from the west coast, it became apparent to her that he might, in fact, arrive in Amherst before she did. She implored him "to be very, very cordial to Mr. D. for he has been as true as steel" and to be "very sweet" to the rest of the Dickinsons—"Ned included"—when he saw them. "Get yourself on a very happy basis with the family by the time I come . . . and keep me informed of your every movement." She reminded David of her love for him. And, she stated, "Mr. D. says there will be no difficulty whatever about your getting five hundred dollars more on your salary next year," and added, lest David forget, "He is poised to do every thing possible for you, in all ways."[19]

David's letter back to Mabel might also have made her keen to protect her incipient relationship with Austin. It contained insinuations that he was "getting on quite well with some of the ladies" he met in California, who were "very agreeable to me." In addition, Mabel no doubt would have felt some dissonance when, in a letter a few days later, David suggested, "You see, I have an idea, darling, that we are going to make our final home out here, and you will not then regret having spent this last season at Amherst."[20] Of course, at that point Mabel was not regretting her decision to have come to Amherst in the least. In fact, she could not wait to return.

As 1882 drew to a close Mabel wrote a longer and more reflective entry in her diary, as had become her custom. Indeed, 1882 had been a banner year, one that she realized would change her life. Although she was clearly concerned about what might await her when she returned to Amherst, Mabel's abounding optimism and sense that she remained the star at the center of her universe prevailed. It was already winter's start but she somehow found one of her seemingly omnipresent four leafed clovers to mark the date. "I am glad this is such a big four-leafed clover on this page. I shall take it over into my new diary and let it there mean more success and happiness than it has ever. I am in a bout of complication these few days." She went on, "But I awoke feeling free & happy and I know everything is going to turn out delightfully. Things always do for me. The day is perfect and promising everything for tomorrow."[21]

⁓

At the beginning of 1883, Mabel was reunited with David—and with Austin. She recorded in her diary that she felt "safe & protected again, & my soul was filled with joy" to see David, for he was "my darling, my beloved." But in the same entry she also noted her delight that Austin came over the evening she returned. Just a couple of days later after she and David had spent an evening at the Dickinsons', Mabel suggested to Austin that she had been extremely distressed at the "horribly chilling . . . cruel atmosphere." Mabel was likely reacting not only to whatever snubbing she felt from Sue but also to the fear that her own social position in Amherst might be jeopardized without the largess of her primary mentor.

The loss of Sue's respect and friendship must have felt a considerable blow. Perhaps even when Mabel first sensed Sue's changed attitude toward her and her altered position in the constellation of the Dickinson household, she also realized that Austin's position would remain unchanged. Mabel told Austin she had "wept the bitterest tears I have shed for years." She went on to say that her feelings for him remained constant. In fact, she insisted, "I am the same to you as ever. Please do not ever lose sight of that." She wrote, "I truly think that my lighthearted and careless exultation in life has gone for always—I am going through a most bitter experience and it has suddenly changed me from what was almost a child's irresponsible joyousness into a woman's somewhat sad and somber outlook on life. . . . I have grown years in the past few weeks and it does seem to me now that I can never look at anything just the same I used to do."[22]

It's clear from her private writings that Mabel felt her entitlement to happiness in life had been deeply compromised by Ned's turncoat actions and Sue's subsequent jealousies. "I am not very happy just at present, I am sorry to say," she recorded at the beginning of February 1883. "I always count time of sadness as so much lost of my life. It is my right to be happy."[23] Mabel never took responsibility for the situation; her diaries never mention the irony of Sue's having introduced Mabel to her home, to her town, to her son and to her husband.

From that point forward, Mabel lived and justified her life invested in two primary relationships. On the one hand, she maintained her marriage with David, continuing to write in her diaries and journals entries such as "David and I spend hours talking with each other. We think of nothing definite and do very little. It is such a joy to be together" and "all the time my dear David and I are very happy and tender and devoted companions. My married life is certainly exceptionally sweet and peaceful and satisfying, and his nature is just the one to soothe and rest me."[24]

Theirs was a seemingly functional relationship. Mabel supported David in his work, assisting him by copying his scientific records, helping him to write reports and articles (indeed, she probably ghostwrote a number of things he bylined), and accompanying him on many astronomical expeditions around the world, across a period of many years. Mabel always hoped that he would enjoy more success than he ever did. They clearly maintained some kind of sexual relationship as documented by the symbols in Mabel's diaries, and on at least one occasion—after the emotional relationship with Austin had begun but before any sexual relationship had commenced—had a pregnancy scare: "It wasn't a little child, after all. And I am glad, for I would rather do that important work intentionally. I am light-hearted and happy," Mabel concluded.[25] And for Mabel, David provided stability and an ostensibly acceptable public veneer, despite the whispers.

It was clear to Mabel that her relationship with David in no way matched the depth of her love for Austin. "I love my dear David inexpressibly," she wrote in her diary in January of 1883, "but I am not in a whole-souled way cheerful of it."[26] Certainly David's continuing infidelities with any number of women over the years contributed to Mabel's ongoing justification of her own unorthodox relationship with Austin. As she opined in her journal in 1890, "I do not think David is what might be called a monogamous animal. While I know he loves me to the full of his nature he is not at all incapable of falling immensely in love with someone else and having a very piquant time of it. . . . But I am the one woman for all time for Austin, I, just myself because it is I. There is something unspeakably solemn in the giving up of a man's soul like that."[27]

Elsewhere Mabel drew a distinction between her behavior and David's: "I have discovered that I can be loyal. I can live for an ideal. If I were to be separated from him [Austin] for ten years I should still be the same as the day we met that I am now. I should know that no distance nor time could make me other than his whole life to him, and I am his equal in loyalty. I can never flirt. I can never have any little affairs on hand. My life is holy since he came into it."[28] For Mabel, loyalty had more to do with her relationship with Austin than her relationship with David. And her relationship with Austin was noble and enduring, whereas David's many flings were often with women whom Mabel considered to be unworthy and transient. But they had an understanding about each other's other relationships, and it worked. Or at least it seemed to at the time.

In a journal entry from 1885, Mabel tried to explain her different feelings for these two men in her life. "David is to me just as dear as he ever was. I have not changed toward him one particle, & he knows it. But if a part of my nature, of which I had not heretofore suspected the existence, has grown & expanded into proportions to fit the universe, whose fault is it if I find a nature to respond to every bit of that great new growth? . . . Austin has descended to the deepest depths of my soul."[29]

Mabel often referred to Austin as "my master" or "my king." In so doing she did not mean that he was the superior and she the supplicant— rather, she honestly believed Austin's love for her to be "truly noble" and that this, in turn, dignified and elevated her. And in 1889 she acknowledged, "Nothing stirs me from him [Austin], or alters my conviction for one moment that he is my absolute mate for all eternity. My dear David gives me all he has, but Austin's is a kind of love which David does not know. . . . The situation is certainly most exceptional. I understand it, and I appreciate both my dear men. I know what one is, I know what the other is, and two entirely separate sides of my nature go to them."[30]

In addition to the intellectual and spiritual appreciation Mabel had for Austin, she also most clearly appreciated him in a physical way. Her journals contain innumerable mentions of Austin's "clear eyes of heaven's own blue" or his "proud and strong countenance" or his "lips I love to distraction."

"What is the matter that I miss you so? I unutterably long for the sight of your face, for a touch of your soft, soft hands, for anything you might choose to say in your splendid voice," she once wrote to Austin, conveying the powerful physical attraction she felt for him.[31]

In Austin, Mabel knew she had found her true soul mate, someone who did not judge her but revered and worshiped the person she was inside and out. He was the person who most completed her in every way. When Austin wrote her in 1890, "you are a splendid woman—you don't half understand and appreciate your power and your qualities, as compared with other women. It is so native to you to be charming, fascinating—satisfying, you think nothing of it," Mabel responded, "You are right—I do not quite estimate myself sufficiently."[32]

Beyond simply feeding Mabel's sense of self-importance and con-curring with her own opinion about the boundlessness of her potential, Mabel believed that Austin understood her as no one else did—with the possible exception of her father—and that they were able to inspire each other as no one else could. "He calls out always my highest, and meets me exactly at all points of sensitiveness and delicacy and fineness and intensity and strength. He says we get, and will get, all we can together here, but that to eternity he looks for the fullest blossom of what has so wonderfully budded here. He knows, and I know, what Heaven means to us both."[33]

The language that Mabel and Austin often used to describe their love in their journals and in their letters to each other was frequently akin to the religious fervor that had swept the country earlier in the nineteenth century during the Second Great Awakening. In one journal entry from 1884, Mabel offered perhaps the fullest explanation for her love for Austin, how it differed from any other love and why she felt it to be an almost religious experience for her:

But the greatest proof I have ever had that I am different from 99 others, and that my girlish hope that I had something rare in me—was well-founded lies in the great, the tremendous fact that I own the entire love of the rarest man who ever lived. And the thing which makes it certain that nobody ever approached him is not only that he is noble and strong and true in character nor that he is impressive in look and manner (the finest looking man I ever saw), nor that he comes from a staunch old New England family, nor that he is sensitive and tender and lovely, nor that he loves nature exquisitely—nor even all these dear things together. But emphatically that his nature is lofty and spiritual beyond that of any one I ever met, unless it is my blessed father. And he shows me my highest always. . . . But Austin Dickinson has re-awakened my almost dormant longing for God, my latent wish for a nobly spiritual life. . . . My whole soul is stirred, and I can never again be shallow or frivolous. . . . He is heaven-sent. It is beyond words.[34]

Indeed, their love letters to each other over the years used language that furthered this pseudo-religious fervor; they believed that their relationship was destined, and that in its exquisite purity it was above and beyond the bounds of socially accepted morality. Austin wrote to Mabel, "Conventionalism, is for those not strong enough to be laws for themselves, or to conform themselves to the higher law where harmonies meet . . . [we are] part of one existence forevermore."[35]

Mabel and Austin also believed their love superior to the love of anyone else. Austin wrote of this highly idealized state in a letter to Mabel: "Was ever woman to man what you are to me! Was ever man to woman what I am to you! Was ever ideal so completely realized as mine in you and yours in me! . . . Such mutual desire, such mutual gratification! It is no where portrayed. It is ours alone—ours to keep."[36] A quarter of the way through their years together Mabel also captured this sentiment in her journal: "I have read a great many stories, and I have had a good many love letters, and I have heard a good many lovers talk, but I never heard or read or imagined such a wonderful . . . or so divine a love as he has for me. No souls were ever so united, no love story approaches it." She maintained this attitude well after Austin died, once scribbling on an envelope a list of "famous lovers," including Romeo and Juliet, Dante and Beatrice, Antony and Cleopatra, and then penning an essay in which she compared her love for Austin to those great lovers of history: "Once in a while, in a generation perhaps, a human love is born to last into eternity; a love unmoved by vicissitude, strength and by pain, made steadfast by separation, and in which the thrill of newly awakened passion never fades, but becomes the accompanying measurement of a growing and perfect oneness which death itself has no power to dissolve."[37]

Thus commenced a dynamic within which Mabel and Austin's relationship not only survived but thrived. Because of the general reluctance to engage in open discussions about anything sexual, in American Victorian-era marriages "unofficial divorce, and therefore technical bigamy, were not uncommon," writes historian Stephanie Coontz.[38] Though Austin probably felt the desire to leave his marriage, he didn't have to. For Mabel, the situation was different.

Throughout the course of their thirteen years together, Mabel experienced a life of constant pain and marginalization in being the Other Woman. Austin's vaunted position in Amherst shielded him from being an object of overt scorn, but Mabel had no such protection. She lived a life of perpetual hope that she and Austin would someday be able to live life together openly, but perennial frustration that they could not.

———

As winter turned to spring, Mabel wished that Sue's attitude toward her would also begin to thaw. She wrote in her diary that after the initial coldness she had experienced, Mabel felt that she needed to put some distance between herself and Sue so that relations could be stabilized. She spent most of the spring of 1883 in Washington, and then spent the summer months in Hampton, New Hampshire, with her parents and Millicent. During these periods she corresponded with Austin in letters sent care of Lavinia, and during the summer Mabel traveled to Boston to meet him on several occasions. Her letters to Austin reveal her ongoing distress with the situation, along with her hope that things would become more comfortable. "It is true I have suffered terribly," she complained, "and I can hardly bear to think of again placing myself where I may have renewed cause for pain." A couple of months later she said, "I would give anything if I were coming back to an entirely serene environment."[39] In her journal, Mabel recorded both David's and Austin's assurances to her that Sue's anger seemed to be subsiding: "David said that Mrs. D. was lovely again, extended her hand pleasantly to him again, and talked cordially. And Mr. D. says everything is going to be all right for me. He will make it right. I suppose it will be long before things are back on a really trustful, friendly basis. But I am sure if there are no more accidents, that they will get back at last."[40]

Mabel's diaries, however, suggested that while there were some renewed social events at The Evergreens during the time she spent in Amherst in the late spring and fall of 1883, relations had hardly normalized. She resumed giving Mattie piano lessons and she attended some social events at the Dickinsons', almost always in the company of David or Grandma Wilder. But the majority of her diary entries show that Mabel was more often at The Homestead than The Evergreens, where she would sing and play for Lavinia and Emily, who continued to listen from behind a door. This was clearly where many of her assignations with Austin took place. Writes Polly Longworth, "The Dickinson sisters not only were aware of their brother's intimacy with Mabel, they became accessory to it."[41]

The stresses of keeping her love for Austin secret in the small town weighed heavily on Mabel. But the more Austin told her about his marriage to Sue, the more justified she felt in her relationship with him. "Mr. Dickinson has told me a great many things since I last wrote, and he is more absorbed in me than I can write. It seems he and his wife have not been in the least happy together although for the sake of appearances and the children, they have continued to live together. Notwithstanding the utter lack of love between them, the fact that he is so interested in me has stirred her far beyond the power of words to express. And she makes it pretty dreadful for him at home. . . . Mr. Dickinson's life has been barren and I understand him thoroughly."[42]

Mabel continued to blame Sue for how she had "abandoned" Austin. "She has gone her own way all these years, & never tried to keep him, doing all the time things morally certain to do worse than alienate him from her . . . the greatest joy in life lay beside her for years, & she never moved to retain it, even pushed it from her. Now it has left her irrevocably."[43]

Mabel recorded in her journals over the years all of the things that Austin purportedly told her or alleged about Sue: that she did not stimulate him intellectually; that he felt her social aspirations and materialism made her shallow; that her anger was volatile and unpredictable; that she trended toward shrewishness; that her father had been an alcoholic; that her fear of childbearing had caused her to abort and to attempt to abort pregnancies and made her physically distant from him; that Ned's epilepsy was a result of her attempts to abort her pregnancy with him; that she was snobbish and pretentious in ways that were both distressingly obvious and out of alignment given her working-class familial roots.

Mabel's perceptions of Sue's character also clearly influenced Millicent's ideas in later years. In Millicent's 1945 book *Ancestors' Brocades*, she wrote that Sue "assumed an attitude of lofty aloofness scarcely deigning, as she drove about town in her barouche, to acknowledge the greetings of her former schoolmates . . . pretense and pose came to be her most notable characteristics."[44]

Mabel once stated that Austin had told her he felt like he was "going to his execution" upon marrying Sue. Mabel put some of the darkest "revelations" about what she said Austin had told her in an envelope labeled "Austin's statements to me," in which she wrote, among other things, that Sue was responsible for Austin's "entire disappointment in all so-called married life, destruction of various children" and "carving knife thrown at you & other fits of diabolical temper." There were some allusions Mabel made that suggested Sue, like her father, might have had a problem with alcohol. Though she begged Austin to write these things down as a kind of insurance policy for her should anything ever happen to him, he apparently never dared commit such thoughts to paper. Or if he did, they were destroyed. More likely, though, for some reason Austin never thought that this was as important to do as Mabel did. He wrote in early 1884, "Yes, my darling, I did promise you that sometime I would put into your hands the story of my life to use as a shield, if ever, when I am not here to answer for myself any attack should be made upon my love for you, or yours for me, or our relations to each other. And yet is it not better and nobler that I say nothing which involves any other, reflects upon any other! . . . Is it not better to begin with my meeting you and for the first time feeling clear sunshine!"[45]

Mabel also recorded the insinuation that Austin had "begun to feel, as I know, that it does not do for persons of entirely different social grade to marry"—this with regard to an assertion that Sue's father had been a "common farmer" and tavern owner. Despite her own meager economic circumstances, Mabel, of course, believed herself of the same "social grade" as Austin because she had roots going straight back to John and Priscilla Alden.

Mabel also wrote on several occasions that she believed Austin was very disappointed in his two older children, whom he thought of as socially ambitious and as materialistically vacuous as their mother. But Austin's feelings for little Gib were different. This was the child in whom Austin invested all of his hopes and dreams. When eight-year-old Gib contracted typhoid fever in the fall of 1883, Austin was frantic. Mabel recorded in her diary, "I went to see Miss Vinnie. Her brother is almost killed by his anxiety and distress—oh! I pity him so." Gib died the next day. Mabel wrote, "My heart is breaking for [Austin]—oh! That dear man, how he is suffering." Weeks later she reflected, "The Dickinsons have had a great sorrow in the death of little Gilbert, and no one has seen anything of them. Of course I have seen my dear friend Mr. Dickinson often. . . . Mr. Dickinson nearly died too. Gilbert was his idol, and the only thing in his house which truly loved him, or in which he took any pleasure. He said he should wish to die if it were not for me—I am the only gleam of light in his horizon."[46]

Gib's death may have been a watershed moment in Austin's relationships with the two major women in his life. Rather than turn to Sue in their shared moment of grief, he turned to Mabel. And he never turned back.

In December 1883, Mabel and Austin took their relationship to a new level. They consummated their relationship in a rendezvous that

AMUASBTEILN
Dec. 9. 1883.

occurred in The Homestead. The actual date is not entirely clear: noting indications from Mabel's and Austin's diaries that they met at The Homestead, as well as a symbol in Austin's diary, historian Polly Longsworth cites December 13 as the most likely date. Longsworth also states that the date was marked by Mabel and Austin with a neologism: "AMUASBTEILN"—the intertwining of the letters of their names. However, the piece of paper with this neologism held in the archives at Yale is dated December 9. It is possible that the neologism was created as a romantic gesture signaling the couple's intent to become more deeply involved rather than actually marking the date on which they did. Longsworth suggests that this tryst occurred "with the knowledge of David Todd, who was fully aware of the depth of feeling between his wife and Austin, and was not alienated by it."[47]

There is a fair amount of evidence that David not only countenanced his wife's relationship with Austin Dickinson but that he actually enabled it. Starting in the fall of 1883, there were many times when David suggested to Austin that he accompany him into Boston when Mabel was already there, and encouraged Austin to join the Todds in Chicago in 1893 at the World's Fair. David acted as a courier, bringing Austin's letters to Mabel and Mabel's to Austin. And on the evenings when he knew that Austin was with Mabel in the Todds' home, David signaled his return late at night from the observatory by whistling a tune from the opera *Martha*. This was a routine Millicent knew well, but whose significance she claimed did not occur to her until much later in her life.

Certainly David recognized Austin's real and potential role in helping to advance his career and knew that as treasurer of the college, Austin signed his paychecks. But more than that, he seems to have truly respected Austin. David and Austin spent time together when Mabel was away and each wrote admiring things of the other in their respective diaries and letters. The delicate balancing act going on in Mabel and David's marriage of allowing each other enough space for other relationships, continued in earnest.

Starting from the time that Ned Dickinson tipped off his mother and Sue began to monitor Mabel and Austin more closely, the lovers began to use new strategies and new rationalizations for their deepening relationship. David's complicity helped. Historian Polly Longsworth points out that in 1885 when the Todds moved to a rented home on Lessey Street, entries in Austin's diary reveal that he spent much time there, both alone with Mabel and also with Mabel and David, together. He referred to it as "the third house." Longsworth goes so far as to suggest that in Austin's diary from this period of time his apparent symbol for having sex (==) is frequently accompanied by the phrase "with a witness"—however, since Millicent was also living there at the time it's not clear exactly whom Austin meant nor what, if anything, that "witness" had witnessed.[48]

Mabel and Austin had rendezvoused first at The Homestead and then starting in 1887, at Mabel and David's house, The Dell. This house was built on a piece of land that Austin gave them on the other side of what was then known as Dickinson Meadow, with funds that he had fronted them and a design he had suggested—including a back staircase with direct and discreet access to the second floor. It was there, as Millicent recalled in one of her "Reminiscences," that Mabel and Austin spent many long evenings together "by the upstairs fire alone, behind locked doors by the hour."[49] Mabel's diaries from these years are peppered with notations like, "a dear friend at 9:30 for a few minutes" or "I had a call in the afternoon, and again in the evening, so it was a pleasant day." Her diaries continued to be the more public record of her life and meetings with Austin, while her journals expounded in great detail her feelings for Austin and about the ongoing highs and lows of conducting their hidden relationship.

As time went on, Mabel became increasingly bitter about Sue's place as Austin's wife when she believed herself to be Austin's true wife in the context of eternity. Sue did what she could to marginalize Mabel by excluding her from social activities and by asserting her rightful role about town as Mrs. Austin Dickinson in ways Mabel found objectionable. Both Sue and her daughter, Mattie, found innumerable ways to snub Mabel or to make life generally unpleasant for her. Mabel's journals are filled with comments comparing her own relationship with Austin to his relationship with Sue, who "was not made to understand him."[50] Increasingly both Austin and Mabel disparaged Sue, referring to her as "the great big black Mogul" (referencing her long period of dressing in mourning for Gib) or as the "incubus."

And of course, they believed their love was beyond the bounds of any conventional social mores. Mabel wrote to Austin, "Your love has completely mastered me . . . I recognize your supremacy and with it the most thrilling gratitude to God for this greatest gift. I spiritually lay my hand in yours with a peace I never knew before. I know God loves us—I know he has an infinite tenderness for us, and for the rare love he has made."[51]

Mabel came to believe that a love given by God trumped any law created by mere mortals to govern relationships. Writing of a biography of George Eliot she'd read in 1885, Mabel opined, "What possible spiritual difference could it have made whether or not a lawyer had spoken the necessary words of release . . . the law of God to me is so far higher than calfskin and parchment, and God and men do not always think identically. Far from it. When two noble natures receive each other . . . they [rise above] the confusion and mist which men throw over life, and know clearly that each is the fitting and perfect complement to the other . . . this is undoubtedly revolutionary doctrine, but so was the first thought about abolishing slavery."[52]

This notion was tested mightily when Mabel's parents came to visit in the fall of 1884 and first began to suspect the true nature of their daughter's relationship with Austin Dickinson. Mabel was so upset by her parents' insinuations that her life and reputation would be ruined should she continue to go on private carriage rides with a married man—even a man of Austin's impeccable credentials and reputation—that she couldn't bring herself to expound too much about it in her journal, including mention of a few "terrible talks" with her mother. But she also let Austin know: "People in general are fools—there is no denying that. . . . If people only realized that the more they try to keep lovers apart, the more they brood upon and think of each other. . . . I am most weak-mindedly near to tears all the time. . . . But I can remember—and I know what is coming, and so I can bear. And only you can know the sorrow; my own!" Austin replied, "We are not to be frightened—we are not of that cheap stuff. We are not afraid of the truth. . . . And is love anything to be ashamed of? Our life together is as white and unspotted as the fresh driven snow. This we know—whatever vulgar minded people, who see nothing beyond the body—may think. . . . God forgives us if there is in that any wrong, but our love for each other will give up life for our love. I would do this over and over again."[53]

After Molly and Eben returned to Washington, Grandma Wilder, who stayed on to help with Millicent, filled them in on Mabel's continuing visits with Mr. Dickinson. Eben wrote to Mabel that her actions had caused her mother to "take to her bed from sorrow" and "were killing her." Mabel was furious. She confided in her journal her anger at Grandma Wilder's surveillance and betrayal and at her mother's prejudices. "My mother and father have heretofore held a standard of life and morals far above mine, but through Mr. Dickinson I have jumped at one bound to a plane far above even theirs," she wrote. "I feel that, now, for the first time in my life, I have emerged from the mists in which every young person's life is encased, and can see myself and life clearly. My emotions and ambitions are all handed and made infinitely higher. And this through and by a man . . . whom they beg me not to associate with so much because he is a married man." Mabel continued this diatribe against her parents with the further justification that Austin was someone who "has always lived his life as honored as no one else ever was before, not since his illustrious father and grandfather and great-grandfather, who have always held every office of trust and responsibility in town. But that is not it . . . every one knows that he has been wretchedly disappointed in his domestic life, and all universally respect him." She concluded by writing of how her mother's "cruelly low" criticisms of her relationship with Austin held little sway because their "doctrine of love" was on a different plane than the love of anyone else.[54]

While both Austin and David urged Mabel not to care so much—indeed, to cut off all relations with her mother—Mabel could not quite bring herself to do this. Instead, she complained about her mother in letters to Austin and in her journal. In one journal entry she delineated the charges Molly had made in a long letter to her: "She denounces me in every way. . . . Every phase of my life comes into her general scourge. Millicent has not clothes—her boots were of the cheapest, while when I was a child no money was spared on me—I am inordinately vain, abominably selfish, as weak as water & only stubborn. This, after pages of abuse of my dear Austin, & his sisters—cynical, carping, irreligious people." What seems to have hurt Mabel the most was the knowledge that through her relationship with Austin, she had caused her mother "the most agonizing suffering."[55] Eventually Mabel apparently reached an accommodation with Molly; though the two would never agree about Mabel's relationship with Austin, her mother backed off her direct criticisms and leveled them in a more veiled way that mitigated direct confrontation.

Even when relations with her parents seemed to have calmed, they were mostly writing her with ostensible concerns about how much she was doing and how tired she appeared in recent photos she'd sent to them—Molly and Eben apparently were trying another tactic in appealing to Mabel's vanity. When Mabel had the opportunity to spend the summer of 1885 traveling in Europe with her cousin once removed, Caro Lovejoy Andrews, and her husband, John, Mabel jumped at the chance to remove herself from Amherst.

Molly and Eben certainly encouraged Mabel to go. In one of Molly's typical letters, written in tiny, almost indecipherable handwriting, with many words underlined multiple times and sentences accentuated by exclamation points, she urgently wrote Mabel, "What we have to say is, you UNDERLINE{MUST} go to Europe with Caro . . . it is greatly needed in your case. . . . Your father says, 'don't fail to tell her she must go now before it is too late! For her pictures show the nervous strain she daily goes through!!!' Leave everything, make any arrangements—only—GO—and may God take and keep you from all harm!"[56] Molly knew that any suggestions about the diminution of Mabel's appearance and putting words into the mouth of her beloved father would resonate with her.

Austin came with Mabel to Boston and spent several days with her prior to her departure. Mabel wrote in her journal that their parting did not fill them with sadness for they recognized that "it was the best thing for now. He and I understand each other fully and time and distance have no power over either of us."[57] Mabel, Caro and John departed for Ireland at the beginning of June 1885, waving from the ship to both David and Austin, who had accompanied her to the dock.

Before she sailed on the *Pavonia*, Mabel gave Austin a book to read in her absence. In her journal she had drafted the note, which accompanied this book: "And do you remember, my dearest, the drumming of the partridges in those spring woods? . . . We have heard it many times, dear, but that day was a holy spot in our lives. And I am going away, and here is this book for you to read—full of everything under the sun—but reaching at last the real peace and joy and unattestable fulfillment of my life in you, Austin; whom I love so that I am lifted solemnly to God by it—so that, as you said yesterday, neither of us can ever be lonesome again. That is over forever. Each has found his and her absolute ideal—living or dead, we are always mated to each other, and loneliness is past. Oh! Darling, darling!"[58] And Austin's farewell note to Mabel was equally effusive: "What in this hurry and excitement can I say for my last word my darling, but the old I love and I love you. We have learned what these mean, how much they hold for us, and that they hold more with each new day. Our separation is for comparatively short, and no separation in the future will be but temporary. . . . Whatever may come or go, we abide—and change not, each the others hope and joy, inspiration and strength."[59]

On the journey across the Atlantic, Mabel reveled in the sights and the sensory delights of sailing. While others retreated to their cabins, seasick, she proudly wrote, "I quiver with ecstasy, and when the great waves completely darken the little fronts, striking the heavy glass with a noise like thunder, I feel a thrill about my heart like my earliest girlish joys which warms my whole being like mutual wine and champagne. The freedom of yesterday afternoon and evening I cannot describe."[60] In letters home to both David and Austin, Mabel noted that she was spending much time with the captain of the ship and crew who were impressed with her ability to stay above deck no matter what the conditions, and that she was known as "the life of the steamer."

For the next three months, Mabel and the Andrews couple traveled throughout Ireland, Scotland, England, Holland, Germany, Switzerland and France. Mabel and Austin wrote each other frequently. Austin's letters document that during this period, he and David saw each other very often, sometimes spending time planning the house that they would build for the Todds.

At the end of July 1885, Austin included along with his letter one that his sister Emily had written to Mabel. In this letter, Emily expressed her pleasure in Mabel's friendship ("I trust you are homesick—That is the sweetest courtesy we pay an absent friend"), her appreciation for a painting Mabel had given her ("Your Hollyhocks endow the House, making Art's inner Summer, never Treason to Nature's") and asked Mabel to "Touch Shakespeare for me."[61] Mabel was moved and delighted to have Austin's sister acknowledge their mutual connection to great literature.

Though Molly and Eben certainly counted on the enforced separation when Mabel spent the summer in Europe to stem the flow of Mabel and Austin's passion, it seemingly had the opposite effect. "I am getting on better than at first, bearing the separation more philosophically, but it is not easy, and I chafe under it," Austin wrote to Mabel while she was in Europe. "I ought to have gone too, and if I had—and had had it in mind long enough to put all my matters clearly before my sisters—I doubt if we should have returned." And Mabel responded, "Dear darling your letter of yesterday . . . was like wine to me. I have been a new creature ever since. . . . Home of my soul, to which I am coming most joyfully back. I shall not want to travel alone, very soon again. I love you."[62]

When Mabel returned to the United States on September 13, David met her in Boston. The next day he returned to Amherst to teach, and Austin arrived to spend some time with Mabel before she went to Hampton, New Hampshire, with her mother, grandmother and Millicent. The dance between Mabel and her two men continued.

For the next decade, Mabel periodically indulged in lengthy journal entries in which she expounded on the injustices of Austin having to continue in a marriage to someone as wrong for him as Sue, of how she felt herself a "martyr," of the bouts of unhappiness she had when, despite Austin's frequent reassurances of his love for Mabel, he never saw fit to extricate himself from his marriage or to adequately protect her from Sue's wrath.

Mabel lived with a constant sense of twoness. Her real life, she felt, was with Austin. But that was not how she really lived, and it made Mabel all the more bitter. She had constant reminders that their proximity to each other was only temporal, with events large and small demonstrating that though Austin told her she was the center of his life, she was in fact on its periphery. Mabel was constantly frustrated by her inability to share things or be spontaneous with Austin. She was reminded of her marginalized role by an unending parade of milestones they could not celebrate together, numerous separations and holidays spent apart.

"My soul [and I] are becoming very well acquainted of late," she wrote in 1885. "I have a strange sort of life—it is not a bit like anybody else's and it is often far unhappier, it is sometimes infinitely happier. . . . But not always can I live in the ideal. And then I suffer."[63]

As the years of her relationship with Austin wore on, she periodically felt the need to leave town and escape. "It has been good for me to be here [away] this minute, to get out of the pain and endurance and the ruts in Amherst," she wrote in her journal. "I live under a dead weight in Amherst. O! That my particular pain might never, never crush me again. I so dread a return of my 8 years of agony."[64]

Mabel was even more specific in a letter to Austin, marking their seventh Thanksgiving apart: "That standing-aside-and-looking-on sort of feeling that I have always had used to hurt me and make me very lonely. I am used to it by now . . . truly pain has come to be so constant a state with me that I take it rather as a matter of course. . . . But I see the world slipping from me—I see it becoming daily more impossible for me to live in the little town which is yours. I see myself more and more alone. . . . I see power over all this lying idly in your hands, and you the only person able to cope with this terrible thing."[65] She rarely blamed Austin in this manner; if she ever thought that his inability to affect true change in his life was a weakness or fault, she never saw fit to commit this to paper. Never once did she write that Austin was too irresolute to leave his marriage; not once that he was too ambivalent.

On a dozen or more occasions in her journal and in letters, she hoped they would not have to wait for eternity to live together and be able to publicly avow their love while they were still on this earth. And there were moments during their thirteen-year relationship when it appeared things might change.

Mabel sometimes addressed Austin in her letters as "my sweet husband." In 1887, Austin gave Mabel an engagement and wedding ring. In one of her reflections on her childhood, Millicent

MABEL SAVED THIS SCRAP OF PAPER ON WHICH SHE WROTE HER NAME AS SHE TRULY WISHED IT COULD APPEAR.

recalled how mortified she was when her mother had taken off the wedding ring she'd received from David and wore instead the one she'd gotten from Austin to a function at Amherst College.

Then in 1888, Mabel and Austin attempted to conceive a child. They referred to this as "The Experiment." Many of their letters between 1888 and 1890 refer to this obliquely. In sharp contrast to the relief she felt when a pregnancy scare with David turned out to be nothing, Mabel invested much hope in the idea that she and Austin could produce a child. In particular, she expressed disappointment when they failed to conceive. (From looking at the range of symbols Mabel used to document when she got her period and when she and Austin had sex, it is not at all clear that she understood any more about when ovulation occurred than she had when she accidentally conceived Millicent.) It's hard to know what they thought they would have done if Mabel had become pregnant. Would David have claimed it as his child? Would they have banked on Austin's reputation around Amherst to ensure that an illegitimate child would still be treated with respect because it was his? Did they think about or consider what Millicent's reaction to such a sibling would be? Or Ned's, or Mattie's? Would this have been what finally made Austin decide that he could leave his marriage, leave his beloved Amherst and start over somewhere else? Polly Longsworth suggests that Austin's trip through the Midwest and South to New Orleans in 1887 "may have been, at least in part, a scouting trip to see how life together in the West would work."[66] Mabel's diaries and journals are certainly sprinkled with allusions such as "Austin and I are looking into life together a good deal."

But it was not to be. The two never saw a successful conclusion to "The Experiment," and they never attempted to leave Amherst for a new life elsewhere. Their two homes were separated by just a meadow, but their lives remained separated by so much more.

It was perhaps in this way that Mabel came to understand Emily's separation from the world and her need to express emotions and insights through words on a page. As Emily wrote in a poem Mabel would later title "Lost Joy":

I had a daily bliss
I half indifferent viewed,
Till sudden I perceived it stir,—
It grew as I pursued,

Till when, around a crag,
It wasted from my sight,
Enlarged beyond my utmost scope,
I learned its sweetness right.[67]

No doubt the joy lost because of the strains coming from her relation-ship with Austin made Mabel receptive to poetic messages like these. Without experiencing this intense period of the greatest love, the greatest sadness and the greatest exclusion, it is unlikely that Mabel would have had the emotional depth to understand the poet and her poetry in quite the same way. It was also this dichotomy between the joy and pain of Mabel's relationship with Austin that set the stage for the tumult to come.

$\mathcal{D}$ICKINSONIAN INSPIRATION: MABEL'S CREATIVE OUTPUT (1883–1893)

"Strange cadences" and "the gift of expression"

"27! I! It seems impossible in most things. I feel like a child—in fact it always seems true that I am 18 and I suppose I act so," wrote Mabel in her journal in 1883.[1] Though Mabel expressed similar sentiments on her birthday for the next several years, in truth both her personal and professional lives were taking on a new character. Her relationship with Austin continued to deepen and mature at the same time as her professional aspirations and accomplishments began to soar. It was a period of enormous productivity and creativity for her. During the next decade of her life, Mabel became an even more sought-after musician in the Amherst area, she continued to refine her painting and she began to publish prolifically (in this period she had several dozen articles appear in print and published the first five books that she either wrote or edited). It was during this decade that Mabel launched many of her civic endeavors, several of which she believed aligned her more closely with the Dickinson family. Mabel began to travel widely and started to write and lecture about her adventures. The development of her art, music and writing as well as the perspective that her international travels gave her, positioned Mabel to achieve what was arguably her most significant professional accomplishment—the editing and publication of Emily Dickinson's poetry.

As she would later write in her preface to the second volume of Emily's poetry, "Like impressionist pictures, or Wagner's rugged music, the very absence of conventional form challenges attention. In Emily Dickinson's exacting hands, the especial, intrinsic fitness of a particular order of word might not be sacrificed to anything virtually extrinsic; and her verses all show a strange cadence of inner rhythmical music."[2] Indeed, Mabel's own work as a musician, artist and writer, and her exposure to non-Western forms of artistic expression, prepared her for and would govern and deepen her understanding of Emily's "strange cadences."

Mabel recognized that while she had many innate artistic talents, these talents were finite. Even in her early twenties, she knew her lasting gift to the world might not be in any one of the areas she cultivated. In her journal she predicted she would look back on her life and see "the flower pictures I painted, the sonatas I played or the writing I did . . . all these seemed mere loopholes."[3] Her talents would, in fact, prepare her for her most lasting contribution—just not in the ways she originally envisioned.

Mabel always took her music seriously. She practiced religiously and performed widely. Even as an adult Mabel strove to continue learning. Not content only to master the performance of new repertoire, Mabel truly wanted to understand more about the structure of the music she was learning. During the winter of 1883 she took a correspondence course in harmony with one of her former professors. And in 1890, she took vocal lessons from famed Italian singing teacher and composer Augusto Rotoli at the New England Conservatory of Music.

Mabel also was an avid consumer of music. The scrapbooks she kept throughout her life are filled with programs of concerts she attended, including performances by legendary musicians such as pianist Arthur Rubinstein and opera singer Enrico Caruso. Though she enjoyed playing Bach and Beethoven, the music that seemed to resonate most with Mabel was the complexly textured and richly orchestrated Romantic music being written in the late nineteenth century. In a journal entry Mabel described her rapturous reaction to a cello concerto by another contemporary Romantic composer, Robert Volkmann: "[the piece] affected me most powerfully. . . . Lo, I waited, and as the tears fell fast and my heart throbbed with longing, I saw myself—blindly but with a passionate truth seeking for peace and right and surety through the one struggle of my life. . . . I felt my soul in those sorry, trembling chords which tried so hard to find this one solitary note of joy and peace and content."[4]

But it was perhaps her interest in non-Western music that would later prove to make Mabel receptive to the nontraditional rhythms of Emily Dickinson's poetry. In her travels around the world on eclipse expeditions with David, Mabel heard and fell in love with music as diverse as Javanese gamelan, Japanese *min'yō* folk music and traditional Hausa music in Libya. Whenever Mabel traveled abroad, she tried to capture her observations in words, in sketches and in passages of music she wrote out in her journal. "A strange, hypnotic quality characterized the native music of Tripoli," she wrote. "There is more in it than mere sound. I have been myself transported bodily into the depths of Sahara by these monotonously chanted tales, I have felt the free winds blow in my face as the racing dromedary bore me on to strange scenes over moonlit sands."[5]

In addition to her music, Mabel continued to take her art very seriously. From the time she arrived in Amherst throughout the next decade, Mabel spent a significant amount of her time painting and worked hard to refine her art. She maintained her relationship with Martin Johnson Heade and periodically studied with him until his death in 1904. Eager to extend her artwork beyond canvas, Mabel learned to paint screens and clothing and took china-painting lessons in 1890. She began to sell some of her art and gave painting lessons as a means of bringing in additional family revenue.

Mabel's favorite subjects were those found in nature—the same source for many of Emily Dickinson's powerful metaphors. Her painting of monarch butterflies on milkweed was selected by famed nineteenth-century entomologist Samuel Scudder to be the cover illustration for his classic twelve-volume study of butterflies, published in 1888. Just as Emily Dickinson would masterfully capture a minute bit of nature in words, Mabel attempted to do so in art, though she was never fully satisfied with her efforts. (Years later, in 1965, Millicent donated about sixty of her mother's flower paintings to what was at the time known as the Hunt Botanical Collection at Carnegie Mellon University. The curator described the collection as "evocative of the Victorian age, but, for the most part, mercifully free from sentimentality." That said, Carnegie Mellon ultimately concurred with Mabel's own assessment of her paintings: they deaccessioned them in 1986.)[6] But Mabel clearly felt her paintings of flowers were worthy efforts because she gave one of them to Emily.

The years of 1883–1894 were also years when Mabel's relationship with Austin Dickinson inspired her to become more deeply involved with Amherst's civic life. Austin, of course, was at the epicenter of the town in which he'd grown up. He had a hand in everything in Amherst, from its infrastructure to its aesthetics.[7] For her part, Mabel's civic activities ranged from the organization and leadership of local Amherst clubs and organizations to fund-raising for social causes to participation on national boards. She would later use her platforms as a writer and public speaker to promote some of her civic work, and she often utilized her talents as an artist and musician to extend the reach of her civic endeavors.

In 1893, Mabel started to work with others to found the Amherst Woman's Club and also the Amherst Historical Society, which officially began in 1899. In 1894, Mabel helped to start the Mary Mattoon chapter of the Daughters of the American Revolution (DAR) in Amherst. She presided over the group for years, and served as regent to the national board of the DAR until 1903. She was also instrumental in the founding of organizations outside of Amherst—for example, a conversation with author May Alden Ward and newspaperwoman Helen Winslow at a tea Mabel hosted in her home led to the formation of the Boston Authors Club (BAC), an organization that honors books and authors with Boston-area ties. Mabel was one of the original officers of the BAC.

Mabel was, in her own way, also involved in issues of racial equality. She was proud of her grandparents' involvement with the abolitionist movement in Concord, Massachusetts, and referred to it frequently in her journals. Millicent told a story in her 1960 "Reminiscence" of how, in about 1892, Mabel had discovered that "when two Negro boys invited their guests to Commencement," the "Southern boys refused to go to the promenade if the Negro couples were permitted to attend. Having heard this, my mother invited them as our houseguests . . . along with Katherine Garrison, granddaughter of William Lloyd Garrison—and had a reception" for them.[8]

Mabel sometimes donated artwork to raise money for charitable causes. She was once so moved after hearing a lecture about the plight of Native American children that she organized an art exhibition and raised funds for the Ramona School for Indian girls in Şanta Fe, New Mexico, a school endowed by royalties from former Amherst resident, author and Dickinson friend Helen Hunt Jackson's book focusing on a Native American heroine, *Ramona*. Mabel wrote in notes she took in March of 1886, "We trust that all will attend this exhibition . . . in the interest of the school for Indian girls," and went on to discuss her realization that her artwork could be used to help raise awareness about a cause.[9]

It wasn't Mabel's actual involvement in civic activities that was truly noteworthy compared with her nineteenth-century female peers; it was her vision of it. For Mabel, civic engagement meant playing a guiding role. In a paper about Mabel's contributions, Millicent stated, "Nowadays we should call it leadership—that quality by which any woman in the town who had anything to give was marshaled into line for service which was thenceforth rendered not grudgingly, under compulsion, but gladly, for the sake of the cause in question."[10] And Millicent was right—Mabel was always elected chair or president of every organization of which she was a part.

While her musical, artistic and civic ventures were quite productive during this period of time, it was perhaps in her writing that Mabel took the biggest creative and professional leap. And it was, perhaps, her ardent desire to be known and remembered as a writer that would compel her to associate herself closely with the genius of Emily Dickinson.

In September of 1883, Mabel wrote excitedly in her journal, "my really beloved story 'Footprints' was published in the *New York Indepen-*

dent. And I had 25 dollars from it!"[11] The story of two lovers' discovery of each other, "Footprints" was something Mabel had started writing early in 1883, just months after her Rubicon moment. Though fiction, it was a tale that had great resonance for Mabel. Her protagonist, Dr. Henry Arnold, is clearly based on Austin: "he was past the first flush of his youth—youth which had brought him much pain, a good deal of endurance, many longings which were principally unfulfilled. . . . His life had been such that Nature had become more to him than father, mother or brothers." The two main female characters, Lilian Dwight, "a stylish elegant girl" with a "rich contralto" voice, and Mildred, "the one person, the only person he knew, who had ever responded to his subtle thoughts, or to whom indeed it had ever seemed possible to express them," could be read as an amalgam of herself. Henry identifies Mildred initially by the footprints she leaves on the beach, and the story concludes with Henry and Mildred's footprints in the sand, side by side, together.[12]

Inspired by the publication of "Footprints," Mabel became determined to refine her craft. Several years after the publication of this story, Mabel wrote in her journal after returning from a sleigh ride with Austin and reflecting on the lovely winter scene, "If I have any genius it then awakes and I could write, write freely, brilliantly, strongly, as long as it lasts. . . . I can remember well the delicious joy of creating, as I wrote, and my joy and belief to be unequalled for me by anything else in the world. I have a perfect passion all the time to write."[13]

Indeed, of all her many talents, the one that Mabel found to be most compelling was her writing. She was thoughtful and reflective about the craft. "Expression of writing is absolutely easy and natural to me, and is always a delight . . . but I say, unconsciously to myself a good deal—there is plenty of time, you are ripening and mellowing and strengthening all the time," she ruminated on one occasion in her journal. On another, she commented, "If I had the time there would be nearly every day recorded thought which I know would be worth refining and saving permanently."[14]

In addition to her public writings, of course, Mabel was a devoted diarist and journal keeper. In the times when she, herself, was unable to maintain her diary (right after Millicent's birth in 1880 and again in

1913 when she had a cerebral hemorrhage) Mabel prevailed upon David and Millicent to fill in for her and dictated to them what she wanted written. It was not only a sense of her own importance and the worth of recording the minutiae of her daily life for posterity, or even the cultural custom of so many nineteenth-century women to maintain a diary that inspired Mabel to write each day; Mabel knew that a writer needed to maintain discipline in writing. In 1888 she observed, "My love for writing in itself is immensely increased—every year makes it stronger."[15]

Mabel also knew that an important part of the writing process is revision. This became critical in her work on Dickinson's poems. She once wrote a story entitled "Stars and Garden," which she described as something that had "lain so near my heart so long." When she read it to Austin, he was impressed with it but felt that she needed to edit it and rewrite the ending, for "if it turned out as people say, badly, it would be more artistic and affective. Of that I was myself absolutely sure, but it rent my heartstrings to change it."[16] Mabel reworked the story several times, and after a series of rejections, finally published it in installments in the *Home Magazine* in 1900.[17]

Mabel also tried her hand at writing drama. In the summer of 1900 she drafted a play "based on some little paper-covered novel."[18] But like fiction writing, playwriting was never a modality in which she found any true success.

Mabel did experience more success in her nonfiction writing. Over the course of her lifetime she published more than two hundred articles on an astonishing array of topics that appeared in periodicals ranging from the children's literary magazine *St. Nicholas* to the *Century Magazine* to *Harper's Magazine*, and in newspapers from the local *Amherst Record* and *Springfield Republican* to national papers including the *Boston Transcript* and the *New York Tribune*. She had a regular job reviewing books for a number of magazines. She wrote or edited a dozen nonfiction books that were published. "I know I have things to say," Mabel once reflected in her journal, "and I know I have the gift of expression—a 'great power of observation and description,' as dear Louisa Alcott said of my very girlish writings. But if I were to become sufficiently well-known to be asked for articles and stories, that sort of stimulus would be very sweet to me. I do long for a little real, tangible success. That is not the motive to me, for my writing is done from a love of the doing per se, but it is so beautiful to be appreciated!"[19]

Mabel began to realize a little tangible success from her writing after she went on an astronomical expedition to Japan with David in 1887. Mabel's careful descriptions of the "exotic" things she saw and experienced found their way into a series of articles she wrote that was published in the *Nation*, entitled "The Eclipse Expedition to Japan." She subsequently wrote and later published two other articles about this trip, "Ten Weeks in Japan," which appeared in *St. Nicholas* and "Ascent of Mt. Fuji the Peerless," which came out in the *Century Magazine*. The interest generated by these unusual travelogues that described things and people few Westerners had seen served to launch Mabel into the world of newspaper and magazine journalism. Mabel also began to learn to use some of David's photographic equipment on this expedition, ensuring that not only would the journey be well documented with words but also with photos. Her connections to some of the leading editors of the day would prove useful in years to come as she publicized Emily Dickinson's poetry with articles about it in newspapers and magazines.

It was on this trip to Japan that two other important facets of Mabel's writing became apparent. The first was her ability to articulate her own role in some very unusual circumstances and bring this before the reading audience: a ride down a crowded Japanese street in Tokio [*sic*] in a jinrickisha, experiencing a strong earthquake, living in a castle atop a mountain awaiting the eclipse. A highlight of this trip was the ascent up Mt. Fuji. Mabel became the first Western woman to successfully make the climb. Her article about this trek, ostensibly cowritten with David, focused on the wonders of ascending this peak of over twelve thousand feet, the "mountain sickness" experienced, the Japanese pilgrims paying religious homage to the mountain, the sights and sounds along the climb. "Grandeur and majesty, with desolation and loneliness, unspeakable, form the crown of Fuji-San," they concluded in this detailed, if often flowery description.[20]

The second facet of Mabel's developing narrative style that became more apparent than ever on this expedition was her ability to spin events and present them in a more positive light than they probably deserved. Despite months of planning, shipping heavy equipment trans-pacifically and the arduous process to set it up atop a Japanese mountain, and traveling thousands of miles to get there, when the night of the eclipse came about in mid-August, the clouds closed in, obscuring the view. Privately Mabel observed in her diary, "The clearest day for weeks, until almost an hour before the eclipse. Then clouds arose in the mist and spread all over like the finger of ... fate. ... I am so sad for David beyond words. He bears it nobly."[21]

But in the second of the series of articles she wrote for the *Nation*, Mabel stated, "Sixteen thousand miles of continent and ocean traversed for three wonderful minutes, and unremitting labor during every clear night, and on all days for whatever sort, all for that little time, which may or may not be cloudy, at its own sweet will. Such are the chances of an astronomer's life, but glorious his compensation when nature is kind."[22] Of course nature had not been kind to David. It never would be. But in writing this article, Mabel demonstrated her ability to parlay the experience into something that helped to shape and advance her own career.

And yet, as Millicent was to observe many years later, the one thing for which Mabel most wished to be known and for which she would have given up all her other talents—her writing—was ultimately not to be her legacy. Mabel wrote to David in 1926, "I ought to have written the great American novel," and a few years later opined, "I should like immensely to write something that would be really popular and would stay in the world for at least a few years."[23] Millicent stated in one of her "Reminiscences" that her mother "cared a great deal about writing and she wrote from the time she was a little child ... she published little stories, but she never succeeded in doing the one thing that she wanted most to do and that was to write either a great novel or a great play. That she never did do."[24] As Longsworth notes, "Mabel had a clear enough eye for genius in writing to recognize ultimately that she herself didn't possess it."[25]

MABEL TITLED THIS POEM "LOST JOY." THE IMAGE ON THE LEFT IS EMILY'S ORIGINAL MANUSCRIPT, THE IMAGE ON THE RIGHT, MABEL'S HANDWRITTEN TRANSCRIPTION OF THIS POEM.

But Mabel certainly could recognize genius in writing. She had seen this immediately when Sue Dickinson shared some of her sister-in-law's poems. It would ultimately not be as a writer, but as an editor of these poems, that Mabel would most lastingly leave her mark.

CHAPTER 5

——

$\mathcal{L}$INGERING PURITANISM AND MILLICENT'S SENSIBILITIES (1884–1897)

"Am I really of their era rather than my own?"

In 1887, when Millicent was seven years old, her father taught her how to take and record the daily temperature each morning. In an interview seventy years later, Millicent stated, "I don't know whether it was because he wanted the temperature, or . . . to teach me to be methodical and systematic from the very early days."[1] Whatever David's intent, he instilled in his only child a habit she maintained for the rest of her life. It established early in Millicent's life a pattern of work and personal practice—a desire to record the world around her— that was not only disciplined and systematic but also bordered on the obsessive. Recording and organizing her world ensured some kind of dependable foundation and control: a way of ordering a life that must have often felt in disarray.

As a child, Millicent compulsively kept lists. In addition to the records of daily temperatures, she kept inventories of the species of birds she saw, the books she read and the places she traveled. She believed that these habits were not only a way of recording the world around her but also "a more observable gauge of my industriousness." Millicent's childhood obsession with list making was certainly in accord with the general Victorian fascination with systems of order and control.[2] Later in life this drive to systematically catalog the world around her would make Millicent feel kinship with Emily Dickinson, whose careful botanical observations and herbarium paralleled Millicent's own lists and collections.

Like her mother, Millicent saved and organized letters, programs, calling cards, newspaper clippings, report cards, doodles, dried flowers, ribbons and other souvenirs in a series of scrapbooks that she began in childhood and continued through midlife. Some of Millicent's scrap-books are so stuffed that their leather bindings cracked long ago under the weight of their contents. She not only meticulously recorded her life but seemed to be gripped by a fanatical desire to preserve it. Later, this propensity to collect and save would cause personal angst as well as con-tribute to the debates surrounding Emily Dickinson's papers.

Around the same time that she began recording the daily tempera-ture Millicent began to keep a daily diary. By the time she was fifteen, Millicent was, like Mabel, writing daily in both a journal and a diary. In a series of notes for an autobiography she never got around to writing, Millicent recalled, "I began at the age of seven to write a daily diary. It became a habit. . . . The diary took on more and more the role of confes-sor, the only companion, as Emily Dickinson said her 'lexicon' was. It has served me well for long periods of time."[3]

Sometimes, Millicent's journals contained imaginary conversations with other people, at times going on for pages. Often dealing with objects of her affection, these imaginary dialogues were conversations Millicent wished for but didn't dare have in real life. For instance, in 1896 she melodramatically wrote of her first real crush, "Millicent, I've noticed you so often walking down the street but never dared to do more than smile"; "Oh Alden, I, too, have only but dared to smile at you, though I have longed to talk to you and tell you so much that is in my heart." Millicent continued to indulge in these types of imaginary dia-logues in her journals as she grew up, with the conversations becoming ever more complex. In a 1911 dialogue, she constructed a conversation with another romantic object, whom she simply called "C"—possibly representing Carol Fleming, one of several women with whom Millicent might have had some kind of romance.

"C: I can't understand you at all."

"M: How, if you love and care, can you cease to care? Is love like a spigot you turn on and off? If you don't care for me, then I'll just have to put that behind me."[4]

Late in life, Millicent mused, "What is the deepest undercurrent? What the surge that has driven me from first to last? When I was quite small, my dear grandfather said: 'The trouble with Millicent is, she takes care.' Maybe so. He was [a] wise man."[5] Millicent recalled that David had once said to her, "You live in your own world—apart." She quipped, "Where else?"[6]

Where else, indeed? From the start, Millicent's childhood was significantly different from those of her peers. Her worldview was colored by an inherited set of morals and values that indelibly influenced all of her personal relationships and made her different from other people in her life. She was acutely, painfully aware of this divide, as well as what she saw as the marked disparity between herself and her mother. In this isolation, Millicent was perhaps able to understand better than most how for Emily Dickinson, too, one's inner life and poetic imaginings could become more real and meaningful than actual social interactions.

In notes for her autobiography, Millicent pondered "Am I really of their era rather than of my own? I wonder. My faults and virtues are certainly those of a Puritan, tightly controlled and inhibited by all sorts of critical judgments and moral anxieties."[7] For Millicent, much as she craved to be like others and to cultivate close friendships and romantic relationships, this Puritan mentality perpetually set her apart. She always felt as if she were living in the wrong century.

⌒

Many of Millicent's early childhood memories and reflections on the seminal influences of her life are about her grandparents. As a child, Millicent lived as much with her grandparents as with her own parents, staying with them when Mabel and Austin began their romantic relationship and when Mabel and David traveled abroad on astronomical

EBEN JENKS LOOMIS, CIRCA 1910; MARY ALDEN WILDER LOOMIS, 1879

expeditions. In fact, she did not live in Amherst with her parents full time until she was eight, nor did she travel abroad with them until she was nineteen. This meant Millicent had extremely close relationships with her maternal grandparents, as well as with her great-grandmother, who lived with them until her death in August 1893. Millicent described the day she died as "the most indelible date of my childhood."[8] In her auto-biographical notes, when Millicent mentions the "paramount influences of my childhood," she names her grandparents and great-grandmother before her parents.

There is a lovely anecdote that opens a book Millicent wrote in 1913 as a tribute to her grandfather. She recounts how the previous summer she and Eben had been sitting in a car in Newport, Rhode Island, awaiting the return of a family friend. A girl walked past the car, glanced in, and then circled back. Through the open window, she said to Millicent, "Excuse me, but will you tell me that old gentleman's name? He shows so much thought in his face." Millicent wrote, "A mind so filled with fascinating facts, so clear in its understanding and interpretation of them, a spirit so exquisite in its trust and its power of direct beholding had quickened a mere passer-by. The poor girl asked his name. It was her way of getting a little nearer to the beautiful nature she perceived."[9] Millicent remembered Eben as having "a nature as open as the sunny meadow and as filled with light as the June sky."[10]

Millicent donated two portraits of Eben to the Smithsonian Institution's National Portrait Gallery collection. Both were painted by Edwin Burrage Child in 1910. The first depicts a kindly looking man with shoulder-length white hair and a full beard. He is dressed in an immaculate white suit, almost like the famous photographs of Mark Twain, and he sits before a full bookshelf. In the other portrait, Eben appears slightly rumpled, tired, his face worn by the years and by long hours spent outdoors. He holds a thick book in which the fingers of his right hand are marking a place about two-thirds through. The artist seems to have caught Eben midchapter.

Though his own formal education was limited, Eben was by inclination a scientist and a naturalist. In her tribute, Millicent referred to Eben as "a child of Nature. He was part of the great outdoors; his brilliant eyes always alert, his fine nostrils vibrating to that other sense which we sometimes envy wild animals, and his ears, Indian-like, adjusted to the significance of a cracking twig or other slight wood noise."[11] Eben's own observations were so acute that Asa Gray, the most noted nineteenth-century botanist, and naturalist/biologist Charles Darwin lauded his descriptions of an unfolding fern frond.[12] Millicent spent a great deal of time with her grandfather, learning to observe and to systematically record her observations of nature. She recalled, "He inculcated in me at that age a love of nature and love of the out of doors and he taught me the common birds from the time I was so little that I don't remember."[13]

Millicent spent a number of summers in her early childhood with her grandparents in Hampton, New Hampshire. In a 1959 interview she recalled how Eben took her for long walks in the salt marshes adjacent to the beaches and taught her to identify migrating shore birds. Millicent remembered once hearing a man announce that he wished to have sandpiper pie for lunch, going out and shooting a "bag full of birds," but selecting only two for his meal. Millicent was so horrified and disgusted that she reflected, "I think this turned me into a conservationist at the age of six."[14]

In addition to giving his granddaughter an appreciation for nature and inspiring in her a lifelong belief in the need to preserve the natural world, Eben also encouraged her to become an avid reader. Millicent stated that even well into his eighth decade, Eben spent several hours a day devouring books. Millicent was amazed by his ability to recite arcane knowledge from a variety of sources. From him, Millicent picked up a love of reading about natural history, a genre that she preferred to any other.

But it was perhaps her grandfather's pairing of a scientific mind with a poetic soul that affected Millicent most profoundly. "He was more and more a poet throughout his life, an artist in his attitude toward science and toward life. This combination was his intellectual power; the scientist perfecting his observations by the poet's vision, the poet resting in his flights of fancy upon a carefully trained scientific habit of thought. He was supported in each realm by his love of the other."[15]

Millicent shared Eben's love of nature and poetry with her mother, an important common thread despite their contrasting personalities. It also provided them both with insights about how observing nature could open up new insights. This would help them understand and relate to Dickinson's enigmatic poetry, so much of which employs nature's imagery.

So close was Millicent's relationship with her grandfather that in one of her "Reminiscences" she wrote poignantly, "The last word, the night before he died, as I sat beside his bed and said, 'Grandpa, I love you,' which was hard for me to say even to him whom I loved best. The last word he whispered was 'And I love you.'"[16]

Millicent's relationship with her grandmother Molly was perhaps less close than her relationship with Eben, but no less influential. Molly instilled in her granddaughter the importance of their shared matrilineal line. "I think my Grandmother Loomis was more responsible for what I turned out to be than any other one person," Millicent reflected in 1959. "She was a Puritan of the Puritans. She was very proud of her descent from John Alden. She brought me up to think that nothing that I could ever do as long as I lived would begin to measure up with what had gone before me. . . . She was . . . very conscientious with all of the virtues which the Puritans held [and which] she hoped to see in me. . . . Her standards were my standards."[17] Molly continually impressed upon Millicent the importance of being a "Wilder woman," and the principles incumbent to this heritage. Discipline, subordination of personal desire and self-denial were some of the Puritan virtues Millicent believed her grandmother passed along to her. In a letter written to Millicent in 1897, Molly stated, "The heroic spirit is always strong and clearly defined and keeps us alive and even happy in spite of circumstances."[18]

The photographs of Molly, which Millicent lovingly preserved, show a woman with a severe profile, a sharp aquiline nose, and hair meticulously braided and arranged atop her head. She never smiles and never looks right at the camera; indeed, most of the photos depict her only in profile.

In 1933, Millicent recalled that Molly was "the embodiment of the Moral law. A descendent of two generations of Puritan divines, she upheld the Right, which sometimes became the Intolerant, against all compromise." Millicent recalled her grandmother's extreme Puritan parsimony: "She worked for my future betterment, she saved for me out of her meager store, even walking to save a carfare so that its equivalent might be added to my savings bank account."[19] This emphasis on frugality and living a lifestyle that was thriftier than one's means necessitated was something Millicent grew to embrace and practice throughout her life.

Inspired by her grandmother, Millicent's emerging beliefs about faith tended to be dualistic. Beginning in childhood but continuing throughout her entire life, Millicent saw the world in stark black and white contrast. In a paper she wrote in 1945 titled "The New England Way," Millicent reflected that the Puritan influence was "firm as the granite which moulds the surface features of a New England scene were the convictions of its people a hundred years ago."[20]

In 1905, Millicent expounded on the development of her faith in one of her "Reminiscences": "the evolution of prayer is one of the most characteristic of a person's most intimate trains of thought." Her own prayers, thoughtfully and meticulously recorded, reveal her developing personal and professional aspirations, as well as the strict moral standards she expected from herself and others.

In later years, Millicent added prayers that reflected on her desires and fears about relationships and a career, such as "do no sins"; "give me a noble purpose in life"; or "may I have a noble, true gentleman for a husband." One of the prayers that Millicent added in was to "love Mamma more dearly."[21]

As an adult Millicent became acutely aware of how her prayers reflected her hopes, dreams and concerns—especially as they related to her highly ambivalent feelings about her mother. "I had a solemn feeling that I should act according to the commandment and love Mamma more than anything in heaven above or by the earth below," she reflected in 1905. "Therefore, this sincere prayer that I might love her more dearly than I did." Millicent recognized this prayer might have been "a strange request for a child," reflecting a "gnawing desire that I could become more Christian so that I could make my Mother more so. I can't remember when I hadn't the intuition as a little child that Mamma having no faith, lacked something which perhaps I could sometime give her."[22]

As a young girl Millicent was also passionate about music and writing. Mabel was convinced from early in Millicent's life that she had enormous musical talent and strove to teach her little girl piano from the moment she could lay hands on the keyboard. But like so many children, Millicent rebelled. In a 1959 interview, Millicent recalled being so appalled at the idea of "being taught by my mother that I felt as if I would scream but, of course, I never did . . . she decided and I concurred, that I better try something else than the piano. What a relief! So we tried the violin. She could not instruct me."[23]

Nonetheless, Millicent remained a gifted and agile musician. She became an excellent violinist and singer and, though she had railed

MILLICENT, AGE 10. SHE CHOSE
TO LEARN THE VIOLIN BECAUSE IT
WAS AN INSTRUMENT HER MOTHER
COULDN'T TEACH HER.

against it, played the piano quite well. But she gave them all up for three principal reasons. First, long weeks of traveling internationally with her parents in her late teens and early twenties meant no time for serious practicing—and being a perfectionist, Millicent knew that this would render attaining musical excellence impossible.

Second, Millicent was both blessed and cursed to have perfect pitch. In some ways, this made it easy for her to become a good musician. But in other ways, it meant that even the slightest flaw in intonation or instruments not being perfectly tuned to one another made playing music almost unbearable for her: "the tones I produced fell so far short of what I demanded of myself that I got only agony out of it."[24] She was inordinately sensitive to issues of pitch even outside of music: dogs barking or car horns blaring made her exceedingly uncomfortable and anxious throughout her life.

Finally, Millicent felt the need to differentiate herself from Mabel. "My mother, of course, was practicing all the time. . . . She was very outgoing. She was not a scholar. She was just a person of enormous ability in anything she wanted to do, and she did it without the slightest feeling of effort."[25] For Mabel, music brought her together with other people; for Millicent, music set her apart. Though Millicent was always a devoted consumer of music and avid concertgoer who retained programs of every concert she attended, her own musicianship all but ended as a young adult.

Writing also became an important form of self-expression, relief and companionship for Millicent early in life. "I sometimes wonder why I want to write things down? Is it the desire to get rid of a thought in order to have the individual free for a succeeding one? Or is it to preserve what unpremeditated moments my experience may have had. It relieves emotional pressure. . . . A unique life, strange and interesting though it may seem, is not as useful as that which can express the joys of little things."[26] Millicent, ever analytical, was certainly correct that her writing served many purposes. And because she considered it important, she saved it. All of it.

In addition to her diaries and journals, Millicent also sought to express herself through various forms of creative writing. When she was about nine years old, Millicent wrote about a new invention she called the "Snoring Extinguisher." Her description reveals something of the kind of child she was—thoughtful, creative and yet reticent to engage directly with people. "I thought of this queer thing last summer, for someone in the hotel with me used to wake me up at night with snoring," she explained. "It is composed of a flexible tube with an open end. The other end is a round, bowl shaped thing, which fits onto the mouth, and is fastened on by an elastic, which goes around the head. . . . The end . . . fits onto the ear, and when a person snores the sound will go through the tube and into the ear. So the sound will wake the person up, and then he will stop snoring."[27]

Periodically in later life, Millicent allowed herself to indulge in other forms of creative writing, mostly limericks or poems. But for the most part, once she left childhood, she left this vehicle for creativity and self-expression behind. However, these early roots would serve her well in editing the Dickinson poetry that would otherwise have been lost to the world. Her love of writing and early inclination to use language creatively, combined with a reclusive nature she shared with Dickinson, made her uniquely prepared to edit the poet's work with remarkable insight. Millicent's three books about Emily's life would later exemplify the ways in which Millicent understood the poet; in *Bolts of Melody*, the heretofore unpublished Dickinson poems, Millicent would purposively select only words Emily herself had offered as possibilities for unfinished poems, even if these selections were unusual.

The normal developmental urge most children have to start differentiating themselves from their parents was perhaps especially pronounced in Millicent. Just as she refused to play the piano because her mother was such a gifted pianist, she gave up writing any type of fiction because she knew that this was something that Mabel herself aspired to do. Even though her fledgling childish efforts had shown creative promise, Millicent felt the need to pursue other paths.

Another reason Millicent might have abandoned creative writing was that her formal education encouraged more structured and analytical means of expression. During the first few years of her life, her parents and grandparents homeschooled Millicent. By her own reporting, she could read independently by age four and learned about nature and the scientific method from her father and grandfather at an early age.

Millicent began attending "a school for young ladies" in Amherst when she was eleven. She attended this school for six years, during which time she studied writing, literature, mathematics, Latin, French and deportment. An excellent student, her monthly report cards (of which she saved every one) show that she shone particularly brightly in languages—and always received a perfect "100" in deportment. Years later Millicent recalled one of her greatest drives was that "[I] liked to be better than anybody else in school."[28] Indeed, her drive to excel in academics became a common theme of Millicent's life and she berated herself for her inability to achieve perfection in all things, obsessing about it in countless journal entries throughout her life.

Mary Stearns, the widowed daughter-in-law of a former Amherst College president and founder of the school Millicent attended, proved to be not only an influential teacher for Millicent but also enormously important in the development of her outlook on the world. Writing in 1963 about the people who most influenced her life, Millicent stated, "Mrs. Stearns, generous and understanding, yet uncompromising on moral standards and conduct. She reinforced Grandma Loomis' attitude which became my own."[29] So profound was Mary Stearns's influence on Millicent that after Stearns's death in 1905, Millicent wrote a book in tribute.

As much as Millicent got out of her education at Mrs. Stearns's school, Mabel and David felt that their daughter was still not quite prepared for the rigors of a college education. They arranged to have Miss Heloise Edwina Hersey, a well-known women's educator and Vassar graduate, test Millicent's preparedness. In her 1901 book *To Girls: A Budget of Letters*, Hersey wrote, "Education, like religion, we may say reverently, is to be known by its fruits." She went on to extrapolate about the elements that must comprise a good and fulfilling education for women which she incorporated into the mission of her school: discipline, a sense of proportion and a way of "vitalysing [*sic*] the process."[30] This educational philosophy of preparing women not only for a liberal arts education but also for finding concrete ways to apply it, became influential for Millicent throughout her life.

When Miss Hersey determined that Millicent's education had been "very hit or miss—absolutely nothing systematic in it whatever," Millicent spent a year in Boston filling in the gaps in her education "to get me into shape before I presented myself to the Vassar authorities."[31] With the supplementary training she received at Miss Hersey's school, Millicent was able to matriculate at Vassar without taking any additional examinations. Millicent parlayed her education at Vassar in French literature and language skills into a number of real-world uses; her subsequent decision to pursue graduate degrees in geology and geography was similarly not just a quest for knowledge but a quest for expertise that could have a number of practical applications.

A solemn child who spent more time in her formative years with her grandparents than with her peers, Millicent would observe the world but not question it. Looking back on her life in her eighty-third year, she suggested her early life led her to "an acceptance of a state of mystification, bathing in impenetrable mystery, my natural state, and it means— silence. This may have been what Emily Dickinson meant when she wrote to my mother, referring to 'the quaint little girl with the deep eyes, every day more fathomless.'"[32] Millicent certainly believed that the bond she felt with the poet emanated from whatever brief meeting might have occurred in the halls of The Homestead—that somehow, Emily managed to see into young Millicent's eyes, divined her nature and perfectly encapsulated it in a dozen words, as sparse and as insightful as one of her poems.

Millicent believed that her parents and her grandparents kept her in a bubble. "My mother kept me over-protected. There was no mention of anything important in childhood. The main idea was to shield me, never any arguing in my presence. Result, I lived in a world of my own. My thoughts and feelings were entirely suppressed." When she looked back on her youth and adolescence, Millicent felt strongly that this overprotection adversely affected the development of her social interactions. "They kept everything from me, or thought they did. They never spoke of Dickinson . . . or the fact that Grandma had cancer, or that it would be fatal."[33]

For these reasons, it's not surprising that as Millicent's girlhood yielded to adolescence, her romantic attachments were characterized by great reticence and self-doubt. Through her father's teaching at Amherst College and her mother's socializing with David's students, Millicent was exposed to a revolving door of bright and eligible young men. Her diaries and journals reveal that she did develop crushes on a number of Amherst students, but she never acted on her feelings. "Boys were as remote from me as a Japanese Buddha," she recalled. "They were a race apart; but I could worship from afar."[34]

One young man, in particular, caught Millicent's eye. Alden Hyde Clark grew up in Amherst before moving to New York when his father, renowned economist John Bates Clark, accepted a professorship at Columbia. Alden returned to Amherst to attend college. As a teenager, Millicent was smitten with "the supreme object of my hero-worship." Alden was the first person with whom Millicent carried on lengthy imaginary conversations in her journals. Though it appears that Millicent mostly admired Alden from afar and did little or nothing to engage with him, she carried her torch for him for many years. Still stewing about it at age eighty-three, Millicent wrote of her love for Alden: "from whom I could not expect more than a smile in passing. . . . And yet he occupied my thoughts to the exclusion of all else—any other boy."[35] Ironically, later in her life Millicent would turn her affections to Alden's younger brother, John Maurice Clark, who would also spurn her. But for the duration of her life, Millicent often thought of Alden Clark. He was her first unrequited love.

———

Even as a young child, Millicent had complicated feelings about her mother. On the one hand, she dutifully loved and admired many things about Mabel, felt incredibly protective of her and devoted to her. But on the other, Millicent found much about her mother questionable, perhaps in part because Mabel so often left Millicent with her grandparents or great-grandmother, and partially because of her own unyielding Puritan values.

Looking back on her childhood many decades later, Millicent reflected that, like most children growing into adolescence, she simply wanted to be like everyone else, to fit in. But Millicent's parents were markedly different—from the way they decorated their home to the ways in which they behaved. "Other people's fathers stayed at home, indulging in no outside activities," Millicent recalled. "My father was perpetually travelling. Each expedition to a foreign country resulted in a welter of heathenish objects which we housed on the return." And as for her mother, while Mabel painted, played music, had a public speaking career and wrote well, "She indulged herself in doing them. Of course I did not approve. Other people's mothers did not do that sort of thing. They were *hausfraus*. They stayed at home and they were cooks and my mother never went near the kitchen."[36]

Millicent's mother was also beautiful, charming and vivacious—and she knew how to use all of these gifts to her advantage. Young Millicent was in awe of her mother's charms, but began to resent them as she began to realize that she herself lacked the same charisma. "She was extremely pretty and she had great allure and I didn't approve in the least, because I felt people should earn what they had not just by looking at a person. . . . I felt it was a graft of the worst variety." Millicent was horrified when "once I opened my mother's bureau drawer . . . and I found a little pot of rouge! Well, I can't tell you what a horrible shock it was to me to think that anybody would disguise anything that they were by nature. It was simply so dishonest that I could not tolerate it and I really felt very disapproving of my mother."[37] Millicent was equally disapproving of her mother's proclivity for wearing fashionable clothes and high heels.

As Millicent grew into adolescence, Mabel would urge her daughter to go out and "have fun." Often Mabel would take Millicent along with her to Amherst College dances. But Millicent hated going to cotillions because it was her mother who was the life of the party, her mother whose dance card was always quickly filled by eager young college boys and her mother who would dance until dawn. Millicent sat on the side, watching. "Mamma talked and held people better than I did. She danced better than I did. The boys at a dance preferred to dance with her than with me. In a word, there just wasn't any use in trying to compete. And I never did. Also I never thought about it—it was just one of those things one accepts like the fact of one's parentship."[38]

Years later, Millicent pondered what her life and character would have been like if she been able to elicit male attention the way her mother did. Mabel, she wrote, had all the qualities that drew men to her "like flies on sticky fly paper." Millicent wondered if she, too, had been able to attract people as her mother had, might this have changed "my point of view . . . not to mention my technique of living?" Yet for Millicent, these differences represented a huge gulf between herself and Mabel. "Unthinkable! But such was my mother. How stupid to have ever imagined that I could understand her, or her me. We inhabited—except for our industriousness—a different world."[39]

Indeed, Millicent grew up seeing both of her parents perpetually engaged with an enormous number of ventures. Millicent recalled in 1958, "I think this is the most characteristic thing about my mother—that with her beauty and with her charm—she was [still] a very hard worker. I never saw her sit down without a book in her lap." She also recollected how her parents were always beginning the next project before the current one was done: "It was just a whirl of work in every room in our house. There was a room devoted to this or that or the other subject."[40] Millicent believed her many lists and scrapbooks were some measure and record of how she had spent her time. She believed she had inherited the Puritanical "idle-hands-do-the-Devil's-work" emphasis on perpetual labor—and on product rather than process.

Millicent felt that for her mother, "Everything was easy! She was complimented and praised and admired without trying. . . . If one accomplishment didn't fit an occasion, there was always another to fall back on."[41] Millicent, on the other hand, though talented in many areas, worked very hard for everything she achieved and envied Mabel's ability to take pleasure from her talents.

Millicent also came to resent a certain affected performance-like quality to Mabel's everyday interactions. "Walking along the street together in silence, someone approaches. My mother begins to talk to me in an interested manner, but without any significance in her remarks. I cannot remember the time when I did not know that it was for the sake of the effect on the passer-by. And how I hated it! She worked hard over her music, her singing and playing. But when she performed before people it was the effect which mattered. . . . I only knew that she was different with an audience, even with an audience of one, not a member of her family. And I writhed against her showing off."[42]

⁓

Although at various times in her adult life Millicent would profess that she knew nothing of the relationship between Mabel and Austin, it's very clear that she did. Millicent's diaries and journals from childhood note "Mr. Dickinson's" visits to her home and carriage rides she took with her mother and "Mr. Dickinson," and make occasional mention of other members of the Dickinson family.

In her "Reminiscences" from 1927, Millicent remembered the time that Austin Dickinson spent in her home, how austere and aristocratic he seemed to her, how he was the "terrible center of the universe, though why he was such I could not have said." She recalled having watched Austin and her mother walk through a meadow one day, and another day, wrote of a ride she and Mabel had taken with him: "I was sitting between Mamma and Mr. Dickinson. I felt them lean together behind me. What transpired I do not know. I could have been borne rigid to a burning pyre before I would have turned my eyes.... Unaware they thought me!" Later that year she recalled, "I began at so early an age to suffer within myself, because of the ever-growing weight of mystifying complexities which surrounded me as in a mesh, that I began also at an early age to be oblivious to usually accepted sources of annoyance and legitimate excuses for fear."[43]

In a 1959 interview Millicent said, "Mr. Dickinson was a very magnificent looking man.... I never addressed him and he never said anything to me that I can remember except 'Hello Child.'... He was a presence—an omnipresence I may say—and a constant visitor every day at our house."[44]

That wasn't all Millicent remembered seeing or thinking about during her early years. "I remember a reception at the President's house—it must have been in the '90s—when I saw her left hand bare and her right with the engagement and wedding rings which Mr. Dickinson had given her.... I felt sickened by such a sense of shame, such a chaotic, profound, devastating, nauseating emotion, all the more corroding because it could not be expressed, either in words or even to my own mind.... I knew without knowing for I had not been told, and never knew what the rings were actually a symbol of."[45]

Millicent also suffered from the ways in which her mother and Austin's relationship was perceived in Amherst, which were not so much articulated as implied. "I was a repository... of the disapproval and moral condemnation of the community. No tangible effulgence spilled over to me, that was theirs and theirs only—but there was disapproval enough to supply all. I did not bask in exaltation but in wonder and dumb unhappiness—a monster which oppressed me, an unhappiness I did not recognize nor understand."[46] In her adult years, Millicent admitted to being puzzled as a child as she came to realize that her mother was frowned on—if not actively censured—by some portion of Amherst society. She recalled that this feeling seemed to emanate from Sue and Mattie Dickinson, whom she suggested were "a race apart. They walked about the village streets scattering venom as they walked . . . half the town seemed to agree with their vitriol."[47]

Millicent summarized her strange emotional state due to Mabel and Austin's affair in a 1932 "Reminiscence":

> As a child it was bewilderment, which with adolescence turned to disapproval, which called forth, however, a still fiercer loyalty, though silent, before the world. Disapproval of her coquetry, of her manner of dressing, so different from that of other Amherst mothers, of her giving talks, which also they did not do, of her exaggeration, of her dancing—and of some deeper thing which underlay all those things which I could name, or could have, had I ever been required to articulate on the subject—egged on, as I now think of it, by my grandmother from whom the disapproval doubtless emanated in the first place.[48]

Indeed, elsewhere—even in some of her journals—Millicent noted that Molly's disapproval of her daughter's relationship with Austin Dickinson filtered its way to Millicent, encapsulated best in one phrase that read, "Grandma has poisoned my thought of Mamma."

Even though there were so many ways in which Millicent sought to distance herself from Mabel, so many times that Millicent harbored quiet resentments of Mabel and found her anywhere from mildly objectionable to downright immoral, Millicent still loved her mother dearly. She felt extremely protective of her and inordinately responsible for her. This would take many forms throughout the years. Above all, Millicent felt unstinting loyalty to both of her flawed parents. "It must be that the keynote of my character was loyalty—blind, unquestioning—for no questions were ever asked of anybody. . . . I stored all things in my heart and pondered them there."[49]

In later life, Millicent often claimed that as a child she accepted things that she observed unquestioningly. She once wrote that she was "the solemn little child with great eyes, whose earliest remembrance is of bewilderment and wonder."[50] The emotional turbulence she experienced through her mother's unorthodox relationship with Austin Dickinson affected her deeply starting from childhood when she observed things that seemed not quite right. These unsettled feelings would reverberate throughout her life, often in ways she repressed, sometimes in ways she could not easily articulate. Despite her "bewilderment and wonder" as a child, through inclination and training, Millicent learned to approach the world in a systematic and meticulous way. These traits would become key in both her personal and professional life, coming into sharpest focus when she chose to embrace the editing of Emily's poetry and letters. The little girl who took the temperature every morning and methodically recorded it in a notebook became the woman who did the very same thing.

⌒

CHAPTER 6

EMBRACING EMILY'S POEMS (1886–1897)

"Emily wrote in the strangest hand ever seen"

Change was in the air in the mid-1880s. Grover Cleveland became the first Democratic president in an era of Republican-dominated politics. America's four-year economic depression ended but residual anxieties culminated in a general strike and the Haymarket Riots in May of 1886. Racial and ethnic tensions plaguing the nation boiled over in anti-Chinese riots in Seattle and in the murder of twenty African Americans in Mississippi. For many Americans, the dedication of the Statue of Liberty in New York Harbor in the fall of 1886 was meant to symbolize a hope and unity by welcoming immigrants, but to some it represented policies that were creating economic, labor and ethnic unrest.

But it was perhaps some of the issues not making the pages of national news that troubled Mabel the most. She, too, was living through a period of unrest, her circumstances a precarious balance that could easily be toppled.

What she perceived as the chilling presence of Sue Dickinson continued to make Mabel uncomfortable as she and David settled in to their rented house on Lessey Street in 1885. Mabel was learning to live a

EMILY DICKINSON, CIRCA 1848. IN 2012 ANOTHER POSSIBLE PHOTO OF EMILY SURFACED, BUT THIS DAGUERREOTYPE WAS THE FIRST—AND POSSIBLY ONLY— VERIFIABLE IMAGE OF HER.

double life, though the whispers around Amherst did not abate. Sue assid-uously avoided Mabel, including leaving the First Congregational Church after Mabel began singing as part of a quartet there, and forbidding her daughter Mattie from attending parties that Mabel chaperoned. Polly Longsworth suggests that Sue also "became intensely, almost obsessively absorbed in Ned's and Mattie's lives, as if this compensated her for loss of control of Austin and absolved her from the humiliation Mabel inflicted."[1]

Sue's actions, recorded through letters Ned wrote to his sister and (perhaps less reliably) through Mabel's diaries and journals, reveal a woman focusing on her two living children and continuing to make her home a haven for the arts. But this did not relieve the building pressures. In January of 1885, when Austin "positively forbid anything being done [at The Evergreens] . . . mother began to pull off the paper" from the walls, Ned told Mattie in a letter. This fit of pique demonstrated the simmering fury Sue fought to control.[2]

Sue was bedridden for most of the winter and spring of 1885 with a mysterious illness treated with small doses of arsenic. David was away frequently, and Grandma Wilder was there to care for Millicent. Com-bined, these circumstances left Mabel and Austin free to pursue their relationship. Austin continued to bring Mabel to The Homestead to sing and play piano for Lavinia and Emily. Life, for the moment, had settled into a routine, if a temporary and discomforting one, with fester-ing tensions ever present just below the surface.

Mabel lived life reactively. Though very much in love, she and Aus-tin were still not able to openly declare their affection or plan their life together. In May of 1885 she wrote in her journal, "I am destined to live greatly—principally—in emotions. Sometimes I positively sigh to live for awhile just a serene, constituted commonplace life."[3]

At the same time, Mabel, David and Austin were busily planning a new Queen Anne–style cottage for the Todds on land that Austin had given them, across the meadow from The Evergreens. This would be the first home that Mabel ever owned and, as someone who had grown up in a series of rented properties and who aspired to enter a different class, she was thrilled at the prospect. Austin took charge of siting and landscaping the new house, as well as cutting a road between his home and the new property; David supervised its construction; and Mabel took over the bookkeeping responsibilities, planned the décor and decided upon a name for the new house. Mabel originally wanted to call the house "Birchbank," but settled on "The Dell." "Austin suggested it as being on the whole best [name]," Mabel later wrote.[4] They moved into their new home in 1887, before it was entirely completed.

But even a new home could not quell Mabel's increasing bitterness that her love for Austin had to remain hidden. "Is it true that the soul expands in misfortune and unhappiness, and finds god in it?" she queried in her journal. "I hope so! I want this—and still I am tired of suffering."[5]

Mabel was not the only one silently suffering. Emily Dickinson's health had started deteriorating.

After enduring decades of poor health, Emily truly began to decline in 1886. Years earlier she never completed school at Mount Holyoke and suffered from various respiratory, eye and "nerve" ailments throughout early adulthood. Her illnesses continued and worsened in later years. In an extended remembrance, her cousin Clara Newman Turner, who lived with Austin and Sue for a number of years before Mabel's arrival in Amherst, wrote that following Gib Dickinson's tragic death, Emily "had a chill . . . and was taken home unconscious" and had similar "attacks" during the next two years.[6] Dickinson biographer Richard Sewall notes that Emily never fully recovered. Sue Dickinson, who penned Emily's obituary in the *Springfield Republican*, wrote that Emily had been an invalid from 1884 to 1886.[7]

Mabel had long been aware of Emily's seclusion, if not her infirmities. She'd written in her journal in 1882, "no one has seen her in all those years except her own family. She is very brilliant and strong, but became disgusted with society & declared she would leave it when she was quite young." (Sewall wrote of Emily making deliberate decisions to withdraw from religious life in Amherst; it's not clear whether this issue was one Austin raised with Mabel, leading her to conclude as she did about Emily's "disgust" with society.) In 1885, Mabel chided Molly for not responding to a note from the Dickinson sisters—Mabel had introduced her parents to Vinnie and told them about Emily—suggesting, "She and her sister live, in great measure, in their correspondence." While there is no record in Mabel's private writings nor in Mabel's and Austin's letters of the period indicating his growing concerns over Emily's declining health, Mabel noted briefly in her diary on May 13, 1886, that Emily was sick, and on the subsequent day that Austin was "terribly oppressed."[8] Emily died the next day, perhaps due to complications from Bright's disease. This turned out to be a watershed moment for Mabel, and ultimately, for Millicent, too.

Sometime after Emily's funeral, her sister Lavinia discovered hundreds of poems Emily had written and saved. In an unpublished paper called "Emily Dickinson, Poet and Woman," Mabel suggested it was just "a day or two after her death her sister came upon a sad yet delightful surprise in finding a locked drawer filled to the brim with manuscript poems."[9] Some of the poems were gathered in close to sixty small collections Emily had hand-sewn together with twine. Vinnie referred to these as "volumes," while Mabel would coin the term "fascicles" to describe them (Literary theorist Virginia Jackson suggests that Mabel preferred "the botanical term for a bundle of stems or leaves to Lavinia's image of a series of bound books." Perhaps it was Vinnie's image of the poems as books, a valued commodity in the Dickinson home, that convinced her they were not part of Emily's private papers, which she had promised to burn.)[10]

Lavinia would continue to find poems for several years after Emily's death, some written in the margins of saved newspapers, some on scraps of paper or the backs of envelopes and shopping lists and even on brown paper bags from the grocers'. Poet, visual artist and Dickinson researcher Jen Bervin writes, "Dickinson's writings might best be described as epistolary. Everything she wrote—poems, letters, in drafts, in fascicles, on folios, individual sheets, envelopes, and fragments—was predominantly composed on plain, machine-made stationery." In the catalog publication paired with a 2017 exhibit at the Morgan Library of Dickinson's manuscripts, scholar Marta Werner utilizes a map metaphor for explaining how one can assess the poet's various manuscripts: "They are aids to our navigation of the world; they give meaning to the ideas of near and far . . . form a kind of poetic atlas, her many unbound poems on single sheets or partial sheets seem like close-ups or bright fragments torn from an infinite but now vanished map."[11]

Vinnie sought to preserve each poem or partial poem she found. Though Mabel quipped many years later, "Vinnie went away to school, though there was no inspiration of intellect to take her,"[12] Lavinia nevertheless knew enough to recognize her sister's genius, and it was of utmost importance to her that others should also acknowledge Emily's gift. She quickly determined that she would not destroy the poetry, but instead would share it widely with the world.

Lavinia's staunch belief in the significance of her sister's poetry came from her experience in the role of Dickinson family facilitator. Born in 1833, the youngest of Edward and Emily Norcross Dickinson's children, Vinnie, who once wrote of herself, "I had the family to keep track of," grew up to play a pivotal role in the lives of her parents, her siblings, her sister-in-law and her brother's lover. Richard Sewall's multifaceted assessment of Vinnie suggests that while Emily considered her sister to be "the uncomplicated Dickinson," Lavinia had greater depth. Her quirky humor, dedication to household tasks and above all, her devotion to her family reveal her to have been the glue in a set of complex family relations. "As Emily's closest associate for more than fifty years," writes Sewall, "she became indispensable to her in many ways." Vinnie became Austin's confederate once he began bringing Mabel to The Homestead, enabling their relationship. Vinnie also developed an independent relationship with Mabel, who came to call on her frequently, and also with David. After Gib and Emily Norcross's deaths and during her sister's increasing illnesses, "Vinnie's life was not a happy one . . . about the only solid pleasure in her life during these years seems to have come from her friendship with Mrs. Mabel Todd."[13] So it is not surprising that when Vinnie discovered the treasure trove of Emily's poems, she felt compelled to do something with it.

In her 1945 recounting of the "literary debut of Emily Dickinson" in *Ancestors' Brocades*, Millicent recalled her mother had said, "shortly after Emily's death her sister Lavinia came to me actually trembling with excitement. She had discovered a veritable treasure—a box full of Emily's poems that she had no instructions to destroy. She had already burned without examination hundreds of manuscripts and letters to Emily, many of them from nationally known persons, thus, she believed, carrying out her sister's wishes. . . . Later, she bitterly regretted such inordinate haste. But these poems, she told me, must be printed at once. Would I send them to some printer—as she innocently called them— which was the best one, and how quickly could the poems appear?"[14]

Apparently, Mabel was Vinnie's third choice. She first brought the poems to the attention of Sue Dickinson, with whom Vinnie had had a difficult and complicated relationship. Richard Sewall and other Dickinson biographers have pointed to Vinnie's loyalty to Emily and consequent distrust of Sue for the many times she had disappointed Emily. Sewall suggests that Emily's relations with Sue were "uneven": on the one hand, the two had been extremely good friends prior to Sue and Austin's marriage, they exchanged many letters and poems over many years, but on the other, Emily ceased visiting her sister-in-law sometime in the late 1860s and there appeared to be a breach in their friendship. Sewall also posits that in her role as observer of family tensions Emily saw too many examples of Sue's "deceptions"—actions that Sewall never spelled out fully—and that Vinnie was well aware of Emily's ambivalence. Vinnie was also fiercely loyal to Austin, and she knew that Sue made him unhappy. Sewall mentions letters from other Dickinson neighbors and friends suggesting Vinnie was "Curiously in fear of Sue; Vinnie's charge that Sue shortened Emily's life with her cruelties . . . and treated them [Emily and Vinnie] as strangers or worse." He quotes Vinnie's friend, Mary Lee Hall's 1935 comment: "Sue was relentlessly cruel to Miss Vinnie in every possible way. . . . I was called to Miss Vinnie's many times to quiet her nerves and help her recover from Sue's verbal blows." Sewall admits that while "it is almost impossible to determine the acts here," that anecdotal evidence, such as Vinnie's suggestion that

Sue had "set her dogs on Vinnie's cats" might show why Vinnie would have had her own ambivalence about her sister-in-law.[15]

But whatever her feelings for Sue might have been, Vinnie knew that Emily had given Sue some of her poems. In fact, some sources suggest Emily sent Sue hundreds of poems over the years.[16] While Vinnie knew that Sue "professed great admiration of Emily's work," and Vinnie believed Sue a knowledgeable advocate for great art, Sue envisioned only a small private printing of the poems, hardly the grand circulation Vinnie imagined. When Sue did not move with alacrity to organize and prepare the poems for publication, Vinnie grew impatient. She later wrote in a letter, "Mrs. Dickinson was enthusiastic for a while, then indifferent & later utterly discouraging."[17]

Mabel's rendering of this story was more pointedly accusatory. After the first volume of poetry was published in 1890, Mabel reflected in her journal, "Susan and her progeny are still outraged at me. . . . Why is still a mystery to me, for they had the entire box of Emily's manuscripts over there for nearly two years after she died, and Vinnie urging them all the time, with fierce insistence, to do something about getting them published." She went on to write, "Susan is afflicted with an unconquerable laziness, and kept saying she would, and would perhaps, until Vinnie was wild. At last she announced that she thought nothing had better be done, they would never sell, they had not enough money to get them out, the public would not care for them . . . in short, she gave it up."[18] (Mabel's recollection was skewed, or exaggerated—in fact, Mabel began copying the poems in 1887, just nine months after Emily's death, not two years.)

Vinnie next turned to Colonel Thomas Wentworth Higginson. During her lifetime, Emily had sent him many letters and nearly one hundred poems, over a period spanning almost two decades. Emily initially wrote to Higginson, who was known for his work in many of the social reform movements of the day but also widely known as an author and respected literary critic, following the publication in 1862 of his inspirational "Letter to a Young Contributor" encouraging would-be authors. Emily's letter asked him if her verse was "alive," and enclosed four poems; he was intrigued enough to write her back immediately and

find out more about the mysterious "E Dickinson." Through their subsequent correspondence about her work, Emily came to refer to herself
as his "scholar" and called Higginson her "preceptor." Higginson offered
his thoughts and advice but never suggested she publish her poetry.
"Higginson had always admired Emily's dazzling thoughts," suggests
Sewall, "but had consistently deplored the form of her poems."[19]

When Vinnie wrote to Higginson about the project to publish her
sister's poetry, he replied "that he was extremely busy, and that the con-
fused manuscripts presented a nearly insuperable obstacle to reading
and judging such quantities of poems. Though he admired the singular
talent of Emily Dickinson, he hardly thought enough could be found to
make an even semi-conventional volume."[20]

And so, twice discouraged, Vinnie turned to Mabel.

From Mabel's diaries and journals, the letters between Lavinia
and Mabel and some of the Dickinson biographies, it is clear that
Lavinia greatly admired Mabel's
social graces, energy and ambition. She knew that Mabel was
well connected and could get the
poems published. Lavinia also
knew that her brother loved Mabel
passionately, and she did all she
could to enable the relationship:
allowing their assignations to
occur in her house while ensuring that Sue would not be there,
delivering messages from Austin
to Mabel and vice versa and at
times even addressing envelopes
for her brother to throw off suspicion. Mabel, for her part, seemed
to welcome the connection with

COLONEL THOMAS WENTWORTH
HIGGINSON ALREADY HAD ACCOLADES
IN MANY FIELDS BEFORE TAKING ON
THE TASK OF CO-EDITING THE EARLY
VOLUMES OF EMILY DICKINSON'S
POETRY.

Vinnie. Her diaries note many times when she went to "call on Miss Vinnie" or "went to Vinnie's at two—a very sweet and lovely hour." Mabel would often shop for Vinnie (Millicent recalled, "my mother seldom went to Boston without making some purchase for Miss Vinnie"[21]) and brought her items from her trips abroad. She tolerated Vinnie's many eccentricities (her multiple cats and her extreme devotion to them, her peculiar modes of discourse and dress, her general paranoia) and she put up with Vinnie's visits to The Dell, made late at night because, as Millicent observed, "[Vinnie] merely disliked having her movements known to her neighbors and so made her calls after dark."[22]

Vinnie knew that Mabel would share her own aspirations for a wide printing and circulation of the poetry, as well as her conviction that the poems were brilliant, and prevailed upon Mabel to get them published. Historian Sharon Nancy White suggests "Mabel's immediate and steadfast admiration for Dickinson's poetry," from the time Sue first shared one of Emily's poems, "underscores Mabel's readiness to respect her as an artist." As Mabel noted in her journal, Vinnie "always knew that I had faith in the poems."[23]

Upon looking through the materials Vinnie brought her, however, Mabel saw the enormity of the task. "I told her that no one would attempt to read the poems in Emily's own peculiar handwriting, much less judge them; that they would all have to be copied, and then be passed upon like any other production, from the commercial standpoint of the publishing business, and that certainly not less than a year must elapse before they could possibly be brought out. Her despair was pathetic. 'But they are *Emily's* poems,' she urged piteously, as if that explained everything." Mabel later recalled that Vinnie had no clue of how many poems there were, nor that Emily's handwriting—always somewhat difficult to read—shifted in three different styles. Nor did Vinnie realize that many poems were "written on both sides of the paper, interlined, altered and the number of suggested changes was baffling." Mabel estimated that "the mere copying . . . if pursued for four hours each morning, would occupy two or three years," and if one attempted to understand and incorporate Emily's own edits, that the task "might take much longer."[24]

Mabel didn't initially commit, recording in her journals that both David and Austin urged her not to take on the poems, suggesting that the project was likely to eat up years of her time. In 1930, Mabel stated that she had "tried at first to persuade Lavinia to place the poems with someone else. I hesitated to take on so much work and study, as well as to assume the responsibility necessary for the successful launching of a new poet on the sea of literary criticism. But she was unalterably determined that mine should be the hand which should help Emily sail."[25] Scholar R. W. Franklin suggests that Mabel's hesitation also came from "her own literary aspirations. . . . Editing Emily's poetry could interfere with her own work, for, as she knew, she had more ideas than time in which to realize them."[26] Though Mabel was incredibly industrious— she sensed that she could work on the poems and still pursue her own projects—she was still reluctant.

Vinnie persisted, making frequent late-night visits to Mabel's home urging her to undertake the work. "She . . . begged me vehemently to begin, only *begin* on the poems. One winter evening she arrived just before midnight. She was more than ever certain that I *must* undertake it. . . . Lavinia almost went on her knees to me that night, and it hurt me to see her so intensely in earnest over what might prove disappointing. But at last I did promise to put the poems in shape, try to find a publisher, and to begin the very next day."[27]

The first clear indication that Mabel decided to take on the task of copying Emily's poetry is a brief mention in a February 1887 journal entry. Mabel knew that she would be accompanying David on the first astronomical expedition to Japan from June to October. But starting in November 1887, after she returned from Japan, there are more frequent entries in her diary about spending several hours per day copying the poems; she sometimes noted bringing them over to The Homestead to share with Vinnie.

Polly Longsworth suggests that Mabel might have interpreted Vinnie's request to copy Emily's poems and get them published as a task "tangential" to Mabel's own literary aspirations. Longsworth believes that because Mabel's letters to Austin in 1887–1889 do not reflect much about her work on the poetry and because there are only scattered and rote entries in Mabel's diaries about working on this project, it was one Mabel undertook "principally as a favor—an enormous favor as it evolved—to Vinnie."[28]

However, Mabel's reflections from just a few years later suggest another interpretation. "The poems were having a wonderful effect on me, mentally and spiritually," she recalled. "They seemed to open the door into a wider universe than the little sphere surrounding me which so often hurt and compressed me—and they helped me nobly through a very trying time. Their sadness and hopelessness was so much bitterer than mine." Notes for lectures Mabel gave a couple of years later support the idea that she came to see her work on Emily's poetry as an activity that freed her from other more depressing aspects of her life and inspired her to persevere.[29]

It is clear from Mabel's journals, diaries and letters that the years during which she copied the poems were trying ones. Austin neither left his home nor his marriage, and Mabel's parents continued to write her letters implying her "activities" with Austin were wearing her down. Mabel periodically admitted to herself that she wanted to be more central in Austin's life. She tried to change things in the late 1880s by attempting to become pregnant. That truly might have altered everyone's life, but, as Mabel wrote to Austin in March of 1888, "I am more and more disappointed with the failure of the experiment."[30]

Mabel's journals evidence her growing bitterness and the ongoing tensions associated with having her relationship with Austin in shadow rather than in sunlight. But copying Emily's poetry offered her a new and productive outlet for her frustrations: "The winter was very trying for me from a new cause—or a new manifestation of the old cause—but on the whole I got through it pretty bravely and accepted a very great deal of work."[31] Work, for Mabel, was a salve. And she found that her musical and artistic training, her love for literature and for nature and her passion for Austin aligned with Emily's poetry, making her appreciate it all the more.

Mabel recalled that when she first took the box of poems, "The outlook was appalling. Emily wrote in the strangest hand ever seen, which I had to absolutely incorporate into my innermost consciousness before I could be certain of anything she reflected." Mabel also noted the difficulties she had because Emily often wrote "six or eight" different words she was considering using in a particular point in a poem, with additional choices that "would run around the margins."[32] In her 1930 *Harper's Magazine* article, Mabel wrote, "In the so-called 'copied poems,' tiny crosses written beside a word which might be changed ultimately and which referred to scores of possible words at the bottom of the page were all exactly alike, so that only the most sympathetic and at-one-with-the-author could determine where each word belonged."[33]

Mabel might not have been Vinnie's first choice of an editor, but it turned out that she was an inspired one. Mabel worked diligently and methodically on the poems, sometimes for hours each day to decipher, interpret and transcribe them. She called David and even seven-year-old Millicent into service to help. (Looking back, Millicent reflected, "Initiation into the vagaries of Emily's handwriting is one of the earliest rites I can recall.")[34] After laboriously copying different versions of each poem by hand, Mabel would type them up on her new borrowed Hammond typewriter. When she was more comfortable with the machine, Mabel sometimes typed poems without first copying them by hand. She worked fairly consistently from the time she returned from Japan in 1887 for the next two years, decoding, copying and typing hundreds of poems.

But Vinnie was impatient. Mabel wrote that when her other activities took her away from the copying, it often resulted in late-night visits from Vinnie. "She could not see why it took so much time. And I knew I was doing it as fast as a mortal could accomplish it, unless one devoted all one's time to it—and frequently I gave three or four hours a day to it."[35] Yet Vinnie continued to press Mabel, even admonishing her when she took a brief vacation in 1888 that she should stay on holiday only if "you fatten in strength & then be ready for poems!"[36]

In March of 1889, after she had already copied and typed over 300 poems, Mabel hired a young woman named Harriet Graves to assist her in copying the poems. Though Harriet copied almost 150 of them, Mabel soon realized that her assistant could not read Emily's handwriting properly and consequently transcribed words incorrectly. "I could not stand it. The absolute lack of any approach to understand or sympathy in what she was copying, although she did mechanically well enough, made poor Miss Graves seem to me a shade more than an insensitive machine—and some of her mistakes in Emily's mad words were so ludicrous as to be pathetic. Besides, it took more time to put her copies into fit shape than to do it myself."[37] Mabel also later suggested that Harriet's lack of understanding of the poems "seemed irreverent to the helpless poet to allow her verses to be so mangled. Loyalty to Emily's patient ghost swept over me and I permanently gave up hope of any mechanical assistance."[38]

By the end of the summer of 1889, Mabel had completed the copying of the seven hundred poems. She had to give up her Hammond typewriter and instead continued her work, either writing poems out by hand or typing them on a slower World machine. As literary analyst Ralph Franklin has written, "The World, a more primitive machine than the Hammond, had only capitals and was operated by rotating a letter into place and pressing down—slow and tedious work indeed—yet the 'few' Mrs. Todd did on this machine totaled nearly ninety. All forty of those extant have purple ink," whereas the ones typed earlier on the Hammond were done with a black ribbon. This has proven significant for later literary scholars trying to better and more authentically understand Emily's use of capitalization. In his doctoral dissertation, Franklin suggested, "Mrs. Todd revered accuracy, and she tried to be faithful at the time of copying, only introducing changes later." He observed that when Mabel worked on the Hammond machine ("one of the earliest to have small letters as well as capitals"), she could adhere to Emily's "capricious" use of capitals; the World machine was not capable of this "literal rendering."[39] In any case, after an initial version, either typed or handwritten, had been copied, then further editing could commence.

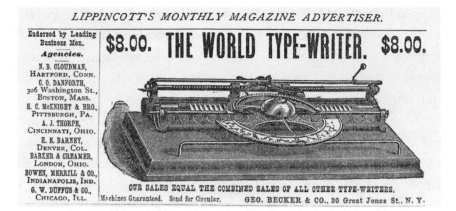

NEWSPAPER AD FOR A WORLD TYPEWRITER, SIMILAR TO THE ONE MABEL HAD.

Mabel was savvy enough about the publishing industry to know that Emily's poems would need more than simple transcription to receive any kind of publication contract. They needed editing to make them less idiosyncratic, and they needed a credentialed literary champion.

Mabel certainly not only knew of Thomas Wentworth Higginson by reputation but had actually met him on at least a couple of occasions prior to any of their collaborative work. Mabel had spoken with him at Emily's funeral; her mentions of Higginson's contributions to the event are found in both her journals and in letters she wrote to her mother. Mabel recalled Vinnie reported Higginson's refusal but also his stipulation that "if this tangle of literary wheat and chaff could be put in easy shape for consideration, he would be glad to go over it carefully."[40] In her 1930 *Harper's* article, Mabel wrote that Vinnie told her of Colonel Higginson's "quaint friendship" with Emily and asked that Mabel "have him co-operate in launching the poems."[41]

In the fall of 1889, after Mabel thought she would accompany David on an astronomical expedition to Angola only to discover at the last minute that no women were to be allowed on board the U.S. Navy ship, Mabel, who had already packed three trunks' worth of clothing and gotten the house in Amherst ready to be left for several months, decided to spend the time in Boston, instead. Along with her mother, grandmother and Millicent, Mabel rented some rooms for the winter. Once in town, Mabel arranged for a meeting with Colonel Higginson, determined to show him a large pile of copied poems. She brought with her the "immense file" that "weighed many pounds."

"He did not think a volume advisable," Mabel wrote in 1890. "They were crude in form, he said, and the public would not accept even fine ideas in such rough and mystical dress—so hard to elucidate." But certain of the poems' worth and determined to convince Higginson to sign onto the project, Mabel "read him nearly a dozen of my favorites—and he was greatly astonished—said he had no idea there were so many in passably conventional form." Emily's "strange cadences" came alive when Mabel read them aloud.

Higginson asked Mabel if she would classify the poems into three groups (A, B and C), organized by her own judgment of which were the best ones ("not only those of most original thought, but expressed in the best form"), a second group of poems "with striking ideas, but with too many of her peculiarities of construction to be used unaltered for the public" and a third group that she "considered too obscure or too irregular in form for public use, however brilliant and suggestive."[42] If she did that, Higginson said that he would look more carefully at the categorized poems during the winter months. Mabel was thrilled, though from the distance of many years later, noted she believed Higginson had not initially exuded confidence: "he indicated to me my herculean task, and I began alone."[43]

After Higginson agreed to assist with the project, Mabel stepped up her efforts to get the rest of the poems classified. She worked quickly and sent Higginson her selections on November 18. He responded a week later, saying, "I can't tell you how much I am enjoying the poems. There are many new to me which take my breath away & which also have form beyond most of those I have ever seen before. . . . My confidence in their availability is greatly increased & it is fortunate there are so many because it is obviously impossible to print all & this leaves the way open for careful selection."[44] He suggested that among the poems

Mabel selected in her first category, some were more worthy of publication than others. Further, he posited arranging the subset of poems thematically: those about life, those about nature, and those about time, death and eternity.

But then Higginson fell ill. Mabel noted, "for weeks nothing was heard from him except bulletins as to his illness. Vinnie was cast down, nearly wild in fact, and said the fates seemed in sorry shape against her." Undeterred, Mabel went to visit Higginson at his home in Cambridge "and he said if I would have patience enough to let him keep them until I returned from Chicago he would look them over and see what he thought of a volume." When she returned from a visit to her cousin, Mabel found Higginson had read through her selections, selected about two hundred poems and "in almost every case had chosen my A's."[45] Having arrived at their selection of poems for the volume, Mabel and Higginson would then launch what was perhaps the most daunting task of all, as well as their most controversial act: their editing of the poems.

—

After the first volume of poetry had been published, Mabel admitted in her journal that the poems' "carelessness of form exasperated me. I could always find the gist of meaning, and I admired her strange words and ways of using them, but the simplest laws of verse-making she ignored, and what she called rhymes grated on me. But she could not hide her wonderful power, and I knew she had genius."[46] Mabel also may have thought at the time, and certainly knew upon consideration years later, that the poems' "unconventionality might repel publishers."[47]

Higginson also felt that the poems defied too many conventions of nineteenth-century verse. Biographer Brenda Wineapple notes that some of Higginson's initial thoughts about the poetry Emily sent him are lost, for while he "preserved a large number of Dickinson's letters to him, most of his to her have mysteriously vanished. . . . Because those letters are missing, one has to infer a good deal."[48] Vinnie, however, destroyed much of Emily's saved correspondence, and did not catalog what she burned. In an essay published in the *Atlantic Monthly* in 1891, Higginson recalled that the first few poems Emily sent him left a powerful impact. He wrote that "The impression of a wholly new and original poetic genius was as distinct on my mind at the first reading of these four poems as it is now, after thirty years of further knowledge; and with it came the problem never yet solved, what place ought to be assigned in literature to what is so remarkable, yet so elusive of criticism."[49] Higginson noted from her very first correspondence Emily's sparse and idiosyncratic use of punctuation and capitalization—even when he looked over Mabel's copies of the poems that rendered them more readable, Higginson still had concerns about the form in which many of them appeared.

In her journals, Mabel suggested that while Higginson concurred with most of her selections, they "changed words here and there in the two hundred to make them smoother."[50] Sometimes Emily's variant word selections were used—for example, in "The Humming Bird" (one of the few poems she actually titled), Emily had offered four alternates to the word "revolving": "delusive, dissembling, dissolving, renewing."

"In this case," wrote Mabel, "as in many others I retained the word she evidently preferred by using it in her own final copy." But in other poems, Mabel clearly substituted words she felt better conveyed meaning (though these changes have often reverted to Emily's original choices in more recent publications). For example, in poem XXXI in *Poems* (poem 258 in Johnson's later rendering), Mabel substituted the word "weight" for "heft":

There's a certain slant of light,
On winter afternoons,
That oppresses, like the weight
Of cathedral tunes.

R. W. Franklin's exhaustive analysis of Mabel's and Higginson's editing demonstrates many other instances in which they altered Emily's word choice. Other scholars have suggested that in so doing, they might also have altered her poetic intent.[51]

Millicent's later interpretation of this work wavered between staunchly defending the editorial practice and taking a more contemporary critical view. "Emily placed a great responsibility upon her editors by leaving to them so often the choice of a key word. For it authorized them to color her thought with their taste. Obliged so often to make a choice, they might be tempted to go further, to *change* a word to fit their own preference—a dangerous leeway, for the thought is timeless while taste may change,"[52] she wrote in *Ancestors' Brocades*. Millicent also made clear that even when her mother altered Emily's word choice, these were decisions not made easily. According to Millicent, her mother seemed aware that in compromising with Higginson's view of what might be acceptable, she might also have undermined Emily's poetic intent.

In addition to altering words, Mabel and Higginson made other textual changes. Among other things, they sometimes altered words to make lines rhyme and conform to a more typical a-b-c-b rhyming pattern. Franklin writes, "By the editors' conventional standards, Emily Dickinson's poetry frequently had no rhyme or rhythm, and much of the editorial surgery was directed toward giving it some."[53] They altered her spellings, too. Millicent's explanation for this was that only "habitual mistakes in spelling were corrected," though other critics more recently have suggested that some spelling alterations "which seem[ed] innocuous enough . . . sometimes involved removing a New England pronunciation that she might have been trying to indicate."[54]

They also changed what Millicent deemed "grammatical vagaries" or "Emily's grammatical irresponsibility"—including swapping out "he" for "him" and "she" for "her" in some poems. Several more recent scholars suggested that Emily's grammar might have reflected spoken usage of the day rather than written usage, though this is not certain. Others posit that Emily's pronoun use might have been deliberate and its suggestiveness in tying "she" with sensual imagery rather than "he" was something Mabel and Higginson purposively sought to change to make the poems more acceptable to potential readers.

At the same time there was some difference of opinion between Mabel and Higginson about whether to correct Emily's grammar. The often-cited example is Higginson's apparent insistence on altering the final line, "I wish I were a Hay" to "I wish I were hay." Mabel reflected, "The quaintness of the article really appealed to me, but my trusted collaborator was decided on that line. 'It cannot go in so,' he exclaimed, 'everybody would say that *hay* is a collective noun requiring the definite article. Nobody can call it *a hay*!' So I retired, feeling that of course he was right with regard to the public. But I have always had a sneaking desire to see a change back to the original version!"[55] (Contemporary publications of this poem have restored the article; Mabel would be pleased.)

In a few cases, these first editors decided to omit a stanza of a poem. Writing about this practice in *Ancestors' Brocades*, Millicent stated, "while omitting a stanza might sometime improve a poem, it was more often a mistake."[56] At times Mabel and Higginson left off a stanza because Emily, herself, had used it in slightly different form as a standalone poem; in other cases, they made a decision to delete a stanza because they found different versions of the same poem without the stanza in question.

Mabel and Higginson also made editorial decisions that, according to Millicent, "were not so much matters of taste as of typographical convention." These had to do with Emily's idiosyncratic, seemingly random capitalization of words and her use of punctuation, including underscores, quotation marks and especially dashes. Each of these issues has been the subject of considerable academic debate. Franklin points out that while Higginson believed that Emily capitalized every noun, that is not correct and, while Mabel explained that "all important words begin with capitals," that seems not to be consistently the case, either. The debate over whether Emily truly had a system for when she chose to use capital letters continued well into the twentieth century.[57]

Similarly, several theories have been posited about whether Emily used punctuation consistently, with any particular reason or for any particular effect. Millicent wrote, "As Emily grew older, she dispensed with punctuation more and more until at last she was using dashes for the most part, with an occasional comma or period. What should be done about those dashes? To what conventional forms did they most closely correspond?"[58] More recent theories include dashes being "merely a habit of handwriting" that Emily used inconsistently, conventions of informal writing of the nineteenth century and simple habit that is "usually not consciously controlled."[59] Another contemporary idea is that Emily's use of the dash is more akin to musical phrasing, suggesting pauses of different lengths that she intended readers to make between different words or phrases.[60]

Apart from editing the poems to put them into a palatable form for the late nineteenth-century reading audience, Mabel and Higginson also ordered and titled the poems, practices that later Dickinson scholars and literary analysts have mostly decried.

To suggest that there is confusion and debate about how Mabel ordered and numbered the poems, whether her system was accurate, and if it was she or David who decided on the ordering and numbering, is an understatement. Millicent intimated that decisions about how to number the poems were David's. Perhaps the title of Franklin's meticulously researched chapter on this issue best summarizes his conclusions: "Manuscript Order and Disorder." Other scholars have suggested that Mabel put the poems "in no particular order," which left to future researchers the task of figuring out their chronology and an appropriate ordering. In 1955, Thomas H. Johnson published a three-volume "variorum" of Emily's poetry that not only brought together all of the poems for the first time but also attempted to place them in an approximate chronological order. In 1981, Franklin utilized clues from the original papers—marks, punctures and other pieces of physical evidence—to reorder the poems in a different chronology. Since then, some scholars have advocated for thematic groupings of poems, more like what Mabel and Higginson originally devised.

Few of Mabel's and Higginson's decisions have drawn more ire than the decision to title poems that originally bore no name. Emily herself gave titles to only a few of what proved to be nearly eighteen hundred poems. Scholar John Mulvihill suggests that Emily left the vast majority of her poetry untitled both because she did not publish it, and thus had no need to yield to this convention, and also because titling poems tends to draw a reader's attention to a particular image or interpretation. "Left untitled, one can argue, a poem can more simply *be*, or seem to be."[61]

Mabel had reservations about titling the poems. In 1890 she wrote that while Higginson wanted to put titles on the poems, "I do not believe, myself, in naming them; and although I admire Mr. Higginson very much, I do not think many of his titles good."[62] Mabel thought that Higginson was often off base with his titles, and that a title such as "A World Well Lost" for the poem that began "I lost a world the other day. / Has anybody found?" completely misrepresented Emily's thought.

Contemporary practice for the identification of Emily's poetry is to utilize the numerical system devised by Johnson in the 1950s, along with the poem's first line rather than use a particular title, or to use the numerical system Franklin established in the late 1990s in his chronologically arranged three-volume edition of the complete poems utilizing newer methods of dating the poems. This is a decision Mabel probably would have embraced. But Mabel yielded to Higginson on the titling of the poetry, as she did on other editorial decisions. As Millicent explained, "My mother was ready to accept as final Colonel Higginson's judgment regarding the poems. Though a lesser figure he had been coeval with the greatest and that sufficed."[63] For Mabel, his judgment trumped her own, even though she often retained and recorded her own opinions. As literary scholar Elizabeth Horan points out, while Mabel "maintained all her prerogatives as a 'lady,' she got her way because she willingly deferred to men. . . . She was careful not to appear pushy and to take others' interests into account when she proposed new lines of action."[64]

Reflecting on the early work done by Mabel and Higginson, literary analyst Virginia Jackson concludes:

> Most readers would agree that Dickinson's early editors imposed conventional poetic form—including titles, regular rhyme, and standard punctuation—on the published verse that in manuscript evaded or swerved away from such conventions, and most would also agree that editors since Higginson have brought Dickinson's

published work ever closer to its original scriptive forms, so that in moving forward from the nineteenth to the twentieth to the twenty-first century we have gradually moved back to discover the "original poetic genius" early editors failed adequately to represent in print.[65]

Mabel most surely would dispute this assessment. More than anything, she insisted that she "felt the genius" of the poems. She drew a sharp distinction between her own copying and editing of the poems and what she felt had been the "rough handling" they experienced at the hand of Harriet Graves, who missed "their dainty and veiled meanings"; the poems, she thought, required that they "be gently and understandingly wooed."[66] Mabel firmly believed she, unlike Miss Graves, had carefully, honestly and successfully rendered Emily's poems.

Partway through their process of "creative editing," as Millicent later termed it, Mabel and Thomas Wentworth Higginson decided that they should move forward on attempting to find a publisher for Emily's poetry. Mabel was certainly feeling increasing pressure from Lavinia to find "a printer," and she was no doubt wondering whether all of her hard labor on copying, typing and editing the poems would bear fruit.

In a footnote in *Ancestors' Brocades*, Millicent suggested her father told her that Colonel Higginson, who had been a "reader" for Houghton Mifflin in Boston, wanted to bring the poems there first. According to David, Houghton Mifflin rejected the manuscripts: "the poems, they said, were much too queer—the rhymes were all wrong. They thought that Higginson must be losing his mind to recommend such stuff."[67]

Mabel and Higginson decided to take the poems to Thomas Niles Jr., the head of Roberts Brothers publishing in Boston because, as Mabel later wrote, "Emily had had a sympathetic correspondence with him, and we thought it best to have someone pass judgment upon the poems who had known something of the shy writer," even though in the past Niles thought that to publish Emily's "lubractions" was a risk.[68] At the end of May 1890, Mabel brought the poems to Niles's office.

According to Millicent, David followed up the next week by going to Boston and speaking with Niles, himself. Millicent consistently believed that her father's role in getting Emily's poetry edited and published was an underreported and overlooked part of the story; in both her "Reminiscences" and in other writings, Millicent pointed out the hours David spent editing and copying poems, as well as his role in insisting that the poems deserved a full print run. In mid-June, Mabel received a letter from Higginson enclosing a note from the publisher and one from the poet Arlo Bates, to whom the poems had been sent for review. While Bates felt that "there is hardly one of these poems which does not bear marks of unusual and remarkable talent; there is hardly one of them which is not marked by an extraordinary crudity of workmanship." Bates believed that the poems needed more editing and more judicious selection. Niles commented to Higginson that given Bates's assessment, he felt it "unwise to perpetuate Miss Dickinson's poems. They are quite as remarkable for defects as for beauties." However, he continued, if Lavinia were willing to pay for the plates necessary to reproduce the poems, he would be willing to publish a small run. Higginson concluded in his note to Mabel that he thought the critiques excellent, that they should do the work and that he had told Niles that "you [Mabel] would probably approve his offer."[69]

When Mabel presented this proposal to Vinnie, Vinnie was furious. According to Mabel, Vinnie's blind loyalty to Emily and impatience to get the poems published made her "inarticulate with rage." But, Mabel suggested in her journal, she was persuasive. She presented to Vinnie a sense of what was realistic with regard to getting such unconventional verse of an unknown poet published, and ultimately cajoled Vinnie into agreeing to the deal: "I conferred with Vinnie (who has about as much knowledge about business as a Maltese cat) and I accepted the offer."[70]

Mabel and Higginson, though disappointed Bates suggested eliminating a number of key poems (wrote Higginson, "My opinion of Mr. Bates has gone down greatly, for he certainly wished to leave out several of the best"), elected to move forward. Throughout the summer of 1890 they had a lively correspondence in which they debated further edits, the issue of titling poems and the reinstatement of fifteen of the poems Bates suggested eliminating. Mabel later told Millicent:

> During all this time we were discussing at intervals the question of naming the poems, and of the changes either of us might wish to make, independent of her [Emily's] own multitudinous corrections and suggestions. But upon this subject we never wholly agreed, Colonel Higginson looking at it more in the light of the reading public as well as of the publishers, while I, with fewer books and articles to my credit than my much older co-worker . . . was exceedingly loath to assign titles to any of them, which might not be unmistakably indicated in the poem, itself.[71]

As the editing progressed, Mabel and Higginson made additional plans for publication of the poetry, many of which were driven by Mabel, who understood marketing long before the term became commonplace. She knew that in order to build excitement about the poems, there needed to be some prepublication chatter, that the aesthetic appeal of the volume to women (whom she believed would be the most likely purchasers and thus the target market) needed to be built, and that the poems' publication needed to be followed by well-placed endorsements.

They decided that Higginson would write an article to be published in conjunction with the collection. Part of this article would also be used for a preface to the volume that Higginson would write based on his own personal history of two decades' worth of correspondence with Emily about her work. Higginson opted to place his article in the *Christian Union* in September 1890. In addition, Mabel wrote to her friend William Dean Howells, the so-called Dean of American Letters and editor of the *Atlantic Monthly*, to let him know about the forthcoming volume. Howells was enthusiastic and offered to write an article about it.

Mabel decided to use her panel of Indian pipe wildflowers for the cover. This was the painting that she had given Emily and about which Emily had written her such a stunningly well-crafted thank-you that Mabel copied it into her journal. "Mr. Higginson thought they might

WITH AN INSTINCTIVE SENSE OF WHAT WOULD SELL, MABEL DESIGNED THE COVER FOR THE FIRST VOLUME OF EMILY DICKINSON'S POETRY.

be almost being too appropriate and spectral at first, but they were done, and are very effective."[72] But for Mabel, the choice was both sentimental and practical—she suspected it would sell.

Mabel also selected the cover color (white) with a gilt top, and the title and author's name in gold. Mabel reportedly told Millicent, "The gray, white and silver of the first edition thus, by happy intuition, expressed somewhat of Emily's 'cool and nun-like personality'. . . the dainty binding, devised partly with this symbolism in mind, partly in the hope of beguiling Christmas shoppers into buying the book for the beauty of its cover, was protected not only by a plain jacket but also by a shiny white pasteboard box made to fit."[73]

All seemed to be going along smoothly until the middle of July 1890, when Mabel received a puzzling query from Colonel Higginson. He sent her a letter he had received from Lavinia, annotating it in pencil, "Can you interpret the words underscored?" The letter to Higginson expressed Vinnie's gratitude for his work on the volume, as well as her disappointment that not all of the poems were to be included. She then noted, "the poem so long watched for in the 'Scribner' will appear in August number" and concluded, "I dare say you are aware our 'co-worker' is to be 'sub rosa,' for reasons you may understand."

Mabel was stunned but she also instantly and clearly saw what was going on. Without Vinnie's knowledge or approval, Sue had sent one of Emily's poems to Scribner's Magazine. Vinnie, who considered herself the sole proprietor of Emily's poetry, was furious at this transgression. Adding insult to perceived injury, Sue kept the money she received from the poem's publication. She had also apparently misread one of the words in the poem and sent it transcribed improperly. There was also Vinnie's knowledge that she had first asked Sue to edit the poems but that she delayed so long that Vinnie moved on to the next possible editor. Mabel also knew the other piece of pertinent information—that despite her fury, Vinnie was fearful of Sue. "Vinnie did not want my name on the book because she didn't want Sue to know that I had anything to do with it," she told Millicent. "Sue would have annihilated her if she could. . . . She was scared to death of Sue."[74]

Mabel wrote back to Higginson and deciphered Vinnie's almost unreadable handwriting for him. Mabel clearly interpreted Higginson's request as one to help him read *what* Vinnie had written, not to understand *why* she had written this. Mabel asked him, "what we should do about this, a species of treachery beyond my imagining." Higginson, she reported, knew that "I was her representative, and acting for her," and responded, "my name must appear on the volume somewhere, and before his, since I had done the hardest part of the work."[75] Mabel asked Higginson to place her name where he thought appropriate, and in the end, the volume was listed as "edited by her friends, Mabel Loomis Todd and Thomas Wentworth Higginson."

Just after the poems' publication Mabel reported that Vinnie "plucked up a great deal of spirit. The more indignant Susan is now the higher Vinnie holds her head."[76]

Poems, by Emily Dickinson, was published on November 12, 1890. Roberts Brothers did an initial press run of 480 copies. Mabel was sent six copies, and she later told Millicent, "The sense of actually holding it in our hands was one of exultation." But, as Millicent noted, with the publication of this volume, "A great calm seems to have enveloped them all—an oppressive quiet, like the eye of the storm."[77]

Much to the delight of the "two of her friends" who edited the first volume of Emily's poetry—and to the great surprise of her publisher— the first edition of *Poems* sold out in weeks. By the end of December, the third printing "was exhausted," said Mabel. The book's "commercial success kept Roberts Brothers more occupied than either Niles or the editors had anticipated. . . . The Christmas demand made another [printing] necessary in less than two weeks, and yet another in January."[78] Reflecting back on this time, Mabel wrote, "And so the book had more than justified my years of toil with little encouragement except a sustaining belief in the greatness of Emily's poetry. She, perhaps, would have been the most surprised of her readers, could she have seen from some upper realm the astonishing reception accorded her 'mind.' "[79]

Higginson wrote to Mabel of his joy in their collective triumph: "Pardon me if I bore you, but . . . you are the only person who can feel as I do about this extraordinary thing we have done in recording this rare genius. I feel as if we had climbed to a cloud, pulled it away, and revealed a new star behind it."[80]

Despite decidedly mixed initial reviews, sales suggested that the public did, indeed, have an appetite for these unusual poems. Arlo Bates echoed his earlier praise of the poems' genius but had reservations about their odd form, while William Dean Howells declared, "If nothing else had come out of our life but this strange poetry we should feel that in the work of Emily Dickinson, America, or New England rather, had made a distinctive addition to the literature of the world."[81] Wrote Mabel: "The notices are beginning to pour in. Of course there is some notice taken of the lack of form, but all agree that it is a marvelous volume, full of genius, and a legacy to the world. And there are hundreds [of poems] yet unpublished which I have here, equally as fine as those in the volume."[82] Mabel and Higginson immediately got to work on selecting and editing another set of poems for a second volume.

Concurrent with the editorial work, Mabel launched into another phase of her marketing campaign. She initiated a series of talks about the life and poetry of Emily Dickinson. These talks were specifically designed to build interest and intrigue among the audience, but also "gave her greater clout with publishers."[83] Mabel suggested in her diary that her initial paper, to be read for a Women's Club in Springfield, Massachusetts, in April 1891, would be "interesting and in a not-deep way rather a comprehensive sketch of her life and personality and work and literary characteristics."[84] From her lecture notes and drafts of her talks, it's clear that Mabel began each one of her lectures by reciting one of Emily's poems (usually either "Success" or "How many times these low feet staggered"), and then launched into a discussion of when she believed Emily had started writing poetry, an analysis of her handwriting and discussion of the structure, punctuation and use of capitalization in the poems. "Emily Dickinson scrutinized everything with clear-eyed frankness," she wrote in her notes for these talks, "even the somber facts of death and burial, the unknown life beyond. She touches these themes sometimes lightly, sometimes almost humorously, more often with weird and peculiar power, but she is never by any chance frivolous or trivial."[85]

Mabel also spoke about Emily's life, in an effort to both build and clarify the image of the poet, which she believed would add to sales: "She had tried society and the world, and found them lacking. She was not an invalid, and she lived in seclusion from no love disappointment. Her life was the normal blossoming of a nature introspective to a high degree, whose best thought could not exist in pretense."[86]

At the time, Mabel was giving many other lectures, including talks about her trip to Japan, astronomy and other topics. Her talks were given to women's clubs, literary organizations and university clubs and to increasingly large general audiences. Mabel was a natural and dynamic public speaker, and she knew it. After the first public talk she ever gave, in May 1890, she recorded, "My talk in Boston . . . was very enthusiastically received. It was really the first elaborate one I ever gave, but I knew I could do it more than well. . . . I had thought out quietly what I wished to say, but I found that dozens of bright things came to me spontaneously which I had not intended and the flow of words and pictures was smooth and inspired. My mother, who is a most severe critic, said it was the best thing she ever listened to, and she was thoroughly enthused by it."[87]

As her public speaking experience grew, Mabel wrote that she could easily "talk to an audience and make them desperately enthusiastic, rippling with laughter one minute and their eyes filled with tears the next." On her talk at the Sixth Biennial of the General Federation of Women's Clubs in Los Angeles in May 1902, she reported, "I captured them at about the third sentence. How much I wish I know what I possess that does this! But the quality which takes, and keeps, an audience in the hollow of one's hand is . . . what comes to be when I stand before a waiting audience."[88] Her talks on Emily's life and poetry began to attract large audiences and launched Mabel's career as a public speaker and a rare female public intellectual. She relished both of these roles.

As they set out to prepare the next batch of poems for publication, Mabel, with David's assistance, undertook the task of compiling a complete alphabetical index of all the poems copied to date. This comprehensive list numbered almost one thousand, and certainly made the task of identifying and locating any particular poem far easier. She and Higginson were in very close touch during this time. Their letters and notes, held in the Amherst College Archives and Special Collections and reproduced in detail in Millicent's *Ancestors' Brocades*, show that they were immersed in a large number of small details in trying to understand Emily's life. Their collaboration was engaged and mutually respectful. (Millicent wryly commented that though the two editors differed in opinion, "It sometimes seems as if the more their opinions differed, the politer they became.")[89]

Although they continued to make a significant number of changes to the poems, there were some they left relatively untouched. In April of 1891, Higginson wrote to Mabel, "Let us alter as little as possible, now that the public ear is opened"—although he continued to suggest a number of changes that he thought would make the poems more acceptable to the general public. Mabel, for her part, preferred that much of Emily's wording be left intact, and maintained her stance that titling the poems seemed wrong, though she continued to defer to Higginson on this point.[90]

Mabel selected over a hundred poems for the second volume, including some at Vinnie's request, which she sent to Higginson for his consideration. When Higginson returned the poems to her, he also included some Emily had sent to him that he felt should be added. By the end of July 1891, Mabel sent him back the copy arranged, punctuated and edited as they had agreed.

Concurrently, she was already thinking ahead to collecting, editing and publishing Emily Dickinson's letters. She had thought of this idea while working on the first volume of poems—"I mean, also, to collect her letters gradually and arrange them for a prose volume. They are also startlingly fine."[91]

To continue their momentum, the editors knew that they needed to have a preface to the second volume of poems that would build the interest in Emily and her poetry. They also needed a well-placed article in a major periodical close to the publication date. They agreed that Higginson would write an article for the *Atlantic Monthly*, to be published approximately to coincide with the publication of the poetry (his article came out in October 1891, a month ahead of the poems). Mabel would write a preface to the book and Higginson would edit it. She completed a draft toward the end of July 1891, and sent it to Higginson along with a letter in which she explained that she knew the preface was a bit long, "but I have tried to answer, point by point, the things said of her by the critics." This included correcting the notions being bandied about in reviews that the poetry was irreverent, and also correcting statements that Emily had been a recluse since childhood, that she never left Amherst and that she had been "cruelly disappointed in love." Mabel told Higginson that Austin liked her introduction and did not think it too long, and that Vinnie had also signed off on it. Higginson, however, did feel it too long, and took her at her word that he should edit it. He made a number of suggestions and concluded by telling her, "In publishing this, I would suggest that your name be signed to it, as was mine to the other preface & that we equalize matters as we did then, but now by putting my name first on title-page."[92]

Mabel received the galleys of *Poems, Second Series* in mid-August. The plate proofs she received after that had more errors to correct, but the book was finally published on November 9, 1891. Within days of its publication, David received a letter from Roberts Brothers informing him that "the book seems to go like 'Hot Cakes,'" and that the publisher had already put a new printing to press. (Why this letter was sent to David rather than Mabel is not clear.) Sales were almost as brisk as they had been with the first volume of poems, only this time Roberts Brothers printed 960 copies in its first run. The first volume went through eleven printings in just two years; the second volume ran five printings in the same time period.

The reaction to *Poems, Second Series* in some ways mirrored critical reception of the first volume: reviewers were divided in their praise for Emily's genius and originality and their criticism of her form. The public seemed more intrigued than anything else. Millicent wrote in *Ances-*

tors' Brocades that "the editors were deluged with letters," which, Mabel told her, demanded further information about Emily's life and composition process, as well as requests to reprint poems and "some letters [that] were just outpourings of the heart in admiration."[93]

Vinnie was pleased that Emily's work was being shared with the world, but became indignant at every review that was less than fully favorable. Though she was delighted to have received some royalties from Roberts Brothers, she was loath to split them with Mabel and Higginson, who had done all of the work. Mabel wrote, "Vinnie has reaped a harvest and she will have another large check on July first."[94] In all, Lavinia paid Mabel and Higginson each just one hundred dollars for their work. The fact that there were never any contracts explicitly spelling out compensation for the editors would later become the heart of an issue that ensnared the Dickinson and Todd families for years, and would erupt in volcanic fashion a few years later.

The other issue simmering just below the surface was the ongoing tension between Vinnie and Sue. In addition to the years of building resentment over her perceptions of Sue's treatment of all three Dickinson siblings, Vinnie was still seething over Sue's having sent one of Emily's poems to *Scribner's.* Sue, for her part, felt completely justified. Emily had sent *her* the poem, after all. In fact, just after the publication of the first volume of *Poems,* Sue wrote a letter to Colonel Higginson, in which she expressed both her surprise and her outrage that the volume had come out at all: "I was so dazed by the announcement of Emily's poems in the *Xtian Union* that I do not rally easily. It was my first intimation that stranger hands were preparing them for publication. I planned to give my winter, with my daughter's aid, to the arrangement of a vol. to be printed at my own expense sometime during the year subject to your approval of course, with an introduction also by yourself." She went on to state, "I am told Miss Lavinia is saying that I refuse to arrange them. Emily knows that is not true."[95]

Lavinia wrote to Higginson around the same time, "I had naturally looked to her first (with you) for help, supposing 'twould be her highest pleasure, but I found my mistake. She wished the box of poems there constantly & was unwilling for me to borrow them for a day, as she was fond of reading them (the verses) to passing friends. Mrs. Dickinson has fine ability but lacks mental energy to complete. She has many ideal plans for work worthy of her talent, but the world will (probably) not see any finished."[96] The stage was set for a pitched battle between Sue and Vinnie.

Not surprisingly, Mabel's rendering of the situation placed the blame squarely on Sue: "With all her delight and satisfaction in the success and appreciation of the book, Vinnie has had a great deal of pain through Susan. Neither she nor Mattie has spoken to her since last September when they first learned of the cousin volume. And Susan sent two poems of Emily's that she had to the *Independent*, and kept the money for them. That is illegal, for the right to publish the poems rests wholly with Vinnie."[97]

The dynamic among Sue, Mabel and Lavinia seemed clear in 1891, with Mabel taking Vinnie's side. But this dynamic turned out to be unstable, with alliances shifting in the years to come.

———

Publicity during the 1890s consisted of a two-pronged approach: go out on the lecture circuit and release a book of letters. Mabel believed creating a brand meant not just excitement but consistency in the form of a memorable image. And that's just what she created for Emily Dickinson.

Mabel knew that the success of the second volume of poetry meant capitalizing on the success of the first volume—emphasizing in talks not only the strange beauty and brilliance of the poetry but also the quirky life of the reclusive poet. So Dickinson would become widely known as the mysterious, poetic genius dressed in white. Her intrigue would generate more readers—and more sales.

Mabel was "fortunate that Higginson was well regarded but over-extended," writes Elizabeth Horan, "for his need to attend to other projects gave Todd free rein, especially in identifying the market and creating demand for the books."[98] Indeed, Mabel had many ideas about just how to do this.

In 1891, during the preparation of the second grouping of poems, Mabel recorded that Colonel Higginson gave a talk where he read from some of Emily's letters to him—a talk Austin attended. The general audience—and more importantly, Austin—felt that Emily's letters offered the personal insights into the poet that the public craved. This confirmed what Mabel had written in her journal during the preparation of the first volume of poetry: that a collection of Emily's letters, "startlingly fine" as they were, would help to build interest in the poet's life. An entry in Mabel's diary from the month after *Poems'* publication, December 1890, shows that Austin had already started to bring her packets of Emily's letters.[99] Mabel was well aware, as she would later write, that "the chronicle of her life is to be found elsewhere . . . in only one way—by reading her own words. They alone can give an authentic account of her strange life."[100]

Following a talk Mabel gave in December 1891 in Westfield, Massachusetts, a woman approached her. Forty years later Mabel recounted, she "told me she had been a schoolmate of Emily's at Amherst Academy, that she never forgot her extraordinary compositions, and *where* might she read some of Emily's prose?" When Mabel responded that Emily had not kept a diary but that she was hoping to find some of her letters, the woman told her she had kept many girlhood letters from Emily and would send them to Mabel. This woman, Mrs. A. P. Strong, had been Emily's childhood friend Abiah Root. "So a chance meeting was the spark which touched off a long train of events culminating in the publication of those two volumes of letters in 1894," Mabel wrote.[101]

In her journal Mabel recounted a conversation with Amherst College president Julius Seelye, in which he purportedly told her that it seemed to him a horrible idea "to publish the letters of that innocent and confiding child." (A later reviewer of the published volume of letters agreed, noting, "to take over little wayside, woodland Emily Dickinson, who really did shun publicity or at least never thought of such a thing, and print her prattlings, is unkind.") But, Mabel argued, though Emily believed that "her verse might see the light of print, only by hands other than hers," she had relinquished control of her letters by sending them to other people. Besides, Mabel reflected, "Austin smiles. He says Emily definitely posed in her letters—he knows her thoroughly, through and through, as no one else soon did. He tells me many things quite unsuspected by others"—and Austin approved of collecting and publishing his sister's letters.[102]

For the next three years, Mabel worked on the considerable task of finding, arranging and editing Emily's letters for publication. This work required both detective skills and diplomacy. Because Lavinia had destroyed almost all the letters Emily had received, as per her request, Mabel had no idea to whom Emily had written. Austin and Vinnie helped her identify and approach likely letter recipients, including family members and friends. In *Ancestors' Brocades*, Millicent quotes her mother as saying, "In this arduous task, Austin Dickinson was an indispensable help, as he was an encyclopaedia of information. He had kept for many years articles relating to early Amherst days, as well as a mass of historical material which he had inherited."[103] Austin's materials proved invaluable both in identifying potential recipients, and also in ascertaining the approximate dates of the letters (the majority of which were undated) through their context and references.

Vinnie assisted too, at least initially. She helped to brainstorm possible correspondents and aided Mabel by writing to them and requesting their letters from Emily. But as the project went on, Vinnie became impatient, as she had been with the work on the volumes of poems. Millicent suggested, "Miss Vinnie's impatience was steadily increasing. She wrote to Mr. Niles at shorter and shorter intervals," about when a volume of Emily's letters could be published. She could not understand why Mabel's editing process took so long. In addition, midway through the collection of letters, Vinnie came up with another project for Mabel to do: "At Miss Vinnie's request my mother soon embarked on another venture for the 'magnification' of Emily. This time it was a 'Birthday Book,' a type of daily reminder then in vogue containing a quotation for each day in the year. It is hard to think of any writer whose work would lend itself better than Emily's to a selection of epigrams." Mabel launched into this project and soon gathered two hundred quotations. Many of these were lines from poems that she and Higginson had deemed too flawed for publication, but which had "occasional bolts of melody" that could be used well in this type of project.[104]

Mabel obtained Thomas Niles's approval to go ahead with the project; he concurred with Mabel that it would sell. But in the story that Mabel told Millicent and that Millicent subsequently recorded, Vinnie changed her mind. "She may have discovered that its preparation would take time and would interrupt work on the letters."[105] Mabel wrote in her diary of Vinnie's volatility: "She is edgy about everything . . . the letters, that I don't come over enough, that she never sees Austin, that her garden isn't attended to every minute, that she doesn't want a 'Year Book' & a dozen other woes."[106]

While the idea that Vinnie lost interest in the project might have had some truth to it, there is another reason the idea of an "Emily Dickinson Year Book" never came to pass: E. D. Hardy, who succeeded Thomas Niles at Roberts Brothers, wanted to wait to see how sales of the volume of *Letters* would be before going ahead with the other project.[107] Mabel wrote to him that she thought the "birthday book" would "make the most brilliant year-book ever issued" and "daintily bound for Christmas" would be a big seller. Furthermore, "if I do not do it, some one else will want to, because E.D. abounds in epigrams."[108] But Hardy did not agree. And so Mabel turned her full attention and energies back to working on Emily's letters.

In total, close to fifty different people ultimately contributed letters to the project, though by some estimates, this probably represents only about a tenth of the letters that Emily would have written to various correspondents throughout her lifetime.[109] Some recipients of Emily's letters were loath to part with them. As Millicent explained, "Publishing private letters was considered a sacrilege. They were a sacred trust. But though never shown, neither were they destroyed . . . letters were hoarded irrespective of whether or not they had intrinsic value. Indeed, that had nothing to do with the case, since a moral code was involved." This is where Mabel's charm came into play. Mabel was more diplomatic than Vinnie, and far more able to woo recalcitrant letter hoarders

into releasing them for publication. Mabel also believed that "it was fortunate that our efforts to collect the letters came so soon after Emily's
death that many of her correspondents were still alive, and in consequence, their little bundles of letters from her still intact."[110] Mabel used
this point for leverage in convincing Emily's correspondents that it was
important to gather and publish the letters while those to whom they
had been sent were still alive to share in this glory.

But there remained those correspondents who refused to part with
their letters, others who were not approached and some who could not
be found. Thomas Wentworth Higginson, for example, sent Mabel all
of the letters he had received from Emily "except for a few letters which
he thought too personal to print." Austin declined to have all of Emily's
letters to him published. Sue, though certainly a key correspondent of
Emily's for many years, was probably not approached to contribute the
letters in her possession for obvious reasons.

As Millicent recounted in her 1954 book, *Emily Dickinson: A Revelation*,
Austin had also given Mabel an envelope filled with letters to Emily and
indicated "that it was something very special and personal. A glance was
enough to show her that the drafts it contained were indeed different.
Obviously love letters, my mother did not ask Mr. Dickinson how they
came to be in his possession, wondering though she did how they could
have escaped destruction, for Emily had tried to erase every vestige of
her feeling toward those she cared for most. . . . My mother did not even
consider the group in question."[111] None of these letters from Judge Otis
Lord, a friend of Edward Dickinson's and possible love interest of Emily's in later life, made it into the volume. Similarly, some draft letters
Emily had written, today referred to as "the Master letters," were not
printed. These passionate letters to an unknown recipient or recipients,
have been a source of intrigue since their discovery after Emily's death.
Mabel and Austin, and perhaps Vinnie, concluded that these were too
personal and revealing to be printed.[112]

And then there were the letters that could not be found. Mabel and
Higginson were convinced that Emily's childhood friend, the poet
Helen Hunt Jackson, had also been one of Emily's correspondents.

After a trip to the Columbian Exposition in Chicago in 1893, Mabel traveled on to Colorado Springs, where she met with the deceased poet's husband, William Sharpless Jackson. Though he was certain that Emily's letters to his wife existed somewhere and had not been destroyed, he was never able to locate them.

Once in possession of the letters, Mabel followed the same editorial process she used with the poems. First she copied them, often noting in her diary the difficulties in dealing with the different styles of Emily's handwriting. Sometimes, she observed, the letters "are immensely wordy—one letter often uses fifteen pages in copying, although it is usually but three foolscap pages in the original, or rather, octavo. The writing is microscopic."[113]

Next, Mabel worked to regularize Emily's use of capital letters and punctuation, as she had in her editing of the poems. And then she attempted to order the letters. She decided to arrange them by correspondent and then within that, to attempt to put them in chronological order—not an easy task, because Emily rarely dated her letters. Sometimes the recipient had noted a date on the envelope (postmarks at the time did not include dates). Sometimes Mabel relied on references to contemporaneous events, or cross-referenced mentions of people, places and events with Austin and Vinnie. Occasionally, she wrote to the letters' recipients, and other times she employed the variations in Emily's handwriting as a way of dating the letters.

Mabel discovered there were a number of poems embedded within some letters and observed that Emily's epistolary writing style evolved over the years, whereas in the poems, she had seen "no advance in style." In an unpublished essay, written sometime in the mid-1890s, entitled "The Evolution of Style: Reading Emily Dickinson," Mabel wrote:

A great many letters have been found, all unusual, many more beautiful and striking than the verses and their publication has seemed the more desirable in that the poems, often but the reflection of a passing mood, do not always truthfully represent herself—rarely, indeed, showing the dainty humor, the frolicsome gayety, which continually bubbled over in her daily life. The somber and even gruewsome [*sic*] outlook upon life, characteristic of many of the verses, was by no means a prevailing condition of mind; for while apprehending to the full all the tragic elements of life, enthusiasms & bright joyousness were yet her normal qualities, and stimulating moral heights her native dwelling place. All this may be glimpsed, often satisfactorily, in her letters.[114]

Another measure of how important a poet's letters could be in building her reputation, as well as evidence of how popular Emily's poetry was at the time it was published, came in a letter Vinnie received offering a most peculiar potential addition to the collection in progress. Gardner Fuller claimed to possess a number of letters Emily had written to him and threatened to publish them, himself, unless Lavinia paid him a large sum of money. While Vinnie was "outraged and angered out of all proportion as to the importance of the affair," Austin's cooler head prevailed. He had Fuller investigated and discovered that he attempted to sell these letters to the *Nation* and to Roberts Brothers, claiming to have "twenty odd letters and some verses (about 19,000 words, more or less) written by this talented authoress during the war (1861 to 1864) which are probably the only letters in existence giving a clear insight into that beautiful and secluded life. These letters are worth their weight in diamonds."[115] Austin, however, was convinced that this was all a hoax. He wrote in a note, "I take no stock in Gardner Fuller. I don't believe he has any of Emily's letters," and felt this was an extortion attempt. Austin was right to call his bluff: Gardner Fuller was never heard from again.

Mabel submitted the completed manuscript of *Letters* to Roberts Brothers toward the end of 1893. An entry in her diary noted that she was looking at proofs as early as January of 1894. However, there were doubts about the arrangement of the letters, and the question of whether the work should appear in one or two volumes. The Panic of 1893, the worst economic depression seen to that date, lent additional uncertainty to the venture of publishing two concurrent volumes. But it was eventually resolved to adhere to Mabel's ordering of the letters by recipient, and to publish the letters in two volumes, to be released simultaneously.

In addition, the publisher wished to have some image of Emily in the book. This posed a major problem because camera-shy Emily had only appeared in one known daguerreotype. Neither Austin nor Vinnie wanted that to be the image reproduced, thinking that it made their sister look "too plain." Vinnie advocated for a reproduction of a childhood portrait of the three Dickinson siblings by O. A. Bullard; Austin did not wish this image to be used. An artist's rendering, depicting Emily with curly hair, and a retouched photo were also rejected. In the end, they decided upon a somewhat altered version of Emily's image from the Bullard painting for the frontispiece.

Tensions over the books of *Letters* were growing in other ways, as well. Lavinia wrote to E. D. Hardy that she would not relinquish copyright of the volume to Mabel. "This I shall never do. If Mrs. Todd wanted such ownership she should have told me at the outset & then give up the work if my answer was not satisfactory. Collecting the letters was my own idea," she claimed. Vinnie wrote that this idea was "endorsed by all my friends. . . . Emily would be indignant at any attempt to rob her sister." Furthermore, Vinnie insinuated Mabel had done no more than copy the letters, and therefore Vinnie should be the sole recipient of any royalties—just as with the poems—and that she might then consider giving Mabel a fraction of the money earned.

Mabel was outraged. Neither David, Colonel Higginson, nor Austin felt that Vinnie's proposal was right or equitable. Austin stepped in, writing to the publisher in September of 1894, "I have had a talk with my sister today. She had accepted the idea that Mrs. Todd had done a little something about the letters—though I think she believes the main work was in copying them into an intelligible hand, and that she did this for love (as she did) and so it would be base to offer to pay for it." However, Austin did get Vinnie to agree that while the copyright would be held in her name, royalties should be divided equally between Vinnie and Mabel. Two days later Mabel also wrote to the publisher: "I have been of course somewhat annoyed, but also amused, at Miss Lavinia's

THE THREE DICKINSON CHILDREN IN THE O. A. BULLARD PORTRAIT FROM 1840.
AUSTIN REJECTED THE IDEA OF USING EMILY'S IMAGE (*FAR LEFT*) FROM THIS
PAINTING. AUSTIN AND VINNIE ALSO REJECTED AN ARTIST'S RENDERING OF
EMILY (*RIGHT*). THEY EVENTUALLY COMPROMISED AND USED A SLIGHTLY REVISED
IMAGE OF EMILY FROM THE BULLARD PORTRAIT IN THE FIRST EDITION OF *THE
LETTERS OF EMILY DICKINSON*.

evasion of the contract matter, but Mr. Dickinson says it is all settled
now, and as we wish. He will have her sign it as soon as it comes, as he
wrote you. It has annoyed him a great deal."[116] As usual, Mabel believed
that Austin's word prevailed; but as usual, it would turn out that he had
not quite protected her adequately enough.

The copyright issue and division of royalties weren't the only sources
of contention. While Mabel was putting the finishing touches on her
preface to the volumes in October, she read it to Vinnie. Vinnie's reaction, according to Mabel, was extreme: "She apparently heard nothing
of it except the first sentence, in which she was mentioned. Did not
think it sufficiently prominent." Vinnie insisted that Mabel's sentence,
reading, "The lovers of Emily Dickinson's poems have been so eager for
some of her prose that her sister has asked me to prepare these volumes
of her letters," be changed to "The lovers of Emily Dickinson's poems

have been so eager for her prose that her sister has gathered these letters, and committed their preparation to me."[117]

But here again, Austin intervened. He sent a telegram to Roberts Brothers, instructing them to print just ten copies of the book with Vinnie's corrected sentence; all the rest would contain Mabel's words. Millicent suggested years later, "her brother thought it necessary to deceive her. So far as I know, the ruse was successful because she could not see to read. Having examined, by proxy, the first paragraph in any early copy of the book, she would have been satisfied once and for all that it was to her liking."[118] The books finally were printed in late November of 1894.

As she had with the two volumes of poetry, Mabel set out to publicize *The Letters of Emily Dickinson* with a series of endorsements, articles in significant periodicals and a sojourn back out on the lecture circuit. Aided by generally positive reviews (the *New York Times* said of the book, "a most remarkable woman is revealed in this collection of letters, a woman who lived in recluse in the college town of Amherst, and who wrote poetry . . . [which is] remarkable for its epigrammatic quality, its terseness and vigor," and the *Boston Herald* reviewer noted, "Mrs. Mabel Loomis Todd, the editor of these letters, likens Miss Dickinson to Emily Brontë").[119] In November of 1894, Mabel wrote an article on Emily's letters for a publication called *The Bookbuyer*. She also published "Emily Dickinson's Letters" in the inaugural issue of *Bachelor of Arts Magazine* in 1895.

Mabel also increased her talks on the life and work of Emily Dickinson. In 1891 she gave four talks on Emily; in 1892–1893 she gave seven; and between 1894 and 1895, thirteen. But the talks, too, became an ongoing source of tension between Mabel and Lavinia. Millicent noted, "Most of all, she resented my mother's talks. It was not so much that she objected to the '$10 and expenses' which my mother sometimes received for her lectures about Emily . . . but that my mother was somehow or other capitalizing some aspect of Emily—some emanation which she, Lavinia, could neither reach nor control. . . . But in her youthful strength and buoyancy my mother continued to go right ahead with the work, unaware of the rancor eating into Lavinia's soul."[120] Millicent also stated that Vinnie's attitude was consistent: any work Mabel or Colonel Higginson had done to get Emily's messages out to the world was simply copying what was there—"in doing the work they were only parts of the machinery, automatons, and should so consider themselves." Millicent suggested that Vinnie probably felt any information about Emily was solely under her jurisdiction, that it was her right to impart it. When she realized that people were increasingly turning to Mabel as the authority on Emily's life, Vinnie's jealousy and resentment grew.[121]

Though the sales of the initial print run of 1,000 copies were brisk and Mabel optimistically hoped for "a dozen editions before Christmas," the subsequent editions did not sell as well. While the first series of *Poems* sold 10,000 copies, *Letters* sold a disappointing 2,000. Contemporary Dickinson scholar Marietta Messmer points out that, "of the 1500 copies [of *Letters*] issued in December 1894 as a second edition, 1200 were still unsold by 1898. This surprising lack of interest in Dickinson's letters can at least in part be attributed to a discrepancy between the readers' expectations and the editorial format in which Todd chose to present them."[122] Messmer suggests there was a disconnect between Mabel's desire to "highlight the chronological development of Dickinson's epistolary style" and the public's desire to understand more about the person behind the poems. However, by reading Mabel's journal entries, it is evident that she believed she was doing the latter.

It wasn't until 1958 that a complete edition of all of Emily's letters was published in three volumes, edited by Thomas H. Johnson and Theodora Ward. What became clear from the initial publication of Mabel's *Letters of Emily Dickinson* in 1894 is that the stage was set for growing tensions between members of the Todd and Dickinson families. These tensions would not soon abate.

—

Even with two volumes of Emily's poetry published, Mabel was still in possession of many other poems that she had laboriously copied. She made a preliminary selection of poems for a third volume in July of 1891, before she had even received the page proofs of the second volume. She had great ambitions for all of the poems she copied that had yet to be printed. She wrote to E. D. Hardy at Roberts Brothers that she had "unpublished poems enough for at least six more volumes like the first Series and Second, and sometime we may want them."[123]

Even when she was preoccupied with her work on collecting, ordering and editing Emily's letters, Mabel was still working to transcribe poems. She also continued to submit individual poems to magazines, in a clever attempt to keep the poetry coming out in a controlled manner, and the public clamoring for more.

In September of 1895, Mabel spoke with Colonel Higginson about the possibility of editing a third volume. However, as she noted in her diary, he had taken seriously ill and could not promise that he would be able to assist her. Mabel had been in touch with Mr. Hardy at Roberts Brothers, who agreed to publish a third volume. Vinnie, of course, urged her to press forward.

Although Higginson could not commit to being a coeditor on a third volume, in fact his imprimatur was already on many poems. Some of the selections Mabel made for the third series were poems that the two of them edited and ultimately rejected from the first two volumes. Even without Higginson fully present to push for it, Mabel continued the practice of giving many of the poems titles. Years later, Millicent suggested, "In spite of her own dislike, more than half of the poems in the *Third Series* appeared with titles, many of them suggested in Mr. Higginson's handwriting on this printer's copy."[124] It might well be that Mabel, as the consummate marketer, understood that titling poems for the nineteenth-century audience would add to their appeal and felt they had developed a saleable strategy with the first two volumes.

In addition, Mabel continued the editorial practices she and Higginson had followed in the first two volumes with regard to punctuation, capitalization and word alteration, supposedly to improve the rhymes. Years later, Millicent observed that she found a carton containing her mother's manuscript of the *Third Series*. She noted, "This manuscript is important because, by comparing it with Emily's originals, one fact is made clear— that my mother copied the poems exactly. The fact should be emphasized that in copying my mother did not alter anything Emily had written. . . .

Any corrections were made subsequently on my mother's own copies and are plainly indicated. This will eventually make it possible to restore to their original form those poems in which changes occur."[125]

Mabel submitted the manuscript for the *Third Series* to Roberts Brothers at the very end of December 1895. At the time, she was also busily engaged with a number of other projects: completing her own book, *Stars and Telescopes*; editing her father's book, *An Eclipse Party in Africa*; helping David with *A New Astronomy* and "an anonymous friend" with *A Cycle of Sunsets*. She was also preparing to leave the country for several months on the Amherst eclipse expedition to Japan. According to R. W. Franklin, Mabel was so busy that the third volume went to press with several errors uncorrected: "The result is that the third series appears to be the most altered of the three nineteenth century editions. It was probably not deliberately so." Franklin's assessment is linked to Millicent's account in *Ancestors' Brocades*, in which she detailed the numerous punctuation changes Mabel had attempted to correct in the plate proofs—however, since she "was to be gone for more than six months, an interval during which the book was to be published, she had no opportunity to check final corrections."[126]

Poems, Third Series came out at the beginning of September 1896, while Mabel was in Japan. Reviews of the book were once again a mixture of praise and criticism, though altogether the book garnered less critical acclaim than had the previous two volumes. (Wrote one reviewer in the *New York Evening Post*, "It is needless to say that Miss Dickinson's poetry achieves its success, in spite of all its flagrant literary faults.")[127] Nor was this volume the commercial success that its predecessors had been. R. W. Franklin suggests, "The temporary Dickinson vogue was over, and the fame that belongs to Emily Dickinson escaped her for a while longer."[128]

Of course there could not be another volume of Emily's poetry published, nor the attendant lectures given and articles written, without Lavinia's notice and growing resentment of the attention Mabel received. When Mabel wrote to E. D. Hardy shortly after submitting the manuscript, she related, "I have said nothing to Lavinia about contracts. I will see her soon—but of course she will want everything, as usual. The next time I am in Boston I will come see you about it."[129]

Mabel had reason to be concerned. Sales from *Letters* were such that they only covered the plates for the books; despite the agreement Austin had brokered, neither Vinnie nor Mabel received any royalties for this book. Vinnie retained the majority of royalties from the first two books of poetry. It wasn't clear, and it was very concerning to Mabel, what might happen with subsequent books she might publish. In 1895, Austin sought to "make things a little more even" by deeding some of his land to Mabel. But this idea was derailed before it could be actualized. Mabel's lack of insistence on being adequately compensated for her work because of her relationship with Austin and her unflagging belief in him turned out to be a most fateful decision.

Mabel still had many more copied poems she had not included in any of the first three volumes of published poetry. And yet, these poems would not see the light of day for decades to come. The potential of publishing the complete works of Emily Dickinson came to an abrupt and most unexpected halt.

Millicent wrote, "The year 1895 marked the end of an era. There are losses which prostrate; there are bereavements which stupefy; and there are Acts of God which smite and paralyze." In August 1895, she observed, an event occurred "which combined all three."[130]

$\mathcal{L}$OSING AUSTIN, FINDING MABEL (1895–1904)

"Without a particle of zest"

The publication of Emily's poetry and letters took Mabel's public speaking career to new heights; she was called on as a Dickinson authority as the public, the critics and the press increasingly recognized the life and work of the poet. Mabel's other work was thriving, too: her book *Total Eclipses of the Sun* was published in 1894, and her articles were routinely accepted by major papers and magazines with national circulation. Mabel was recognized around Amherst for her civic work and for her leadership of the Amherst Woman's Club and the Mary Mattoon chapter of the Daughters of the American Revolution (DAR). She gave music and art lessons and performed on a regular basis. Her life, as she observed in her daily recounting of it, was full and bright. But as the year opened, there were already ominous clouds gathering.

"Dear Austin is pretty sick, with symptoms of pneumonia," she wrote in the very first days of 1895. "Dr. Cooper came over, and a trained nurse has come from New York. I cannot do anything, or put my mind anywhere, except upon that dear man at whose side I do so long to be. The tears stream from my cheeks all day. I am so helpless and terrified."[1]

This entry marked one of the first times Mabel used her diary, rather than her journal, to discuss her feelings about the events of a given day. It was also one of the first times in her diaries that she referred to Austin intimately; usually "dear Austin" would be found in her journals, while "Mr. Dickinson" was more typical of her diaries, the more public record of her life. Now Mabel wrote about Austin's health with equal emotion in both her daily diaries and her journals.

During his illness, Mabel wrote frequently to Austin and had Vinnie deliver her letters. "I really believe I have suffered more during your sickness than you have," she wrote on January 5. "I am without a particle of zest. I am completely unnerved today. The news this morning was that you are comfortable, that Dr. Cooper was over, and you are getting on all right. Yet I cannot eat or work, and I do not know what I shall do."[2]

As 1895 wore on, Mabel continued to report the ups and downs of Austin's health in her diaries and journals. She recorded every respiratory infection, she observed how pale he was and how markedly different his new, slow gait was from his normal "springy, elegant step." Each time he fell ill, she was filled with frustration that his marriage to Sue prevented her from being his caregiver. She was also filled with terror at what his recurring illnesses might portend. Despite her busy speaking schedule, she did not travel far from Amherst if Austin was ill. Every time he improved she rejoiced; each time he relapsed she was despondent. She wrote, "I tried to do things but absolutely couldn't. I seem to almost have been unnerved by the terror to me of my dear Austin's illness."[3]

After a long winter of poor health, Austin seemed mostly recovered by April. Relieved, Mabel wrote of some planting they would do together on the strip of land that he wanted to give to her as partial compensation for the work she had done on Emily's poetry and letters. Austin's attempt to "make things a little more even," caused Mabel to write: "Austin and I struck down stakes for trees on my new east line— they will comfort me a great deal."[4] Austin was also setting out trees at the new Wildwood Cemetery, another of his pet civic projects, and coming to call on Mabel in the evenings for short periods of time.

June 1 felt like the first real day of summer. Mabel described it in her daily recounting as "excessively hot." She wrote, "dear Austin came by for me to go to Wildwood with him, which I did, & found it lovelier than a dream, & quite a good breeze. It was a very happy time, and he said things to me coming back that make me insensitive of any earthly pain or irritation or discomfort, forever!"[5]

But forever didn't last. As the hot summer officially began a few weeks later, Mabel's fear returned as Austin's health took a turn for the worse. Each day in July, Mabel recorded what Austin conveyed about how much or how little he had slept and what he was or wasn't able to eat. These bulletins often came via Vinnie; Mabel was not able to see Austin unless Sue and the children were not at home. Austin, Mabel reported, was "very weak and tired from this oppression in his breathing. I would give ten years of my life to have him perfectly well now. . . . May God take me too, at once, if anything happens to Austin. I could not live without him."[6] Unable to be with him or to take care of him as she so desired, Mabel tried to comfort herself by balancing his checkbook—one of the few things she could do to help. Still, it didn't come close to what she wanted or needed. "My heart is every second of time with Austin. I do not eat, I sleep badly, and I am checking all the time. He is so tired and ill, and so strangely short breathed."[7]

On July 18, Austin finally had enough strength to meet Mabel at The Homestead for a short time. "He seems very weak & it almost broke my heart," Mabel noted. His racing heartbeat and difficulty breathing alarmed her greatly.[8]

The Dickinsons' family doctor called in a specialist from Boston to examine Austin and determine the cause of his continuing illness. Dr. Knight was "not very encouraging," diagnosing problems with Austin's heart. Austin told Mabel, who dutifully recorded that the outer walls of his heart were too thin and could not properly send blood to his lungs. At the end of July, the Dickinsons brought in a second nurse from Boston to aid in his care.

In her writing, Mabel described the fear and panic that almost paralyzed her and prevented her from focusing on her work or anything else.

She tried to enjoy the beautiful summer days but could not; she learned how to ride a bicycle and went out riding for longer and longer periods of time, trying to distract herself with exercise. Yet, at the end of the day, writing in her diary, Mabel gave voice to her true feelings: "All day on and off I wept and cried, I rode and tried to read to ease my mind and went to bed almost spent with grief [and] fear . . . O Austin, my Austin!"[9] Mabel's word choice was not incidental, alluding to Whitman's 1865 poem "O Captain! My Captain!" about the death of Lincoln. After all, she believed Austin had been her own emancipator, freeing her to pursue love and her own ambitions in new ways.

Desperate to help her ailing love, in the beginning of August, Mabel traveled to Boston, and from there, to Wayland, to consult a faith healer. She wrote that throughout the journey she was "completely broken up" and "I begged God to save him." She explained the circumstances that "undermined Austin's health" to the faith healer, Mr. Bishop, who found the case was "most transparent" and suggested he help Austin with "absent treatment" for three days. (The belief that healing through the prayer of nonmedical practitioners gained many adherents in nineteenth-century America.) Mabel felt sure that she had "struck the right thing." Her faith restored, she claimed, "I feel strong for him—he will get well!"[10]

She wrote to Austin about this meeting, and sent the letter care of Vinnie. "What I have been through since the day, July 18, when you were last out and saw me, no human being can ever know. Even you, my beloved king, can scarcely tell my suffering." She told Austin of the "terrible day when I heard things that stopped my breath, and I besieged God with frantic entreaties to save you, or else kill me too." But after her visit with Mr. Bishop, "It was the first time in my life that God ever spoke to me," she said, "but He did that time, and told me you would get well. . . . I have solemnly promised God that when you are well again, and I feel your beloved arms around me again, and I know I have you safe, that from that hour I will live up to the best and highest there is in me, and make you happy as I never did before."[11]

Mabel was heartened when Austin seemed to rally a bit right after this "absent treatment." He slept better; he seemed to be breathing more easily.

On August 12 she noted, "My darling is much better. Dr. Cooper says it's the first time he has been able to say so with confidence. I solemnly thank God."[12]

Feeling somewhat reassured but thoroughly exhausted from the continuous anxiety, the heat, and the "effort to keep my mind tranquil for [Austin]," she consented to go with David on a short excursion to an event in nearby New Salem, where he had been asked to represent Amherst College. They departed on August 15. They returned to Amherst on the evening of the sixteenth. But they were too late.

There is a one-sentence entry in Mabel's diary on Saturday, August 17: "My God, why hast thou deserted me!"[13]

The day that Austin died, fifteen-year-old Millicent wrote in her diary that the doctor "told us to one hour or so that he had died at seven o'clock. Mamma is nearly dead and told Arthur [Curtiss James, a close family friend] that she has had her death." Millicent understood both her mother and her father were intensely shaken and in deep mourning. The next day she noted, "This has been one of the very saddest days that I have passed in my life. Mamma has been crying all day and papa has cried some and has looked so sad that I have been perfectly bewildered. It seems to be a universal grief."[14]

Throughout her long life, Millicent saw the death of Austin Dickinson as "an all-engulfing disaster," whose ripples indelibly affected her and her parents. It also heightened the feud between the Dickinson and Todd families. Millicent believed that while Austin was alive, he "carried" all the members of his family and kept their incipient tensions in check. "Without his controlling presence, they were all unleashed."[15] And, as she wrote in 1945, Austin's death had one other important consequence: it "brought about a stalemate which blocked publication of a large part of the poetry of Emily Dickinson."[16]

When she was approaching the end of her own life, Millicent went back and read her mother's diaries from the fateful year of 1895. The day Austin died, Millicent wrote, "put an end, among other things, to my childhood."[17] Mabel's prolonged state of mourning and insistence on wearing black, as an ersatz widow, caused people around Amherst to whisper even more. (Mabel, for her part, wrote, "the whole town weeps for him but I am the only mourner.") Millicent may also have felt that her childhood ended after Austin's death because Mabel, slowly but with certainty, began to shift her dependence on Austin into reliance on Millicent.

"He was a strong man, strong in his convictions, strong in loyalty to his ideals, strong in his likes and dislikes, strong in words and in action," stated the writer of Austin's obituary in the *Amherst Record.* "He looked upon the town of Amherst as one of the most beautiful places in the world and was ever seeking to add to its natural beauty and alert to anything that might menace it."[18] Under the headline of "Amherst Loses a Strong Man in the Death of W. A. Dickinson," the *Springfield Republican* noted Austin's death was "due to overwork" and that "William Austin Dickinson, the most influential citizen of Amherst . . . was a strong and forceful personality. He had an open, frank and vigorous way of speaking to and looking at the world that commanded respect and confidence from the moment that he appeared — but his nature was all gentleness and refinement. . . . No man in Amherst has done more to beautify the town than Mr. Dickinson."[19]

All of Amherst shut down on the day of Austin's funeral. Millicent observed in her diary, "Mr. Dickinson's funeral was at three o'clock but neither Mamma nor I cared to go." She added, "I have never seen mamma in any such condition as she is now, and as for papa, he looks so sad and mopey."[20] What Millicent couldn't fully articulate at the time was that Mabel would not have been welcomed at the funeral. She also did not know that her mother had already said good-bye to Austin privately. Longsworth writes, "at noon that day Ned Dickinson had quietly let [Mabel] in at a side door, while Sue and the rest of his family were at the dining table, so Mabel could say goodbye to Austin and place in his casket a token of their love."[21]

"I am utterly crushed and heart broken. I have had my first true grief; and it is so overwhelming and stupefying that I do not realize how completely I have had my death-blow," wrote Mabel that evening. She continued:

My Austin has left his dear, beloved body, and gone, I do not know where, but away, out of sight. I kissed his blessed cold cheek today and held his tender hand. The dear body, every inch of which I know and love so utterly was there, and I said good-bye to it, but all the time I seemed singularly conscious that my Austin himself was out in the sweet summer sunshine, more light-hearted and blithe and strong and happier than he has ever been before since he was a boy. But oh, the tragedy of it, and the unthinkable bitterness to me! . . . There never was such a love, as his for me and mine for him. I have lived in and by and through and because of him for thirteen years; every breath I drew was for him; no success or praise or gain seemed anything until I had told it all to him, and we had talked it over and put it away in our mental reserves of pleasantness.[22]

Mabel's tortured journal entries for the next several days and weeks outlined her belief that Austin had worked himself to death because he would never take a vacation if he could not take it with her. She insisted it was Sue's unrelenting grip on him that had shortened his life, keeping him from true happiness. "While the crickets sing tonight, my master, my mate, my king, lies up at his dear Wildwood, at peace, at rest, after a life that was actually sucked out of him for forty years, and in which I was the only bright spot. One of his doctors told him he had no organic disease of the heart, but he had a 'tired heart.' Tired! He was tired to pathos . . . I alone knew the pathos and from where it had emanated."[23]

A bright red Columbia bicycle arrived at the Todd residence on the morning of August 17, 1895. There was no card attached, no envelope, no clues about who had sent it. "I have never known who gave it to me," Mabel wrote in her journal a few months after the bicycle arrived, "and the man in Springfield from whom it was bought refused to tell me who ordered it—said he had promised not to tell. It is a most curious thing."[24]

Millicent observed that day, "This morning a most beautiful elegant Columbia bicycle . . . came and nobody knows anything about it. Mamma is crazy to find out who sent it and she wonders if dear Mr. Dickinson did."[25]

Mabel was convinced that Austin had purchased the bicycle for her. However, Austin died the day before the bicycle was delivered to her home and he had been sick and housebound for many weeks before that, nearly constantly attended to by his family.

For months after Austin died, Mabel wrote in her diaries and journals about the long bike rides she took by herself throughout the Pelham hills that surrounded her home. "All I can do is ride,"

MABEL SPENT HOURS RIDING THE NEW COLUMBIA BICYCLE THAT MYSTERIOUSLY APPEARED THE DAY AFTER AUSTIN'S DEATH. SHE EVEN RODE IN HER MOURNING ATTIRE (DETAIL).

she wrote. "I really think [the bicycle] saved my life, for I never should have ridden again if it had not come," she reflected, "but such a beautiful present seemed to make it incumbent upon me to ride, so I did."[26]

But even these long rides, which must have taken great effort given the late summer heat, the hilly terrain and the fact that Mabel was cycling in the long skirts of the day, weren't enough to curb her sorrow. Everything she saw and smelled and heard reminded her of Austin: "the warm mellow silences, the insects in the grass, the scent of tobacco and corn, and above all the sound of crickets at supper-time . . . I hear them and my heart breaks anew." Three months later the pain wasn't any better. "My heart cries out to be with him . . . I am overwhelmed with grief . . . I cannot breathe for sorrow, I sit in the pastures and talk to Austin. I cry and cry and cry. What CAN I ever do?" Mabel wrote that Austin took her former "zest for life with him."[27]

A few months after Austin's death she reflected, "It does not grow in the least easier. In fact, I think the wear and tear of every day life makes his absence constantly harder. . . . I feel adrift, rudderless . . . the reality of his absence is so crushingly constant."[28]

It took Mabel many weeks to gather Austin's letters and put them in a tin box in her vault for safekeeping. The velvet hat he had left hanging on a peg at The Dell remained there as long as Mabel lived in that house: "I still leave it where he always kept it—and when I have been away the first thing I do is go and kiss it and hold it to my cheek, the moment I get back," she wrote. She wanted to be buried with that hat in her hands.[29]

Months later, Mabel recalled how she and Austin spoke often of being together in Wildwood Cemetery. In fact, she wrote more than a year after Austin's death that he had wished to be buried not just beside her in adjacent plots, but with her, right next to her in the same coffin. He had struggled to orchestrate this, even considering willing Mabel his body. But he died before he could take any such steps.[30]

Poignantly, she recorded the words to a joint prayer she and Austin had uttered. "We had a little creed which we said together, alternately, and had, for years: 'For my beloved is mine, and I am his, what can we want beside? Nothing!' the last word in unison. He and I, with the noblest emphasis on his part and the deepest belief on mine. I begin it now, half mechanically from habit, and he always seems to take it up as he used to."[31]

Though still grieving, in the fall, Mabel threw herself back into her work. She resumed giving some talks to publicize Emily's *Letters*, and in September, the month after Austin died, she took up editing the third volume of Emily's poetry alone, Colonel Higginson's own illness preventing him from collaborating. She also began writing and editing five other books at the same time. "Thank God for work!" she wrote, "IT is my salvation. I have never been so rushed in my life; and if it were not for that very fact I should probably be dead—or crazy." As she worked steadily on editing the third book of poems, Mabel found some solace in the words of Austin's sister:

We learn in the retreating
How vast an one
Was recently among us.
A perished sun

Endears in the departure
How doubly more
Than all the golden presence
It was before![32]

Sometime in the year after Austin's death, Mabel made the acquaintance of Dr. Albert Josiah Lyman. Lyman, minister of the South Congregational Church in Brooklyn, New York, was making a name for himself by speaking on such topics including "new thoughts on salvation after death." In 1897, Mabel engaged in an extended correspondence with him about her love for Austin, her grief, and questioned how her life might productively continue without him. She admitted in her journal that she probably should not keep Lyman's letters since they were about Austin and her continued connection to him, but she copied extensive passages from them. "No one can help you much. No! only two. One is yourself. And the other is the one whom you loved and love. For a part of his soul is in you now and if that can not help you, then he is deprived of his own," Lyman wrote.

Lyman told her that pain was not at odds with the spirit of life, but that she needed to endeavor to find that spirit again. He convinced her that she had the special gifts to do this: "All your letters, dear my friend, confirm my thought of you as one form of God. . . . It is impossible for a woman's soul to harness love and sorrow together to become the chariot of the mind's nobler resolve. It might be difficult for most women—I will not believe it is impossible for you." And in another letter, Lyman urged her to "Let work be the wing that carries you over the monstrous stretches. There will come occasional peaks, where your feet will touch ground, rock under you, sky over you, sunlight on you. Then you can fly again."[33]

Dr. Lyman's letters convinced Mabel that she had more of life to live. They fed into her belief in her natural "brilliance" and her many gifts. They also managed to convince her that death was not the end of her relationship with Austin; in some way—perhaps one that she could not touch—he was with her, still.

Mabel and Austin had always been certain that they would be together for all eternity. They wrote innumerable letters to each other about their conviction that in the life beyond, they would be united. After Austin's death, there were times when Mabel was certain that she felt him with her, and other times when she just couldn't sense his presence. "There are days when I am distinctly conscious of him, of his intimate presence—when a glowing certainty that he is with me and fills me wholly for a time, and buoys me up," she wrote at one time, and at another, "Well, my beloved Austin, there is no need to say good-night—you do not go away at all. I feel you here in me, enfolding me, this instant. You <u>know</u> how eternally I love you." But on another date she penned, "Austin is in heaven, and so heaven is where I want to be—and it is full and sweet there, and it is home. My home is Austin only, and so I am hurrying to get there. . . . I am lonely to suffocation, in spite of feeling distinctly at times that he is close to me. I long to touch him, to hear his deep voice. His body lies in Wildwood, but that is not where he is. If only I knew where his soul had gone, if only I could speak to him! Oh Austin!"[34]

For many years to come, Mabel would wonder where Austin was and how to reach him. On New Year's Eve in 1900 she wrote poignantly:

> I know that when my beloved Austin died I came into the strang-
> est and yet most sweet and normal relation to the unseen. And if
> I had or had known how to follow it up I should have heard him
> speak to my inner sense. I even did, as it was; and certain sentences
> from him were borne in upon me most singularly. At times I have
> felt him very near I have KNOWN he was with me. And then I
> felt like the grub down in the water which dimly sees the gorgeous
> butterfly above in the sunshine but cannot talk to it. Yet knows

it was once a companion and will be again. Or like the prisoner in thick stone walls, who hears his friend knocking, but cannot understand what he is trying to say through the impassive granite. Something is between I cannot break down. But if I only knew how, I could hear him. It is my fault, not his.[35]

To try to break down this wall, Mabel turned to the supernatural.

Mabel had always been superstitious and interested in the occult. In addition to her constant collecting of lucky four-leafed clovers, she put horseshoes in her homes and believed in the magic of rainbows. Despite her own authorship of several papers and books about astronomical phenomena, she believed that the universe could not be explained by scientific principles alone and that larger forces beyond humankind were at work. Mabel had a more than passing interest in theosophy (the philosophy of religion founded by spiritualist Helena Petrovna Blavatsky in 1875) that included beliefs about reincarnation; she retained some of their publications including a booklet entitled "Scientific Evidence That the Dead Still Live." She was fascinated—even a bit obsessed—by the story of the Salem witch trials. She frequently wrote and spoke about witchcraft or supernatural events in her lectures; had gone to a faith healer in her desperate attempt to make Austin well; and starting around the turn of the century, she began to pay periodic visits to palm readers and to mediums. Several years after Austin's death, still desperate to reach him, Mabel traveled to a place others had suggested she might be able to do so.

At the turn of the nineteenth century if you wanted to reach your dearly departed, there was one place to go. The small hamlet of Lily Dale in upstate New York, organized in 1879, had become widely known as the epicenter of the Spiritualist movement. By this time there were perhaps a million professed Spiritualists in America, with more than seventy newspapers and other vehicles for spreading the word about the movement. Stemming from this Spiritualist impulse, Lily Dale literally became an occultist cottage industry, with house after house owned by mediums who would guarantee visitors a clear connection to the other side.

In 1902 a somewhat skeptical Mabel traveled to Lily Dale, though, truth be told, there was a part of Mabel that desperately believed it was indeed possible to connect with the spirit world. Lily Dale "did not sound attractive to me as a place, only as a curiosity," she wrote in her journal. "The whole thing seemed to me pitifully cheap."

After two weeks in Lily Dale where she attended countless séances that she derided as "tricks," there was one session Mabel simply could not explain. "How, supposing he had desired to cheat me," she wrote of the medium, "could he have known that it was Austin, and Austin alone I desired? And if by any . . . chicanery he could have found out his name in the few hours between his arrival in Lily Dale and my coming to him, how could he have known that the middle name was the one I called him by? And how could he have imitated that voice! And said the characteristic things with certain reiterated words just as Austin did! It was wonderful to stupefaction."

She recorded in detail what was said: "You kept me nine months on the Earth after my body was dead—your grief and loving kept me. But I have wanted to speak to you for seven long years." Mabel added, "he went on with things that kept me breathless for nearly an hour."

This remarkable encounter "tore my heart strings so that for weeks I walked in a daze. The voice was identical with what I had so longed for years to hear. . . . Some things just could not have been invented. But what does it mean?"[36] Mabel could not explain it. It was an experience that stayed with her for the rest of her life.

⌒

"I wish my heart were in anything; but I look at myself as from outside somewhere, and long for any real interest to make me care for life again. I probably shall never feel any real zest again, but . . . these delightful experiences are doing me physically and probably mentally good, though my soul is with Austin, only waiting to be awakened in his arms," wrote Mabel in the late spring of 1896.[37] Mabel was writing from the spectacular Volcano House overlooking the caldera of the Kilauea volcano, on the Big Island of Hawaii, where she had traveled with David on the

Amherst eclipse expedition to Japan, part of her attempt to live a life without Austin.

Two days before departing, Mabel turned in revisions of the third book of Emily's poetry. That done, she felt she could depart the country. This long journey lasted from April through the end of October. Though Mabel recorded wondrous natural sights throughout the trip, she also wrote many nostalgic, painful and heart-wrenching entries in a special journal she kept.

This expedition was David's second attempt to photograph a total eclipse of the sun from a mountaintop in a remote area of Japan. David spent months planning the expedition, as well as gathering, assembling and shipping more than twenty telescopes and cameras with which he would attempt to do what had never been done before—provide a complete photographic record of the eclipse as it passed through the Hokkaido region of northern Japan. David would test his "hi-tech" hybrid lenses and refractors to take nearly five hundred quick photos of the corona. (Quipped Mabel in her book-length account of the expedition, *Corona and Coronet*, "So who could complain if tubes and valves and pneumatic arrangements and object-glasses and electric devices of every sort strewed the drawing-room and measured their innocent length on every floor throughout the house?")[38]

The journey began in New York, where a crowd of journalists, Amherst College alumni and the Amherst Glee Club gave them a rousing send off. From there they traveled by train to Chicago, where they were met by the president of the Great Northern Railroad, who lent Mabel and David his private car for the trip across the country to San Francisco, "so we are crossing in the greatest possible comfort and every luxury," Mabel recorded.[39]

As the trip went on and the Midwestern prairies yielded to the snow-capped Rockies, and the mountains eventually gave way to the verdant Northwest, Mabel could not help but think of Austin: "As I sat there gazing upon the beauteous mountains that could make one's heart ache, I became sure but strangely conscious that my Austin was distinctly with me, his dear arms were as clearly around me as when we stood together on the Transportation Building at the World Exposition . . . and he held me as if he could not let me go, ever. I believe he never has, and cannot."⁴⁰

At the end of April, the expedition team set sail aboard the *Coronet*, a yacht bound for Hawaii. "Although I had twice crossed the Pacific by steam," Mabel wrote, "yet its magnificent immensity was almost unappreciated until this voyage in a sailing vessel." As usual, Mabel was able to stay above deck while others were seasick, and got to observe pods of dolphins and whales, masses of Portuguese man o' war and great schools of flying fish.

Mabel found Hawaii to be heart-stoppingly beautiful but heartbreaking. Whether it was going for a horseback ride on the beach at Honolulu, observing the lushness of a coffee plantation or seeing a spectacular eruption of the Mauna Loa volcano, it all somehow brought her back to Austin. "Not until this my trip have I thoroughly realized how utterly alone I am in this world. Most persons would say my life is brilliant, and so it is . . . but no soul meets me—my real innermost self as Austin did."⁴¹

Hawaii also brought another Dickinson to Mabel's mind. She began a chapter of *Corona and Coronet* with an Emily Dickinson poem to which Mabel added the title, "Hawaiian Volcanoes." The poem, itself, does not mention Hawaii. In fact, in the third edition of *Poems*, Mabel had titled this same poem "Reticence." But so immersed was Mabel in the editing of Emily's poems that she could not experience anything in her own life without seeing some relevance of Emily's work, and in turn, filtered the poems through her own life and activities. Her diaries reveal she increasingly connected her own work to Emily's, just as she believed her life continued to be connected to Austin, even after his death.

At Ka'awaloa, near Kona, the *Coronet* picked up another passenger: the well-known journalist and actress Kate Field. She was very ill, attempting to get back to Honolulu for treatment. The doctor aboard the *Coronet* did what he could for her, but she was in the final stages of a deadly pneumonia. Mabel stayed with her, told her that she was not likely to see another sunset, took down a letter she dictated, and pointed out the cliffs of Maui to her as they sailed past. "Where did you say your expedition was going?" the dying woman asked her. "'The Amherst eclipse expedition,' I replied, 'and we go to Japan to observe a total eclipse of the sun August 9.' 'The Amherst eclipse expedition,' she said brightly; and those were her last words on earth." Mabel also recorded this event in her journal, commenting: "Poor woman! So infinitely alone! My heart ached for her, and I wanted to give her a little love to get to heaven on."[42] She later reflected on the poignant experience in an article she published in the *Chicago Times-Herald*. As she wrote in her journal, it gave Mabel some comfort to be with Kate Field when she died; she had not been able to be with Austin and now it gave her a little solace to know that she had been able to be there for someone else. In a way, the experience of being with Kate Field as she died began to help Mabel start living again.

"Danger of disenchantment lurks about a return to distant lands whose memory has been for years enshrouded in a rosy atmosphere," Mabel wrote in *Corona and Coronet*. But Japan did not disappoint; in fact, Mabel found it more charming and more fascinating than she had almost a decade earlier. They arrived at the port in Yokohama at the end of June. "Japan is changing, and noticeably," she wrote. "The past had perhaps been canonized, and the present was different, but there was no disenchantment. The old-time charm exerted its spell as before."[43] Its charm extended to Mabel's interest in artifacts, including a jinrickisha that she shipped back to Amherst, where riding around in it along the New England country roads made "spectators greatly interested."

But perhaps the true turning point of the entire trip occurred for her as she looked out on an Ainu fishing village. "I felt a gleam of something more like real peace than I have had before for months—as if Austin's real self had bade me to be cheerful and really take up life again. I felt as if something may still remain for me of comfort and accomplishment, but always and ever in and for him whom I love with an endless intensity and a near-failing devotion. He is never out of my mind and soul for one single instant. I believe most solemnly that my Austin is actually with me—here in Hokkaido, and looking out for me and loving me. My king and my master!"[44]

From that point forward, Mabel set her mind to reclaim her life.

MABEL HUNG A PORTRAIT OF
AUSTIN IN HER HOME AND WROTE
THAT IT GAVE HER SOME COMFORT
TO GAZE UPON HIS IMAGE EACH DAY.

She decided to "think a great deal about my dear Millicent," and wrote repeatedly, "my chief interest in life is the success of this expedition." Knowing David's track record, of course, there was reason to be concerned. Mabel continuously entered prayers for a clear viewing in her journal. Alas, when the day of the eclipse dawned, it was not to be. Clouds closed in once again and thwarted a view of the eclipse. "Nature knows how to be cruel, or possibly it is mere indifference. But until, in his search for the unknown, man learns to circumvent cloud, I must still feel that she holds every advantage. On that fateful Sunday afternoon the sun, emerging from the partial eclipse, set cheerfully in a clear sky; the next morning dawned cloudless and sparkling."[45]

But as usual, Mabel managed to make the best of a bad situation, at least for her own career: she turned the Amherst eclipse expedition into a book, at least a dozen articles published in national magazines and newspapers (including the *Nation*, the *Chicago Herald-Tribune*, the *Century Magazine* and *Atlantic Monthly*, among others), and a series of lectures that she gave for years afterward.

As they sailed back toward the United States, Mabel wrote: "Last night there were showers all around the horizon and a perfect linear rainbow, brightening as the moon came out from the clouds, until even the secondary bow could be followed. It was an exquisite and mysterious sight, elusive, fairy-like. I once believed in the happy promise of a rainbow, and dried my tears for an hour or two—but it was only an elusive arch of promise, and so I do not believe in them anymore." She continued, "This last year is aging me before my time. Up to a year ago people always thought I was at least ten years younger than I am. . . . But now I see, when I part my hair, far under the brown, some white hairs, and I am beginning to see a line of pain in my forehead." She concluded, on the train that this time took the southwest route on the journey back to Amherst, "Austin's dying has shown me my own soul."[46]

When Mabel and David finally reached Amherst on October 24, the leaves were past their colorful autumn apex. Though delighted to be home at last and thrilled to see Millicent and the friends who welcomed them back, Mabel could not help but find her return to Amherst bittersweet: "Ah! But it is Austin's town, and his oak leaves, and his blue flowers, and his stacked corn—and I miss him and want him and need him beyond even anything I have known before."[47]

Mabel went to visit with Vinnie soon after her return. Vinnie didn't offer any explanation for not having answered any of Mabel's letters, but she did seem glad to see her. She was glad, as well, to hear that Mabel had purchased some new china for her that would be arriving from Japan. Other than Austin's absence, nothing seemed amiss.

But, as Millicent later wrote, "It was a different home-coming from any she could have anticipated . . . my mother soon discovered that sinister plans had been brewing in her absence."[48]

On November 16, Mabel was served with papers: Lavinia had filed suit against Mabel and David over the strip of land that she had deeded over to them, claiming that her signature had been obtained by misrepresentation and fraud. The tensions that had simmered for years finally erupted, an explosion no less spectacular than the one Mabel had seen in Hawaii. Mabel was blindsided.

CHAPTER 8

SUING THE "QUEEN OF
AMHERST" (1897–1898)

"The wicked injustice . . . kills me daily"

An article in the *Hartford Courant*, headlined "Emily Dickinson's Poems: The Bitter Trouble They Have Made between the Sister and Friend," trumpeted, "College and society circles in Amherst and Northampton Massachusetts are agog over a unique lawsuit that involves persons of high social standing. It is an interesting story from the beginning—and the end is not yet in sight." Even the *New York Times* weighed in: "The unique poems and letters of the late Emily Dickinson attracted the attention of all literary circles two or three years ago. Out of the editing of these poems and letters has arisen a peculiar lawsuit, in which the editor, Mrs. Mabel Loomis Todd, well-known as an author and lecturer, and wife of the Amherst College Professor of Astronomy, is the defendant."[1]

Another well-known Amherst resident would have been mortified had he known that his failure to enact legal documents triggered a case that "attracted as much attention as any that has been before the Northampton court" and was likely to "furnish gossip for afternoon tea in the Connecticut Valley for a long time to come."[2] But Austin Dickinson was no longer alive to see the headlines or the spectacle that was about to unfold.

Twenty-seven years older than Mabel, pragmatic Austin knew that he would die long before her. His intent was to provide for Mabel in death as he had in life, but without fueling a public scandal and subjecting Mabel to more shame. In November of 1887, he drafted a will in which he left The Evergreens and his real and personal property to Sue; his share of the family property, including The Homestead, stocks and bonds to Vinnie; and two paintings to Mabel. He wrote to Mabel that this was "not quite as I wanted it but best for now. I have left all my share of my father's estate to Vin with the request that she turn it over to you. She has promised to do this, so you are protected in any case."[3]

In addition, Austin told Mabel of his intent to "make things a bit more even" in the compensation she was due for editing and publishing Emily's poetry by giving her a strip of land along the eastern boundary of the Dickinson meadow. The only problem was that he never actually deeded her the land.

THE DELL, THE HOME MABEL AND DAVID BUILT ON LAND GIVEN TO THEM BY AUSTIN. THIS PHOTO SHOWS THE STRIP OF LAND THROUGH DICKINSON MEADOW THAT BECAME THE BASIS OF THE 1897 LAWSUIT.

Why someone trained as an attorney, facile with real estate deals and fully cognizant of the importance of proper documentation to avoid problems in land transactions did not draft the proper legal papers to will Mabel the land is a mystery. In fact, as Dickinson scholar James Guthrie points out, Austin, like his father before him, was a "skilled advocate" for his "clients' landed interests, and for [his] own."[4] To suggest he wanted to spare Mabel further embarrassment or scandal is perhaps too generous. To think he simply fell ill and ran out of time before executing these legal documents, as Mabel wanted to believe, is also perhaps unrealistic, because for months he was sick but not completely incapacitated. It's possible that, despite the multiple times Vinnie tried to cut Mabel off from sharing in the royalties from Emily's poetry, Austin trusted Vinnie would keep her word to him and hand over the property to Mabel after his death. But this, too, seems less than credible, since he knew that Vinnie had consistently failed to behave in an equitable way toward Mabel. Surely the dire medical news he had received for at least a year should have signaled the need to codify transferring the land to Mabel. It is possible that this brilliant man was frozen with regard to this transaction, just as he had been unwilling or unable to extricate himself from his marriage. Austin seemed to be stuck. Whatever his motivation, his failure to act left Mabel in a precarious situation.

Less than two months after Austin died in August 1895, Mabel went to see Vinnie to ask about her share of Austin's inheritance. Mabel recorded in her diary her disbelief that Vinnie appeared poised to ignore Austin's request: "She is, as he always told me, utterly slippery and treacherous, but he did not think she would fail to do as he stipulated in this. . . . If he knows, how sorry he must be!"[5]

After her brother was no longer around to advise her, Vinnie turned to family friend and neighbor Dwight Hills. Hills, a bank president, was well acquainted with the business world, unlike Vinnie. According to Polly Longsworth, Hills "agreed . . . to draw up the necessary papers and secure legal services when she had made up her mind about the meadow, but he declined to tell her what to do, only warning that she should not take any steps without his knowledge." Vinnie was also acutely aware that Mabel was still in possession of hundreds of Emily's unpublished poems, and one of Vinnie's dearest dreams was to see *all* of Emily's poetry in print. Moreover, even while tensions with Mabel had become exacerbated, Vinnie was still quite dependent upon both Mabel and David, paying them innumerable late-night visits and welcoming their company. Longsworth writes, "Vinnie would have been forlorn indeed had she cut off her relations with the Todds, who in many ways were more like family to her than the Evergreens' residents."[6] So, in December of 1895, according to Mabel, Vinnie apparently suggested that if a deed for the strip of land were drafted, she would sign it.

In notes she dictated to Millicent in the early 1930s, Mabel said that Vinnie "always wished to do everything in secret—the checks she received from Roberts Brothers she asked her brother to cash in Boston so that the Amherst bank might not know how much she was getting for the poems, and she did not wish to examine the land in daytime, but came across by moonlight and walked all over it."[7] When it came time to sign the deed, Vinnie similarly insisted to Mabel that she bring the attorney Timothy Spaulding to witness the signing after dark. Mabel wrote in her diary that they went to The Homestead on the evening of February 7, 1896, and Vinnie signed the paper. "A great weight is off my mind, to have even that, which Austin had given me, but had not finished the deed."[8] But the deed was not finished. Not wishing to arouse Sue's suspicion or make things worse with Dickinson relations, Mabel asked Spaulding to defer recording it until he heard from her.

Weeks went by, until just before Mabel and David were to leave for Japan in April of 1896. Finally, Mabel felt the time was right to have the deed officially recorded on April 1—probably because she would be out of the country for many months. When Dwight Hills discovered that Vinnie had made a business transaction without his knowledge, he found himself in a compromised position and declined to advise her further.

Longsworth writes, "Caught doing what she had promised Mr. Hills she wouldn't do, caught doing what she knew Sue would kill her for, Vinnie reacted like a child with her hand in the cookie jar. She said she *hadn't* done it, which immediately got her into deeper trouble . . . while

Susan cleverly decided to hold Vinnie to her lie and insist she get the land back."⁹ Whether or not Sue Dickinson was the behind-the-scenes force in getting Vinnie to file suit against the Todds (Longsworth and Sewall suggest she was, based at least in part upon statements from Mabel; Dickinson biographer Lyndall Gordon suggests otherwise), Mabel and David were served with papers in November of 1896.

In the months leading up to the trial, Mabel sought advice and assembled a legal team to defend herself and David. Part of their strategy was to file a countersuit, clarifying that Austin had wanted to deed the Todds this land as partial compensation for her work—and David's assistance—in the preparation and publication of Emily's poetry, work for which she had received exceedingly little money. The countersuit accused Lavinia of slander, and sued her for $25,000. But when the Todds' answer to Vinnie's lawsuit and their own countersuit were filed, Lavinia immediately disputed them, and both cases were placed on the docket for the district Superior Court for February 1897, but then continued to the following fall.

Attorneys for Mabel and David, and for Vinnie, took depositions from potential witnesses. One deposition, in particular, caused Mabel and her team great concern. Dickinson family servant, Maggie Maher, told of the many times she had observed Mabel and Austin meeting alone at The Homestead, at The Dell—and even on one occasion—at The Evergreens. She described how their meetings took place behind closed doors, and how their carriage rides would sometimes take up an entire day. Maggie's testimony would have been a great embarrassment to the living members of the Dickinson family, as well.¹⁰

Maggie's deposition was never used in court, but attorneys on both sides were keenly aware of its explosive potential. Judge Everett Bumpus, a friend of Mabel's who had been part of her legal team, recused himself. Dwight Hills, who had been scheduled to testify on behalf of the Todds, apparently lost his nerve upon learning of the evidence Maggie provided. According to Longsworth, he "became more cautious,

[and] eventually took to his bed through the trial."[11] Perhaps both Bumpus and Hills realized that the trial was likely to hinge on the question of reputation, and that a close alliance to Mabel Loomis Todd was something that could damage their own standing.

Mabel wrote of Maggie's deposition, "It is nearly all false, the bits of truth interwoven to make different meanings from the real, and only one or two unimportant facts. She has been very skillfully coached and manipulated." She added, "I am too angry to sleep—only she is such a cowardly traitor she is not worth my wrath. It is cheap and low beyond even the imagination of Maggie's measurement."[12]

Before the trial commenced it was clear that friends, relatives and neighbors were taking sides. Millicent later suggested, "The area of the feud had spread. The town had taken sides. . . . Partisans took their stand: on one side, those who held that the elderly Squire Dickinson had been too fond of Mrs. Todd—for had they not been seen more than once buggy-riding through the autumn woods together—and, on the other side, those who maintained with equal vehemence that the close relations known to exist had been purely platonic. Excitement was growing day by day. Loyalties were intensified. Families were divided."[13]

Mabel continued to puzzle over Vinnie's behavior, reinforced by her conviction that she had simply been following Austin's wishes to procure for her what she deserved. "Darling Austin, what WOULD you say if only you had not put things off so long!" she lamented. In the spring of 1897 she summarized her feelings ahead of the trial: "What a beautiful world to look at, and what a heartbreaking one to live in."[14]

Adding to the anxiety Mabel felt ahead of the trial was something she recognized as perhaps one of the greatest ironies of her life. At the same time as she was being sued by Lavinia for the strip of land between The Homestead and The Dell, Mabel was busily packing up all their belongings to leave it. She and David moved one mile away into Amherst College-owned Observatory House. She wrote in her diary, "In a way it breaks my heart to leave my beloved little Dell. In another way I feel infinitely relieved to have new surroundings. I have suffered so much in the little red house! Dear Austin, I love every tree and shrub, but I have been too much cut to bear it here."[15]

The presiding judge dropped Mabel and David's slander countersuit due to scheduling disagreements, but *Lavinia N. Dickinson v. Mabel L. Todd & Another* was called to order in the Northampton Courthouse on March 1, 1898. One of Vinnie's attorneys, William Hammond, gave an opening statement in which he articulated the long-standing importance of the Dickinson family to Amherst's community and institutions. He gave a summary of Lavinia's main arguments: that she had been tricked into signing a deed when she thought she was simply agreeing that no house should be placed on that land, that the land had significant mone-

LAVINIA DICKINSON, KNOWN TO ALL FOR HER MANY ECCENTRICITIES—AND HER MANY CATS.

tary value and that the deed to the Todds should be set aside since it had been procured with misrepresentation.

Vinnie took the stand as the first witness. She testified, "I never had any talk with Mrs. Todd subsequent to the death of my brother which referred to the land near her house . . . I never had in mind an intention to deed this lot to Mrs. Todd." Vinnie also spun a very different story about Mabel's work on Emily's poetry than the one that Mabel would later tell. "I intended to have them published, and had been urged very much to have it done by very distinguished people, and my wishes were to have it done," she said. However, she claimed, "I did not make appeal to any other parties. I did not make appeal to any one. Not to my niece nor to any person. Mrs. Todd asked for the privilege of doing it . . . I wished them copied. Mrs. Todd copied them." Furthermore, Vinnie claimed that Mabel's work on Emily's letters emanated from her own desire to have them published—not Vinnie's. "Mrs. Todd asked to do it. I knew that she thought it would be for her literary reputation to do it, and it made her reputation."

Vinnie went on, "There had been no conversation nor arrangement nor agreement between Mrs. Todd and me." She claimed that attorney Spaulding had not witnessed the signing of any documents—that he had been in the dining room looking at her china when Mabel asked her to sign. "He did not say anything to me at all. I did not see him take the paper at all. I do not remember he made any remark about it . . . I do not recall Mr. Spaulding's speaking to me on the subject."[16]

Vinnie also claimed not to have sent Mabel any notes about the land transaction, and when on cross-examination she was shown notes she had sent Mabel, only said she didn't recall sending them—though she admitted that indeed, the notes were written in her handwriting. She claimed not to have surveyed the land, nor to have made any late-night visits to the Todds, at all.

Local businessman and executor of Austin's estate Dwight Palmer next testified as to the value of the land. Though a witness for the plaintiff (the only other one), his testimony contradicted Vinnie's. His estimate of the land's worth was not nearly as high as Lavinia asserted.

Mabel's take on this testimony was optimistic. She wrote, "Vinnie appeared and was the first witness. She perjured herself right along for an hour. It was appalling to see a person lie so composedly."[17] Millicent's later rendering from her reconstruction of the written testimony and from what her mother told her, was similar: "Lavinia Dickinson's testimony was a repetitious fabric of misrepresentations and contradictions. . . . [She] stood alone without support from any quarter."[18]

In the afternoon, Mabel took the stand. Questioned by one of her attorneys, Wolcott Hamlin, Mabel told her side of the story. "I told my straight story," she recorded in her diary that night, "and was cross-examined for nearly three hours. It was terribly exhausting, but everybody, even the lawyers on the other side, said I was a splendid witness. The papers said my evidence was not shaken in the least."[19]

Mabel's testimony focused in large part on the story of how Lavinia came to her to ask for help in getting Emily's poetry to print. Mabel recounted in great detail all of the work she had done to prepare and edit the poetry, the hundreds of hours spent and the great difficulty of deciphering, organizing and editing the poems. She clearly articulated her lack of compensation and Austin's desire to deed her the land as a way of retroactively acknowledging her work.

But on cross-examination, Mabel had to admit that she was not certain whether the plot of land on which The Dell stood had been purchased or given to the Todds by Austin, and that Mr. Spaulding had never sent her a bill for witnessing Vinnie's signature on the deed. Upon intensive questioning from another of Vinnie's lawyers, Mr. S. S. Taft, Mabel was also forced to admit that although she claimed a close association with the poet whose work she had edited, she had never even seen Emily Dickinson face-to-face. The partial transcript from the trial reads, "I never saw Emily Dickinson except as I saw her flitting through a dark hall. I never spoke to her."[20]

Taft's argument suggested that though Mabel worked on Emily's poetry and letters after her death, in life she could not possibly have had a close relationship with her. He implicitly planted doubt about how Mabel's work could have been so expansive if she had never even met Emily. Through his insinuations about Austin's other real estate largess to the Todds, he raised the issue of whether Austin would have wanted to leave Mabel his family property as compensation for work on the poetry had it not been for their inappropriate relationship. Mabel's credibility had been partially—if not irreparably—undermined.

David was called to testify next. He described Vinnie's peculiar perusal of the land in question by moonlight, and her late-night visits to the Todds'. David stated, "She remarked that she had been all over the strip of land, and that she understood about it, what its boundaries, in a general way were, and that she was prepared to complete the deed at any time."[21] But Taft's cross-examination of David revealed that he and Mabel had not paid anything for The Dell, and suggested subtly that Austin's gifts of land came with strings attached.

The account of this day's testimony in the *Springfield Republican* included Vinnie's uncorroborated testimony that Dwight Hills had "warned her against deeding the land to the Todds, for, he said, 'They are leeches, leeches, leeches.'" In fact, this quote was sensationalized because Dwight Hills did not testify in person at the trial and his own testimony offered in writing was entered on behalf of the defendants, not the plaintiff.[22]

The *Dickinson v. Todds* trial resumed on March 3. Attorney Timothy Spaulding testified on behalf of Mabel and David, stating he had been clear with Lavinia that it was a deed she was to sign, indicating that she knew precisely what the deed was for, and concluding that he had witnessed her signature himself. He said that Mabel asked him to delay recording the deed because "Mrs. Austin Dickinson and she were estranged, there was a good deal of feeling between them, and Mrs. Austin Dickinson would make it very uncomfortable for Lavinia; that is the word she used; and that on account she wanted it, the record of it, delayed."[23] This testimony opened the door for Vinnie's attorney to insinuate that Mrs. Austin Dickinson's ability to make anything "uncomfortable" for his client had more to do with Mrs. Todd's relationship with Mr. Austin Dickinson than any concern Mrs. Todd might have had for Miss Lavinia.

Following Attorney Spaulding, Dickinson family friend Frances Seelye testified as to her knowledge that Austin had intended the land to be deeded to the Todds as partial compensation for their work on Emily's poetry, and that Lavinia had told her that she would, indeed, honor Austin's intent. Next, Dwight Hills's deposition was read. He stated Vinnie had "repeatedly talked over with him the matter of deeding the land to the Todds."[24]

Mabel's recounting of the day concluded that her own case "had all the law points, theirs took it out in personal abuse of me and for an hour I was hit in the face and pounded. It exhausted me terribly. The little judge looked rather tired of it all and I came away feeling black and blue."[25]

In his summation for the plaintiff, Attorney Taft emphasized that Vinnie was the elderly surviving member of the honorable Dickinson family. She "knew little of the world and nothing of business." He argued Vinnie's lack of worldliness sharply contrasted Mabel's, who had "business experience which one necessarily derives from extensive travel and the occupation of a public lecturer." This acumen, he concluded, enabled Mabel to deceive Vinnie easily into signing over her ancestral land.[26]

In the *Springfield Republican*'s final accounting of the trial, the unbylined reporter suggested Lavinia's attorney gave "one of the most lucid and forceful arguments that has been heard in a Northampton courtroom in some time." Attorney Taft asked the judge to set aside the Todds' claim on the land because, apart from any issue of fraud, the two parties were of such different minds about it.[27] Another contemporary newspaper reported, "The Connecticut valley was divided into two hostile camps—the Toddites and the Dickinsonites."[28]

Those who observed the trial were equally partisan. Millicent recounted a conversation with Smith College professor Mary Jordan, who sat through the entire trial. She told Millicent: "It was generally recognized that Lavinia was putting up a ludicrous testimony. But the onlookers enjoyed it. It was very amusing. It was in fact *opera bouffe*. For instance, when the question was raised as to whether she had signed the deed, and she was asked, 'Is this not your signature?' she replied, 'Yes, that is to say, that is my autograph. I understood that someone in Boston wanted my autograph. I thought that was what I was doing when I wrote that.' No one thought for an instant that Mrs. Todd had deceived Lavinia about that strip of land."[29]

Twentieth-century assessments of the trial help to contextualize it. Dickinson biographer Richard Sewall points out ways in which the trial demonstrated the deep tensions among members of the Dickinson family, and the ongoing strife between the Dickinsons and the Todds. Speculating that Sue, "who wanted nothing more than Mabel's public humiliation," might have encouraged Vinnie to be "disloyal to Austin's wishes and to her friendship with both the Todds," Sewall suggests that the trial deepened the rift between the two families.[30] Elizabeth Horan's assertion that "the very facility for promotion that Mabel Todd used on behalf of the *Poems* undid her" in the trial is also worth considering. Horan posits that by setting up Vinnie as a "gentlewoman" versus Mabel as "a woman of the world," Taft subtly but powerfully evoked generational and class differences between the Dickinsons and the Todds.[31]

In the end, it seems that this trial was less about what was explicitly stated than what was implied. It was about the credibility of the last surviving sibling of a venerable and respected old New England family versus the credibility of a woman who was whispered to have had an inappropriate and immoral relationship with the scion of that family. It didn't matter that Vinnie contradicted herself on the stand, or that Mabel had more credible witnesses testifying on her behalf. It didn't matter that Mabel and David had respected careers, or that Mabel had done the great majority of the work to copy, edit and publish Emily's poems and letters. It seemed to be a trial about preserving the reputation of an esteemed and moneyed family. While Mabel and Austin's relationship was never mentioned directly, it was almost certainly the subtext that underscored the entire trial. And though she didn't appear as a witness, it was also a trial about Emily Dickinson—whether the poet and her editor ever could have had much of a relationship and whether Emily's editor was entitled to more compensation for her work on the poetry.

On April 3, Judge Hopkins came in with his ruling—for the plaintiff. He ordered Mabel and David to return the land to Vinnie, and to pay her court costs, all $49.55 of them.

⁓

Mabel was stunned. She couldn't even write of it until weeks later:

> The Judge has given his decision against me in the law-suit. It seems incredible, in the face of five witnesses on my side, and none but herself on Vinnie's. The whole town is amazed, and aroused, and it has brought out more expressions of sympathy from heretofore neutral people. Nothing but the Spanish war equals it in their minds for interest. That such a perversion of justice is possible speaks ill for Massachusetts, but it was perfectly clear to me from the outset that the judge leaned to Vinnie.[32]

Days later Mabel wrote of how "the wicked injustice of the judge's verdict kills me daily," She then had a series of "bladder attacks" that she knew were brought on by the ruling and that left her in agony. She was especially pained when she heard that a professor at Harvard Law School, Austin's alma mater, was using her trial as an example of how a case where all of the evidence seems to be compelling and weighted in one way can ultimately have a ruling go against it.

Mabel and David, convinced that they had been publicly wronged and humiliated, decided to appeal the verdict to the Massachusetts Supreme Court.

Their argument hinged on two main points: first, that Vinnie's testimony had been contradicted not only by Mabel and David but also by the testimony of their other witnesses—Mr. Spaulding, Mr. Hills and Miss Seelye. They refuted each contradiction and misstatement Vinnie made in her testimony, pointed out that the deed was never about constructing a building on the property as Vinnie suggested, and reiterated that it had been Austin's wish to give them the land because "Mrs. Todd's work on the poems had not been properly compensated." Second, they argued, each of these witnesses were people who should be believed by virtue of their professional attainment or position in the community. Their brief concluded by asking the court to consider whether "a long-time professor of Amherst College, known and distinguished throughout the world for his attainments as an astronomer, and his wife, almost as widely known as himself, have conspired together to defraud this plaintiff . . . in order to obtain this paltry strip of land worth five or six hundred dollars. This imputation wounds more deeply than any pecuniary loss would do." Finally, their attorneys argued, if a signed deed could so easily be undone, "truly . . . a deed furnishes a very insecure title."[33]

Vinnie's lawyers, on the other hand, suggested to the appeals court that because this case had been decided by a judge who had been present to see and hear each witness and who had made a ruling based on all of the evidence before him, that the ruling should stand.

The arguments were made on September 20, 1898. One of the six justices hearing the case was Oliver Wendell Holmes Jr., who would later be appointed to the U.S. Supreme Court. The justices' verdict came back on November 21 and upheld the finding of the lower court. In the Massachusetts Supreme Judicial Court judgment, Judge Marcus Knowlton, writing on behalf of the unanimous ruling, noted, "the judge who sees and hears the witnesses has a great advantage in the search for truth over those who can only read their written or printed words. For this reason it has long been established that upon appeal of a decree of a judge in equity upon questions of fact arising on oral testimony heard before him, his decision will not be reversed unless it is plainly wrong. . . . The trial judge might have been able to tell from the appearance of the defendant whether she was really ignorant of this matter or not. . . . In the present case there was testimony at the trial on which the court could properly find for the plaintiff."[34]

Mabel was in Chicago giving a series of talks about Emily Dickinson when the ruling came in. She was devastated, and wrote in her diary, "My heart is broken. . . . The Supreme Court sustains the lower court verdict, and it seems as if I could not live. How can a lie be endorsed and re-endorsed, and the real truth put in the wrong! I am perfectly crushed. What would my love think now of the treachery of his sister?"[35]

Mabel later told Millicent her theory, that the entire suit had been brought about as result of Sue's pressure on Vinnie: "Vinnie despised Sue, whose father had died in the gutter or poor house, as Vinnie said, and who looked at everybody with her nose in the air. . . . The reason Vinnie sued me was because Sue found out about the land—Sue was awful to her, and Vinnie was afraid." Mabel added, "Perjury always kills."[36]

It is not surprising that Mabel held this view. Ned Dickinson became ill and died suddenly three weeks after the original trial was over (though for some reason the date on his tombstone is incorrectly listed as the year before). Vinnie, herself, died just nine months after the Supreme Court upheld the lower court's decision. And the strip of land that had been the ostensible focal point of the trial? It soon ceased to exist, as well: Vinnie sold it to a developer on July 1, 1899, less than a year after the verdict.

At the end of 1898, Mabel wrote a long entry in her journal about how glad she was to see the year end: "This wretched old year! This wicked, cruel, unjust, perjured old year! Glad indeed am I to see the last of him. And I still believe that the new one will be kinder. That lawsuit has blackened every sunny day, has hurt the quality of every bit of work I have accomplished, has squeezed my heart, creased my forehead, and given me unspeakable pain in every breath I draw. It is horrible beyond words, and I hate to mention it in writing, but I must to begin to put it from once the way it actually was, and then leave it forever."[37]

In retrospect, Mabel remembered this time a bit differently: "It [the trial] didn't have the effect of a gnat's wing on me. I went on being the Queen of Amherst and manipulated it as I wanted to," she said in 1931.[38]

Many years after the trial had reached its denouement, Millicent wrote, "The story of the lawsuit is not drama; it is melodrama. On the face of it, it is incredible. To the end of her life my mother never understood it."[39]

Despite her inability to understand what had happened, immediately after the trial, Mabel could think of only one way of dealing with the hurt and betrayal she felt. She took all of the remaining copied but unpublished Emily Dickinson letters and poems in her possession—655 poems—as well as other Dickinson papers, and put them carefully away in a camphorwood chest. She locked it, placed it in storage and did not speak of it or its contents for three decades, leaving Millicent to wonder what was in the chest and why her mother was so uncharacteristically silent about it.

CHAPTER 9

TRAVELING AND TRAVAILS (1899–1917)

"Cloudy eclipses"

Though the unpublished Emily Dickinson poems remained locked away, out of sight in the camphorwood chest, they were far from being out of Mabel's mind. Each of the momentous activities and events that occurred in the next twenty years helped to shape how Mabel, and then Millicent, dealt with their most important professional work to come, and reinforced their complicated bonds with each other. Mabel's longing for Austin was ceaseless and her desire to become known as a writer, unrelenting; Millicent's thwarted search for personal and professional fulfillment grew through a series of events that made her wonder if she'd ever find her true path. The upheavals that each of them experienced during this period of their lives refined their understanding of Emily's poetry. Seeing new cultures would enrich their abilities to find human universals in diversity; experiencing loss deepened their perspectives on life. Both Mabel and Millicent would reflect that in the pause from active editing of Emily's poetry and letters, their life experiences made them better understand the nuance and brilliance of her work.

In the first decade and a half of the new century, Mabel and Millicent would travel (to four continents and more than thirty countries), earn new professional opportunities and endure personal turmoil. These years brought both life-changing technological improvements— electricity, more rapid transit, the telephone, and moving pictures—and major events overseas that catapulted nations into the First World War. On New Year's Day 1900, when Millicent wrote, "This doesn't seem the least bit like the beginning of a new year, and what a controversy we do have over whether it is the beginning of a new century as well,"[1] she could not have foreseen just where their lives would go in the near and foreseeable future.

The summer after her freshman year at Vassar in 1899, Millicent traveled through Europe with her good friend Elizabeth Sawyer. Millicent's first year at college had been extremely successful academically, but while she was elected president of the freshman class and seemed to enjoy some popularity, her diaries show her still feeling awkward and uncertain in most social situations—and acutely aware of how this contrasted with her mother. She was still pining for Alden Clark and unwilling or unable to let herself look elsewhere for romance. By the end of the spring semester, Millicent was ready for a change of scene. Her journey with Elizabeth took her across England, Holland, Switzerland, Germany, Italy and France. It was the first time she had traveled abroad, and Millicent was enchanted by the art, the music and the history.

That summer Mabel was also ready for a change of scene after a year of trying to put all things Dickinson behind her. "The lawsuit still hurts my feelings indescribably, but I have had so many expressions of splendid friendship about it that I ought to feel better." Reflecting on Vinnie's death at the end of August 1899 she added, "And I am glad that it is Vinnie and not I who had to go into eternity with perjury on her soul. I think probably hers had shrunk so that there was nothing left to go anywhere when she died."[2]

Though her Emily Dickinson work remained on hiatus, Mabel continued to write articles and give talks, traveling throughout the east coast and into the Midwest and South. She also returned to some old

MABEL (*LEFT*) AND MILLICENT (*ABOVE*) AS THEY APPROACHED NEW DIRECTIONS
IN THEIR LIVES.

projects, like painting, and launched new projects, including her local civic work, and she began traveling even more widely.

Mabel had already gone on two expeditions with David to Japan before 1900, and when the opportunity arose to go to Tripoli (then part of the Ottoman Empire) that year, Mabel was thrilled. She later wrote, "If science acquaints us with strange bedfellows, eclipse paths are responsible for enticing their followers into remote and untraveled ways which are extremely likely to prove mines of heretofore unsuspected wealth, in landscape, ethnology, picturesque history and customs, and all the charm of unspoiled humanity."[3]

But like the two Japan expeditions, the expedition to Tripoli ultimately advanced Mabel's aspirations far more than David's. Once again, the clouds thwarted David's attempts to get clear photographs of the eclipse. But Mabel's 1912, book *Tripoli the Mysterious*, might well be the literary highlight of her writing. She was at the apex of her descriptive powers and included riveting anecdotes about her adventures and observations.

Even though her book garnered good reviews ("a fascinating book . . . told in an unusually entertaining style," heralded the *American Review of Reviews*), it was hardly the literary masterpiece for which Mabel yearned, and it would not fulfill her ambition of being remembered as a great writer.

Upon their return to Amherst in September, Mabel kept her life in a state of almost perpetual motion. She gave interviews and talks and wrote articles about the expedition to Tripoli. She worked on getting Observatory House furnished with the "new accumulations" from the most recent trip. Her civic work, her music and her art provided her with a dizzying array of undertakings.

Though today we think of 1900 as the beginning of the twentieth century, at the time there was much debate about whether the new century actually commenced on January 1, 1901. Mabel was a 1901 believer, and so on December 31, 1900, she permitted herself an extended reflection in her journal, looking within, looking back, and trying, somehow, to look forward. "Tomorrow will begin a new year—a new century. I wish I could start all over too. And yet I have achieved some things which I should be sorry to ignore." She wrote of how she was quite certain that the "truly great" advances in the twentieth century would be in telepathy and psychic forces. This would be good, she suggested, because it might connect her to Austin.[4] Much as she wished to move on, there was no denying that Mabel's life was still tied inextricably to the Dickinsons: her pain in the loss of Austin, the ongoing perceived injustices at the hands of Sue and Mattie, and the knowledge that there were still many more unpublished poems of Emily's hiding in the camphorwood chest.

In 1901, Mabel, David and Millicent departed for an eclipse expedition to what was at the time called the Dutch East Indies (modern-day Indonesia). They crossed the Atlantic, sailed through the Suez Canal into the Indian Ocean and on to Asia. Traveling through Singapore and Malaysia, they stopped in Singkep to attempt another eclipse viewing, unsuccessfully, and then traveled on to the Philippines (encountering Governor-General William Howard Taft, who so impressed Mabel that she entered in her journal her conviction that he would one day be president of the United States), to China and finally back to Japan before heading home.

For David, the journey was yet another in a seemingly endless series of professional disappointments. For Mabel, it provided needed distraction from Amherst and more opportunities to further her writing and public speaking career. For Millicent, it proved a rare chance to bond with her parents: "It all seems unreal to me, just as if I were living a languid dream. Two weeks ago I was studying at college, and here I am . . . seeing sights I never dreamed of before. It has been so nice to be able to talk to my father and mother and really get to know them a little in their enforced leisure."[5]

The year 1904 also marked Mabel and David's twenty-fifth wedding anniversary, and Mabel threw a big party to commemorate the occasion. There was, however, no heartfelt reflection in her journal, only a cursory

ADMITS TO THREE TALKS

BY

Mʳˢ MABEL LOOMIS TODD

AT Mʀˢ G. HENRY WHITCOMB'S, NO. 51 HARVARD STREET,
WORCESTER, AT THREE O'CLOCK

January 7th. "Panama and the Canal"
January 21st, "Lima and the High Andes"
January 24th, "Mars from the Chilean Pampa"

MILLICENT, MABEL, AND DAVID ON THE 1907 EXPEDITION IN PERU; MABEL
PARLAYED MANY OF THESE EXPERIENCES INTO TALKS SHE GAVE BEFORE AUDIENCES
AROUND THE COUNTRY AND MILLICENT FOUND THE TOPIC FOR HER DOCTORAL
DISSERTATION.

description of the event. But that same year on the anniversary of Austin's death, Mabel wrote, "I cried for two hours." She had her palm read the day before, and while she didn't record what she'd been told, she did comment, "Curiously, this is the saddest anniversary of my life."[6]

The following year, 1905, didn't start out promisingly, either. Though Mabel was earning money from the speaking engagements that seemed to keep coming ("I'm answering the telephone every three minutes"), she noted that it still didn't cover their "enormous expenses." Molly and Eben were getting frail, and Millicent, at home and unsure of what her next steps would be, was diagnosed with an inflamed appendix that had to be removed. But once everyone's health stabilized, David, Mabel and Millicent packed up and prepared to depart on the SS *Arctic* in late July, bound for another Tripoli eclipse expedition. "Twice the alliterative delight of 'an eclipse trip to Tripoli' has been ours," Mabel observed in *Tripoli the Mysterious*, commenting on the "coincidence unique in astronomical annals" of an eclipse track crossing the same exact path as a previous one.[7]

For the first time in his career, David Todd experienced and photographed a cloudless eclipse. Encouraged by this success, he planned another expedition to South America for the following year.

Millicent recorded this journey in great detail in a journal she later typed up (150 pages worth), but didn't realize then that the most significant part of the journey was Peru's rugged and contrasting geography, which would become the topic of her 1923 doctoral dissertation "An Investigation of Geographic Controls in Peru." It also became the subject of her book *Peru: A Land of Contrasts*, published in 1917. "Any statement regarding Peru implies a contrary statement equally valid," she wrote. "Contrast is its characteristic quality, true as to the general aspects of the country and ramifying through remote details. It is the obvious point of view from which to study Peru. . . . Contrasts of nature, of people to country, of antiquity to the present—these diverse elements are insistent wherever one turns."[8] The expedition to Peru crystallized Millicent's interest in geography. She became the first woman to receive a doctorate in this field from Harvard, and thought—for a time—that she had finally found her true professional path.

As many people do, Mabel and Millicent experienced midlife as a period of dealing with loss—of learning to handle transitions and uncertainties about the future, including the end of relationships, the decline of aging and commencement toward mortality. For both Mabel, who was solidly within her midlife years, and Millicent, who had just entered them, the early twentieth century was not only about traveling and exploring the world outside of them but also about plumbing and mapping their interior worlds and sense of self.

Apart from managing to find meaning without Austin, Mabel, who had always been pampered by others, found herself in the role of caregiver for the first time. This was a role from which she not only learned things about herself but would also enable her to better understand Emily Dickinson, who had spent years of her life devoted to the care of her invalid mother.

Mabel dedicated herself to nursing Millicent in 1908 when Millicent became ill with diphtheria along with a virulent strep infection and subsequent endocarditis. "I love her so much that I ought to be able to do well for her," Mabel wrote, noting her frustration about both her inability to make Millicent well—and about how Millicent's illness curtailed her own activities. It echoed the ambivalence Mabel felt when caring for Millicent as an infant. Millicent recognized that her illness was not only aggravating for herself but was also exacerbating existing but unspoken tensions between herself and her mother.

Millicent was bedridden and forbidden from even sitting up for four months. When she was finally allowed to get up, she recorded her incremental progress toward recovery, and the ways in which she allowed fiction to play a big part in keeping her mind active. "At present I'm in an interesting laboratory," she reflected. "Effect of novels on a person as a parallel in his own life for most of events described. Is it better to go fresh to live an open wide life upon unlimited things? Or to learn of joy and sorrow from stories of other people, suffering the unreal till the wish of life is round about your own ankles and can be recognized for what it is?"[9] Mabel's nursing made Millicent keenly realize her own obligation to her parents; she knew the caregiving roles would soon be reversed.

Just when Millicent seemed better, Mabel's mother fell ill, and Mabel and David moved her parents to a home near them. Mabel's journals reveal her conflicted feelings between her sense of duty to her mother, her desire to make things easier on her father and her own distaste for caring for the mother toward whom she had felt more than a bit of resentment over the years. "I am getting at my wits' end," complained Mabel, "and almost sick with a score of responsibilities, both mental and physical. But I make long and cheerful calls on Muggy [Mabel's nickname for her mother] every day, tell her all amusing things, take her books of photographs and postcards, one at a time, which she delights in, and work in every way to have this a happy year."[10] Her mother's final illness lasted ten months, into the sweltering summer.

By mid-September, Mabel was beside herself. "I feel like a wreck," she admitted, "and I am on the verge of dysentery all the time." Her mother finally passed away on September 20. "Poor little Muggy," Mabel wrote, "her tumultuous, volcanic enthusiastic, appreciative, happy, disappointed, prejudiced, intense, sensitive, affectionate life was over. We shall understand one another much better when we meet again."[11] To the very end, Mabel's relationship with her own mother remained conflicted and unresolved.

But Mabel would find no respite. In 1911, David became ill and was diagnosed with painful, life-threatening kidney stones that had to be surgically removed. Then Mabel's beloved father began to decline precipitously. After several weeks during which Eben's strength seemed to wane and he had "faintish turns," he suddenly became worse and it was clear that his heart was failing. "My beloved father is dying tonight, and I am sad, sad. I love him so dearly—and we have been always such comrades all my life! . . . His beautiful eyes already see a light that never was on sea or land, and I am lonely, lonely, already." Eben was buried beside Molly, in a plot at Wildwood Cemetery just up the hill from where Austin, Ned and Gib already lay. Mabel penned in her diary, "We went to Wildwood, flowers, sunshine, and we left him on the east slope he loved so well . . . the house is so empty. I want him so much."[12]

Reflecting on this time a few years hence, Mabel recalled, "My mother's really terrible final sickness, lasting ten months, my darling Millicent's endocarditis after diphtheria, David's illness & operation & then my blessed father's death—all had worn me more than I knew—and I lay in my long chaise . . . day after day, not even caring to read—singular lack!—except an attic full of family letters, & my mother's collection of an epistolary life-time."[13] But in truth, this was just the impression she wished to leave, for Mabel had kept herself as busy as she was able to during this time—writing and giving lectures. She also engaged in a new pursuit—acquiring land.

Mabel found the idea of purchasing land to preserve it from development compelling. In 1909 she bought land in Pelham, just outside of Amherst, determined to save it. "Pelham Knob," as it was known, was where she and Austin had walked many times. Mabel wanted to preserve both a part of Amherst history and Austin's legacy; it was a way of keeping him alive.

Then that same year, on a trip off the coast of Maine in Muscongus Bay, Mabel first laid eyes on Hog Island. Millicent later wrote "The Story of Hog Island," in which she described Mabel's new mission: "My mother . . . was a woman of wide interests and talents artistic, literary, civic and social—but most of all she was interested in the world of nature and in the preservation of forests and their wild inhabitants. As it happened, a short time before their visit . . . one of the strips of forest on Hog Island was cut. . . . There were threats that the entire island might be similarly cut over. My mother was shocked. 'Oh,' she exclaimed, 'they must not destroy any more of it! This island is too wonderful, it must be preserved, what CAN we do about it?' "[14]

Later in 1909, Mabel embarked on a complicated scheme to buy up the island by having her friends purchase some parcels, while she and David purchased others. By the end of the year, Mabel and her associates were finalizing the deeds. The Todds eventually gained majority ownership of the three hundred-acre island, a manifestation of Mabel's belief in the sanctity of the environment, which she stated came to her

MABEL AND DAVID IN THE EARLY YEARS OF THE TWENTIETH CENTURY.

from her father and underscored her shared love of the natural world with Austin and Emily.

Because of the various eclipse expeditions, and the financial uncertainties and family illnesses they faced, the Todds were delayed in starting to build their own camp on Hog Island until 1915. Once the camp was finished, Mabel and Millicent spent many long summers on Hog Island and it became an important place for them. It was on Hog Island that mother and daughter began the editing that led to the reissue of Emily Dickinson's letters and a new volume of poetry.

Mabel's relationship with David was also starting to change, and it would have many lasting ramifications that would confront her with uncertainty, transition and ultimately great loss.

"For thirty-three years I have absolutely refrained from putting on paper one single thing which under any circumstances could do my dear David any harm," she wrote in November of 1911. "I have even allowed misrepresentation and reproach to attach to myself, to be thought the gay and flirtatious one of the two; and never a word, written or spoken, has come from me to show that I had the faintest justification for anything I have been supposed to do. If I should write out the facts it would be appalling!" Next, the words "David" and "unmoral" are crossed out in dark ink.[15] Just what the facts were, or what this "unmoral" transgression was, we will never know for sure, because either Mabel or Millicent cut several pages from the journal. What is clear is that David's serial indiscretions were becoming less discreet, and that his behavior was becoming more erratic.

———

In May of 1913 an event of cosmic proportion occurred in Mabel's life: Sue Dickinson died. Mabel inscribed in her diary, "Poor old Susan died last night. A very curious nature, full of (originally) fine powers most cruelly perverted. She has done incalculable evil, and wrought endless unhappiness. At times she seemed possessed of a devil—yet could be smoothly winning and interesting."[16] Mabel told Millicent years later, "She was my most bitter enemy, no one in the world except possibly her daughter Mattie held such unchanging hatred toward me as she. After a fashion I felt a bit relieved and freer in my mind and occupations for her departure. For several days, even weeks, I was much more completely myself than before."[17] It felt like the end of an era to Mabel.

Less than two months later, at the beginning of a very hot day in July, Mabel decided to go swimming at the Amherst College pool after doing some errands. She felt a bit odd as she walked up the hill but assumed it was just the heat. She dove into the pool, felt awful, climbed out, and then, as she recalled years later, "remembered no more." She had had a stroke. Millicent reported that the very first thing Mabel said when she regained consciousness several days later was, "Sue has finally got me." Her mother was certain that it had been the ghost of Sue Dickinson that came up behind her, pushed her into the pool and caused the blood vessel in her brain to burst.[18]

Toward the end of her life, Mabel retold this story to Millicent, along with other memories of her years in Amherst and relationships with members of the Dickinson family. Millicent typed these up in three separate manuscripts that Mabel edited in pencil, and placed them all in a folder she labeled, "Scurrilous but True." Mabel recalled that on that hot summer day in 1913, "It was distinctly an unfriendly push or hand laying-on which startled me. I got into the pool feeling more and more under the hatred of some near-by influence, and I swam up to the end of the pool, ninety feet away, becoming there very helpless—very different feelings from any other I had ever felt . . . completely in the power of any unfriendly influence being exercised against me." She concluded, "I could not help feeling certain she [Sue] had stricken me in her pleasure to be able to work her will upon me."[19]

"Everything in the world changed then," said Millicent, years later. "It was Mamma's stroke that sealed the doom. . . . The entire family ended in me and so, of course, there was nothing for me to do but stay and do what we could to get her well again."[20] This was a turning point for everyone; the roles had reversed and Millicent became the caregiver for her parents. Toward the end of her own life, Millicent thought back on this time and wrote of "the fatal year, 1913. I was visiting the James' in Newport, when the telegram came telling of my mother's stroke. That tightened the cord so fast, it was never loosened again."[21]

For a time, Mabel was paralyzed on her right side, could not walk, and had no use of her hand. Millicent did all she could for her mother, including noting for Mabel in her diary some of the milestones of her recovery: the day she managed to cut her steak with her right hand, the day she played a scale on the piano, the day she dressed herself, the day she walked across the room with "barely a limp."

With her typical determination and resilience, Mabel soon graduated from a wheelchair to a cane to being able to walk independently, though her right foot never regained full function. "As fall days became cooler I began to feel my normal energy awakening. I determined to walk. I would not be wheeled about—except for the luxury of it—I gradually got to three or four miles a day," she recounted. Mabel taught herself to write again with her left hand ("I wrote too—but oh!—fitfully"[22]) and was eventually able to regain enough motion in her right hand to write with it, and then relegated almost all writing to typing, as she was never able to recapture her former penmanship.

A few months after Millicent had moved back to Amherst to help care for Mabel, she met a young academic named Walter Van Dyke Bingham. He invited her to the Winter Carnival at Dartmouth College. Walter, a psychology professor, was smitten with Millicent as soon as he met her. The feeling was not mutual. Though Millicent's journals and diaries contain only the occasional reference to Walter, such as "Bingham could make no impression," Mabel noted a number of times he came to lunch or took Millicent out to tea. At one point, Mabel wrote, "Professor Bingham has turned up again. His devotion is pathetic, since I suppose she will not accept him."[23]

It was true, Millicent had little to no interest in Walter, nor in much else. "I have no joy. I never laugh. Pretty soon no one will enjoy me—it is a blank ahead. There are but three things a woman can want supremely— a man, a child, a faith. I have none of the three."[24] Millicent filled her journal with pages asking why she couldn't find someone to marry, and questions about whether it would be acceptable to marry someone whom she did not love. She found it all disheartening. And so, disappointed yet again in love, worn down by the deaths of her beloved grandparents and the care of her mother, Millicent eventually resolved to turn her energies elsewhere.

Luckily for Millicent, another astronomical expedition soon came along. It surprised neither Millicent nor David that just a year after her stroke, Mabel was somehow well enough to board the SS *Rotterdam*, bound for Denmark, en route to Russia. Austria-Hungary had declared war on Serbia only weeks

WALTER VAN DYKE BINGHAM. ALAS, POOR WALTER: MILLICENT REJECTED HIS EARLY ADVANCES.

before, but the Todds thought it unlikely to affect their travels. Looking back on this many years later, Millicent wondered, "How could I have consented? My mother, dragging her foot and partially recovered from her stroke, my father was possessed by the pursuit of eclipses. So off we went in pursuit of that shadow to cross Russia in August, 1914."[25]

Mabel kept only the sketchiest and most sporadic diary entries on this journey, but Millicent retained an extensive travel journal. They traveled as far as what was then St. Petersburg, Millicent noting, "everything was all right. We saw no sign of war." But at the Kiev railway station, a messenger came running up to them and handed David a note in French, suggesting that the Todds should travel no farther. The next day Germany declared war on Russia.

Millicent wrote, "in the grey dawn of Friday the 7th of August an astronomer from a far country, marooned in a great city by the impending war, arose to finish his calculations of the sun's total eclipse he had come thousands of miles to see."[26] The Todds made a hasty and perilous journey out of Russia. Eventually, they were able to get to Stockholm, where they boarded a steamer bound for Britain, dodging German U-boats on the way. The frightening journey ended safely in Liverpool, where the family was able to board a boat headed for Boston. They landed in the fall of 1914. "We went back to Amherst soon. I immediately came to the conclusion that although my mother had been so gallant about this experience—she had come through it so beautifully—I thought more than ever that I was going to have to be the support of my father and mother before very long," wrote Millicent.[27]

Millicent agonized about whether she needed to stay in Amherst to take care of her increasingly needy parents, or if she should go to Harvard for her graduate degree. Feeling that she needed to be involved in "a pursuit of systematic learning, the forging of a point of view, focused so that I could become a teacher and support my disintegrating parents," Millicent began graduate studies in geography, which also included coursework in geology and anthropology, at Radcliffe College in Cambridge, in 1916. Surely, Millicent believed, she had now found her path.

In a tribute to David, his former student Charles Hudson later wrote, "Perhaps it was the thought of these disappointments, lost opportunities over which he had absolutely no control, which in his last years unsettled his brilliant mind."[28] Indeed, in the early years of the twentieth century, David Todd's behavior became more and more concerning to all around him. In Millicent's tortured thoughts about her father's descent into mental illness, she often attributed it to his thwarted genius, as well as to his general dependence on Mabel and her social skills, and to "the impact of Austin Dickinson."

After a series of cloudy eclipses, David began to turn his professional attention to other endeavors, including an attempt to contact the "intelligent life" he was convinced lived on Mars. Not surprisingly, these efforts were often met with derision from his colleagues. At this time, he also became less reliable about attending meetings or even teaching his classes at Amherst College, often disappearing without explanation.

Though it is difficult to know exactly from the sketchy notation and coded language both Mabel and Millicent used to describe David's behavior, what they observed certainly seems manic. He was awake much of the night and slept at odd hours for short intervals. He engaged in reckless sexual behavior, irresponsible spending and had periodic unexplained absences. His significant mood swings were frightening to behold.

In May of 1917, Amherst's president, Alexander Meiklejohn, wrote Millicent to say that her father had been given "an indefinite leave of absence." The Todds were asked to "vacate [Observatory House] at once." Millicent reflected that this, along with the increasing numbers of young men she knew who were being drafted and the news of the growing war overseas, paralleled how confusing and unsettling everything in her own life then seemed. "Life will never be the same again," she wrote.[29]

The year 1917 proved to be one of significant upheaval. David was "retired" from Amherst College; Mabel made the momentous decision to leave Amherst and move to Florida, where Arthur Curtiss James (the multimillionaire who had financed some of David's expeditions) enabled them to purchase an elegant home in Coconut Grove; and Millicent, torn between continuing her graduate studies at Harvard and "the call to 'make the world safe for democracy,'"[30] decided to put her education on hold and joined the war relief effort. As she packed up Observatory House for her parents, Millicent knew that this was the end of an era in Amherst for her family. She recognized her parents' reluctance to have anything thrown out as part of a desire to retain the past. But she could not understand why her mother insisted upon the special care she should take in ensuring that the mysterious, locked camphorwood chest be moved but not opened.

CHAPTER 10

"SINCERELY, JOE THOMAS" (1918–1919)

"Just as vibrant as love can be"

Looking back on her life in a 1959 interview, Millicent reflected, "I don't know how to tell people of this modern generation about our feeling about that war. There was a feeling of such consecration—a feeling of such tremendous idealism—uplift. We felt that if there was anything that we had in the world that we could offer to help the country to win that war it was all too little."[1]

Though the "Great War" had been raging on European soil since 1914, America didn't formally enter the fray until April of 1917. Now intent on entering the war, the United States had to staff it. The passage of the Selective Service Act drafted close to three million American soldiers; by 1918 about ten thousand men were sent off to France every day. Belief in the righteousness of the cause ran high and Millicent increasingly felt that she needed to demonstrate her support not just through words but through some kind of action.

Opportunity knocked when the YMCA put out a call for volunteers to aid the war effort by staffing canteens that would, in the words of General John Pershing, "provide amusement and moral welfare" to American soldiers. For the first time ever, the Y opened its doors to women. More than five thousand American women went to France to support American troops, assist at hospitals for the wounded and provide educational programs for soldiers. A YMCA recruiting poster from the time depicts a robust-looking woman, dressed in black with a stylish cape and hat, wearing a tie, extending a cup of coffee in one hand and holding a book in the other. She appears supremely capable, intelligent and ineffably kind. It was exactly the sort of image that resonated with Millicent.

Millicent and the others in her YMCA contingent departed for France in early April of 1918. "For the first time I have a grasp of the glory of the canon for which I am going to work," she wrote in her journal. "Free, free, free of a personal consideration!" The group arrived in Paris on April 19. "As our great, grey steamer sailed to the enchanting shores, lush, green, misty, a great garden from end to end, unspeakably beautiful, we began to see the sight that was to accompany us all the way. Every woman, every child, every old man waved from the shore and cheered."[2]

But once Millicent got into the war-fatigued country, things looked a bit different. "Here we are again, in this most heavenly spot on earth," she wrote to Mabel of the place they'd traveled to together, "but it is strangely changed. Everybody in the streets looks so sad, so tired."[3] Millicent went on to tell her mother that soon the delegation would be stationed at a place she could not mention due to censorship rules, near the front but "far away from the firing line, so I shall be entirely out of danger."[4] Millicent's canteen was actually in Angers, about three hundred kilometers southwest of Paris. This became her base for six months, until October, when she moved to Grenoble.

Millicent felt in her element. She was finding ways to use her education and intelligence to bring her closer to a wide variety of people. This was the epitome of the "vitalized" education she'd embraced at Miss Hersey's school. Appreciated for her talents, Millicent felt that she was making a real contribution. "The work is too delightful for words. I really can't tell you how happy I am to be doing the smallest bit—it is all there is in the world just now," she wrote to Mabel.[5]

But as time went on and the wounded poured in, the work was anything but delightful. Millicent recorded some of the horrible, poignant

MILLICENT TEACHING FRENCH TO A CLASS OF AMERICAN SOLDIERS AT BASE
HOSPITAL 27, ANGERS, FRANCE, 1918.

scenes she saw: "Shell shock boy calling for me, but not time to go
there.... The boy with the broken back is failing fast—can't eat anything and just whimpers . . . I wrote three letters for a gassed fellow with
swollen eyes . . . a little boy brought in tonight, his legs all crushed by a
truck that had run over him, he died just as taps were sounding."[6] The
images were still vivid years later, when she recalled the time: "From
eight in the morning until ten at night at Base Hospital 27, I was hum-
bled by the sight and sound of young men who had returned from the
front maimed. Their backs one great mustard gas blister, shell-shocked,
eyes blown from their sockets by a too close exploding shell, or perhaps
worst of all, lungs partially burned out by mustard gas."[7]

On balance, though, Millicent still felt good about the work she was
doing and was glad to be part of the war effort. She wrote to Mabel, "I
wish I could even in [a] thousand years tell you how great the experiences we're having here are, but I can't. There is one thing I can say.

That is that the courage and sublime unselfishness of these everyday soldiers is the biggest thing in this world, and I know it. The American private is the man who should be honored and worked for with the last ounce of one's strength. I for one intend to do it, although all I can do for them seems so insignificant."[8]

There was another reason Millicent initially felt so satisfied with her life in France during the war: she was in love.

———

In June of 1918, Sergeant Joe C. Thomas, crippled by shrapnel wounds in his knee and exposed to mustard gas, causing him crushing headaches and affecting his lungs, was brought to Base Hospital 27. He and Millicent began to talk and quickly felt a connection. The first thing he shared with her was that he had already earned a Croix de Guerre (literally "cross of war," a medal for bravery awarded by the French starting in 1915). He told her he was an engineer by training, a doctoral graduate of the University of Chicago, where he'd been captain of the football team and an All-American baseball player. He oversaw many engineering projects throughout the Southwest and Mexico prior to the war, and would have much work to return to. The two had a mutual affinity for discussing world affairs and philosophy. Millicent felt that she and Joe shared not only interests but also a sensibility about life.

Joe told Millicent that though his father was a man of great wealth from his success in the oil fields, he was also a physician by training, a surgeon general in the Army. He reported that his grandfather had been a famous Confederate general in the Civil War. Joe also shared that he'd had a sister named Virginia who, like Millicent, was a Vassar graduate. Joe and Virginia had been very close, inseparable as children, but she'd been in a devastating accident and had died far too young. Joe said he always felt her watching over him on the battlefields.

"I count each day lost that I don't spend time with Sergeant Thomas," Millicent soon confided in her diary. "I am mute in [his] presence— his understanding, his wisdom, his quiet, his modesty."[9] Millicent also marveled at his boyish good looks and at the ways that other men seemed to respect Joe.

THOUGH MILLICENT DIDN'T LABEL THE PHOTO, THIS IS MOST LIKELY JOE C. THOMAS; THE SAME SOLDIER APPEARS IN MANY OF HER UNLABELED PHOTOS FROM FRANCE.

But of all of the things Millicent appreciated about Joe, she was most taken when Joe told her quickly and definitively that he was falling in love with her.

"Dear Millicent, I shall call you Millicent if you don't mind. 'Miss Todd' means hardly anything but 'Millicent Todd' means much more than I ever dare tell," Joe wrote her in a note early in their relationship. As Joe recuperated from his wounds throughout the summer of 1918, the two spent long hours talking. Though Joe told her he might never be able to walk again, he was soon not only up on his feet but taking walks in the countryside with Millicent. He credited her for his recovery. Millicent's feelings for him deepened with each passing day, yet she still couldn't believe that what was happening between them was real. At the beginning of August, she wrote to Mabel, "Have you ever known Surgeon General Thomas of the Army? His son is here at present, a most interesting fellow."[10] Given Millicent's past history of unrequited love and unfulfilling relationships, as well as her insecurities about how attractive and vivacious her mother was, it's perhaps not surprising that Millicent was so reluctant to share the full extent of her feelings for Joe. But there was another reason lurking in the background, a reason given voice only in Millicent's most private writings.

"I haven't told him that I am eight years older than he is," she confided to her journal. "Though I know it will make no difference, I just have to tell him. Perhaps he would not have fallen in love had he known!"[11] At thirty-eight, Millicent had some reason to be paranoid about this. U.S. Census data reveal that between 1910 and 1920, the average age for white women to marry was twenty-six, and fewer than 10 percent of all American women thirty-five and older had never been married.[12] Millicent's future prospects for marriage didn't look too encouraging. She lived in fear that Joe would discover their age discrepancy and leave her. She continued to vacillate agonizingly between apprehension and denial: "Joe Thomas . . . is the most powerful man I have ever met as I love him enough to defy all the printed papers of statistics in the world," she wrote in her journal.[13] But despite her frequent self-reassurances that the age difference wouldn't be a problem, she couldn't bring herself to tell him about it.

October brought change for Millicent, for Joe, and for their relationship. Millicent was offered an opportunity she couldn't pass up: a chance to travel to Grenoble to work with Professor Raoul Blanchard on a history of French geography. Considered the "father of modern geography," Blanchard's primary work focused on exploring and recording the Alps. He was one of the first geographers to propose a theory of regional geography, a way of thinking about spaces of the earth as regions that have their own unique environment, topography, economy and culture. Millicent had met him two years earlier when he was a visiting faculty member at Harvard and she was thrilled with the chance to work with him again. She helped him to collect and organize his data and to translate them from French to English. In her notes from France, she wrote that Blanchard wanted her to "be the hyphen between France and America via geography. It is a big, wonderful plan, to translate his geography which is something entirely new to Americans, and then to amplify it."[14] Their seminal work, *Geography of France*, was published in translation in 1919. Working with Professor Blanchard enabled Millicent, who was technically "on loan for educational work" from the YMCA, to get back into the field in which she had been doing graduate work at Harvard. For Millicent, this felt like a professional homecoming.

Though the written record is a bit unclear, it appears that sometime in early October of 1918, Joe was sent back to the front. However, his previous injuries were not entirely healed and his lingering, hacking cough began to bring up some blood. He returned from the battlefield to seek additional treatment.

He also, apparently, began to speak to Millicent of marriage. She could barely believe her good fortune. Though some of Millicent's letters home telling her parents about her plans to be married no longer exist (she apparently destroyed them), letters from Mabel to Millicent about the upcoming nuptials remain. "I long to see the miraculous man who has actually conquered you!" Mabel wrote to her daughter in November of 1918. "Ah! Millicent, it is a happy thing to be conquered, really! If you come before spring, come here, which is a community of friends, and have a beautiful, tropical wedding in the little St. Stephens by our very good friend the rector, Mr. Solper, and then have a lovely reception in our new and impressive house. Really, it is a house designed for a wedding reception. . . . Will you give my love to Mr. Joseph Thomas and tell him I want to see him extraordinarily?"[15]

Yet Millicent was still plagued with worries, which she regularly wrote about in her diary and journal. She fretted about the giveaway gray in her hair. She agonized about whether she should have told him about her age long ago. "Joe, my beloved, who speaks of marrying him immediately! Does he really love me as much as he thinks he does? Would he if he knew how old I am? I can't seem to write mamma about it. If I did everybody would know. . . . But is it fair to mamma not to?"[16] Millicent's urge not to disappoint her mother tortured her almost as much as the thought of losing Joe.

In addition, Millicent began to have some other doubts about him, doubts that she barely dared admit to herself even in her private writings. She was disturbed by his "awful grammar," which, given his educational credentials, she simply couldn't understand. Millicent started to catch Joe in a series of small untruths, something she found very unsettling. He told her he would be at certain places at certain times but then was not. He told her that he was going to do things that she subsequently found out he did not do.

She began to hear disconcerting things about him from third parties. "There is one thing that disquiets me, and so I am going to ask him point-blank. 'Are you clean?' . . . Youthful affairs may be one thing, but relations with a girl or two . . . that he could be tainted, no, that I couldn't forgive." In addition to worrying that perhaps Joe had been exposed to "a source of infection" going around in the Army, Millicent also began to hear rumors that he was, in fact, already married.[17] Millicent could not understand why nurses would have started whispering about this, despite Joe's reassurances to her that it was all rumor. She agonized when a YMCA colleague related that Joe "told his regiment that his one idea of a good time was a bottle of cognac and a French woman."[18]

Millicent's need to believe that Joe loved her trumped her desire to find out the truth. This often led her to bouts of mental wrestling, cognitive dissonance, and intensive rationalization. "Until unreasonably—if it proved to me that he has lied to me time and time again, I shall know he did it to win me. I shall fear perhaps the kind of lies he may tell again if he has told such now, but I shall marry him anyway, unless he does not love me—but that can't be so. What we have is just as vibrant as love can be."[19] Millicent often convinced herself that doubting Joe was a sin far worse than any untruth he'd uttered. At times she even managed to believe this.

When she finally revealed her age, Joe told her that he knew she was a few years older than he was. "I'm 38," she told him when he visited her in Grenoble shortly after peace was declared in November 1918. "Oh, I didn't know it was that much," he replied. Millicent wrote later in her journal, "I could have died on the spot."[20]

Millicent's fears were not unjustified. Joe did not write to her as frequently after his visit to Grenoble. After the celebratory moment when the war ended, he let her know that he would likely be discharged from the Army but that the blood he'd been coughing up might indicate that he had tuberculosis. He would need to seek treatment. Millicent was frantic, urging him to be treated at a hospital in France, but he didn't tell her where he was, nor where he would be receiving treatment. He only told her that he couldn't marry her right away because he needed to "clear out [his] system" first. Then he told her he must put off their marriage, indefinitely.

Though Millicent was both devastated and panicked, she admitted her feelings only to her journal. Publicly, she reported nothing amiss. She wrote to Mabel, "Gas in the lungs means that he is very sensitive to damp and cold, and the physicians feel that he ought not to cross the ocean until warmer weather. It is the most hideous instrument of torture that was used in that hideous war."[21]

Around the same time, the Todds' great family friend and patron Arthur Curtiss James, sent Millicent a letter. She recorded its contents in her journal, but apparently destroyed the actual letter, for it does not reside anywhere in the voluminous files of correspondence that she preserved. Arthur, suspicious of this unknown man in Millicent's life, had him investigated. He wrote Millicent that though Joe had said, "he graduated from Chicago, class of 1912, he had not." Though Joe had claimed to be captain of the football team and an All-American baseball player, "someone who was a spokesman for that never heard of him." The sister who'd gone to Vassar? "No record of this, no such girl." Arthur also wrote that someone reported that, in fact, Joe was already married.[22]

Though Millicent didn't know this at the time, the real story was even worse. U.S Census records from 1920 reveal that Joe C. Thomas's father did not list himself either as a World War I veteran or as a physician. The Census listed Joe's birth year as 1896, which would have made him just twenty-two—not thirty—when he and Millicent met. And perhaps most damning of all, Joe's "dear dead sister chum," Virginia, the one who'd died in that devastating automobile accident? She was alive and well, living with her parents in Muskogee, Oklahoma.[23]

Millicent couldn't bring herself to believe Arthur's letter. "I don't

ARTHUR CURTISS JAMES, AMHERST
ALUMNUS, MULTIMILLIONAIRE. HE
FUNDED SEVERAL OF DAVID'S ECLIPSE
EXPEDITIONS, BOUGHT A LARGE HOUSE
IN FLORIDA FOR THE TODDS, AND PAID
FOR A PRIVATE INVESTIGATOR TO LOOK
INTO JOE THOMAS.

care if all is false," she wrote in her journal, "<u>He</u> is not. He is a reality. He loves me as I love him. . . ."[24] Yet Millicent needed to see Joe, to talk through what she had heard, to reaffirm their love. She begged him to meet her in Dijon a few days later, and he consented. Millicent traveled there and waited for Joe at the café at which they'd agreed to meet. But he didn't come. Millicent stayed in Dijon through the end of 1918, waiting for Joe. But there was no sign of him, nor any word from him, at all.

Millicent eventually found that Joe had been sent to a sanitarium in Germany, and then to one back in America, in Denver. She acted quickly and booked her own passage across the Atlantic, then traveled from New York to Denver. But at the VA Hospital in Denver, she discovered that Joe had been furloughed to his hometown. She boarded yet another train, this one to Muskogee.

The next morning dawned and the heat climbed quickly. Millicent, trained since her earliest days to record the daily temperature, noted that it was a blistering 110 in the shade. Along with the temperature, she recorded, "The day has come; I hardly slept at all."[25] She was plagued with doubts about whether she should have made this journey. It turned out that Millicent should have been doubting Thomas much more than she did.

Later that same day, Millicent wrote in her diary, "Joe came at about noon and stayed two hours. I did the worst thing I possibly have done for him, for me, for our relationship."[26] And with that, Millicent noted that she took a 4 p.m. train out of Oklahoma. She did not write in either her diary or journal for two weeks.

When she could finally stand to relive the scene, Millicent wrote, "Tomorrow will be two weeks since that fatal day. I have gone about and done my work—and there has been much—in a trance. People are intolerable. I never want to see another man." But then she declared, "I must write it. Yes. Then I shall leave this journal and write no more."[27] In excruciating detail, Millicent delineated her final encounter with Joe C. Thomas.

—

He met her in the lobby of her hotel. She told him she couldn't speak with him there and asked him to come to her room. There she took both his hands in hers. "I should have known then that all would be all right and that he loved me," she wrote. But it wasn't all right. It couldn't have been more wrong.

Millicent asked if it was his health that had been the trouble, the reason he'd fled, the reason he'd been so out of touch, the cause of his distance from her. He replied that it was not his health, at all. Joe admitted that he had lied to her about everything. "I'm sorry for that. . . . But I didn't want you—I don't want you."

Millicent was stunned. She couldn't believe what she was hearing. But "the climax was the worst of all," she wrote. Millicent reached for the catch on the chain to take off the ring Joe had given her, the one he said was a temporary promise of their future until he could get her a proper engagement ring, which she wore around her neck. But the catch stuck. She asked Joe to help. He assisted her with the catch and she took the ring off the chain and handed it to him. He put it in his pocket and then removed it. He looked at it for several long moments, and then threw it to the floor and stamped on it. And then he walked out the door and let it slam behind him.[28]

—

Millicent returned to Harvard to continue work toward her doctorate. She threw herself into her studies, working fifteen-hour days, trying to shut everything and everyone else out. Years later she told an interviewer, "It was a great solace to me because I had had a very devastating experience in France. I can't say much about it but we were all living on such an idealistic plane, and there was a soldier . . . I believed in him. . . . It was a very awful experience. So I just plunged into hard work as hard as I possibly could."[29]

But even work couldn't shut out the experience with Joe or her feelings for him. Not completely. And not ever. Almost forty years later, Millicent reflected, "The sense of utter annihilation, the return to Cambridge to finish the work I had started—all feeling was dead."[30] The failed romance with Joe made Millicent even more entrenched in her beliefs about morality and keener than ever to do what she could to right the injustices she perceived done to herself and to her parents. Ultimately, this life-changing incident paved the path for Millicent to doggedly pursue her work on Emily Dickinson. She would later suggest to a psychiatrist, "I espoused Emily's cause largely, I think, to right a wrong." And the erstwhile relationship with Joe convinced Millicent of the ambivalence of Emily's views of love, something that would significantly color Millicent's subsequent writings about the poet and her work. Millicent clearly related to Emily's bittersweet views on love as embodied in the poem Higginson and Mabel titled "Bequest"— poem 644 in the later Johnson edition:

You left me, sweet, two legacies,—
A legacy of love
A Heavenly Father would content,
Had He the offer of;

You left me boundaries of pain
Capricious as the sea,
Between eternity and time,
Your consciousness and me.[31]

Even during the time she spent with her mother shortly after the scene in Muskogee, Millicent still could not bring herself to tell Mabel the truth about Joe. There are few other events in the course of their relationship that so clearly demonstrate how their efforts to protect each other from difficult truths in fact prevented them from ever having a full and honest relationship. Eventually, Millicent wrote to Mabel: "I hardly know how to tell you, because I can't bear the thought of making you grieve. But my engagement to Joe is broken. It is final and can never be remedied. I do not want you to feel badly. It is best this way. Sometime when I can I will explain. I cannot write about it. Somehow you and I . . . we will get something good out of these terrible experiences. It is not all loss."[32]

Joe did send a letter to Millicent after the incident in Muskogee. In it, he wrote, "Can't you be happy, Millicent? To know that you had forgiven me and that you were happy would mean very much. . . . Sincerely, Joe Thomas."

Millicent was flabbergasted. "I am numb tonight," she wrote in her diary. "A letter from Joe. . . . He signed himself 'Sincerely'? . . . I sat in the room in the geography lab and tried to read; I am absolutely aware of failure, complete failure. . . . It is perfectly ghastly."[33] The formal salutation spoke volumes to Millicent.

As 1919 drew to a close, an old acquaintance resurfaced in Millicent's life. Walter Van Dyke Bingham, the academic psychologist whom she'd initially met—and rejected as a potential suitor—years earlier, once again sought a romantic relationship with Millicent. She wrote in her journal that she thought she perhaps should not see Walter Van Dyke Bingham (she insisted on writing his full name each time she referred to him) because her heart still belonged to Joe. "Of course I must tell him I am not free at present. I have got to wait. I shall not go into details with him—that would be a desecration. Oh Joe, my darling, my adored—shall I go through life alone without you?"[34]

⌒

Early in December of 1920, the Miami newspapers told of a fabulous wedding held at Matsuba, the home of Professor David Peck Todd and Mrs. Mabel Loomis Todd. It was the "beautiful tropical wedding" with the service at St. Stephens and the party at "the house made for a wedding reception" that Mabel had outlined in her letters to Millicent in France. The house was resplendent with ferns and exotic flowers. Guests arrived from faraway places. The wedding announcement cards were from Shreve, Crump and Low. And the name of the groom was Walter Van Dyke Bingham.

CHAPTER 11

FIGHTING TO DEFINE EMILY DICKINSON (1920–1929)

"May I accomplish all I can"

"Once again the far southern tip of Florida and Boston are in friendly accord," noted an article in the *Boston Transcript* in December 1920. "This winter . . . the fair southern town of Coconut Grove, one of the most beautiful and choicest of Florida resorts was the scene of the marriage of Miss Millicent Todd and Professor Walter Van Dyke Bingham. Miss Todd is the daughter of Professor David Todd, for over 35 years Professor of Astronomy and Navigator and Director of the Observatory of Amherst College, and his wife, Mrs. Mabel Loomis Todd, all of them with intimate connection in Boston." The article continued, "On Saturday, the 4th of December, the wedding occurred, surrounded by all the tropical wealth of southern Florida . . . a mass of superb blossoms making of the house, 'Matsuba,' which Professor and Mrs. Todd have built there, a veritable bower of beauty."[1]

Millicent's scrapbook from her wedding is large, perhaps six inches thick, its binding now cracking. It contains the formal invitation and subsequent printed announcement from Shreve, Crump and Low that Mabel had so desired. There are wedding notices from several newspapers in Massachusetts, Florida and Pittsburgh (where Walter was work-

MILLICENT WAS MARRIED IN MATSUBA, MABEL'S GRAND NEW HOME IN FLORIDA.

ing at the time), and also, typical of Millicent, a set of lists: those who were invited, wedding gifts received, music she wanted played. There are also notes from many friends. Quite a number of people expressed surprise at the announcement of the nuptials. "My dear Bingham," wrote a former colleague of Walter's, "I see the great event has finally happened. At last you have found 'her.' Astonishing!" There's also a telegram to Walter saying, "Your surprising letter just received and I hasten to wish you all possible joy and happiness." One friend of Millicent's commented, "My dear Millicent, the news of your engagement was a complete surprise to me!"[2]

There are fewer than a dozen photos in the entire album. Among them are elegant photos of Mabel's home, Matsuba (a Japanese word for a pinecone pattern found on trees and on red koi, which Mabel found particularly aesthetically appealing). In one shot, a stylishly dressed

Mabel sits, hair elegantly coiffed atop her head, with Millicent standing beside her in her bridal gown and veil, hand on her mother's shoulder, looking unexpectedly dowdy. They appear to be gazing intently at each other, but they do not smile. Perhaps most surprising, there are no photos of Millicent and her groom together.

Many years later, Millicent recalled why she decided to finally accept his marriage proposal. "I had received a death-blow," she wrote. "I felt that emotion would never be revived. There was nothing but work—hard work—for me. And of course, anxiety. . . . And so, working as I never worked before, I entered my forties. During the summer of 1920 Walter Bingham came to the island. . . . He told me that he still loved me and wanted me to marry him. I told him that I could not respond—that I was emotionally dead. He said he didn't care."[3]

For Millicent, Walter was her salvation from the disappointment and despair Joe's rejection had caused. Walter and Millicent were the same age and he really *did* have a PhD from the University of Chicago. At the time he proposed, Walter was in the middle of developing his theories of industrial psychology (theories that would become seminal in the field) and had a position in the Division of Cooperative Research at what was then called the Carnegie Institute of Technology (later known as Carnegie Mellon University). Walter was safe, Walter was sure. Even though Walter knew she did not return his love, he wanted to marry her, nonetheless. Millicent even hoped that perhaps she and Walter could begin a family. It was a relief; she would not be alone. Perhaps even then she sensed what she would recount in a 1959 interview: "Walter Bingham assumed from the very beginning my responsibilities and my burdens."[4] And so, as she later wrote: "Without announcing our engagement, we set the date for our marriage"—just four months hence.[5]

After one month of marriage, Millicent wrote in a new journal, "I am married, the incredible, much-thought about, much postponed, great big wonderful thing has happened." Only she wasn't finding it so wonderful. While she wrote of Walter's devotion and willingness to help take on the increasing burden of caring for her parents, Millicent still had doubts. At first it was just little things—his table manners were awful, or he was "too meticulous" in his grooming. Just two months into the marriage, she learned that Walter had had several prior sexual relationships. Given her extreme Puritan values and how sensitized and intolerant she was about sex outside of marriage, Millicent found this unforgivable. She admitted in her journal that though she was "not infatuated" with Walter, "love means self-sacrifice and permanences."[6] Many years later she reflected, "My ability to respond to Walter's love in kind, was gone—dead forever." Though she would learn to respect him, and certainly appreciated all that he did for her parents, it would

A RARE PHOTOGRAPH OF MILLICENT AND WALTER TOGETHER.

always be "love, yes, but not the dazzling, frightening intensity of which I was capable."[7]

There would be no children, and in later life she pondered whether not marrying Walter when he first proposed in 1913 had been her greatest mistake:

> As for a child? Did I not think of that? Did I ever consider my duty to my family? The line ends in me. Did I ever consider my biological reason for existence? . . . Had Walter and I married then, and had a family, who knows, the tension might have been released. My mother might not have had a stroke, my father might not have been broken. . . . And as for me, I might have had ties that bound me tighter than those to my mother. Children, they say, do.[8]

In the middle of 1922, there was a small crisis in their young marriage. "I intend to talk to Walter about his sex standards," Millicent wrote.

Though she didn't dare to record her thoughts in her bound journals, Millicent did write out a series of notes on individual pieces of paper that she saved. All of them focused on the issue of his fidelity. "Suspicion . . . what are the suspicions founded on? . . . Your lying to me was a great blow, it simply put you down on the level with the common herd."[9]

Millicent's fears about Walter's "sex standards" and her recognition that there was no great physical chemistry between them were not the only problems in their marriage. Millicent was disappointed in Walter's lack of connection to the world of academia—he had held several adjunct academic positions over the years but never managed to get a full-time professorial appointment. Millicent was also dismayed that even with a master's degree from Harvard and a PhD from the University of Chicago, Walter was still not affiliated with a similarly prestigious institution. ("And how I HATE to have him put down as coming from Stevens in the Harvard Catalog. All our friends are getting top notch recognition," she wrote privately during the time that Walter had an adjunct instructorship at the Stevens Institute of Technology.)[10] She was extremely concerned about Walter's general lack of ambition and inability to bring in money. While her mantra was "May I accomplish all I can," his productivity and work ethic were quite different.

Walter's position at the Carnegie Institute of Technology was abruptly terminated in 1923, the same year Millicent completed and defended her doctoral dissertation. It was becoming increasingly clear to Millicent that she would have to be the main provider not only for her parents but also for Walter and herself.

When Walter became the director of the Personnel Research Federation of New York, it meant moving from Pittsburgh. At first, she was pleased. They had moved into a large apartment on Washington Place, in Greenwich Village. Millicent picked up part-time teaching jobs in geography at Sarah Lawrence College and Columbia, worked on translating the *Principles of Human Geography* by Paul Vidal de la Blache from French to English and wrote several articles about the geography of Peru, which were published in the *Encyclopaedia Britannica* and elsewhere.

But Millicent soon found that she didn't like New York's pace or crowds or dirt; the city sounds kept her up at night—as did her incessant worries about Walter and about her parents. Millicent was so troubled that in 1927 she did something extremely unusual for the day—she sought psychiatric help.

As with everything else in her life, Millicent took notes and meticulously documented her psychiatric sessions, although she did not type up her notes or even use the doctor's first name. There were clear themes emerging from her work with Dr. MacPherson: how she loved Walter but felt no passion, how she longed for Walter to be financially stable so that he could "operate on all cylinders," but feared he never would. There were Millicent's concerns about her obsessive need for "productivity" and her "acquisitiveness" (by which she meant her inability to throw anything out). She also discussed the very long and growing list of genuine and psychosomatic ailments that resulted from her anxieties.

There were the issues with her parents: her recognition of her mother's affair with Austin Dickinson; how it made her feel as if the entire town of Amherst had been against her mother and herself; and her revulsion that this relationship occurred outside of marriage. There was also Millicent's own "false sense of loyalty" to her parents and her fear that this would derail her own work and life's purpose. She despaired that Mabel had squandered so many of her talents and would only be remembered for her work on Emily Dickinson, something of which Millicent was acutely aware, even then.

When the stock market crashed in 1929, Walter lost his job at the Federation. He took out loans and borrowed money from Millicent in a vain attempt to keep the organization afloat. She wrote, "My concern about Walter is not only financial. It is even more that he does not seem to have a sense of what his own services are worth, or getting anything like a fair wage for his grueling work. . . . But it is awfully hard for me to sit and take it, as it is, when I disapprove and resent the situation so." However, Millicent added, "my own affairs would cause me no end of worry if Walter's were not so much worse."[11]

Millicent's own affairs had much to do with those of her parents.

David's odd and erratic behavior was becoming more acute. In 1920 he launched a series of "experiments" attempting to "signal Mars" from a balloon. An article in the *Kansas City Star* quoted David as saying, "If there are human beings on Mars . . . I have no doubt that they have been sending us messages for years and are still wondering at our stupidity in replying."[12]

Not surprisingly, the press evinced more than a little skepticism, while the scientific community and David's former colleagues largely ignored him. David launched other projects that he didn't complete, and on which he spent unreasonable sums of money. One of these was a movie about the Everglades, for which he had "put mortgages on the Florida house up to the hilt," according to Millicent, who attempted to pay off her father's debts and save the house when the bank was ready to foreclose on it. Millicent retained many folders' worth of papers delineating the bills David left unpaid, which she, Walter or Mabel had to somehow cover. David sometimes sent Millicent on errands that made her question his sanity. He would ask her to fetch something from a person who turned out not to exist. He told her to find friends he wished to see, only to send her to incorrect or nonexistent addresses. "I got very tired from all of those wild goose chases,"[13] she noted.

In 1922, David decided to go South America to set up a giant telescope in the mountains of Chile, to observe Mars more closely. Millicent and Walter went to see him off at the New York port from which he was scheduled to depart. But David failed to show up. At that point Millicent and Walter had David evaluated by a psychiatrist, and "the result was that he was placed in Bloomingdale [Insane Asylum] in White Plains, where he stayed for a year or two."[14]

The decision to institutionalize David was wrenching for both Millicent and Mabel. Mabel captured some of this in her journal: "Last spring in Coconut Grove my dear David grew queerer and queerer . . . I can't write of it, it's too heartbreaking. But we found him in New York . . . he was found to be suffering from 'circular insanity' and immediate treatment was insisted on."[15]

STARTING IN THE EARLY YEARS OF THE
TWENTIETH CENTURY, DAVID PECK TODD
TURNED HIS ATTENTION TO TRYING
TO SIGNAL THE INTELLIGENT LIFE HE
BELIEVED EXISTED ON MARS. SOME OF
HIS EFFORTS INVOLVED ASCENTS IN HOT
AIR BALLOONS WITH EQUIPMENT HE
INVENTED TO SEND AND RECEIVE SIGNALS
FROM MARS. 1909.

Millicent recalled, "I shall never forget my first visit to him there in Bloomingdale. . . . He was lying on a settee out under a tree with dark glasses on and he would hardly speak. The tragedy of his life then became clear—I had a glimpse of it but I knew very little at that early date as to what the trouble would be."[16]

For the rest of his life, David Todd would be in and out of mental institutions, nursing homes, and other care facilities. He escaped or disappeared from some facilities, causing Walter to go off in search of him. Even the most secure and well-staffed facilities still had problems with David: once Millicent was asked to stop sending her father stamps, because David had been sending out letters with "very inappropriate messages"; another time David was caught contacting potential investors about his various "fanciful and extravagant schemes," only to have them back out when they realized they were visiting a patient at a mental institution. David often prevailed on Millicent to have him released because he was so miserable, and she often felt guilty enough to do so—until the next incident of his "asocial" behavior or "failing mental capacity" precipitated another stay at a different institution.

In 1925, David traveled to Amherst to attend his fiftieth college reunion. Millicent received an urgent letter from George Daniel Olds, then president of the college: "I am very sorry indeed to have to write you about your father . . . to be perfectly frank, he is giving a great deal of trouble. Reports come from various sources absolutely trustworthy that he is accosting people, especially ladies, in a rather disagreeable way. I understand of course that he is not responsible for his acts." President Olds concluded by asking Millicent to come to Amherst and remove her father. Millicent recalled, "The result was that he was shut up over night in the hospital and then taken to the hospital for the mentally ill in Northampton under very humiliating circumstances."[17]

Millicent and Walter had David transferred from the Northampton State Hospital to McLean's Hospital (known at the time as Waverly), a private facility outside of Boston. "I wanted him to be in a more agreeable place," Millicent wrote. Arthur Curtiss James set up a special fund to help cover the costs of David's care. Millicent and Walter spent that summer living in Professor George Herbert Palmer's house in Cambridge (Palmer, an old family friend of the Todds', had officiated at Millicent and Walter's wedding); Walter was teaching a course in the Harvard summer school and Millicent made frequent visits to see David. "I remember him saying to me after one of these visits, 'What have I ever done to you that you should put me in a place like this?' and it was so devastating that I would go out onto those lovely grounds and sit under a great tree and try to pull myself together before I started back to Cambridge to see what I could do to get him out of an institution which he felt so humiliated to be in. I took him out in spite of the doctors saying he would do himself injustice if not harm."[18] To Millicent, it seemed as if her father's "brilliant mind" was still there, but was as clouded as the eclipses he'd long hoped to photograph. And her guilt at institutionalizing David was so significant that it overshadowed her own judgment, as well.

For Mabel, the 1920s was a decade that roared. Her move to Florida meant a fresh start. Her work on Emily Dickinson was on indefinite hiatus, but she periodically made sure that Millicent knew that the camphorwood chest was secure. Despite her increasing worries about David, Mabel was able to carve out a new existence. She operated in a separate sphere from David, their worlds only occasionally intersecting. Though David wasn't around, Mabel often seemed to pretend otherwise; she always referred to herself as "Mrs. David Todd" and the many newspaper notices about the events at Mabel's home refer to it as their home, though they almost never mention David having been there. He wasn't. From the time he was institutionalized in the spring of 1922, Mabel and David never lived together again.

Mabel delighted in her grand new home that with the help of the trust that Arthur Curtiss James set up, she was able to decorate as she wished. Millicent wrote, "Matsuba was a center of cultural life in the community."[19] Mabel spent several months each year in Florida; from June to October she went to Maine and lived at the camp she and David had built on her beloved Hog Island.

Although Mabel's Florida winters and Maine summers suggest the leisurely life of a retiree, she was anything but. As she had in Amherst and throughout her life, she placed a high premium on industriousness. Despite her age and the stroke she'd suffered, she continued to be energetic and vital, involved in a variety of artistic, civic and environmental endeavors. "Although she is the wife of one of America's most eminent astronomers, Mrs. David Todd does not shine by reflected glory," observed an article in the *Miami Herald*. Another notice in the social pages titled "With the Women of Today" read, "Mrs. Mabel Loomis Todd, wife of Professor Todd, the noted astronomer, has been one of the most familiar figures on the lecture platform for a quarter of a century. In addition to her lectures she is known as an astronomer, poet, editor and author. The story of Mrs. Todd's active life reads like a page each from 'who's who,' travel and adventure."[20]

Mabel's scrapbooks from the 1920s are filled with newspaper notices about her many talks on a range of subjects from world travels to astronomical events. There are articles about her election as president of the local chapter of the Audubon Society and her work to make the Everglades a national park. The scrapbooks are stuffed with programs from concerts, plays and art exhibits she attended and with printed cards announcing the multitude of events she held at her home, including many receptions for local artists.

One of the artists she encountered was Howard Hilder. Hilder, a British expatriate decamped to the American South, and described by the *Miami Herald* as "the leading interpreter of the scenic beauty of Florida," was known for his large murals as well as for smaller oil paintings. He and Mabel hit it off instantly. Soon Mabel was introducing him to prominent collectors, featuring his works in her own home, and creating social opportunities at which he could display, donate or promote his art. He also became her escort to innumerable events. Mabel provided Hilder with studio space on her properties in Florida and on Hog Island. She lent him money, even though she was concerned about David's increasing debts. Hilder took charge of the cleanup at Matsuba when it was severely damaged by a hurricane in 1927. He drove Mabel to and from her residences each October and June, and he often would help her by closing up the houses at the end of each season.

Even when they were not together, they maintained an intensive correspondence that lasted from 1919 until 1932, sometimes writing each other every day. They always addressed each other as "My dear old pal" or sometimes, "Hilder of Hog." From their letters, one can clearly discern a deepening relationship: they move from speaking only about art, sales and logistics to discussing David's bizarre behavior and the need to keep him institutionalized and Hilder's relationship with another married woman.

The nature of Mabel and Howard Hilder's relationship is not quite clear. At the time, Mabel was writing only the most cursory entries in her daily diary and rarely wrote in her journal. Lines in her letters to Hilder suggest that she wanted to tell him more than she could write. Whether this was a function of her inability to write long passages by hand after her stroke or some hesitation about conveying intimate thoughts on paper after the relationship with Austin is uncertain. They certainly were great cheerleaders for each other—she referred to him as "the Chopin of painters," and he wrote her: "Your hidden (so far) talents are brilliant even unto purposeness, my dear."[21] He painted several pictures of Matsuba for her, as well as her portrait.

Millicent was very suspicious of this relationship. In the write-ups from her psychiatric sessions in 1927, Millicent included notes about her belief that Mabel was being ridiculous in thinking of Hilder as one of America's greatest painters, and that, by catering to him, her mother had stooped to depths she had never before been capable of. She was disgusted by Mabel's lavish praise of Hilder, appalled that she had loaned him money, and truly horrified that Mabel had somehow used her contacts and wealthy friends to enable Hilder and Jack, his son from a prior marriage, "with their love of whiskey and painted women," to purchase a tract of land on Hog Island. In a rare moment of true vulnerability, Millicent admitted to her fear and jealousy that her mother had grown closer to Howard Hilder than she was to her: "Doubtless he is much nearer to her than I am," she wrote, adding that the patterns of her mother's relationships with men other than David "wakes me up at night and torments me."[22]

———

"Not knowing when the dawn will come / I open every door," wrote Emily Dickinson in the poem Mabel titled "Dawn" (poem 1619 in the Johnson edition). As the 1920s progressed, neither Mabel nor Millicent would clearly know when their dawns would come. But the events of the past two decades had shown Millicent that the doors once open to both her parents were rapidly closing—their legacies were in doubt, her own was still not in focus. In one of her journals she admitted her fears about never finding her own true path, as well as how her filial loyalties tore her apart—and how the cloud of the Dickinsons hung over them all:

> There is my father, as there is my mother. My father, a curious mixture of doing more than he is given credit for, as well as doing less than he has a right to be. . . . Mamma? She occupies much of my

thought, heart, brain, unwittingly pathetic little soul. I never forget her brilliancy, sometimes pointed to dazzle with dismay. Her gifts, her talents, her achievements, the adoration she has from the world, her prolific service. . . . But oh, Mr. Dickinson, the poison of that for my childish soul—and Madam Bianchi still. . . . Cruel past belief.[23]

Even though Mabel and Millicent had moved away from Amherst, Amherst's legacy stayed with them. They found themselves unable to put it all behind them. Mattie Dickinson would not allow it.

Mattie, now incongruously known as "Madame Bianchi," following her 1902 marriage to Alexander Bianchi, a Russian captain in the Imperial Horse Guards, had inherited her mother's and her aunt Lavinia's papers and homes. The last surviving member of the Dickinson clan, Mattie was facing financial and social pressure because of her husband's gambling debts and fraud conviction. Literary scholar Elizabeth Horan points out that "the family car, various stocks, property in Atlantic City, the land over which Lavinia and Mrs. Todd had fought, all went to pay off Captain Bianchi's debts and to settle lawsuits."[24] When none of Mattie's own literary endeavors yielded any significant income, she decided to release a new volume of her aunt Emily's poetry, possibly in an effort to rehabilitate her own name and help promote her own career as a writer and poet—and raise some much-needed funds. In 1914 she published *The Single Hound: Poems of a Lifetime* by Emily Dickinson. In the preface to this book, Mattie suggested that Emily had sent all the poems to her mother, Sue. While this may be true, in fact, many of the poems in this volume were ones that Mabel and Higginson had previously edited and published. *The Single Hound* contained a total of 143 poems; altogether Mabel's original three volumes of Emily's poetry contained 144. As the editors of the online Emily Dickinson archive point out, Mattie subsequently brought out additional poems in two other volumes that "combined the poems found in the three Todd-Higginson volumes with her own work and published *The Complete Poems of Emily Dickinson*. But this appellation proved too hasty: she subsequently found more manuscript material and released two further installments."[25] Those were only the poems that had been previously published in other places or were in Mattie's possession.

Mabel and Millicent took issue with Mattie's work in many ways. As Millicent later explained in *Ancestors' Brocades*, "Certain poems in that volume . . . differ more or less from the printed text, some by only a word or two, while others are sufficiently unlike as to constitute two separate versions." Millicent provided many specific examples of instances in which she believed Mattie had either misread Emily's manuscripts, or selected an alternative word from among those Emily had suggested but which differed from Mabel and Higginson's word choice. For instance, Millicent pointed to Mabel's transcription of the poem "There is another loneliness," and how the first stanza differed from Mattie's version published in *The Single Hound* (1914), which Millicent believed came "from misreading the manuscript":

MABEL'S TRANSCRIPTION:
There is another loneliness
That many die without,
Not want of friend occasions it,
Or circumstance of lot.

MATTIE'S VERSION:
There is another loneliness
That many die without,
Not want or friend occasions it,
Or circumstance or lot.[26]

One of the clear examples Millicent provided of Mattie having not used the word choice Emily preferred was from the poem "To see her is a picture." Millicent noted that in the Todds' interpretation of Emily's true choice, the third and fourth lines of the poem read:

To know her, a disparagement
Of every other boon.

Whereas in Mattie's published version in *The Single Hound*, these lines read:

To know her an intemperance
As innocent as June.

Millicent wrote in *Ancestors' Brocades* that while Emily did suggest many alternatives in her original manuscript, she also gave clues about her preference, as evidenced by the appearance and location of word alternatives.[27]

Furthermore, Millicent pointed out that some of the poems Mattie published as stand-alone verses were, in fact, fragments of longer poems.[28] However, Mattie did keep most of the poems' original rhyme schemes intact, and unlike Mabel and Higginson, Mattie chose not to title the poems, just as her aunt had declined to do.

The publisher, Little, Brown (successor to Roberts Brothers), promoted the book with ad copy that might have come directly from Mattie, herself: "A memory sketch of Emily Dickinson, written in the desire to establish her identity beyond misconception of hearsay and portray her as she was."[29]

Critical reaction to the volume was mixed. In *The New Republic*, Elizabeth Shepley Sergeant wrote, "There is, I think, less of human passion in this collection than in the earlier ones," though she applauded Emily's creativity and was intrigued by Mattie's introduction, which was "a suggestive preface of anecdote and reminiscence to prove how little the aunt she loved resembled the poetess as she is 'taught in colleges.' . . . *The Single Hound*," she concluded, "is as surprising as a cold douche, as acute as the edge of a precipice, as lambent as a meteor cleaving the night."[30] In *Poetry: A Magazine of Verse*, editor Harriet Monroe wrote:

The present volume may not increase the measure of her spiritual height and depth, or add new luster to her beauty of soul, to the star-like fidelity of her genius or the lithe nudity of her art. These were established by the two earlier collections, published soon after the poet's death. But nothing in those precious books is finer than a few poems in this one, which doubtless represents the final effort of her niece and literary executor to extricate Emily Dickinson's poems from a mass of ragged papers, and preserve them for lovers of her temperamental art.[31]

In 1922 the copyright on Mabel's 1894 *Letters of Emily Dickinson* expired, which Mattie used to her advantage. In a new volume she rearranged most of the letters so that they appeared chronologically rather than by correspondent, added in letters in her possession that Emily had written to her mother and other family members and wrote an introductory essay and a number of chapters about Emily's life to go with them. Houghton Mifflin published her book, titled *The Life and Letters of Emily Dickinson*, in 1924. That same year, Mattie's *The Complete Poems of Emily Dickinson* was published by Little, Brown. Of course, this volume was not truly complete—Mabel still retained over six hundred poems that were stashed away in her camphorwood chest. Mattie wrote, "A high exigence constrains the sole survivor of her family to state her simply and truthfully, in view of a public which has doubtless without intention, misunderstood and exaggerated her seclusion—amassing a really voluminous stock of quite lurid misinformation of irrelevant personalities. She has been taught in colleges as a weird recluse, rehearsed to women's clubs as a lovelorn sentimentalist."[32] This was clearly a shot over the bow directed at Mabel, renewing the battle to define Emily Dickinson. Millicent, outraged over the public wrong she felt Mattie had done to Mabel, decided to step into the family feud for the first time.

Predictably, Millicent's reaction to these publications was to analyze them. In *Ancestors' Brocades* she provides a painstaking list of all the errors that Mattie made in her version of Emily's letters, ranging from simple omissions to outright and sloppy mistakes, including incorrect dates of people's births and deaths—even Emily's. Millicent noted, "Bad as such factual mistakes were, at least they were obvious and would sooner or later be noticed. Many of them have been rectified in a later edition. But misrepresentation of personal relationships is a different matter." Here, Millicent was referring to Mattie's essay about Emily's life, in which she characterized her aunt Emily's relationship with Sue as loving, mutually respectful and genuine. ("The romantic friendship of Aunt Emily Dickinson and her 'Sister Sue' extended from girlhood until death. The first poem, dated, was sent in 1848, and probably the last word Aunt Emily ever wrote was her reply to a message from my Mother, 'My answer is an unmitigated Yes, Sue.'")[33] Millicent retorted that in her own mother's volume of *Letters*, any mention of Sue was taken out at Austin's request and "Emily's relationship to her sister-in-law will repay further investigation."[34] Millicent also pointed out that other than one paragraph on Emily's childhood, Mattie made no mention of Emily's relationship to her brother, though Austin and Emily were very close, nor did she include any photos of Austin in the book. Old wounds, it seemed, were still fresh, and their pain spurred Mattie to try to alter the historical record—at least according to Millicent.

Millicent was also outraged by the "irreparable misrepresentation" of Emily's "love story."

"Not only was the legend of a broken heart revived," wrote Millicent, "it was fantastically embellished. . . . The fact that the niece does not understand her aunt, though regrettable, does not matter. What does matter is that such a statement betrays Emily, because it is not true . . . to misrepresent her in this is to do her the greatest disservice in the power of a relative to bestow."[35] Of course, coming from the daughter of the woman who launched a different—and perhaps not altogether accurate—image of the poet and marketed it to the world through her talks, Millicent's remarks must be taken in context.

"I begged my mother to allow me to refute some of the misstatements in the *Life and Letters*, arguing that a false impression may become permanent unless it is challenged at once," Millicent wrote in *Ancestors' Brocades*. "She refused. I drew her attention to the fact that no acknowledgment had been made to her early volumes. Mrs. Bianchi's name on the title-page implied that she herself had collected and edited the letters. Such effrontery left me aghast. That misrepresentation must not be allowed to stand. I asked my mother why she did not protest. She said, 'Please do not talk about it.'"[36] This may be a bit of revisionist history on Millicent's part, because nowhere in her journals or diaries—or in Mabel's, for that matter—is there a record of such a discussion. In addition, a letter Millicent wrote to the poet Amy Lowell, who was also at the time considering working on her own volume about Emily Dickinson, and who had been in correspondence with both Mabel and Millicent, shows that in 1924, Mabel was already starting to craft how and when to publicly respond to Mattie. Millicent wrote to Lowell that Mabel had shown her some unpublished Dickinson copies: "They are simply superb! . . . What an orgy we shall have when the said MDB [Mattie] steps out one day!"[37]

Elsewhere, Millicent reported that at the time of Mattie's publication of *Life and Letters of Emily Dickinson* in 1924, it was David who urged his daughter to intervene:

> My father, who was by that time in a mental hospital, said to me, "Are you going to sit by and do nothing while the work on which your mother spent years is pirated and her name erased from the title page?" I was indignant, of course, but at that time I felt that if Mrs. Bianchi wished to appropriate the work of another as her own it was not for me to object nor to try to do anything about, but five years later in 1929 when a volume of poems appeared I changed my mind. The title-page reads as follows: "Further poems of Emily Dickinson withheld from publication by her sister Lavinia, edited by her niece, Martha Dickinson Bianchi, and Alfred Leete Hampson." I was shocked, for I knew that the poems had not been withheld by Lavinia Dickinson. On the contrary, her wish, her transcendent wish, had been to have all of Emily's poems published as quickly as possible.[38]

This point also irked Mabel greatly. She wrote in her journal, "the Emily Dickinson revival has given me much reason for thought. . . . Of course Mattie has now posed as the only authority upon her aunt, and she evidently thinks I am out of the running, but decidedly I am not."[39]

When Millicent read the introduction to *Further Poems of Emily Dickinson* in 1929, she wrote, "I am absolutely trembling in every limb. My heart thumps as with a great fear." The cause of Millicent's consternation was a paranoid worry that Mattie had somehow gotten into Mabel's papers, which were locked in a warehouse in Springfield, and stolen not only the poems but "perhaps Austin's letters to Mamma or hers to him." (This statement also provides evidence that even at this point, Millicent was aware of Mabel's and Austin's love letters, something she would deny in later years.) Millicent did not realize at the time that Sue Dickinson had also been in possession of a number of Emily's poems. Millicent worried, "something must be done about this thing. Mamma is absolutely fixed in her determination to do nothing as long as Bianchi lives. But with Mamma's characteristic refusal to face facts she thinks she will outlive Bianchi and then do something! Not realizing that she is ten years older than Bianchi."[40]

Mattie continued to publish books containing Emily's poetry and her own interpretations of Emily's life: *Further Poems of Emily Dickinson* (1929), *The Poems of Emily Dickinson, Centenary Edition* (1930), *Emily Dickinson Face to Face* (1932) and *Unpublished Poems of Emily Dickinson* (1935). Dickinson biographer Richard Sewall comments, "The poems came out piecemeal, unprofessionally edited, with Mabel's holdings, of course, still in the camphorwood chest."[41] In fairness, other contemporary Dickinson scholars (including Ralph Franklin, Martha Nell Smith and Ellen Louise Hart) have stated that Mattie's editing is worthy of "serious study" or had a "serious mission" and should not be dismissed out of hand.

Mattie, it seemed, was responsible for a resurgence of interest in Emily's life and poetry in the years leading up to the centenary of her birth. It also seemed as if she would be considered the authoritative voice on the poetry, and that her interpretations of Emily's life, family, and relationships would prevail. Emily, Mattie wrote, "was not daily bread. She was star-dust. Her solitude made her and was part of her. Taken from her distant sky she must have become a creature as different as fallen meteor from pulsing star."[42]

At the same time, the poet Genevieve Taggard was working on *The*

Life and Mind of Emily Dickinson, a book that would be published in 1930. In the late 1920s she got in touch with some of the surviving people who had known Emily and Vinnie—including Mabel, to whom she wrote that she was "most anxious to be of any service to you, if any occasion arises."[43] Taggard also contacted Vinnie's friend Mary Lee Hall, living at the time in Tennessee. Taggard's research had the effect of stimulating a correspondence between Mary Lee and Mabel, much of which is reprinted in Sewall's biography of Emily Dickinson. Sewall points to Hall's clear bias against Sue and Mattie, evidenced by phrases such as "the awful spirit rises in me whenever Sue and Mattie are in my thoughts," and he suggests these comments reveal Hall's position that both Dickinson sisters were wronged by Sue and her daughter. This position, of course, was very much in line with Mabel's own.

Perhaps it was the confluence of many issues that made Mabel decide, finally, that it was time to act. There had been the publication of Mattie's versions of Emily's poems and letters, with their mistakes and deliberate erasure of Mabel's named work. There was Mabel's belief that Mattie had deliberately understated Austin's presence in Emily's life. There were Mary Lee Hall's letters, with their vituperative accusations of Sue and Mattie, Millicent's indignation at the whole situation and the knowledge of the upcoming centenary of Emily's birth—all of these things made Mabel, with her instinctive sense of timing, know that the moment was right.

In November of 1929, Mabel accepted an invitation to speak about Emily Dickinson on Founder's Day at Mount Holyoke College. As soon as Mattie got wind of this upcoming event, she fired off a letter of protest to Mary Woolley, president of the college, citing Mabel's loss at the 1898 trial as evidence that she was "a cheat and a fraud" and should be disinvited. Woolley responded, "Mrs. Todd, I am sure, will not wish to introduce any controversial material and Mount Holyoke College has no desire to enter into the controversy."[44] In the end, Mabel's stellar legacy of civic engagement in and around Amherst, as well as her publication record, offset Mattie's insinuations. Woolley did not rescind the invitation. Mabel's address at the college, reported in newspapers, reaffirmed her status as an authority on Emily's life. And significantly, she stated that she was in possession of many unpublished poems, piquing public interest.

Mattie, Elizabeth Horan suggests, was "caught off guard. She probably did not realize that she was not in possession of all of Emily's poetry. Wanting to counter Todd, [but] uncertain as to how," she was "absolutely unprepared"[45] for the attack Mabel and Millicent were about to launch in the battle over the right to publish and define Emily Dickinson.

Then Mabel struck again. In 1930 she published an article in *Harper's Magazine* entitled "Emily Dickinson's Literary Debut," in which she retold the story of how Lavinia had approached her and asked her to get Emily's poetry published, and how she had worked with Thomas Wentworth Higginson to get the first two volumes of poetry out. She delineated how she had edited the third book of poems and the double volume of Emily's letters. Mabel concluded the article suggestively: "Emily's debut had been a triumphant entry into the life of that public which she 'never saw' but to which, nevertheless, she had sent her message. . . . And now . . . her place [is] secure for all time not only in the hearts of those who understand her unique ways, and in the love of those who may not criticize but [place her] in the front rank of American poets."[46] Mabel noted in her journal that the article "aroused much favourable comment" and that she was already being urged to write another book. "Everybody else in the literary world seems to already [have] written a book about her, although nobody knew her at all as I did."[47] The article had laid the groundwork. But there was more work to be done, more perceived wrongs to be righted.

That summer on Hog Island, as she lay in a hammock, Mabel looked up at Millicent and said, "It is all wrong, Millicent, everything that has happened. Will you set it right?" Millicent later wrote in her book *Emily Dickinson's Home*, "I said I would try. A simple question and a simple answer. I did not know what I was promising."[48]

⌒

CHAPTER 12

ℬRINGING LOST POEMS TO LIGHT (1930–1939)

"Will you set it right?"

Millicent's promise to "set it right" turned out to be a very complicated one, one that would eventually upend her professional trajectories, lead her to publish four books and create even more complexities in her relationship with Mabel. "I did not know what I was promising. . . . And I realized that if I were to keep the promise it would take a good deal of time," she reflected in 1954. "It was not for me an easy decision, because I was deep in professional activities in another field which I should be obliged to give up."[1]

Keenly aware of the centenary of Emily Dickinson's birth in 1930, Martha Dickinson Bianchi preemptively published *Further Poems of Emily Dickinson*, even though she had published the "complete" poems just five years earlier. Millicent recalled, "I said to my mother, 'What about this? Where did she get these? Where were they?'. . . I'd never mentioned the Dickinsons to my mother before but, of course, the poems were another thing—that was something quite objective with no personal implications, I thought. I said, 'Are these spurious or are they real?' Then my mother said, 'They're real.' I said, 'How do you know?' She said, "I copied them all.' "[2]

Mabel went on to tell Millicent where all the poems she had copied were hidden. "'You know that camphorwood chest that you have carried about from Amherst to Springfield to New York?' She said, 'I would like you to open it.' I had supervised its transfer from place to place all these years without asking what was in it. I knew instinctively that it had something to do with the Dickinsons and the Dickinsons I didn't talk about."

It hardly seems credible that Millicent never spoke of the Dickinsons, but she consistently maintained this story. In the late 1950s, during a taped interview, she suggested, "I had never in my whole life talked with my mother about the Dickinsons. I had been willing to know nothing about it. Although I had grown up from babyhood in the midst of weird tensions I never asked a question . . . after the lawsuit in 1898 the Iron Curtain descended. Until 1929 down it remained, but something sinister—something I did not understand—was always behind it." And in 1963, Millicent wrote that when she was discussing the Emily Dickinson work with a literary scholar:

> he could not understand how it was possible for me, with my universal curiosity, and my intelligence, never to have talked with my mother about the camphorwood chest and its contents—from 1898 to 1929. "How was it possible for you not to ask what was in it? Did no one ever talk to you about the Dickinson situation? Did you never read a newspaper at the time of the trial? How could you have remained unaware?" How, indeed. The Berlin wall is no more effective than the Dickinson taboo was for me.[3]

It wasn't that Millicent was totally unaware of Mabel's relationship with Austin and how it had poisoned all relations with the Dickinson family. She had certainly suspected ever since she was a child riding with her mother and Austin in the carriage, and wouldn't turn around to look at what was happening behind her back. She clearly understood from the many hours that "Squire Dickinson" spent at their house, from his commandeering of their hearth, from his hat that hung on a hook in their home years after his death, that he played a significant role in her mother's life. She was aware of the many times her mother sequestered herself with Austin behind locked doors at the Todds' home, and mindful of her mother's extreme reaction to Austin's death, which Millicent documented in her diary at the time. And she acknowledged that people in Amherst whispered about her mother and shunned the Todd family, writing about it on several occasions over the years and discussing it with her psychiatrist in 1927. She'd written in 1929 about her unfounded fears that Mattie Dickinson had somehow unearthed Mabel's and Austin's love letters. Millicent certainly had her suspicions—she just didn't want them confirmed.

And so it was perhaps with more than a touch of trepidation that Millicent left Hog Island for New York, and set off to retrieve the much-moved and long-locked camphorwood chest.

"I put the key in the lock and when I turned the lock it rang a little bell like all the Chinese camphorwood chests with brass corners which are so equipped that if anybody is a thief the owner may be forewarned," she wrote. "My heart went so fast I thought I should perish on the spot." Millicent looked inside and began removing piles of papers.

Millicent found scores of manuscripts in brown envelopes. There were the poems that Mabel had laboriously copied and published in the first three volumes of Emily's poetry. There were several of the poems Mattie had published in her volumes of her aunt's poetry, copied in Mabel's writing from Emily's manuscripts. But there were also many original poems in Emily's hand that had never been published anywhere—"six fascicles, numbered 80 to 85, containing unpublished poems as well as . . . quantities of her rough drafts and practice pieces—'scraps,' my mother called them. Some of these were perfect poems. Many, though complete, were interlined with alternative readings. Others were mere fragments; jumbled together as they were, they looked 'hopeless,' she thought, and had laid them aside for later consideration." Millicent soon noted, "she [Mabel] had progressed far enough with the work to indicate the lead poem for a fourth series and to select the valedictory for a final volume."[4] Included in this treasure trove Millicent published in *Bolts of Melody* were some of the poems now among the most often cited of the Dickinson oeurve, including "The Soul has Bandaged moments," "Shall I take thee, the Poet said" and "A great hope fell." (It's also worth noting that a significant number of the poems in *Bolts* were included in scholar Helen Vendler's 2010 selection of some of Dickinson's most important works.)[5]

That was not all. "Also preserved in the chest were Austin Dickinson's packets of family letters," many of which had never appeared in print. There was also "extensive correspondence" between members of the Dickinson family and Mabel, as well as bundles of Mabel's and Austin's love letters, which Mabel had painstakingly preserved.[6]

Millicent put aside her shock to focus on the task at hand. "I looked and beheld these quantities of Emily Dickinson manuscripts and I caught my breath because I realized that here was a dilemma." With both her training in geography and fluency in French, Millicent knew she was in an unusual and marketable position both in and outside of the academy. She enjoyed teaching and worried that were she to leave it, she would be abandoning a fulfilling career in which she had invested years of education. No doubt her growing fears about Walter's sporadic employment and the need to provide financially for her parents also played into her concerns.

Though she couldn't express it in writing at the time, her old fears about being a dilettante, about aligning herself too closely with the mother about whom she had such complicated feelings and her own aversion to anything Dickinson all played into her profound ambivalence about the promise she had made to Mabel.

She and Walter left New York for the weekend, to discuss what she should do. Years later Millicent recalled that Walter had finally concluded, "You know, other people can do geography. They can even do French Geography; but there is nobody who has been in this other situation all their life who knew all the members of the family, who understands the situation as you do and who began at the age of seven to read Emily's handwriting—there's nobody so centrally located as you are." And then, Millicent recounted, Walter, "being a psychologist with an uncanny understanding, said, 'I want you to realize just one thing—there is enough power in this situation . . . to get us both before you finish.'" She sardonically added, "Well, that I have thought of many times in recent years."[7]

Millicent's continued reflections on her complicated promise seemed only to have strengthened her resolve: "The decision was made that I should try and set the record straight and put an end to the stifling of a field of literature. It was an obligation, a trust, a compulsion so strong that I had no alternative but to drop geography, take it on and try to inject some integrity into the Dickinson controversy. . . . For me there was nothing else but to do what I could to right a grievous wrong—not only to my mother but even more to Emily Dickinson."[8] Millicent returned to this theme again and again in her private and public writings—clearly this promise to "set it right" was something that went straight to Millicent's core.

As Millicent began to discuss the idea of reissuing and expanding Mabel's *Letters of Emily Dickinson*, she learned that Mabel felt strongly that *all* of Emily Dickinson's work needed to be published. "Even more did my mother deplore the restrictions placed by Emily's niece on her literary output . . . I knew my mother deplored the assertion by that niece as last of the family, of her right to say which if any of Emily's writings should be published, now in 1930, nearly a half century after her death. . . . This stranglehold, maintained by virtue of consanguinity alone, for Emily left no will, nor did her sister Lavinia, to whom her literary remains went . . . was what my mother resented most of all."[9] Millicent came to embrace this belief in the virtue of publishing the unexpurgated content of Emily Dickinson's writings. True scholarship, believed Millicent, who was trained in the methodical rigors of science, is possible only when all of the known data are considered. She felt it was her duty to future scholars of Emily Dickinson's work that its full corpus be accessible and made it her mission to publish all of Emily Dickinson's known writings. In her introduction to *Emily Dickinson's Home* in 1954, Millicent wrote of her decision to include all the family letters, no matter how trivial or personal. A wise historian, she said, told her,

"Individual experiences are the essence of history. For a documentary volume about Emily Dickinson there are no trivia."[10]

Mabel and Millicent were not the only ones to share this view. In an article in the *Saturday Review of Literature*, poet, critic and editor Louis Untermeyer wrote, "Readers waited for Emily Dickinson's niece to affirm, amplify, or repudiate; to say six definite sentences that would clarify the situation; to explain the too-mysterious discovery of the *Further Poems*, variously stated to have been suppressed or buried or withheld by Sister Lavinia. But not a phrase was forthcoming . . . Martha Dickinson Bianchi contented herself with a few generalities by way of introduction to the 1930 edition of the *Poems*, adding nothing and subtracting nothing from her vaguely outlined story." Untermeyer concluded, "We should have an accurate Emily Dickinson, and we should have her complete."[11] Mabel, of course, was thrilled by this proclamation. In her journal she noted, "indifferent people are starting up, with intent to suppress Mattie, who had been smiling in lordly intent to remain Emily's grand relative . . . Louis Untermeyer . . . is of course a very important literary writer, and [his] words will be at least <u>arresting</u>, if not more."[12]

Mabel also firmly believed that Mattie's work had set in motion a series of off-the-mark speculations about Emily and her life. As she wrote in her introduction to the second edition of *Letters*: "For several years, it seems, a feeling has been growing among students of Emily's life that something is wrong. Their picture of her in her setting is not altogether true. They have been coming to me, with increasing insistence as time goes on, begging me to speak."[13] She felt that the images of Emily promulgated by others (principally Mattie) portrayed an otherworldly sprite, not someone with a grounded and profound understanding of the natural world and human nature. She pointed to "a widely used picture" of Emily in a ruffled dress as also giving a false impression of the woman who, at least throughout the last part of her life, wore simple white dresses. Mabel believed that "the careful reader" would look back to her earlier works "to find the real Emily." But since her earlier books were out of print, Mabel—with Millicent's very able assistance—resolved to

MABEL AND MILLICENT ON HOG ISLAND, WORKING ON THE NEW EDITION OF
EMILY DICKINSON'S LETTERS.

step back into the world of Dickinson publishing and present the version of Emily she believed more accurate.

Millicent and Mabel set to work sorting the Dickinson family letters from the camphorwood chest and preparing for a reissue of the 1894 book of Emily's letters with expanded content. They had two goals: first, to correct the errors in Mattie's 1924 edition of *Life and Letters of Emily Dickinson* and restore the original quotes and context to the previously published letters, and second, to add in additional letters that had not been included in her original edition. "We assumed that the original text was sufficiently accurate to be followed without attempting to change the sequence within the different letters to the various correspondents."[14] Among the never before published letters were some regarding Reverend Charles Wadsworth in Philadelphia, one of the men later speculated to be the object of Emily's so-called Master letters. (Wadsworth, minister of the Arch Street Church, maintained an active correspondence with Emily for two decades, until his death, even after he moved to San Francisco in 1862.) Mabel and Millicent also chose to identify some people whom the previous edition of letters had left anonymous, mostly at Austin's behest, or out of deference to those who at the time were still living and who "wanted their identity disguised, or reference to their personal sorrow omitted." As Mabel wrote in her preface to the 1931 book, she believed it important to include these letters and names because "now, after thirty-seven years . . . her life is revamped to suit the taste of the times, and Emily herself has all but vanished in the process."[15] In one version of this preface in her collected papers at Yale, Mabel added handwritten edits suggesting "a second edition affords the opportunity to supply missing parts, thereby giving a more complete impression of Emily."[16]

As Elizabeth Horan points out, "Martha Dickinson Bianchi's editing and memoirs restore[d] Susan's name,"[17] while systematically removing Mabel's. It's also interesting to note that Mattie chose to edit out the Todds with her scissors. In the Martha Dickinson Bianchi papers at Brown University, there's a copy of the "tear sheet" from Millicent's book *Ancestors' Brocades*, describing her mother's efforts to gather and publish Emily's letters. It is literally torn from the book. Similarly, Harvard's Houghton Library Dickinson family collection holds a copy of Mabel's 1894 *Letters of Emily Dickinson* with the title page bearing Mabel's name cut out.

Though Mabel didn't write in her journal very often after her 1913 stroke, a few entries document aspects of her work on this project. In November of 1930 she wrote, "Another whole summer passed without any record here. But this summer I have been especially busy with Emily Dickinson. I have looked over my volumes of

MARTHA (MATTIE) DICKINSON BIANCHI.

her printed letters with reference to re-publishing and re-copywriting, and I have examined my own journals to get out material for that possible book, and I have written a lot of stuff which may be used later." She noted "dear Millicent" spent two months at Hog Island, assisting her with these endeavors.[18]

As she had with her other volumes of Emily's poems and letters, Mabel knew that the best way to publicize them was to create pre-publication chatter by injecting herself back into the world of Emily Dickinson authorities. Her 1930 article in *Harper's Magazine*, "Emily Dickinson's Literary Debut," signaled Mabel's return to this particular public arena. *Harper's* invited her to write additional articles, and she had several in the works. For example, among Mabel's papers at Yale is a draft of one article Mabel titled "The Story of Emily Dickinson," which is really the story of her reediting and reissuing of the *Letters*. Mabel wrote of how "those poignant letters, some of which rank among the greatest ever written, tell a story of herself second in importance only to that of her poetry."[19]

Mabel intrinsically understood the value of a publicity stunt to promote her work. In December of 1930 she threw a large party at Matsuba to mark the centenary of Emily's birth—and made certain that this event got written up in all the society pages. In her journal she recorded that over two hundred people attended despite what was for Florida "an intensely cold night." The party "was exceedingly successful," she wrote. "I gave a truly brilliant talk, about which I have heard continually since then."[20]

Mabel was back.

Harper & Brothers in New York scheduled the "new and enlarged" edition of Emily Dickinson's letters for publication in the fall of 1931. "I have added much new information in the notes connecting them, and there are many letters omitted in the first edition," wrote Mabel. "Millicent has practically spent her whole winter in all this work, and has made all the arrangements with the publishers. I can never be grateful enough to her, and never do enough to show it. I could never have conducted the whole thing to so triumphant a finish by myself." With some chagrin, she admitted, "Although I appear to be a whole person I am far from it. I have to rest, and stupidly must look out for this silly person. The sun stroke which so nearly finished me still take [*sic*] toll; but I do not wish to die until I have published dear Austin's memorable letters to me, and until I have written most of my autobiography."[21]

But of course, Mabel and Millicent's volume would not be published without igniting further controversy. Mattie Dickinson Bianchi wrote to her attorney, "It is in regard to these 'new' letters—and any other unpublished letters in the possession of Mrs. Todd or anyone else—that I feel my rights must absolutely and definitely be established in order to prevent confusion and litigation in the future."[22]

"As soon as it was announced Harpers received a protest from Theodore Frothingham, Mrs. Bianchi's lawyer," Millicent recounted. "He stated that for the past seventeen years since the death of her mother in 1913, Mrs. Bianchi had been the sole heir of Emily Dickinson and that she claimed exclusive right to publish anything written by her aunt and that the proposed book was being published without her knowledge or consent." But, Millicent added, Harper's legal counsel "agreed that assertion of such exclusive rights was not in the public interest and advised going ahead. So the book was published in 1931. Nothing further was heard from Mr. Frothingham."[23]

Contemporary scholar Elizabeth Horan notes, "The 1931 comeback of Mabel Loomis Todd, aided by her daughter Millicent Todd Bingham, was a nightmare for Bianchi, for it was the first sign of an alliance between publishers and critics who viewed Bianchi's claims as an obstacle to overcome. Todd's success in publishing her reedited letters without obtaining permissions from Bianchi or her publishers led the interested parties to work behind Bianchi's back."[24]

Mabel and Millicent's reissue of Emily's letters was still far from a complete rendering. Not surprisingly, they did not include any of the correspondence with Susan Dickinson. They also omitted several letters that were in their possession that Mabel judged too private to present to the world just yet.

Critical reaction to Mabel and Millicent's 1931 edition was generally positive. Writing in the *New York Times*, Edna Lou Walton stated the book was "important," although she noted that in the years since Mabel's 1894 edition was published, "much water has flowed under the bridge" with the publication of Mattie Dickinson Bianchi's books, including her 1924 biography *Life and Letters of Emily Dickinson* and Genevieve Taggard's 1930 *The Life and Mind of Emily Dickinson*, and suggested "there is doubtlessly much data still missing." She also castigated Mabel for not including any of the correspondence between Emily and Sue, and for not shedding light on the mystery of Emily's loves.[25]

But the scholarly community was more enthusiastic, focusing on how this new edition illuminated the context of Emily Dickinson's life and helped to create a sharper image of both the poet and the poetry. Wrote poet Marianne Moore in the January 1933 edition of *Poetry*, "If we care about the poems, we value the connection in which certain poems and sayings originated. The chief importance of the letters, however, is their establishing the wholesomeness of the life." In an unpublished master's thesis on the critical reception to publication of Emily Dickinson's poetry and letters in the early twentieth century, emerging Dickinson scholar Ruth Corrigan concurred, concluding about the importance of Mabel and Millicent's 1931 work: "the new edition brought forth a new Emily Dickinson."[26]

Historian and radical political activist Morris Schappes pointed out that because Mabel's edition still did not contain any of Emily's letters to Sue Dickinson, and the 1924 edition by Mattie did, both volumes should be considered together as a way of seeing the full spectrum of Emily's correspondence. Schappes devoted most of his article to correcting the errors in Mattie's version of the *Letters*, citing Mabel's versions of the letters as the accurate and definitive source in almost every instance.[27]

Amherst College English professor George Whicher wrote an extended review of the 1931 volume of *Letters* in the journal *American Literature*, in which he praised all of Mabel's work on editing and publishing Emily's poems and letters over the years: "That we have an adequate selection from her correspondence in a transcription that can be trusted and with a large number of items at least approximately dated is due to Mrs. Mabel Loomis Todd, whose pioneer services in editing the Emily Dickinson papers have not always been sufficiently acknowledged," he wrote. Though he suggested Mabel and Higginson's groupings and editing of the poems "may fairly be challenged," he called the new edition of *Letters* "the definitive edition," adding, "we may thank fortune that Emily Dickinson fell into the hands of an editor who did not attempt to change her fairy wine into lemonade."[28]

Mabel recounted the achievement of this book in her journal: "Well, I got out the new edition of Emily Dickinson's *Letters*, and it was an immediate and really overwhelming success, the first edition being completely sold out on the first day, November fifth, 1931. And people have asked me for talks." But she concluded this entry by opining that the book wasn't just about her own success, it was also about Emily's legacy: "and she is adored for the genius she is."[29]

Mabel spent the summer of 1932 on Hog Island, as she had spent so many of the summers that preceded it—socializing with those who lived in nearby towns on the mainland and those who came to visit her on the island, passing great amounts of time with Howard Hilder, walking through the woods, and working on a rock garden. Millicent and Walter spent most of the summer with her, Millicent assisting Mabel by getting her scrapbooks more up to date, and helping her to organize other materials in preparation for further Dickinson work.

Mabel wrote only one entry in her journal during the summer season on Hog Island. As ever, Mabel found it important to record how industrious she had been and what she still wished to accomplish. "I really want to finish many important pieces of work before I go," she wrote. "And I have three volumes in progress."[30] But it was work that Mabel was never able to complete.

———

On October 14, Millicent was in Poughkeepsie, visiting a friend. Walter called her to read her two telegrams, one informing her that her mother had fallen ill, and the other, that she had died.

Millicent did not record in her diary or journal anything of her feelings that day, or the several days following Mabel's death. Three days later she noted that she had called her father to tell him about Mabel's death: "From 'Mr. Todd speaking' to 'no' in response to my query whether he had anything to say, his voice betrayed no emotion," she wrote. But Millicent couldn't cry yet, either.[31]

———

"Our dear friend Mabel Loomis Todd died suddenly at her camp Mavooshen soon after noon on Friday last," Howard Hilder wrote to Arthur Curtiss James.

> We had planned to start the drive South next Wednesday, and she was sorting out bureau drawers for packing as I was at my Studio

just a mile off the northeast corner of the island and due to return at noon. I was within a couple of hundred yards . . . so dropped my things and ran. She was on the verandah hammock groaning terribly, she just recognized me, then began retching violently. I held her in my arms and tried to ease her. Occasionally she tried to speak and indicated a violent headache, although she could not pronounce distinctly.

The doctor came after 1 p.m. "Cerebral hemorrhage! Not so good!" . . . I followed instructions and watched. The breathing got calmer and calmer and by 3 I could detect no sign of life. At 4:30 he returned with the nurse and pronounced her dead. I telegraphed Millicent who came with Walter the next morning. . . . It will always be a joy to me that I left her in the morning radiant and happy.[32]

On the evening of Mabel's funeral, Millicent wrote in her journal:

Dear, precious little mamma! Oh, the thing that I can't bear— that I can never bear is that I left her. Part of me is gone—perhaps most of me. She is entertwined with every little flitty leaf and bird note . . . she is a part of every memory—since my earliest childhood, nothing apart from her has ever happened. The bond is the closest on earth—I never knew it before, because of alien points of view because I disapproved of many things, because I didn't understand. She got on my nerves. . . . I could work my fingers to the bone for her, do chores, attend to errands, write books till I dropped in my tracks.

She reflected on the day: "Oh, that beautiful wilderness and the brilliant foliage and now and then a falling leaf on her flower-laden casket creaking down, down into the deep grave, and the mist-laden air and the poignant notes of the white-throated sparrows that filled the trees— trembling, sweet. . . . The woods were aflame with red and yellow."[33]

MABEL'S ENGRAVING OF THE ETHEREAL INDIAN PIPE WILDFLOWERS; SHE GAVE A PANEL TO EMILY DICKINSON IN 1882. THIS BECAME THE COVER OF THE FIRST BOOK OF DICKINSON'S POETRY IN 1890, AND REMAINED SUCH A POWERFUL SYMBOL IN MABEL'S LIFE THAT MILLICENT HAD IT ENGRAVED ON HER MOTHER'S TOMBSTONE.

Mabel's tombstone reads:

IN LOVING MEMORY OF
Mabel Loomis Todd
10th November 1856–14th October 1932
Daughter of
Eben Jenks and Mary Alden Wilder Loomis
Wife of David Todd

That such have died enables us
The tranquiller to die;
That such have lived, certificate
For immortality.

The verse, of course, is an Emily Dickinson poem.[34]

———

As was her habit, Millicent made a scrapbook after Mabel's death. It begins with the two telegrams. The rest of the album, perhaps five or six inches thick, its bindings now broken and leather chipping, is filled with hundreds of condolence notes and letters. They came from around the world: from relatives and friends, neighbors from Amherst and Florida and Maine, colleagues of David's and Millicent's and Walter's. They came from publishers and poets and people in the literary world. The last note Millicent glued into this album came from someone whose name she somehow chose not to record or preserve. But the sentiment it expressed seemed so universally held among those who wrote to Millicent that its authorship almost does not matter. It read in part, "I like to remember her as living. She was so well made for living. She lived so much and so completely, last year at this time, what a ravishing picture, the pink dress, the jewels, the eyes more shining than the jewels. She was carrying forward the beautiful pure spirit of Emily Dickinson."[35]

———

Though the *New York Times* got her name wrong ("Mary L. Todd, Authority on Emily Dickinson," read the headline) and the *New York Herald Tribune*'s headline seemed somewhat off-center ("Mabel L. Todd is Dead; Writer on Astronomy, Shared Husband's Career in Planet Research; Edited Emily Dickinson's Poems"), other newspapers printed more thoughtful, accurate, and Mabel-centered obituaries. Writer, editor and well-known literary critic Nathan Haskell Dole authored an obituary in the *Saturday Review*:

> The useful, colorful, magnetic life of Mrs. Mabel Loomis Todd ended suddenly Oct. 14th. Up to the last moment she had been busily engaged. . . . A man who was helping her asked if there was anything more he could do. "Yes," she laughingly replied, "more than a million things."
>
> "A rather large order," he said, "but I will begin and we'll finish them somehow." A few moments later she fell to the floor, her earthly work was done.
>
> Hers was an indefatigable energy. With all her scientific inter-

ests, Mrs. Todd continued to cultivate her gifts as a painter and a poet. . . . But her most distinctive service to literature was in connection with the poems and letters of her friend and neighbor, Emily Dickinson. . . . It seems incredible that this ever youthful and vivacious spirit should have passed from our midst. But her memory will live.³⁶

And the *Amherst Record* printed several remembrances of Mabel, including an homage by Millicent, entitled "A Friend of Amherst." Millicent's lengthy obituary began, "For nearly 40 years, while she lived in Amherst, she was its devoted friend and was identified with its activities in a multitude of ways." The tribute concluded, "While she lived in Amherst it was hard to think of the town without her."³⁷

Despite keeping meticulous records—as well as all the bills—for Mabel's funeral, Millicent wrote little about it. In a series of interviews taped by J. Donald Sutherland in the late 1950s, she recalled, "She was buried in Wildwood Cemetery, not far from the grave of Austin Dickinson and facing the Pelham Knob which she had bought to save the great hemlock forest on its crest."³⁸

The only other aspect of Mabel's funeral Millicent chose to record anywhere was a brief mention of her decision to keep her father from attending it. At the time she wrote, "We could not have run the risk of having him there. Mamma couldn't have borne it." Of course, it was Millicent who could not bear it. In 1959 she remembered, "He did not forgive me that I did not let him attend her funeral. It was just that I could not bear to think of the possibility of him making a spectacle of himself in the presence of her body and that of a churchful of Amherst neighbors."³⁹

Millicent contemporaneously recorded one other memory. "Such a weird experience," she wrote in her diary a few days after Mabel's funeral. She and Walter had returned to Wildwood with a man who would do the engraving on Mabel's tombstone. Millicent spoke with them, then wandered down the hill by herself, away from the graves of her grandparents and her mother, toward the Dickinson plot. "I went off in the darkness and put my hand on Austin's boulder, and stood on Sue's recumbent stone. The Amherst of my childhood lying silent all around me, as the leaves dropping, one by one."[40]

⸺

In the months after Mabel's death, Millicent, named sole heir to her mother's estate, faced innumerable decisions and enormous unresolved issues. "Mamma died leaving mountainous problems to be settled from Maine to Florida," she recorded in notes from one of her psychiatric sessions in 1942. She recalled in 1959, "The 1930s was a decade of real disaster, beginning with the death of my mother . . . and I was left with problems which seemed so inextricable that I didn't know really just how to begin."[41]

First there were the properties in Florida (Mabel had purchased a second, small home for rental income), which Millicent had to make ready to rent because she needed funds to repair the two houses so they could be sold. Millicent also had to attend to a "storehouse full of papers which had been, some of them, drenched in a series of hurricanes." Matsuba, she noted, "was completely filled with every kind of memorabilia and archives and curios, [enough] for a museum." (Indeed, Mabel had dreamed of establishing just such an institution; in an undated letter to Charles Green [the first director of the Jones Library in Amherst] she pondered whether the Amherst Historical Society might be willing to provide a separate room for "my entire collection of wonderful curios from all over the world.")[42]

That wasn't all. "There was the barn full of papers in Amherst and the books, and there was the partially owned island in Maine," as well as eighty acres of land Mabel had purchased outside of Amherst. And then there were the innumerable Dickinson projects Millicent and Mabel had discussed—to publish the remainder of Emily's unpublished poems, to tell the story of how their publication came about in the first place and to try to tell a more authentic narrative of Emily's life than Mattie's presentation of it.

Millicent knew that while some of these problems required her immediate attention, the most meaningful, which would necessitate years of effort—and though she didn't know it at the time, legal wrangling—was her promise to "set it right" by publishing Emily's remaining work and preserving her true legacy and image. While crafting Mabel's legacy and image, Millicent would be doing the same for her own.

The summer after Mabel died, Millicent spent weeks on the island, meticulously making a detailed inventory of all Mabel's possessions. Millicent recorded mundane household items as well as trinkets from around the world. She delineated each item of clothing, each handkerchief, each book and magazine. She made lists of the shells and buttons collected in various drawers and bowls and containers, and of the various bottles of perfume. There were the many projects in which Mabel had been engaged just the summer before, just as she left them, frozen in time: the unfinished scrapbooks, drafted literature about Everglades National Park, a partially written article, correspondence not yet finished.

And there were artifacts that Millicent found so poignantly affecting that they brought her to tears. She wrote of them separately from her methodical lists:

> a tan silk handkerchief with a black and yellow border, the emotions of forty years were stirred—vague, powerful, indefinable . . . the lamp, freshly filled, by the light of which she has read aloud almost the whole of Dickens, summer after summer . . . a basket containing a moth-eaten hearth-brush. Ah, that hearth-brush! Can it be only what it seems? What would happen if I were to burn up the remains of that little hearth-brush which Mr. Dickinson gave to mamma more than forty years ago? . . . Every link with the past, or rather, every chain that binds me to it cries out "NO." I seem to see mamma's liquid brown eyes beseeching me not to burn it . . . that brush is a symbol.

The vases she found throughout the Hog Island home affected Millicent most of all. "Nothing so accentuates her absence as these empty vases, everywhere. . . . How poignant all these evidences of her belle-like quality."[43]

Yet Millicent was not paralyzed with grief. If anything, the process of making these lists made her ever more determined to move forward. While thinking about what her mother would have most wanted for her beloved camp and the beloved island she had saved from the loggers, Millicent struck upon a novel idea. She would turn the island into a camp that would become "a laboratory for the teaching of conservation to grown-up people." This, she felt, would be a most fitting tribute to Mabel and something Millicent could do to aid the cause of preserving "what we have left in the way of wild nature,"[44] an imperative Millicent felt had been passed from her grandfather to her mother to herself.

In addition to attending to the real estate and the mountains of papers and objects Mabel had left behind, Millicent was also now David's sole caretaker: "My father, the most distressing insoluble problem—oh, the humiliation and agony of it! It was bad enough in the twenties when he was in confinement. But when he was not—after Mamma's death—it was worse." David's manic states became ever more pronounced, and despite his periodic pleas to have Millicent grant him greater freedoms and keep him out of restrictive institutions—and her periodic willingness to indulge him, "sometimes even when I knew his request was foolish"—it became ever more apparent that he needed care that was far beyond her ability to provide.

Toward the end of 1933, David was living outside of an institution but ostensibly under the care of a paid attendant in upstate New York. Millicent traveled to see her father and take him to Lake Ridge, the town in which he'd grown up. When she arrived, though, the housekeeper informed Millicent that the man she had engaged to care for her father was "in fact, a drunkard and this is no place for [David] to be." Her father required significantly more care and supervision than he was getting.

David was not sleeping. He lashed out at people unpredictably. He was unreasonably attached to certain activities, in which he obsessively engaged—reading through a dictionary front to back, entering a contest to come up with a new slogan for a beer, developing theories about what would enable eternal life. He had somehow lost track of the few possessions he'd had with him.

Despite these alarming signs, Millicent still thought that David did not need to be locked up in an institution again. But by the end of her visit, she became convinced that "this was the only thing to do."

Millicent took David to a cemetery in which some of his relatives were buried. Along the way she tried to engage him in conversation about their life in Amherst. David told her about all the work he and Mabel had done on Emily's poetry—"it took hours and hours of my time"—and launched into a discussion of the role Austin Dickinson had played in their lives. "He was a wonderful man, and I loved him more than any man I ever knew," David said, before bursting into tears. "Sometimes it all seems like a ghastly dream. . . . It all might easily have been so different. I want to shut a trap door on the whole thing and get up above it."[45]

In the cemetery, things escalated further. David suddenly turned to Millicent. He "walked up the path between the white marble headstones of his ancestors, wheeled about . . . and lifting his cane in the air began such an invective and denunciation as I have never heard even from his lips. 'You're not my daughter, do you understand? Such lying deception—low-down, skunk—don't come near me as long as you live. I cut you off forever, do you understand that?'" David cursed at her, using language that she primly declined to record. Stunned, Millicent reeled from hurt, surprise and confusion. David's insinuation was further evidence of his deteriorating mental state, because it simply wasn't true.

Then, the manic episode ceased as suddenly as it had come on. Shaken, Millicent brought David back to the house where they were staying. She wrote that evening she "put a chair against my door as there was no lock . . . instinctively afraid of what he might do at night."

As horrible and frightening as the previous afternoon had been, the next morning was worse. When David came down to breakfast, he immediately began interrogating Millicent about what she had done with her mother's wedding ring—why had she buried it with Mabel rather than giving it to him?—and his pension—why was it going directly to Millicent? She had no right to touch his money. David went on, "Does that jackass husband of yours still call you 'little one'—in that sickly sweet voice that Mamita liked so much? Colonel Walter Van Dyke Bingham, yes, I know him—he sickens me." And then David screamed, "Don't ever dare to darken the door of the house I'm in again. You're not my daughter!'"

But then he "stretched wide his arms, 'come darling, come' he sobbed, 'I loved your mother so—and you I love you because I loved her,' and tried to kiss me on the mouth, and thrust his tongue into my mouth with all the accompaniments, and filled me with such horror and loathing that I was faint and nauseated." Millicent froze with revulsion and fear. In writing about this horrific episode later, she concluded, "I never before had such a realization of his insanity—and when I could conquer my loathing—such a heart-breaking pity for him."[46]

After these incidents, David Peck Todd was never out of restrictive care again. Millicent wrote to Arthur Curtiss James, whose special trust was helping to pay for David's care, "Oh, I don't need to tell YOU what the wear and tear is all the time. It is like the dripping of water on the forehead, one drop at a time, which after a time becomes a form of torture."[47]

In the five years that followed, Millicent and Walter had David committed to mental facilities in Vermont, New York, and Virginia. In 1939 his physical health began to decline as precipitously as his mental health, and Millicent removed him from an institution and placed him in a private home with round-the-clock nursing. Though there is neither mention nor record of this in Millicent's many files about her father's illness and care, an article in the *Journal for the History of Astronomy* stated, "It seems, alas, that he suffered from paresis, the end-stage of syphilis. He spent the last years of his long life . . . in hospitals and nursing homes, scheming ways to achieve 'eternal life,' but also horrified at the prospects of the Sun's splitting in two and bringing about the end of the world."[48] David died on June 1.

Millicent had his body moved to Amherst, where Alfred Stearns, president of the Amherst College Board of Trustees, led a memorial service. "Dr. Stearns called him a genius, a man of vision, whom the

Philistines laughed at because they could not understand him." David was laid to rest beside Mabel in Wildwood Cemetery. On David's tombstone, Millicent had inscribed:

IN LOVING MEMORY OF
DAVID TODD
19th March 1855–1st June 1939
Professor of Astronomy in Amherst College 1881–1920
Firmament showeth His handiwork.

There is also an engraving of an eclipse, the sun's corona clearly visible on the stone—clearer, ironically, than David had ever seen it.

Millicent wrote in a special "diary" she had made for her father's final arrangements, "I could not believe that it was the last time I should clean up after him—that this departure was for good and all." She noted, "at sunset we went back once more to the cemetery to look at the mound of flowers . . . and we placed iris on the graves of my grandparents and a wreath of dark purple leaves on both my father's and mother's. And then as evening fell we made our way out among the great fallen trees [left in the wake of the previous fall's tremendous hurricane]. One in particular, an oak at least three feet across the trunk, lay prostrate, no one having the courage so far to attempt to move it. I could not help thinking of it as a symbol."[49] It was Austin Dickinson's "millennial oak"— a massive fallen tree that could not be moved and blocked the path to David's newly dug grave.

In 1937, Millicent developed a case of type 3 pneumonia, a very severe infection that results in death in more than half of those who contract it. "I was taken by the grace of God and my husband's persistence to the Rockefeller Institute for Medical Research . . . they only took cases of pneumonia and heart disease which had been given up by doctors. I was put there and for ten days, they later told me, they thought each breath would be my last." She was placed in a special isolation chamber with experimental breathing apparatus and medication.

Millicent recounted that after she pulled through, Walter told her about the point at which he knew that she would recover. "Walter wanted to see if my mind was working at all, because I apparently was gone. He said, 'You remember that article that you wrote for the American Museum of Natural History?' I replied, 'yes' and he said, 'Well they have sent you a check for fifty dollars,' and I replied, 'Oh, how very nice.' That was that." He told her the same exact thing on the next two successive days, and on the third Millicent replied to him, "Yes, how about those two other checks?"[50]

But this near-death experience was not without lasting consequences for Millicent. Perhaps she realized this had happened to her at almost precisely the same age at which her mother had her first stroke. In any case, the illness made her even more hyperaware of every real or perceived symptom that she experienced for the rest of her life. She became a hypochondriac. She kept thick files filled with her letters to countless doctors recounting numerous ailments. Another folder is stuffed with prescriptions Millicent received. "Pneumonia shattered parts of my personality,"[51] she freely admitted to her psychiatrist—and recorded—a few years later.

Part of Millicent's posthospital recovery was spent in the quiet of her camp on Hog Island. While there, in the beginning of September 1937, she received word from Walter back in New York that their apartment had been robbed. "Walter thinks they disturbed no papers," she typed in a separate series of notes she kept. "They opened every drawer, every closet, every chest, every trunk, whether locked or unlocked, mauled over the contents and took only jewelry, he says. But that he does not know, of course. He wants to put the best possible interpretation on their intentions—think of it, the intentions of such criminals!—so, not knowing what was in anything, he says they took nothing in the way of books, MSS, journals, diaries, etc." Millicent immediately began berating herself and noting the sad implicit ironies: "Strange, I who am so over careful. Who have always locked everything, protected everything, almost to absurdum, so that it is a byword with my friends. I who have been led around by the nose by things and the care of them, so that my whole family . . . all have given me their worldly affair to watch, strange that it is I who have been guilty of this negligence."[52]

The reward Millicent and Walter offered for information leading to the arrest of the robbers never yielded any clues, nor were any of the stolen objects ever recovered. The experience left Millicent feeling incredibly violated and vulnerable. "Why is it that I feel so crushed?" she wrote. "The realization that ... I should not have left the things there? No, though I should not have. That I shall miss them? No, though I shall. That those to whom they were to be given are deprived? No, though they will be. That the precious things are now in the hands of those who not only do not appreciate them, they defile them with their touch. Ah, that is getting nearer to the truth."[53]

She tried to rationalize, to convince herself that the robbery was a sign that she was meant to break with the past and move on. At least the things most precious to her—the Dickinson manuscripts, her mother's letters, all the diaries and journals—were safe in a bank vault. She even attempted to justify it by thinking that the robbery had freed her from the burden of dealing with some of the detritus of three generations that she had been accumulating. Perhaps the robbery had actually *helped* her in this enormous task? But try as she might, she could not make herself believe this. She never got over the theft.

With all that continued to burden her—her mother's death, her father's mental illness, the pneumonia, the robbery—Millicent felt the need to seek additional counsel. In the fall of 1938 she began to see Dr. Alfred Ehrenclou. She would see him consistently for two years, and then sporadically between 1940 and 1952. A neurologist by training, Ehrenclou was one of the first doctors to practice psychotherapy with patients in private sessions outside an institutional setting. He was a Southern gentleman, raised on a horse farm in South Carolina to which he frequently returned and which he regularly referred to in his sessions with Millicent. She kept a special journal of their meetings, which often consisted of Ehrenclou relating parables from which she was supposed to extract life lessons. He frequently used the analogy of his farm or quasi-biblical stories to impart how Millicent might differently interpret her world.

In her sessions, she discussed her insomnia, her struggles to understand her father's illness and her efforts to justify institutionalizing him, as well as Walter's inability to hold down a job, his tendency to do things at the last minute versus her need to plan ahead and the difference in their levels of ambition. She discussed how the robbery left her feeling vulnerable, how her illnesses took an emotional toll on her. She related her fears about being a dilettante in switching her life's work from geography to Emily Dickinson. She acknowledged that her burning desire to be "productive" often paralyzed her. It is not at all clear from her notes whether she felt that her many sessions with Dr. Ehrenclou (which sometimes went on for hours at a time) significantly helped her to cope with all of her troubles.

As the 1930s drew to a close and many countries in Europe entered into World War II, marking "the end of an era," Millicent knew that the decade had been "a very profound one" for her. "I had a realization of my own capacity for emotion for which there was no outlet at all. So I turned to an effort to focus my knowledge into a tool."[54] And at the end of the decade, with both of her parents dead, Millicent knew she still needed to utilize this "tool," both as a wedge between herself and her own unsettled emotions, and in the service of the promise she had made to Mabel to "set it right."

As she later wrote in the preface to the last of her four books about Emily Dickinson, *Emily Dickinson's Home*, "My obligation I construed to be this: to publish all the documents in the chest, whatever they might be—to make them all available. For this was the living material of history." Though Millicent felt that "of first importance of course were the poems, hundreds of them," she also "promptly discovered that even to decipher them would be a fantastically difficult undertaking."[55]

It was an undertaking that would take Millicent years, especially given that she was simultaneously working on four books. Millicent was researching and writing *Ancestors' Brocades* at the same time as *Emily Dickinson: A Revelation* (about Emily's relationship with Judge Otis Phillips Lord) and *Emily Dickinson's Home* (more of Emily's story as told through family letters). But there were still many unpublished Dickinson poems remaining. Mabel had warned Millicent not to attempt to publish any of these poems until after Mattie Dickinson Bianchi died. Mabel and Millicent knew all too well that the battle over the rights to Emily's poetry and Emily's image would not end until the last surviving member of the immediate Dickinson family was gone. Millicent knew that when that milestone occurred, the final path to fulfill her promise to Mabel to "set it right" would be clear.

CHAPTER 13

*D*EALING WITH "DICKINSONIANA" (1940–1955)

"The epic Greek drama"

In 1940, Millicent and Walter were in New York and living off of their savings, Millicent's salary from teaching and translating, and Walter's "driblets" of income, as Millicent called them. However, with the United States ramping up its prewar efforts, the Army suddenly became interested in using Walter's work on identifying psychological markers of leadership to determine rank and thereby strengthen military effectiveness. Walter accepted a job with the War Department, and in the fall, they left New York for Washington, D.C. For Millicent, the Second World War and the war over the Emily Dickinson manuscripts began to converge and significantly affect her life.

Millicent had few regrets about leaving New York. She had never felt comfortable there, a feeling that was exacerbated by her near-fatal pneumonia and by the robbery of their apartment. Though relieved that Walter would be receiving a regular income and recognition for his work, she had always assumed that when they left New York, they would return to New England. Ironically, just as Mabel had worried about leaving Washington behind for Amherst in 1881, Millicent now worried about giving up her dream of returning to New England for Washington.

Walter worked long hours, six days a week, at the War Department. Millicent kept busy managing her family's real estate, papers and other possessions now in her care, which resided in four different states. Millicent had foreseen how problematic this would be. In 1934 she reflected:

> Things, things, things. From the time when grandma bequeathed to me, in addition to books, furniture and other household effects, 28 trunks full of clothes, embroideries, laces . . . I have received accretion after accretion of the ages. I should have taken stringent measures at the outset, but I didn't. For the past 20 odd years I have been hoping for a "permanent" home where I could sort and after seeing what was in a systematic way, dispose of them, also in a systematic way. Meanwhile things that are not "permanent" have continued to accumulate . . . and mamma, the key to the situation, has gone—about the only thing which is permanent, after all.[1]

Millicent managed to sell Matsuba in 1936, but could not sell or rent the other properties because they were still storing items she hadn't yet sorted. "I felt that there must be things that were extremely important because both my mother and my father had insisted that none of these things should ever be thrown away and that I must go through them all."[2] These duties preoccupied Millicent, taking up vast amounts of her time.

But there was still the Dickinson work to "set right": publishing the yet-unpublished poems in the camphorwood chest, correcting the inaccuracies of Mattie Dickinson's publication of Emily's poems and letters and rehabilitating Mabel's image as a Dickinson authority. "That was my task," Millicent recalled. She also called it her "compulsion" to "try to inject some integrity into the Dickinson controversy."[3]

Once she agreed to assist Mabel with the Dickinson work and recognized that this would in all likelihood mean the end of her career as a geographer, Millicent was able to rationalize this decision: "All my study of geography has done is to enrich and clarify my life," she wrote in 1934, but "in it, it seems, I shall have no career. . . . For the first time in my life, duty, and desire, enthusiasm even, coincide and all I want is the time to get at it and see what I can do."4

Millicent's plan accounted for the many complexities surrounding the Dickinson work. She knew it was too risky to publish the work she and Mabel had done on Emily's poems from the camphorwood chest while Mattie Dickinson Bianchi was still alive, so she simultaneously worked on other manuscripts. By 1934, Millicent had drafted a "book on the editing," which eventually became *Ancestors' Brocades*, but continued to work on it for more than a decade before its publication in 1945. Next, she wanted to write the story of her mother's life, "possibly getting Austin's letters in condition to print also though they should not be printed in my lifetime." Millicent knew that Mabel had wanted to present the story of her relationship with Austin to the world, and suspected there was a beauty and power in the letters that would make a compelling narrative. But it was one thing for Millicent to be aware of her mother's relationship with Austin, and altogether different to read the letters, herself. She decided to hold off on that project.

Millicent also planned to write "a vast psychological document" about her own development, which is what she believed her own autobiography would be, and another book on the early Dickinson family letters, which would help to explain the context of Emily's life. And finally, Millicent thought, she would write "the book about her [Emily's] love affairs, culminating with Judge Lord . . . which, if I can do it right, ought to sell like hot cakes."5

The topic of Emily Dickinson's love life has long been another one of the intensively debated issues among scholars and fans alike. Because her poetry contained such "magnificent love poems," as the Emily Dickinson Museum website suggests, and such passionate—even erotic—language, as scholars Martha Nell Smith and Ellen Louise Hart write, speculation abounds concerning the nature of Emily's relationships with a variety of people in her life. Regardless of the men or women who might have been the objects of Emily Dickinson's ardor, it seems clear from poems such as poem VII in Mabel and Higginson's version of the *Poems, Second Series* (249 in Johnson's numbering) that the poet knew something of love and desire:

Wild nights! Wild nights!
Were I with thee,
Wild nights should be
Our luxury![6]

Millicent was determined to address the subject of Emily's passion in the books she knew she must write.

As she conceptualized these projects, Millicent was painfully aware of Mabel's influence. "It reminds me pitiably of dear, precious little mamma, who was always talking about what she would do after Bianchi died. She never once said, nor, I think, thought that perhaps it might be she who died first." Moreover, Millicent ruefully observed, "If I put in all my time for the next twenty years I could hardly more than get through."[7] Time, Millicent realized, was already starting to run out.

To fulfill part of her promise to her mother, Millicent felt she must tell the story of how Emily's poems came to be published in the first place. In an interview she did with Richard Sewall in 1963, Millicent speculated about what might have occurred had Emily sent her poetry to Ralph Waldo Emerson, Henry David Thoreau or Walt Whitman. "If she had sent her poems to a genius instead of to dear Mr. Higginson," then, she mused, maybe Emily's unique brilliance would have been recognized earlier and the poems' long and peculiar path to publication would have been swifter and more direct.[8]

Millicent wrote in the prologue to *Ancestors' Brocades*, "An account of the literary labors preceding the publication of the poetry and letters has historic value. It gives to the readers a glimpse of the task of editing troublesome manuscripts—glimpses also of a poet's workshop. But the story would be a mere collector's item were it not for the fact that interwoven with it is a drama of elemental intensity—a clash of conflicting personalities so insistent and so prolonged that no account of the literary activity can be extricated from the emotional strain in the midst of which it took place."[9] Millicent continually referred to the "epic Greek drama" of the Todd/Dickinson feud, both blatantly in her private writings and in more subtle ways in her public ones.

Indeed, *Ancestors' Brocades*, as several reviewers were quick to point out, was part an impressively documented account of how Mabel came into possession of Emily's poems and letters, part a meticulous report of her editorial processes and decisions and part an attempt by Millicent to vindicate her mother. Writer and Mount Holyoke professor Sydney McLean wrote in the journal *American Literature* that the book was "a painstaking unfolding of a situation which has taken place over half a century to reach an outcome; the explanation of Mabel Loomis Todd's role in the Dickinson melodrama and the defense of her sudden retirement from the stage. Mrs. Bingham, a trained scholar in nonliterary fields, should be commended for her valiant attempt to be dispassionate in her presentation of a story which has influenced her own life." A reviewer in the journal *Poetry* was somewhat harsher: "It is a complicated tale, and tedious for the reader to unravel, as Mrs. Bingham unfortunately has organized her material very badly. But the emotional involvements and the difficulties in elucidating the intricate details were alike so great that, as Dr. Johnson observed in another connection, 'it is not done well but you are surprised to find it done at all.' "[10]

In her journal Millicent responded to one review: "Robert Hillyer (in the *New York Times*) says that I have 'handled this heavily charged material with delicacy, with tact—one might almost say, with mercy.' " Millicent seemed to ignore the part of the review in which Hillyer had written, "One is much in doubt at times, whether Emily is the heroine of the story or Mrs. Bingham's mercilessly executive mother, the first foreign woman to climb Fugi [*sic*], and no less eager to stand on the heights of Emily Dickinson."[11]

As Millicent was gathering information for *Ancestors' Brocades*, she simultaneously began preparing the previously unpublished Dickinson poems from the camphorwood chest for publication. But she knew she had to wait until Mattie died so that she could not launch a proprietary claim on the poetry or a lawsuit against Millicent. When Mattie passed away in 1943, Millicent knew it was time to act.

Harper, which would print *Bolts of Melody* in 1945, wanted to establish beyond reasonable doubt Millicent's right to publish the Dickinson poetry she had inherited from Mabel. The publisher insisted she go through all the letters in her possession about Emily's writings, "including all of those from Austin Dickinson . . . because they wanted to find out the authorization given me in writing for publication of Dickinson material," she related in a late 1950s interview. In the same interview, Millicent admitted that in the quest to find written authorization to publish Emily's poetry, she not only read Mabel's and Austin's letters to each other but also Mabel's diaries and journals. While she didn't find explicit written permission, she did find evidence of the love affair she had for so many years suspected—ever since she was a child knowing there was something odd going on when her mother and Mr. Dickinson locked themselves behind closed doors:

> I met head on a passion so overwhelming that my knees shook and I felt as if I could not breathe. Walter read one or two letters and fell silent. . . . The thing was so mighty and it was so wrong—it had spawned such primitive savage emotions—hatred and revenge embodied in a curse so full of power that it had reached even down to me . . . I could not handle it. I was not fit to handle it. . . . Anyway, I did not have to tackle it yet. I had other things to do first. So until the end of the decade this smoldered beneath the surface.[12]

Although Millicent's mining of Mabel's materials yielded no conclusive written verification, ultimately Harper attorney Cass Canfield concluded that Millicent "had a strong claim, 'based on physical possession—a claim which dated back many years.'" Millicent wrote years later that after Mattie died, "Harpers began to weigh the conditions of her will which seemed restrictive and contrary to public interest . . . they consulted the foremost authority on copyrights, Alexander

Lindey . . . who agreed with Harpers' counsel that my two books should be published. So did [poet] Mark Van Doren, who wrote a foreword to the poems in *Bolts of Melody*."[13] In the end, neither Alfred Leete Hampson (the executor of Mattie's estate) nor Little, Brown (Mattie's publisher) filed a lawsuit. For Millicent, and for Harper, the path to publishing the remainder of the Emily Dickinson poems seemed clear.

—

When Mabel spoke at Mount Holyoke College's Founder's Day in 1929, she announced that she was in possession of hundreds of unpublished Emily Dickinson poems. At the time, Mattie was busily publishing all the poems her aunt had given to her mother as well as reprinting poems previously published by Mabel, to which Mattie laid claim and subsequently, copyright. But as literary scholar Elizabeth Horan writes, Mattie clearly saw Mabel's assertion that she had many unpublished poems as a threat to her own control over Emily's work. This control had given Mattie a source of badly needed income and a way to oversee and define the Dickinson brand.

Later that year Mabel had taken additional steps to ensure her claims on the unpublished poems would be seen as legitimate, including a return to the lecture circuit and the publication of articles about her own work on editing Emily's poetry. She reached out to influential literary critics with the intent that they would recognize her editing of the poems as more authoritative than Mattie's. It worked: as Mattie continued to publish books of her aunt's poetry and letters, reviewers increasingly took her to task for sloppy mistakes and referred to Mabel as having produced more accurate renditions. But Mattie persisted, impervious to criticism, continuing to lay claim to copyright, unwilling and unable to satisfactorily answer the publisher's questions about the existence of unpublished poems. In addition, since Mattie and her newly named collaborator, Alfred Leete Hampson, "had never managed a systematic inventory of their own holdings," Elizabeth Horan suggests, "they could hardly begin to answer Todd's charges."[14] This gave Mabel the upper hand.

Mabel had prevailed upon Charles Green, at the Jones Library in

Amherst (which would later acquire a sizable collection of Dickinson materials), to assemble and publish a detailed set of figures about the number of copies sold of each edition of Emily's poetry. Green, who already knew from previous correspondence with Mabel that she held a number of unpublished Dickinson manuscripts that he had his eye on, was busily cultivating a good relationship with her. At the same time Green was compiling his list, as Elizabeth Horan points out, Mattie Dickinson Bianchi urged Little, Brown and others "not to print the figures that were most valuable to the Todds"—in other words, to suppress sales data that would allow anyone to "figure precisely the immense profits that the Dickinsons had realized from the former editors' work." But Green was persistent; he obtained the data he sought and published them. Green, an ostensibly impartial arbiter and someone with impeccable credentials, clearly demonstrated where profits from Emily's poetry had gone. Green's analysis indicated that while the Todds had done the lion's share of the work, the Dickinsons (Lavinia, then Mattie) had yielded the lion's share of the profits. Mabel and Millicent "gained further advantage by appearing to be more generous than Bianchi, such as by showing unpublished manuscripts to writers Genevieve Taggard, Josephine Pollitt and Frederik Pohl, who further publicized Mrs. Todd's expertise."[15]

Horan points out that "Todd's verbal claims had pushed her rival into a very tight corner" and all Mattie could do was dredge up the 1898 trial and insinuate that its outcome meant Mabel was immoral and untrustworthy. Mattie wrote to Herbert Jenkins at Little, Brown, "I know of no 'friend of the family' who could possess hundreds of unpublished poems of my Aunt Emily Dickinson. The original editor who intimated as such, at South Hadley last November, is the person convicted of a fraudulent land transaction in open Court." Mattie went on to suggest she was certain her Aunt Lavinia had broken off relations with Mabel and it was thus improbable that Mabel somehow was in possession of poems, but if she were, that they were obtained "by false pretenses." In a letter to her attorney, Theodore Frothingham, Mattie wrote of Vinnie's efforts to "eliminate Mrs. Todd from any further connection with her sister's work." She went on to assert that Mabel could not be trusted and concluded, "I have no wish or intention to involve myself in a lawsuit against your advice, but it is apparent that I cannot submit in silence to the gross flouting of my family's wishes or to the intolerable liberties being taken with the family inheritance."[16]

But Frothingham responded to Mattie, "I think that to be doing any further thing now would be doing a vain thing. It would not strengthen our position in any way." As Horan writes, "the publishers were far less interested in unverifiable allegations about morality . . . than in discovering who was holding what properties."[17]

When Mabel died, it fell to Millicent to complete the job of editing those "properties" that Mabel had long held in the camphorwood chest, and to verify that she had legal standing to publish them. Millicent noted in her introduction to *Bolts of Melody* that the unpublished poems could be broadly categorized in two ways: poems that contained Emily's interlined corrections or in which she noted possible word substitutions, and those that were untouched. The latter were often fragments, many times written on scraps of paper, brown paper bags, in the margins of drugstore bargain flyers or the inside of envelopes that, Millicent observed, appeared to be the paper Emily liked most. Millicent found these fragments confusing and often near illegible, even to one familiar with Emily's hand. "Their appearance was so discouraging that I put off grappling with them from year to year, wondering indeed as I did so whether I should ever attempt to disentangle them, whether the time required would not be wasted." But, she found eventually "after laboriously puzzling out a word, a line, a stanza, letter by letter, with all the alternatives one is rewarded by seeing, suddenly, a perfect poem burst full-blown into life. The clarity of the thought shines forth in striking contrast to the chaos of the manuscript."[18]

Millicent spent years working with these "scraps." As she later wrote in the preface to *Bolts of Melody*, this work proved important because "the result has been the discovery of some of Emily's finest poetry, because these are the poems she wrote in her fullest maturity . . . it is precisely because, during her last years, these thoughts were jotted down at white heat and never revised that some of her most powerful poems, dealing with fundamental areas of experience, are contained in this volume. Like the dormant life-germ of a plant these verses, buried for sixty years, are at last reaching light and air in full vitality."[19] For instance, Millicent used the example of an unfinished poem she numbered 600:

The sun in reining to the west
Makes not as much of sound
As cart of man in road below
Adroitly turning round.

That whiffletree of amethyst[20]

Millicent worked diligently to decipher words, put together pieces of torn paper and discern what Emily intended among papers "smothered with alternative words and phrases crowded into every available space." An example of a "scrap" Millicent elected to record separately was one she numbered 623:

Soft as the massacre of suns
By evening's sabres slain.[21]

While she was able to put some of these poems into a more final form, others remained incomplete. Millicent noted even "some of her finished poems are rough, rugged, awkward. But that she intended. In some of these unfinished poems, however, not only is the idea obscured by the form; the idea itself is obscure—not sharp enough to pierce through the words."[22]

With the finished poems, Millicent, like Mabel, first made a fresh copy of each poem, looking both at Emily's original and at Mabel's copies. She stated that it was historically important to have Mabel's transcriptions because "they have correctly preserved a good many poems which might otherwise have been lost" and because in *Further Poems* and

AN EXAMPLE OF ONE OF EMILY DICKINSON'S "SCRAPS."

Unpublished Poems, Mattie had altered some of the poems' words and orderings (although Emily sometimes wrote different versions of poems that Sue might have had and Mabel did not). But in any case, Millicent wrote that Mabel's versions were "available to check the accuracy of the published versions."[23]

Millicent wrote that in her efforts to "discover Emily's own preference," she often ignored Mabel's changes and instead, "in no single instance have I substituted a word or phrase not suggested by Emily herself." Like Mabel, Millicent did attempt to standardize Emily's spellings, but pointed out that she did so only "with great reluctance, I . . . changed archaic spelling to conform to current usage."[24] For the most part, Millicent left Emily's unique punctuation intact.

Millicent also parted company with Mabel and Higginson's practice of naming poems, except where Emily, herself, had indicated a title. Like her mother and Higginson, Millicent chose to place the poems within thematically named chapters. While writing, "nothing reveals the scope of Emily Dickinson's insight more than the variety of her themes," Millicent was also aware of the limitations of such an arrangement. She thought that optimally, "the poems of Emily Dickinson should eventually be arranged in the order of composition as well as by subject matter" because this would best demonstrate "her inner development." Millicent was also keenly aware that the selection of poems "for a definitive edition of the works of Emily Dickinson will be easier in fifty years than it is now," because at the present time, the push was to have *all* of the poems published[25]—an initiative Millicent heartily embraced, feeling it was her responsibility to make "all the data" public. It was part of fulfilling her promise to Mabel.

Either Millicent took a page from Mabel's dramatic playbook, or a clever publicist for Harper realized that the story of these long-hidden poems' reemergence would boost sales. "In 1929, at the request of her mother, Millicent Todd Bingham unlocked the camphorwood box containing the poems of Emily Dickinson," read a flyer advertising *Bolts of Melody*. "There were hundreds of them; over half had never been published . . . the resulting volume is a gift of inestimable value to the large audience which has long recognized the genius of Emily. Although her personal life was shrouded in mystery, the greatness of her work . . . is as fresh and exciting today as it was sixty years ago."[26]

Bolts of Melody, its title derived from the poem "I would not paint a picture" (unnamed and unnumbered in Millicent's version, poem 348 in the Johnson edition), contained well over six hundred poems total, including both finished and unfinished poems. Critical reviews were mixed. In the *New York Times Book Review*, Robert Hillyer said, "no praise can be too high for Mrs. Bingham's editing. . . . The editor's preface is written with masterly skill and gives the key to her method." Richard Sewall at Yale University, who would later write a definitive biography of Emily and also become an important confidant of Millicent's, wrote in *The New England Quarterly*, "In no previous collection have the major problems of editing Emily Dickinson's poems been more clearly recognized, and Mrs. Bingham has made excellent progress toward their solution." In the journal *Poetry*, Babette Deutsch wrote something that must have particularly pleased Millicent. She stated that while she wished Millicent had chosen to arrange the poems chronologically rather than

thematically, "one would not wish to exchange the carelessness and pre-
sumption of Emily's niece, guided, apparently, in her treatment of the
manuscripts by her own view of the quarrel, for a decorous pusillanim-
ity. But for all her hesitancies and some few mistakes of judgment, Mrs.
Bingham has done an admirable job."[27]

But writing in the *New York Herald Tribune*, Amherst College professor George Whicher used the opportunity to excoriate members of the
Dickinson family, cast aspersions on Mabel and David, and insinuate
the Mabel/Austin relationship; he opened up wounds that Millicent
had hoped were healed. Whicher explained to the reading public that
"the Austin Dickinson ménage which Emily had mildly characterized
as 'Vesuvius at home' became more of an inferno than ever, with Sue as
hellcat-in-charge" after Austin's death. (In fact, Whicher was being a
bit misleading in this statement: while Emily probably did know about
Austin's marital issues, the reference to "Vesuvius at home" came from
a line in a poem, "Volcanoes be in Sicily" [number 1705]—it was not a
clear or direct reference to the doings next door at The Evergreens.)[28]
The ensuing trial led by Lavinia, whom Whicher characterized as a
"semi-demented creature," succeeded, he suggested, in getting the public to see that the Todds were the sort of people who would want to pull
the bright stars around them—like Emily Dickinson's poetry—into
their own orbit. When the trial verdict went against Mabel, Whicher
concluded, it alienated her from all things Dickinson so that she hid
away hundreds of poems for decades—an act he compared to Henry
James in *The Spoils of Poynton* . . . with Mabel "in the role of the woman
who defies legal conventions rather than let a thing of beauty fall into
the hands of despoilers."[29]

Millicent was both alarmed and horrified. This review hurt her
deeply "because he spoke of the Todds' 'well-known acquisition habits.'" But what really distressed her was Whicher's insinuation that "the
whole thing [was] rooted in the Dickinson-Todd relationship."[30]

However, Millicent put aside the threat of Whicher's further expos-
ing Mabel and Austin's relationship, the rift between the two families,

and the periodic appearances of Emily's poetry when she saw the vindicating review of both her books in *The New Yorker*:

> The student of Emily Dickinson cannot help but be struck by the marked difference between the poems edited by Mrs. Bingham and those edited by Mrs. Bianchi. The latter's compilations were remarkable for their haphazard arrangement and general tone of carelessness and lack of insight into the material, and Mrs. Bianchi's *Life and Letters* when compared with Mrs. Todd's edition of the *Letters*, is clearly sentimentalized and doctored. . . . Mrs. Bingham brings all this into focus. She is concise, comprehensive, and only a little bitter. The spell cast over the poet's work is beginning to break, and Mrs. Bingham looks forward to a complete, definitive edition once a few remaining obstacles are overcome.[31]

Looking back from the vantage point of 1964, Millicent felt keenly that her own childhood in Amherst and her work on the life and poems of Emily Dickinson had given her an understanding of the poet that few others could match. She wrote that her chief contribution to Dickinson scholarship was "the editing of the poems in *Bolts of Melody*. This meant deciphering the most illegible manuscripts . . . it simplified the work of subsequent editors. It meant a selection of the final word among many variants left by Emily. . . . I knew which word she would have chosen. I feel sometimes as if Emily and I were going it alone."[32] But in the 1950s, Millicent was far from alone in her quest to publish and interpret Emily Dickinson, and she was only halfway through her publishing journey.

Millicent's publication quests took years to realize, not only because of her meticulous research but also because momentous events periodically interrupted her progress. In 1947, Millicent had a hysterectomy that was, she wrote, "performed as a prophylactic based on suspicion." Shortly after that, Walter's health began to decline. En route to a psy-

chology conference in 1951, Walter had trouble breathing and very little
stamina. Millicent was frantic. They got home safely, but shortly afterward he collapsed. Millicent arranged for nursing care and for an oxy-
gen tent "but I did not fully take it in," she recalled. "I thought he was
just tired."[33] But it was more than that—Walter was diagnosed with con-
gestive heart failure.

Millicent and Walter had planned to spend the 1950s "writing about
the things we knew," as Millicent later said. Walter intended to issue a
revision of his book *Aptitudes and Aptitude Testing* (first published in 1937) to
include work he'd done during World War II for the Army, and to begin
working on an autobiography that would also be a history of the industrial psychology movement. Millicent considered a return to geography
(she published a short history of Miami in 1948 and enjoyed the work
so much that she considered doing more), but she mostly felt obligated
to launch the research for her last two books on Dickinson, one on the
early letters of members of the Dickinson family, including letters from
Emily to Austin, and one about Emily's relationship with Judge Otis
Lord, drawing heavily from their correspondence. Millicent's ambivalence about this topic was clear: though she believed that such a book
would be popular and an important contribution to the growing body of
works about Emily Dickinson's life, "I was not at all sure whether those
letters should ever be published at all," she recalled.[34]

Despite concerns over Walter's declining health, the two spent a
great deal of time in the early 1950s "driving hither and yon in New
England and New York State to try to search out people still living who
might have memories or documents that would be useful."[35] Millicent
believed that unraveling the mystery of Lord's relationship with Emily
Dickinson would yield important information about both the poet and
her poetry. She also believed she knew what she might find. In the first
chapter of *Emily Dickinson: A Revelation*, Millicent wrote that when Austin
had given her mother packets of Emily's correspondence, one envelope
was different from all the rest. This envelope contained letters Austin
told Mabel were "very special and personal." Mabel declined to publish
them in either edition of her volumes of Emily's letters, as Austin had

not wished them made public. "A glance was enough to show . . . that the drafts it contained were indeed different . . . my mother did not consider publishing the group in question. She put them back in the envelope and placed it at the bottom of the pile of Emily's manuscripts in the camphorwood chest where it remained unopened for almost forty years." When Millicent opened the chest, Mabel told her "that I would do well to find out all I could about Judge Lord." Millicent claimed to have asked Mabel no questions, but "accepted the challenge and took the first exploratory steps."[36]

Judge Otis Phillips Lord, eighteen years older than Emily Dickinson, a graduate of Amherst College and Harvard Law School, was a close friend of Edward Dickinson's. Lord and his wife, Elizabeth, were frequent guests at the Dickinson Homestead. Emily had known him for her entire life, but it seems that after his wife died in 1877, Judge Lord might have expressed a more-than-fatherly interest in his old friend's older daughter. Millicent cited two pieces of evidence suggesting a bond between Judge Lord and Emily: first, Mabel's recollection that shortly after she moved to Amherst in 1881, Sue Dickinson admonished her not to go to the home of her two sisters-in-law, whom she stated hadn't "any idea of morality." According to Mabel, Sue had told her that one day, she walked into the drawing room at The Homestead and found Emily "reclining in the arms of a man." Mabel did not record whether Sue specifically suggested that the man was Judge Lord, though presumably the judge was well-known to Sue. Millicent argued, "it is worth bearing in mind that this was the time when Emily's idolatry of Judge Lord was reaching its peak,"[37] and therefore, she concluded the man must have been Lord. (Many years later, professor and literary critic Christopher Benfey wrote on Slate.com, "The notion of Emily Dickinson making out in her living room is so foreign to our conception of her that her autumnal tryst with Judge Lord has never become part of the popular lore about her.")[38]

The second and perhaps more independent indicator of a powerful bond between Lord and Emily was Colonel Thomas Wentworth Higginson's description of Emily Dickinson's funeral, at which he had been present. In his diary, Higginson had written that in Emily's coffin Vin-

JUDGE OTIS PHILLIPS LORD MIGHT HAVE EVINCED SOME ROMANTIC INTEREST
IN HIS OLDEST FRIEND'S OLDEST DAUGHTER LATE IN HIS LIFE. EMILY WROTE HIM
A NUMBER OF LETTERS. SOME SCHOLARS BELIEVE THAT LORD WAS THE INTENDED
RECIPIENT OF EMILY'S SO-CALLED "MASTER LETTERS," AS WELL.

nie placed "two heliotropes by her hand, to take to Judge Lord."[39] How
Higginson knew this was never made clear.

Since Emily kept no known or saved diary, other "evidence" would
have to be found in her letters or poetry. Millicent knew that three
extant letters in Mabel's camphorwood chest deserved special scrutiny.
Mabel had published just six lines of one of these letters in her 1894
edition of Emily's letters, and had concealed the identity of the recipient under the heading "To ___ ___," even deleting the title "Master."
While even today the true intended recipient of the so-called Master
letters is contested, there's no debate about the depth of feeling Emily
expressed in them. For instance, in a 1986 publication of the entire
text of the Master letters, Dickinson scholar Ralph Franklin notes that
the letters "indicate a long relationship, geographically apart, in which
correspondence would have been the primary means of communica-

tion. Dickinson did not write letters as a fictional genre, and these were surely part of a larger correspondence yet unknown to us." Franklin's recounting of the Master letters shows how contemporary scholars have attempted to date them by analyzing the formation of Emily's letters and comparing them to her handwriting at different points of her life, a potentially important clue in identifying the identity of "Master."[40]

The Master letters contain some of Emily Dickinson's most beautifully poignant imagery. "I wish that I were great, like Mr—Michael Angelo, and could paint for you," she wrote in the first one. "You ask me what my flowers said—then they were disobedient—I gave them messages—." In the second, perhaps from early 1861, she wrote, "A love so big it scares her, rushing among her small heart—pushing aside the blood—and leaving her all faint and white in the gust's arm." The third, tentatively dated later in 1861, contains the plaintive "Could you come to New England—(this summer—could) Would you come to Amherst—Would you like to come—Master?"[41]

But besides these three much written-about letters were several others, perhaps more definitively meant for Judge Lord. Millicent reported these letters were separated from others that were found after Emily's death, and that unlike Emily's other correspondence, they were not destroyed. She wrote that Austin wanted "to shield [Emily] from the curiosity of those who would pry into her deepest feelings in order to speculate about the nature of friendship which, although he knew it had been sacred to her, he himself did not wholly understand. He knew to whom these letters had been written—imposing, dignified Judge Lord, his father's best friend," and that Mabel, "because of [Austin's] attitude considered them hallowed and left them alone."[42] Millicent was the first person to publish the Master letters in full, in *Emily Dickinson's Home*. But that still didn't make the connection between Emily and Judge Lord complete.

Millicent knew that to truly solve the puzzle of the object of Emily's affection, and possibly the riddle of why Emily chose a life of relative seclusion, she would need to find proof that some version of Emily's letters had actually reached Judge Lord. In addition, she wrote, if "even a single draft of a letter from him to Emily turned up, it would reveal more of his attitude toward her than can be inferred with safety either from her own letters and notes or from his family's attitude or hers toward the friendship."[43]

So Millicent set off in search of proof. Her inquiry sent her to the Library of Congress, then to Salem, Massachusetts, where Judge Lord had lived, to other towns and cities throughout Massachusetts, and to destinations in New York and Connecticut, seeking living descendants who might be willing to share any papers or information. But evidence proved elusive—some relatives were unable to provide information, and others were unwilling to be forthcoming. Millicent meticulously documented her efforts, despite the little they yielded. She later admitted that though she had hoped to find "documentary evidence . . . that some stray letters might have been overlooked by those bent on wiping out all trace of it," in fact she had not found any such documents.

Yet she did find sufficient information about the judge and his family to piece together enough of his association with the Dickinsons that, assembled alongside similar information from Emily and her family, Millicent felt capable of crafting a narrative outlining their story. Millicent became convinced there *was* a love relationship between Emily Dickinson and Judge Lord, that Emily's "messages to the man who during the last years of her life held her 'soul at the white heat' until his death two years before her own" demonstrated this conclusively. And she believed that some of Lord's relatives and descendants either withheld or destroyed information that would shed further light on a romantic relationship with Emily.

Millicent based her conclusions around a number of pieces of "evidence." First, there were Emily's own writings, including references to Judge Lord in a few existing letters she had written to other people, the "My lovely Salem smiles at me" line from one of her letters circa 1878 (the year after Judge Lord's wife died) and seemingly clear references in some of her poems, such as the often-cited lines from one of her poems:

How fleet, how indiscreet an one,
How always wrong is love—

Second, Millicent referenced Mabel's story about Sue Dickinson's warning, and third, she cited the purported attitude of Abigail Farley West, Lord's niece (and Susan Dickinson's good friend), about Emily; she had supposedly described the relationship between her uncle and Emily Dickinson as "immoral," though this description was passed along to Millicent secondhand.[44]

Some later Dickinson scholars have not concluded, as Millicent did, that Judge Otis Phillips Lord played such a primary role in Emily Dickinson's love life. Many have suggested that, among other things, "Master" was really just an amalgam, not a particular person but a muse or imagined figure, citing lack of written evidence to conclude there was any romantic relationship.[45] But some people have thought otherwise. In 2012, John Evangelist Walsh published *Emily Dickinson in Love*, a book in which he attempted to demonstrate and reconstruct a love relationship between Emily and Lord. His many assertions are not well documented in any evidence and, as one reviewer suggested, "Walsh does not let the facts get in the way of a good story."[46] Being the stickler for documentation that she was, Millicent would undoubtedly have found Walsh's book severely lacking, even though he arrived at a conclusion similar to her own. In 2014 poet Susan Snively published *The heart has many doors*, a novel elaborating on Millicent's work in *Emily Dickinson: A Revelation*. While she admits taking "liberties" in putting together her fictionalized account of a relationship between Emily and Lord, Snively writes, "at the heart of this narrative lie many of the poet's poems and letters"[47]— using them as Millicent did, to arrive at a similar conclusion. Scholars at the Emily Dickinson Museum conclude, "A romantic relationship late in the poet's life with Judge Otis Phillips Lord is supported in Dickinson's correspondence with him as well as in family references."[48]

The reviews of *Emily Dickinson: A Revelation* must have done little to quell Millicent's fears about not being taken seriously by literary critics and the academy. Scholar and English professor Walter McIntosh Merrill described the book as "rather slight and even pretentious in its total effect, because Mrs. Bingham tends to overstate her thesis. From the title page on, the reader is kept in suspense; one innuendo after another leads him to expect momentarily a sensational revelation," but that in the end, "the reader feels rather cheated."[49] Writing in the journal *American Literature*, Jay Leyda (who would later write and publish two volumes' worth of *The Years and Letters of Emily Dickinson*) wrote, "the new letters are remarkable. . . . Mrs. Bingham's editorial attitude is admirable—the book's center remains the letters themselves." His generally positive review concluded that other reviewers who were more critical were harsher because "perhaps it was easier for critics to dismiss the book and its implications than to revise their prejudged images of Emily Dickinson."[50]

Though Millicent did receive an honorary doctorate from Dickinson College (no relation to the Amherst family) in early May of 1952, in large part because of her earlier work on Emily, she still worried that because her formal training was not in literature, she would never be fully accepted as a true Dickinson scholar. In fact, the citation for her honorary doctorate of letters read, "You have made for yourself a career in two widely separated fields, the science of geography and the art of biography. You know more, perhaps, than any other woman alive about the physical forces which shaped the world into a theatre for the activities of the human race, and about the spiritual and cerebral forces which brought into being the esoteric meanings, the flashing insights, the awareness of beauty that made the poems of Emily Dickinson true 'bolts of melody,' as you have named them." Though flattered, Millicent reflected privately in her diary, "What Dr. Edel [president of Dickinson College] said of me was quite overwhelming but . . . not true."[51] This honor only seemed to reinforce her belief that her professional decisions rendered her an imposter in both of her chosen fields.

Millicent was likely aware of the many inherent ironies in her writing of a romantic relationship between Emily and the much-older Judge Lord, which had possibly developed while he was still married. Though Millicent never said this directly, the parallels to her own mother's relationship with Austin were unmistakable. Otis Lord and Austin Dickinson were both graduates of Amherst College and Harvard Law School.

Mabel had thought of Austin as more like her father, Eben Jenks Loomis, than any other man she'd ever met; Emily revered Otis Lord in part because of his close relationship with Edward Dickinson. Lord's surviving descendants were every bit as upset about the insinuation of a possible relationship with Emily Dickinson as Emily's family was about a relationship between Austin and Mabel.

The publishing of presumptive love letters between an unmarried couple was certainly something that would have struck a very painful chord within Millicent, who struggled with the decision of whether to publish her mother's and Austin's love letters. In the end, Millicent never published any of Mabel's and Austin's letters (they wouldn't appear in print until Polly Longsworth presented them in 1984). But in the case of Emily Dickinson, Millicent clearly knew her decision meant that she "assumed a grave responsibility . . . my only criterion has been this: will they [the letters] help to bring about a better understanding of Emily Dickinson?"[52]

Looking back on this work, Millicent told an interviewer this book had been "intended as the climax, the last of my four books, [but] because of its brevity, the publishers said that it could be rushed through the press quickly." When *Emily Dickinson: A Revelation* was published in November of 1954, Millicent recalled, "it made little impression. Since it is an enlightening source-book I was disappointed."[53]

There were two other intertwining reasons Millicent had negative associations with this book.

In the early 1950s, as Millicent worked on the interviews and to find written documentary evidence of an Emily/Lord relationship, Walter grew progressively weaker. "I will not enlarge upon the anguish of those months as Walter lay struggling for breath in the next room while I worked against time trying for his sake to finish the manuscript," she said in 1959. When one of Walter's doctors told her she had "an aura of frustration" that was not helping Walter's recovery, Millicent reluctantly agreed to go to Hog Island to finish her work. "It would not take long, we thought. Then I would return refreshed with added strength for the long pull ahead, for Walter would be ill for a long time. And so, against my deepest feelings, I was persuaded to leave him and go to Maine."[54] Walter died just three weeks later.

Millicent's guilt about being apart from Walter at the end of his life never abated. On the train returning to New York after learning of Walter's death, she wrote in her diary, "I was overwhelmed by the realization of what I had been deprived of, doing for him at the last, reading to him each time. I marvel I could ever have consented to leave him, no matter how necessary for me the doctor said it was. How <u>could</u> I?" Weeks after his death she berated herself further: "beating with knotted rope is not good enough for me. I deserve suffering, torture and grief such as paralyzes me now. It is blackness and despair. It does not help to pray." Months later, the feeling had not lessened: "Oh, if only I had tried as hard to please Walter as he did to please me!" she lamented. She pondered whether she should return to Dr. Ehrenclou to help her process these feelings, and then poignantly suggested, "Today, from the depths of my heart, I thought of Emily's solitude and compared it to my own."[55]

Though Millicent would later acknowledge a childhood rheumatic fever predisposed Walter to heart problems, she truly believed that his decline in health emanated from another source: the battles with Harvard University that had begun.

—

CHAPTER 14

BATTLING OVER EMILY'S PAPERS (1946–1959)

"They are reviving an ancient feud"

When Mattie Dickinson Bianchi first began publishing books of her aunt's poems and letters in 1914, Mabel must have been aware that her own collection of unpublished Dickinson poems and letters was an untapped gold mine, worth both literary prestige and a significant amount of money. Someday, she knew, someone would want those manuscripts. Mabel's 1929 suggestion that she was holding hundreds of unpublished poems made literary analysts, publishers and poetry fans wonder what Dickinson treasures might still be out there, and who was in possession of which literary properties. Mabel's reissue of *The Letters of Emily Dickinson* in 1931, which contained many previously unpublished letters, certainly proved that she hadn't teased the public about the unseen documents.

The jousting over who had copyright to Emily's poetry and letters went on for years. Between 1929 and 1942, Mattie continued to claim copyright of all Emily's works. Her efforts are documented by several large files of letters held at Harvard; there are innumerable requests sent to Mattie, via her publisher, asking for permission to read an Emily Dickinson poem on the radio, to put poems to music, to utilize a poem in a play. Mattie tried to control this universe as tightly as she could. Mabel's reentry to the Emily Dickinson space was therefore particularly threatening, confirming that there were letters and poems outside of Mattie's possession. But Mattie was unable to get either her attorneys or her publishers to take up a lawsuit against Mabel and Millicent to rein in their use of any Dickinson materials, in large part because no one was certain of how much original Dickinson material the Todds retained. But these questions took a different turn in 1943, when Mattie Dickinson Bianchi died.

With no biological heir, Mattie named Alfred Leete Hampson executor of her home and estate, and bequeathed to him the copyrights to all her books. Mattie had met Hampson in New York in 1920, shortly after she divorced her husband. As numerous Dickinson biographers point out, Count Bianchi had run up significant debts against Mattie's inheritance that left her scrambling for funds. By 1916, Mattie had had enough drama and enough debt. She consulted a New York–based attorney, a distant cousin by the name of Gilbert H. Montague, about divorce.[1] Four years later, when she made the acquaintance of Alfred Leete Hampson, Mattie was once again a single woman.

Hampson, twenty-three years younger than Mattie, has been variously described as her "secretary," her "literary advisor" and her "devoted companion." After the trauma and theatrics of her relationship with Alexander Bianchi, mild-mannered Hampson must have been a soothing presence. The nature of their relationship has been speculated about in a novel entitled The Path Between and hinted at in some scholarly articles. Elizabeth Horan writes that while Hampson maintained a separate address from Mattie, the pair "spent every summer together in the Evergreens, where he brought order, typing, and planning skills to the Dickinson legacy."[2] Biographer Lyndall Gordon suggests that for Mattie, the "condition for collaboration was not accuracy; it was unquestioning loyalty. Hampson was more than happy to oblige."[3] Hampson became Mattie's coeditor on a series of books, including several volumes of Emily's poetry. He was unquestionably devoted to Mattie, and revered the memory and work of her aunt Emily.

After Mattie's death, Millicent was poised to publish the first two of her books about Emily Dickinson. She wrote, "Harpers lawyers felt that it was in the public interest that they publish both books. They felt the risk that Mr. Hampson would try to stop publication . . . should be taken and they doubted very much that he had any firm ground on which to stand. The right to exclusive possession in publication, even if legally enforceable by a member of the family, could hardly be passed on, they thought, to one unrelated to the family; or at least they thought there was a doubt about it."[4] When *Ancestors' Brocades* and *Bolts of Melody* were published in 1945, there was no lawsuit. It became clear that while Hampson and Mary Landis (the woman he married four years after Mattie's death) had a trove of Dickinson papers in their possession, so did Millicent.

After Mattie's death, questions about finding a permanent home for the Dickinson papers began to arise. Millicent was sixty-three; Hampson was ten years younger but ill with recurring hepatitis. Hampson was also consumed by fears that the deteriorating conditions in The Evergreens meant that the precious Dickinson papers might not be safe.

William McCarthy, an emissary from Harvard's Houghton Library, saw this situation clearly. McCarthy had had his eye on the Dickinson papers for a long time. He'd met Mattie during preparations for an Emily Dickinson centennial exhibition in 1930, and began ingratiating himself. McCarthy knew that to earn Mattie's trust he must pledge allegiance to her and eschew any contact with the Todds; as Lyndall Gordon points out, McCarthy "had gone so far as to declare himself Madame Bianchi's 'slave for life.'"[5] After Mattie's death he befriended Hampson by continuing to insist on a "shrine for Emily," and building on Hampson's fears about the papers going up in flames, stressing the need to find a safer home for them.

McCarthy was a former student of loyal Amherst College alumnus R. M. Smith. Smith believed that the Dickinson papers should go to his alma mater, not Harvard. When he heard from McCarthy about his plans to get the Dickinson papers, he sounded the alarm to Amherst College professor and Dickinson scholar George Whicher: McCarthy, he said, "has designs on selling them either to a prominent national library or to an equally prominent eastern university. . . . Now is the time for an Amherst millionaire to step forward and do a handsome thing for you and Amherst." But Mattie Dickinson Bianchi, who had not liked the portrait of Emily that Whicher had painted in his writing, left specific instructions in her will prohibiting Whicher from quoting Dickinson materials. Correctly assuming that Hampson would similarly cut him out, Whicher responded to Smith that "as long as Hampson was in the picture Amherst College was not interested in acquiring the Emily Dickinson manuscripts." He wrote to Millicent, "in other words, I cannot say too emphatically to the world in general and to everyone in particular that I am through with Emily Dickinson and all her relatives and their hangers on. I have made my contribution toward cleaning up of that mess, and I expect from now on to be concerned with other and pleasanter matters."[6]

At the same time, Gilbert Montague—the same distant Dickinson cousin whom Mattie had discreetly contacted about her divorce—began to evince interest in acquiring the Dickinson papers. A wealthy, bright and self-made man, Montague was imbued with a sense of his own importance. His marriage to Amy Angell Collier had united two prominent New England families. His law practice largely consisted of representing big oil companies and trying to advance private enterprise. Montague thought nothing of reminding people of his wealth, a tactic he used in aggressively pursuing things that he wanted. A man with an acquisitive bent and an inveterate collector of autographs and other papers, once Montague became aware of Mattie's Dickinson papers, he wanted to possess them. But not only Mattie's papers. After the publication of Millicent's books in 1945 demonstrated another Dickinson cache, Montague decided to go after Millicent's Dickinson papers, as well.

Montague invited Millicent to dine with him in New York. At first, the tone of their correspondence was warm, even effusive. "Dear Mr. Montague," Millicent wrote after her visit to his home in November 1945, "I left your house last night all a-quiver. It was not alone the feeling of having stepped through the Bibliothèque National, the Library of Congress and the British Museum all together—but a sense of having somehow been among the height of our culture—the sources of strength for our very existence. I am really at a loss to thank you for one of the most memorable evenings I ever spent."[7]

The following year, after seeing Montague again at a Dickinson exhibit in New York, and learning of his intent to purchase Hampson's Dickinson collection for Harvard, Millicent "wrote an enthusiastic letter to Mr. Montague . . . I congratulated him on his benefaction and said that he would go down in history as the liberator of one of our greatest poets and that we were all to be congratulated that at least scholarship would come before partisanship, or words to that effect."[8] It was not certain that Montague would be able to procure the papers from Hampson; in the meantime, Montague made clear to Millicent that he was interested in her Dickinson collection, as well. But then, he wasn't the only one.

William Jackson, the man at the helm of Harvard's Houghton Library from the time the library opened in 1942, had earned the nickname of "The Grand Acquisitor" for his tireless work adding to Harvard's already considerable holdings. Knowing of Montague's promise to purchase the Bianchi/Dickinson manuscripts owned by Alfred Leete Hampson for Harvard and learning of Millicent's holdings, Jackson sensed another conquest. He approached Millicent, expressing interest in acquiring her collection. Millicent was certainly aware of the potential to make a great collection of Dickinson papers at Harvard. A Radcliffe alumna, she had warm feelings toward her alma mater. However, she explained to Jackson that before she considered parting with the papers, she must fulfill her promise to her mother to complete the books on which she was presently working. Millicent felt that for the sake of future scholarship it would be optimal for all of Emily's papers to be in the same place, but she questioned whether Harvard was the most fitting place. Millicent related years later her belief that "all her manuscripts should be in one place and I hoped and believed that that would be Amherst, for it was Amherst where she was born, where she lived, wrote and died."[9] So Millicent deflected Jackson's initial approaches.

Because of her conviction that Emily's papers ultimately belonged back in the town in which they had been written, Millicent contacted Charles Cole, the newly inaugurated president of Amherst College. Cole, an economic historian, would later serve as the U.S. Ambassador to Chile in the early 1960s—but it is clear that he honed his diplomatic skills while at Amherst in his dealings with Millicent and Harvard over the Emily Dickinson manuscripts. Little did Cole know when Millicent first contacted him in 1946 that he would spend the entire fourteen years of his presidency, and beyond, handling Millicent and issues pertaining to her Emily Dickinson papers.

Soon after Millicent initiated contact with him, Cole traveled to Washington, where he spent two hours with the Binghams. In a confidential internal memo he stated that Millicent "has a collection of curios (and I mean curios) such as Ashanti stools, Japanese rice bowls and the like, collected by her father on his various trips . . . my guess is they are mostly curiosities only." Millicent, he wrote, wanted to give these to Amherst if a designated room could be set up for their display. Millicent also owned an eighty-acre woodlot outside Amherst that she wanted to donate to the college as "an especially good place to study certain warblers." This land, the pragmatic Cole concluded, might "have real value for Amherst if it was ever decided to put up an FM radio station."

"And here is the real thing," he wrote, "She has the bulk of the surviving Emily Dickinson manuscripts in her possession. These latter are of simply inestimable literary significance, partially in view of the many corrections of the different versions through which the poems progressed, and further from the fact that no really well equipped editor has worked on them. Even as a matter of market value, my guess is that these manuscripts would fetch hundreds of thousands of dollars."

Cole concluded, "if we are to get the manuscripts, I think we will: 1) (God help us) have to take the curios and exhibit them somewhere, at least during the life of Mr. and Mrs. Bingham; 2) have to accept Pelham Knob and I see no difficulty in that; 3) have to promise to keep the Emily Dickinson/Mabel Loomis Todd materials together in a room designated thus." To seal the deal, Cole thought, would require

Amherst to "urge her gently from time to time. It may be necessary to talk about warblers," he wryly commented, "but the appropriateness and value to Amherst of the Dickinson manuscripts are such that I think Amherst would be well justified even in expending two rooms on their acquisition."[10]

It's possible that Amherst had attempted to get some of Mattie's Dickinson manuscripts earlier. Millicent had been told by a member of the Amherst College Board of Trustees in 1931 that "when an honorary degree was conferred on Mrs. Bianchi . . . it was given with the hope and expectation that it would result in her presenting her manuscripts to the college. This, as we know, she did not do."[11] So when Millicent told Charles Cole about her own collection of Dickinson manuscripts, the idea of an Amherst College collection was likely already percolating.

Cole also noted in his confidential memo that the Library of Congress was "making terrific efforts to get Mrs. Bingham to promise them the Emily Dickinson manuscripts." Pulitzer Prize winning poets Archibald MacLeish (who had also served as the head of the library from 1939 to 1944) and Robert Penn Warren (the only person to have been awarded a Pulitzer for both poetry and fiction) were dispatched to contact Millicent on behalf of the Library of Congress. They each urged her to give her Dickinson papers to the library. "Following our conversation in my office. . . . It would help us a great deal working toward a solution of a rather thorny and difficult problem," MacLeish wrote to Millicent, if she would consider giving her papers to the library.

But once again, Millicent held out, hoping that Hampson would not sell his papers to Montague, or that Montague would somehow decide to give the papers to Amherst instead of Harvard. Later in life, Millicent would regret having rejected the Library of Congress's approaches: in 1961 she wrote of her "catastrophic errors of judgment," including "not to have given the Emily Dickinson papers to the Library of Congress in 1945," which would have "released me from ten years of anguish."[12]

As the 1940s came to an end, there was still no resolution about where Emily Dickinson's papers would reside. Millicent was holding on to hers, and Alfred Leete Hampson had yet to reach a deal with Gilbert Montague. However, Hampson's lack of income, coupled with the deteriorating conditions of The Evergreens and of his own health, left him struggling with mounting expenses. He and Mary resolved to sell off some of Emily Dickinson's letters to raise cash. But the redoubtable William McCarthy advised them not to sell things in a piecemeal fashion.

McCarthy leveraged Hampson's debts and fears to his own advantage. In 1948, McCarthy left Houghton Library to become a dealer in rare manuscripts. He had been cultivating a relationship with the Hampsons for years, vowing to defend Mattie's reputation and to "care for Emily" by helping them find a home for her papers. That home, he suggested, must be more secure than The Evergreens, and must have sufficient financial backing to make the transactions worthwhile to all parties. McCarthy also assisted the Hampsons by combing through rooms at The Evergreens, uncovering letters long stored in trunks, under the eaves and hidden away in closets. After a few false starts with other potential buyers, in the first months of 1950, McCarthy let the Hampsons know that Gilbert Montague wanted to buy their collection for Harvard.

As a collector, Montague did not want *only* the Emily Dickinson papers in Hampson's possession to go to Harvard. Knowing this, William Jackson apparently told Montague that Millicent had "promised to yield up her own collection" if Harvard acquired Hampson's, too. There is no evidence of Millicent's "promise" in any written correspondence between her and Jackson. But thus assured, Montague provided Harvard with an initial gift of $25,000 to purchase the Dickinson papers from Alfred Leete Hampson.

As soon as Millicent learned of the forthcoming sale of the papers in March of 1950, she was troubled. "The announcement appeared in the *New York Times* and the *Herald Tribune*," she recalled years later. "I was disturbed by several things . . . that I knew to be untrue. The *Herald Tribune* said, for instance, that the gift included 'seventy-five percent of the Emily Dickinson poems.' Who invented that, I wondered? Next, Emily's papers 'passed into the hands of her sister-in-law [Sue Dickinson],' after Lavinia's death. How was that?" Millicent knew, of course, about all the Dickinson papers and poems she retained. Though Walter tried to reassure her that what got reported in newspapers wasn't entirely accurate, Millicent was not comforted. In addition, at the time that Montague's gift was announced, Harvard announced the hiring of literary scholar Thomas H. Johnson to edit a "definitive" edition of Dickinson's poetry. Johnson was quoted as saying, "We have no assurance that any of Emily Dickinson's works now in print is an accurate transcription of her original writing." For Millicent, who had already invested two decades trying to be as precise as possible about her own Dickinson transcriptions, and who was fiercely protective of Mabel's reputation and work on the Dickinson transcriptions, there could not have been a more stinging slap in the face. Or a more public one. "I remembered the years and years I had spent on the poems contained in *Bolts of Melody*, verifying every single word and being as accurate as I knew how having been trained as a scholar in science and accurate to the seventh . . . decimal point—I carried over that accuracy into the editing of the poems."[13] Millicent began to realize how fraught her dealings with Harvard would become.

In fact, the announcement of Montague's acquisition of the Dickinson papers and their subsequent gift to Harvard came about as the result of Alfred Leete Hampson's illness and subsequent desperate need for money. He had resisted McCarthy's attempts to broker a sale to Montague, but Montague became impatient, threatening that such tactics would ruin Hampson's reputation. He dispatched legal emissaries to pressure Hampson further.[14] When Hampson was taken to the hospital and placed in intensive care in late April of 1950, he finally conceded and signed a letter of agreement. In early May, William Jackson sent Montague a celebratory note with the heading "V-Emily Day."

Jackson's promise to unite the papers proved difficult to deliver. Millicent still believed, "it is obvious that all should be in the same place," but by the spring of 1950, she was starting to doubt that this would ever truly happen. Both Harvard and the Library of Congress were still trying to procure her Dickinson papers. In another imaginary conversation in her journal, Millicent wrote about what she planned to tell

Mr. Jackson when he came to call on her including her opinion that a very "competent" editor needed to be hired for the preparation of a new volume of Emily's poetry. She planned to tell Jackson that she needed to retain the papers while she was working on her books, and of her underlying belief that Emily's papers belonged not in Cambridge, but across the state, in Amherst. Rather than seeing it all as a business transaction, Millicent continued to view the situation as part of the ongoing tragedy spawned by the Mabel/Austin relationship. "It seems to me as if now is not the time . . . to go into the sordid story of Austin's disillusionment and the reasons for it, and the effect on Bianchi, not to mention our family, as well as on Emily," she wrote. "The virulence he [Jackson] encounters in the Hampsons is only a reflection of that of the real thing in the midst of which I grew up."[15] At this point, despite her beliefs about where the papers belonged and the offer from the Library of Congress, Millicent was still considering giving her papers to Harvard because more than anything, she wanted a full collection of Emily Dickinson's works to be available for future scholarship. She never considered the idea of selling them. To Millicent, the idea of receiving cash for her collection was repugnant; to do so, she said, "would be inconsistent with my own unremunerated effort as well as with that of my mother . . . it was a labor of love."[16]

Around the same time, in the early 1950s, Millicent agreed to let Thomas Johnson, the Harvard-anointed editor, come see the manuscripts she was holding. Millicent hoped that Johnson's "variorum" edition of the poems (a volume containing different variants of the text) would also be the first to publish Emily's poems in chronological order, knowing the limitations of arranging them thematically.

Johnson, who held a doctorate in American literature from Harvard, was best known for his work on colonial American literature, not the poetry of the Victorian era, or romantic or realism movements. But, in the name of scholarship, Millicent was willing to have Tom Johnson examine her manuscripts. In exchange for this gesture of good will, Millicent hoped and expected that Harvard would not interfere with her own work. She was still not ready to give up her collection to Harvard.

But after Jackson reported Millicent's reluctance about giving up her manuscripts to Gilbert Montague, the distant Dickinson cousin decided that he needed to have a more deliberate hand in the negotiations. Montague began to pressure Harvard. Realizing that Millicent's reasoning revolved around holding the original documents while she continued work on her books, Montague urged Harvard to issue an injunction against Harper. They should prevent the publication of Millicent's next two books on the basis of claiming legal ownership of all Dickinson papers, regardless of who held them. This claim would be made with the rationale that all of Emily's papers had been inherited by Lavinia, bequeathed to Mattie and then to Hampson. Even though Lavinia gave some of the manuscripts to Mabel, she claimed that Mabel did not have their copyright. Therefore, Harvard's position would be that only the Dickinsons and then Hampson had ever legitimately held the copyright— and that when Harvard bought the papers from Hampson they also bought the rights. Montague boldly asserted that Harvard would claim the copyright and control over all past publications and all future manuscripts that drew from Emily's letters or poems. If Harvard did not follow through on these demands, Montague threatened to sue them. This threat escalated and went on for years. Jackson explained Harvard's position in a letter written to Amherst College president Charles Cole: "Bluntly speaking, we are being bludgeoned into it by threats of law suits from a benefactor, and apparently these are not idle threats."[17]

Cole later wrote to Millicent that he felt her willingness to share Photostats of her Dickinson material with Harvard had been a tactical error: "Had you not made the material available to Johnson, I think they [Harvard] would have had to give you permission to publish your books so as to be able to go on with their variorum edition." Elsewhere he wrote that Millicent had "thus lost her major bargaining point with Harvard."[18] But as Walter conveyed Millicent's willingness to Jackson during a meeting in New York, he said that in return the Binghams were expecting that Harvard would "not interfere with my work which was now approaching completion. . . . Mr. Jackson assured him that they would not interfere in any way."[19]

To make certain of this, Walter went to Cass Canfield, the attorney for Harper, and asked him to get something in writing from Harvard. Canfield said he would write a letter to Harvard at once. Thus assured, Walter and Millicent went to spend the summer on Hog Island.

When they heard nothing from Harvard by the end of the summer of 1950, Millicent recalled, "somehow I had a feeling that all was not well; so I wrote to Harpers . . . asking to see what they had heard from Harvard—whether they had had the needed assurance. They replied saying that there had been no answer to Mr. Canfield's letter written in June and they enclosed a copy of his letter." Much to Millicent and Walter's dismay, they realized that Canfield had not asked Harvard for an assurance that they would not interfere with Millicent's books, only that they would grant her permission to see what was in the Dickinson collection they were acquiring from Hampson. Walter felt he had been remiss in not being more insistent or clearer with Canfield and waiting too long to follow up when they had heard nothing back from Harvard. "To the end of his life, Walter blamed himself for this."[20]

In the fall of 1950, Jackson asked the Binghams if he could finally come to D.C. to make Photostat copies for Thomas Johnson. Millicent still felt that allowing Jackson to do this, as she had promised months before, was the honorable thing, and it would promote scholarship, her ultimate goal.

Jackson spent a full day at the Folger Library doing the copying. Late that evening, he returned to the Binghams' apartment. Millicent was already asleep. When Jackson handed Millicent's copies back to Walter he told him "that he was sorry [but] that he could not possibly keep his part of the agreement"—that in exchange for allowing Jackson to copy the original Dickinson manuscripts in Millicent's possession she could continue with her own work to publish them. Millicent later recalled, "Walter told me that he 'hit the ceiling.' 'You mean to tell me that you come and get these Photostats without which your editor cannot do his work and then tell me you can't keep your promise in return?'" Worse, Jackson then presented Walter with a letter. "It said in effect that unless I promised to give everything I had to Harvard—all my Dickinson manuscripts—they would not let me publish my books. I was to sign on the dotted line."[21]

Millicent and Walter were stunned. Walter felt that the box of Photostats sitting at the Folger Library waiting to be shipped to Harvard should not be sent. But while Millicent believed she should "not knuckle under to Harvard," neither did she want to stand in the way of scholarly work. The Binghams allowed the box to be posted, but Harvard returned it, unopened. Millicent never received an explanation of Harvard's seeming turnabout—perhaps William Jackson had become convinced Harvard's actions would force Millicent's hand. Soon they would no longer have need of copies of the Dickinson manuscripts, for they would possess the originals.

In October 1950, Harper told Millicent they had "stopped the presses" on *Emily Dickinson's Home*—Harvard had informed them that Millicent must receive the permission of the Harvard College Library Trustees prior to publication for the right to publish any Dickinson material. They said Harvard held all copyrights, past, present and future. "So this is the way to treat an honorable person!" Millicent wrote in her diary. She knew that Harvard was intent on getting all her manuscripts but commented, "it is certainly a curious way to go about getting them."[22]

Millicent was advised by attorneys not to speak with Harvard directly about their demands. Lawyers at Harper told her they were trying to pursue a "friendly settlement" with Harvard, and that the university was "so gentlemanly and so anxious not to get into an argument." But, as Millicent reflected several years later, "It seemed that several of the executives at Harpers were Harvard men, including Mr. Canfield, and they did not wish to risk a lawsuit."[23] And she believed that Harvard was not using "gentlemanly" techniques.

Millicent felt paralyzed. With her books' publication in limbo, she couldn't bring herself to continue working and spent significant time making notes of arguments she wished to pose to Harper to make on her behalf. Among them, she noted, "lawyers know that they can count on my finding a lawsuit distasteful, which gives them license to put on the screws. But does the fact that these manuscripts have been in my mother's and my own possession since before the turn of the century mean nothing? That Austin entrusted their care to my mother?" She consulted with attorneys and librarians who suggested to her that Harvard's claims of complete copyright control were questionable and might not hold up in court.

Millicent also agonized about the situation in her private writings. On November 10, Mabel's birthday, she wrote, "This morning I am on the point of nausea. . . . I think perhaps it is because Harvard (Mr. Montague) should overlook everything except the mere legal precedents, as if there were any, and insist on their rights . . . it has been my dearest wish that Emily's manuscripts should all be together, as they were in the first place . . . what will this mean? A renewal of the feud . . . even if I should win and be vindicated, a stench would have been added by me to the situation that has filled my life and from which I had hoped to retire with a generous gesture." She also noted, "Walter grows whiter and whiter every day. Only a sense of accomplishment he says, will help him. . . . But evil qualities seem to provide strength, witness Gilbert Montague."[24]

Walter and Millicent's frequent conversations about the situation, diligently recorded in her journals and diaries, reflected a sense of collective disbelief. "My first words to Walter were, 'If it weren't serious it would be comic, for the leading university to go to law with a leading publishing house about a matter of legal rights so attenuated that if brought into the open would seem to be nil, they would both be a laughing stock,'" she wrote at the end of 1950. And at the end of that decade she recalled how Walter had taken it "much harder than me. That a great university, one moreover from which he himself as well as I hold degrees, should use gangster methods to get what it wanted was to him incredible."[25]

But with unrelenting pressure from Gilbert Montague, Harvard continued to hold firm. William Jackson came to call on the Binghams, accompanied by a Harvard attorney. They informed Millicent and Walter that Montague's purchase meant that Harvard owned the literary rights to all Dickinson materials. Furthermore, they stated that Millicent did not legally own the manuscripts "which had been in my mother's possession since the 1880s. Many of the letters had been given to her by Austin Dickinson for the express purpose of preventing them from falling into the hands of his wife and daughter, whose wishes Harvard was now putting into effect."[26] But still Millicent did not yield.

After Walter's death in 1952, Millicent felt not only overwhelming sadness and grief but also a sense that the fight with Harvard had played a significant role in shortening his life. "Harvard's policy of intimidation toward me had a lot to do with Walter's collapse," she concluded at the time. And in a 1959 interview, she stated that Walter's demise came from the "agony of spirit that he could not shield me from the threats which he considered not only cruel but disgraceful, underhanded and dishonest. . . . Harvard's mercilessness to me, what seemed like the determination to obliterate, or at least to disparage my quarter of a century of work for Emily Dickinson seemed too much. There was nothing Walter could do to protect me. It seemed to break the spring, and perhaps . . . the will to live." (Interestingly, perhaps still trying to insinuate himself into Millicent's good graces, several years after Walter's death Gilbert Montague wrote her at Christmas: "you have been very much on my mind this December, for I shall always remember how lonely the first six or eight Christmases were after I lost Mrs. Montague in 1941." Millicent responded crisply, "Your letter of sympathy in remembrance of my loss of all that I held most dear has come.")[27] Ultimately, Walter's death also seemed to strengthen her resolve in the disputes with Harvard.

Over the next few years, as the battle dragged on, Millicent considered her options. One was trying to get Harper to publicly announce that "because of threats from Harvard, they were withdrawing the publication of *Emily Dickinson's Home.* That far from the documents being in the public domain they [Harvard] are reviving an ancient feud and threatening me if I am to publish." Another tactic she thought about was getting some man of "impeccable credentials to speak out against Harvard." Charles Cole, with whom Millicent was in very frequent contact, urged her not to try to embarrass Harvard. Cass Canfield from Harper reiterated to Millicent that Harvard wouldn't budge, and he, too, urged Millicent against saying anything publicly. He was certain that Harvard would not be the party to suffer in the court of public opinion. "Besides, who would believe a lone female against the word of Harvard?" Millicent bitterly lamented.[28]

Millicent briefly considered finding another press willing to publish her book but never followed through on this. She also took a page out of Mabel's playbook and tried to get influential men of letters to rally to the cause of breaking Harvard's blockage of her books' publication. In January of 1952 she wrote, "Mr. [Mark] Van Doren is really involved in my crusade to break the strangle hold on publication, having written the preface to *Bolts*. His reply was to the effect that both editions should be available." In 1953 she wrote to Charles Cole, "A few nights ago I had a talk with Robert Frost who brought up the subject of Emily Dickinson . . . I gathered that he is disturbed . . . that Harvard is still threatening Harpers with an injunction if they publish my books. . . . Mr. Frost understands, I think, that something more is involved than my promise to my mother to publish all of Emily Dickinson's manuscripts in her possession." In a later conversation Millicent recorded, "Mr. Frost said, 'I would eat those manuscripts before I would let them go to Harvard. No, I would burn them first.'"[29]

Yet still they were at an impasse. Millicent refused to give Harvard her papers and Harvard refused to allow her books to be published. In 1953, Millicent wrote in her diary, "I wish I could look ahead a hundred years and see where those manuscripts really ought to be—in Amherst with everything else? In the Library of Congress where the papers of a national figure belong?"[30]

While the stalemate between Millicent and Harvard continued, Thomas Johnson was moving forward with his work to publish the variorum edition of Emily's poetry. In 1952, Johnson visited Millicent and begged her to give him the Photostats of all her Dickinson manuscripts, trying to distance himself from William Jackson's earlier efforts and the unopened box of Photostats Harvard had returned. Johnson knew just how to play to Millicent's sensibilities: he was appealing to her on behalf of himself as a scholar, he said, not as an agent of Harvard University. Millicent's attorney insisted that Harvard was still paying Johnson's salary, and under no circumstances should she release any papers to him. But Millicent was stubborn; as ever, her personal convictions took precedence. She stood firmly by her belief that scholarship mattered above all else, and, despite her growing distaste for Harvard and her doubts about Johnson, she decided to give him her Photostats. When Johnson told her that looking through these papers had entirely changed his ideas about the conditions of the poems' composition, Millicent wrote in her diary, "just wait until you have the letters!" She pondered whether Johnson had any clue of the "torment" that his employer had subjected her to for the past couple of years. "Remember that it is not my fault that everything you now want is not at your disposal," she said to him in yet another imaginary diary discourse. Ultimately, she stuck to her justification for letting Johnson see her materials. She concluded in 1959, "At least it could never be said that I had stood in the way of scholarship."[31]

After Johnson had examined the Photostat copies, he asked Millicent if he could see the original manuscripts. Next, he wanted to see Mabel's original transcriptions of the poems, and after that, the letters. Though Johnson spent weeks examining the poems and their various transcriptions, he spent very little time with the letters, since Harvard University Press had commissioned another scholar, Theodora Ward, to work on a new volume of Emily's letters, which came out in 1951. (Ward and Johnson subsequently coedited another volume of Emily's letters published in 1958.)

After Ward's book was published, Millicent was incensed. "In this book partisanship is shown in several ways," she wrote. "by using copyrighted material without permission or acknowledgment; by using unpublished manuscript letters given to Mrs. Ward by me without acknowledgment of their source; by using 29 letters, the original of which were lost, published by Mrs. Todd in 1894, without mentioning the fact that because of their preservation by Mrs. Todd's publication, Mrs. Ward was enabled to include them in her book." Millicent concluded her diatribe by suggesting that Ward was "presenting Sue in the best possible light thereby making almost credible her daughter's picture of her in *Life and Letters*."[32] This book only hardened Millicent's feelings about the behavior of Harvard University—while she was still willing to allow Tom Johnson to see copies of the materials in her possession, she was not willing to relinquish the originals.

After going through all these materials at the Folger Library, Johnson told Millicent the work had been such a strain on him that he could not sleep, that he thought about it all the time and found himself dripping with cold perspiration. Millicent said she shared his suffering. And then "he told me about his interview with Montague, whom he called a 'curmudgeon'; I said I thought that a conservative estimate." She reported that Johnson told her he was "absolutely convinced" that Montague intended to go through with his threat to sue Harvard; that "Harvard is frightened out of its wits and that Harpers also appeared to feel that there is a possibility that Montague will win a suit."

Thomas Johnson then turned to her, Millicent wrote, and told her that there was one way out of this mess: she must promise to give all her manuscripts to Harvard. "He presented a picture of the preeminent place my mother would occupy in American literary history; and the acclaim that would redound to me because of my generosity. That might not interest me so much, he ventured, but that my mother should be given full credit for what she did . . . he thought should appeal to me. . . . 'Don't you want to place your mother where she deserves to be? It would be a very noble thing for you to do.'"

At the time, Millicent recalled she simply reiterated that her goal was to "free this field of literature."

"What I did not say," she wrote, "was that all Montague is interested in now is . . . to show how clever he is, to gain prestige and power. He does not care about Emily Dickinson at all. He would like to have what I have of course. It would make his collection complete and back up his ridiculous claim in June 1950, that Harvard now has 75% of Emily's manuscripts. His bombast has caught up with him."[33]

Indeed, Harvard was putting the full-court press on Millicent. Gilbert Montague, himself, tried to see her on three separate occasions in 1953, but each time she politely turned him down. "I think if the man had been honest and merely said that he wanted to have a talk with me, without subterfuge, the whole miserable business might have ended then and there," she said. Cass Canfield from Harper told Millicent the publisher concluded Harvard's position was intractable and that she should reconsider her own. Millicent's public stance was unyielding; privately, though, her rationale was becoming a bit unhinged. "Of course, if they choose to bring out the relationship between mamma and Mr. Dickinson they would think they could extort anything from me to avoid that. But in that they are mistaken. I have reached a point where the truth is all that matters. I fear no revelation that they could bring out."[34] There is no indication in written communications from Harvard representatives or from Harper that Harvard was threatening to expose the Mabel/Austin relationship as a way of getting Millicent to turn over her papers. It seems she simply drew this conclusion herself.

During this time, Millicent wrote more and more frequently to Charles Cole at Amherst. Sometimes she wrote him daily. In April of 1953, after he had met with Robert Frost, Cole communicated to Millicent that he would try to "point out to Harvard people the error of their ways." Cole wrote that he and Frost would like to see all the Emily Dickinson papers in her possession ultimately come to Amherst "since we believe that anybody working on Emily should spend some time in the town of Amherst as we feel that she was more closely identified with the town than any poet normally is with a single place." Cole told Millicent he would speak about the whole situation with his presidential counterpart at Harvard, Nathan Pusey. While it is true that Cole was doing what he could to bring Millicent's Dickinson collection to Amherst College, he was sincere in his belief that Harvard, in preventing Millicent's books from being published, was doing something antithetical to the mission of an educational institution. Millicent was thrilled at his offer. "Your talk with Mr. Pusey may result in freeing Emily Dickinson from the exclusive ownership of any one person, which has been my objective for more than twenty years ever since my mother asked me to set things straight," she responded to Cole.[35]

President Cole kept his word. In October 1953 he wrote to Millicent, "Mr. Pusey assures me that Harvard truly did not want to prevent the publication of your two works but that they were more than somewhat entangled in the toils cast about them by the donor of the material they have. He also indicated to me, at the close of the conversation, that he thought you would receive an official communication before too long offering to withdraw Harvard's objection to the publication of the books, provided that the books would bear, in an appropriate place, 'published by permission of Harvard University' or some similar statement." Cole concluded, "This, I think, marks a very major retreat from the position that Jackson originally took with you. . . . My general feeling would be that it would be a very good idea to accept the Harvard offer, if made, so as to get the thing settled and the books out even if it did jeopardize somewhat your legal position in these matters. The last would seem to me to have things drag on endlessly, fruitlessly and with increasing bitterness, at the same time that the public and scholars would be denied access to the very important material in your books."[36]

Believing Charles Cole to be an honorable man who placed scholarship first, who understood and respected the place of Emily Dickinson and who admired her work and Mabel's on behalf of the poet, Millicent acquiesced. Several years later, she said Cole had "talked with the new President of Harvard, pointing out the absurdity—not to mention the injustice—of Harvard holding up the publication of scholarly work in which they themselves were interested in order to gain their end. A good deal of correspondence was involved . . . among the lawyers. They finally agreed that if I would, in both prefaces, publish Harvard's claim to the manuscripts in my possession as well as to all copyrights on my books, they would withdraw their threat to Harpers of an injunction." After many months of wrangling, in June 1954, Millicent signed an agreement with Harvard.[37]

Despite this mandate, Millicent managed to get the last word. While the note preceding *Emily Dickinson: A Revelation* reads, "All writings of Emily Dickinson contained herein are published with the approval of the President and Fellows of Harvard College, who claim all the literary rights and copyrights therein," the note contained within the preface of *Emily Dickinson's Home* repeats that language but also contains another sentence. "But, I add, I think the claim is invalid and made without knowledge of what the writings are or from whom or why acquired."[38]

Jay Leyda, a filmmaker and literary historian working on his Emily Dickinson sourcebook, wrote to Millicent about what he called Harvard's "evil impasse" in not allowing her books to be published. When they finally were in print, he commented, "What a bombshell you're sending the world! And a lovely bombshell, too."[39]

Even though Millicent had intended *Emily Dickinson: A Revelation*, her book about the possible relationship between Emily and Judge Lord, to be the last of her four Dickinson books, *Emily Dickinson's Home*, her book meant to contextualize Emily's life, was taking longer to publish. Harper felt there had already been so much delay that they decided to publish the two books in the reverse order. *Revelation* was published in 1954, *Home* the following year. Though Millicent got some strong letters about these books (critic John Ciardi wrote her, "I have just finished reading *Emily Dickinson's Home* . . . and I cannot put it down without telling you how impressive I found it in both humanity and scholarship" and author Jay Leyda wrote her that *Emily Dickinson: A Revelation* was a gift to the world because it delineated Emily's "period of happiness, even though we sense it mostly through its conclusion. . . . But you were right to print these documents, and in exactly this way"),[40] they were largely ignored by the press. That same year, Thomas Johnson's much-anticipated variorum edition of Emily Dickinson's poetry came out, completely overshadowing Millicent's works. Millicent sardonically noted in her diary that Harvard University Press didn't "even have the courtesy" to send her a copy. When she procured one, she observed that the preface contained Harvard's claim of "sole ownership of and sole right of possession in all the Dickinson manuscripts now in the possession of Mrs. Millicent Todd Bingham and all the literary rights and copyrights therein by virtue of Harvard's purchase agreement in 1950 with Alfred Leete Hampson, heir of Emily Dickinson's niece, Mrs. Martha Dickinson Bianchi."

"How can I express the disappointment, the mounting disillusion-ment, the sense of frustration and futility which built up to a climax in those words in the publisher's preface to the variorum edition of the poems published in 1955?" she reflected a few years later. "Here is the very book which I had made possible, the implication was that I had obstructed the work of the Harvard editor when the opposite was the case . . . indeed, without my help and without my manuscripts the vario-rum edition of the poems could not have been possible. It seemed to me then and still seems to me . . . doubly incredible, in view of the fact that all my mother's work, as well as my own, had been used in the prepara-tion of this very book."[41]

Beaten down but not defeated, Millicent maintained in her pri-vate writings that she had continued to fulfill the "sacred trust" that was her possession of the Emily Dickinson materials she had been given by her mother, materials that had "survived uninjured through any vicissitudes, frequent changes of residence, transfers of one stor-age warehouse to another, Florida hurricanes and after my mother's death in 1932, a wholesale burglary of our house in New York." To Millicent, there was still great meaning in the papers she possessed. "As custodian of these precious documents my part is now finished. The collection has been preserved intact. To scholarship I have ful-filled my obligation as honestly and as carefully as I know how to."[42] At this point she knew she would never give the papers to Harvard. She was convinced, as she had been from the start, that she must send the papers back to Emily's home.

In early March 1956, Millicent wrote to Charles Cole, "It is hard to plead my own cause, and I am not in the habit of doing so. And I have tried in writing this letter not to be influenced by the grievous injury I have suffered, professional as well as personal, culminating in the gratu-itous insult of Harvard's published claims. If my gift to Amherst Col-lege is finally accepted, and the literary remains of Emily Dickinson are at last jointly owned by two distinguished institutions of learning, do you not think the time will have come, seventy years after her death, to stop talking about exclusive claims, to put an end to these prohibitive claims asserted by the last member of her family and still being exercised today by Harvard? Or are the wishes of Mrs. Bianchi to continue to dominate the field?"[43]

By April of 1956, the Amherst College Board of Trustees voted to accept Millicent's gift. In the initial agreement, Millicent gave Amherst all of her Emily Dickinson materials and her family archives. The copyrights to her books were reassigned to Amherst, and what became known as the "Todd Family materials" started to be shipped to the college, where they were stored in Morgan Hall "pending decisions about a permanent location."

The Dickinson poems were cataloged by Jay Leyda at the Folger Library and sent to Amherst in two batches, one in 1956 and one the following year. As part of the agreement, Amherst agreed to pay for Millicent to hire an assistant to help with the cataloging, and to pay the rent for a separate space in which sorting and organizing could take place. Millicent hired Gladys McKenzie to help with the tasks at hand. Gladys was a Swarthmore graduate, a pacifist, a Quaker, and had worked as an archivist for the Library of Congress. She had spent forty years working for the National Council for the Prevention of Wars. Bright, extremely well-organized and very independent minded, she was the perfect person to assist Millicent with the colossal task of going through the Todd family papers.

Charles Cole had been dubious from the start about whether accepting the "Todd Family materials" would be as advantageous to Amherst as accepting some of Millicent's other gifts. But in 1960, President Cole informed Millicent the college could not commit two or more rooms in a new building or library and "a separate building seemed even more impracticable." Therefore, he went on, while the Amherst College Board of Trustees "would have been happy to do anything possible in the way of renovating . . . the room assigned as the Mabel and David Todd Room," they wanted to "release" Millicent from the terms of her gift with regard to the family artifacts and family papers, in the case that she would not find this offer acceptable.[44]

Of course, the real jewels among Millicent's gifts, as far as Amherst was concerned, were the Dickinson manuscripts. But as might have been expected given the tortuous and protracted dealings of the preceding decade among several institutions, once Amherst finally had the Dickinson manuscripts in its possession, the controversies didn't end.

"I have never made any concealment of my belief that Amherst College was the logical donee to hold all the Emily Dickinson material," Gilbert Montague wrote to Millicent in May of 1956. He disingenuously added it was to his "regret that this was contrary to the desire of Madame Bianchi and her heir."[45] Millicent was keenly aware of Montague's many ties with Harvard, which seemed to belie his professed "belief" about where Emily's materials belonged. Millicent also knew that her gift to Amherst was an end game. But there were other issues still to be resolved.

"In 1956, having given all of the Dickinson manuscripts which came to me from my mother, as well as all of my copyrights, to Amherst College, I am no longer in a position to make decisions as to how they are handled, but I do retain the right to express an opinion," Millicent wrote, "and the opinion is this—that when a trade edition of the poems of Emily Dickinson is penned it ought to be edited by a person of top caliber, a man of letters, a poet and critic as well as a person of integrity and high purpose." By this time Millicent was convinced Thomas Johnson was not the man for such a job; she railed on him as "a compiler and not a very careful one at that." Millicent fervently believed Amherst had the right to help find an editor for such a volume. "This thing is bigger than a dispute between Amherst and Harvard over legal technicalities. It is a question of a correct text for the standard edition—the permanent form in which the poems of Emily Dickinson will be known from now on. It demands of the editor expertness of the highest order, no less."[46]

Johnson's 1955 variorum edition of the poems compiled Emily Dickinson's poems from all known manuscripts. He arranged them chronologically, according to his best efforts to date them based on Emily's changing handwriting. The 1,775 poems (including both complete poems and poem fragments) in this volume were assigned numbers that are still often used to identify the poems.

Millicent believed that "if Archibald MacLeish could be persuaded to undertake the job of editing, it would be a face-saver all around." Beginning in about 1957, she and Charles Cole corresponded about whether there might be an "Amherst edition" of the poems, which Millicent believed would be "an inspiration" and which Cole believed was "not something to be entered into lightly, for I think it precludes the possibility of ever reaching an agreement with Harvard and I would much prefer to settle everything by agreement." Millicent took it upon herself to correspond directly with MacLeish about this prospect: "Even more I hope that you will be the editor—the one to decide which version of controversial poems are to be included in a standard edition. It deserves no less." But MacLeish demurred. "I am naturally very much pleased that such an idea should have occurred to you—pleased and honored," he wrote to Millicent. "Whether or not I could accept the task satisfactorily is something you and the Harvard Press and Amherst College should think about carefully. I am not in any sense of the word a scholar."[47]

It's not clear how seriously anyone at Amherst considered the idea of putting out another edition of the poems. But in 1960, Harvard decided to put out a new edition. When Harvard made this announcement, Amherst sought legal opinion about whether Millicent's copyrights, which they now owned—including her copyright on *Bolts of Melody* and all the Dickinson poems in it—would be violated. In 1977, Charles Cole wrote that when he first heard that Harvard was considering putting out a new edition he was dismayed that "Houghton Mifflin was going ahead and would ignore Amherst's copyrights relying on permission from Harvard."[48]

Charles Cole knew the prospect of legal action was something neither institution would undertake easily. But as he wrote to Millicent in 1959, "I think there is no way for Amherst to influence Harvard short of a lawsuit and I am in agreement with you that that is undesirable."[49] Cole wished to continue to pursue other ways of trying to influence Harvard, which included an implicit threat of legal action he probably had no intention of ever taking.

The first attorney Amherst consulted couldn't say definitively whether the statute of limitations to transfer literary rights to the poems from Lavinia to Mabel to Millicent had expired. Amherst went on to solicit opinions from several copyright lawyers, including Francis Plimpton (brother of Calvin, Cole's successor as president of Amherst College), Philip Wittenberg and Eustace Seligman, an Amherst graduate and trustee of the college then considered to be the premier copyright attorney in the United States. Seligman's opinion was that "it would be impossible to determine who had title to the words of Emily Dickinson without a court case. He said that if it went to court Amherst had a much better than even chance of winning and sort of indicated that he would enjoy handling our case." Cole sent this opinion to Harvard's president. "There was a long pause during which I know Harvard sought legal opinions too. My guess is that it was appalled by the thought that it mightn't/didn't have good title even to the material it had bought."⁵⁰

In the years that followed, Cole suggested that there were a long series of negotiations between Amherst and Harvard. All along, he recalled, "Amherst took a high moral stand. We did not want money, but would want justice done to Mabel Loomis Todd and Millicent Todd Bingham for their arduous work in editing and publishing the poems. . . . Amherst also wanted recognition of the fact that publication of poems to which it held copyright was by its permissions."⁵¹

In 1960 incoming Amherst College president Calvin Plimpton and Harvard's Nathan Pusey signed an agreement that stated that a future complete edition of Emily Dickinson's poems should include *both* Harvard and Amherst in permissions, and Harvard agreed to "suggest to the editor of any future edition of the poems that they include suitable recognition of the contributions to scholarship made by Mrs. Bingham and Mrs. Todd." Though not specifically spelled out in this agreement, there was, perhaps, a tacit understanding that were the agreement to be signed, neither institution would take formal legal action against the other. This followed Cole's belief that "agreements" between educational institutions were vastly preferable to lawsuits. Harvard University's Leslie Morris, curator of Modern Books and Manuscripts at Houghton Library, believes a subtext was "an agreement to disagree," for not everything was defined in the agreement.[52]

But perhaps "agreements" are also less enforceable. At the end of 1966, Plimpton wrote to Pusey complaining that recent books contained neither of the stipulations earlier agreed to. In January of 1967, Pusey responded to Plimpton that reprintings of the poems didn't acknowledge Amherst but would in the future, and said that while Harvard couldn't dictate to any editor what she or he should say about Millicent's and Mabel's contributions, "we are calling the matter now to the attention of the various editors of editions already published so that they will have the suggestion before them before any further reprintings are issued." Plimpton reported back to Millicent later that year: "In President Pusey's letter to me, he promised that they would take pains to make sure that any reprinting, as well as new publications, carried the same acknowledgement of Amherst's permission and also they would make the most vigorous urging to make sure that your scholarship and that of your mother's was included   I think, however, in general they sound exceedingly contrite and I think things are back on the tracks again."[53]

Though Millicent wrote in her diary, "Amherst College prefers not to tangle with Harvard," in fact at least two presidents of the college appear to have made a good faith effort to do just that. Charles Cole's consistent correspondence with Millicent over several years demonstrates that he seems to have gone beyond thinking her a difficult person to deal with, and just humoring her, or talking about warblers to get her papers; he had a good deal of respect for her work and worked diligently to broker an agreement with Harvard that he believed was both fair and honorable. Calvin Plimpton, for his part, pursued this agreement, and went on record with his belief that Harvard had violated the spirit if not the letter of the agreement, and he tried to set it right.

———

In 1957, Millicent found herself astonished by something she received in the mail. "On my return last night from New York I found your letter of

January 30, informing me that the Trustees of Amherst College voted to confer upon me the Degree of Doctor of Letters at Commencement," she wrote to Charles Cole. "This is not only a very great surprise, it is an equally great honor, which I accept with gratitude and with humility. Please express to them my deep appreciation of an honor which stamps with their approval my long crusade to free the work of Emily from the exclusive claims which in the past have hampered scholars in their study of her poetry. This honor will compensate for the long years of grueling work and frustration."[54]

The citation read at Amherst's commencement that year noted Millicent's achievements as a geographer and author of scholarly books and articles, and as a conservationist in establishing the Todd Wildlife Sanctuary on Hog Island. But then the citation stated:

> In more recent years you have changed your career and completed the unfinished work of your mother by deciphering, editing and publishing hundreds of hitherto unknown poems of Emily Dickinson; in three books based on careful research and a deep knowledge of this community you have portrayed the ambiance in which that poetry was created. As recognition of Emily Dickinson has grown apace, it has brought with it an increased realization of the debt owed to your mother and to you, not only by scholars but all those whose minds are touched or whose hearts are quickened by the eternal and penetrating beauty of the lines written by America's greatest poet here on Main Street in Amherst Town.[55]

In November of 1960, Millicent wrote in her journal:

> It is curious that I have always felt that my mother's bequests to me were not gifts but trusts.... Emily's manuscripts? They were a trust, a sacred trust, to be returned as Colonel Higginson and as my mother hoped, to Amherst. But those were trusts not to me or to mother alone, but to those yet unborn who will

care for an untouched wilderness . . . and the manuscripts must be placed where they will not only be safe, but revered. To have accepted money for either trust—a precious gift temporarily in my possession—would have been unthinkable—out of keeping with my attitude and endeavor and set of values.[56]

And in this trust Millicent had succeeded.

When the battles over where Emily Dickinson's papers would reside were finally resolved in 1960, Millicent reflected about the toll it had all taken. "I have been trying to think what has motivated me all along," she wrote.

> I have thought it was loyalty to my mother's wishes, whether or not I agreed with her objectives. But I think it is rather the wish to rectify an injustice. It may be that I cannot change this drive until I am destroyed by it. . . . Had I given the Emily Dickinson manuscripts to the Library of Congress in 1945, as they wanted me to do, I should have been spared the past years of anguish the righteous indignation—Walter would have been spared the disillusionment and suffering of the last months of his life . . . and my story, with a different ending from what, if I live, it will have now.[57]

The battles with Harvard left her personally scarred; she could never quite get over them or leave them behind. Having Emily's papers divided between two institutions had certainly not been Millicent's wish, nor her intent. The twisted and complicated machinations that led to the papers' dispersal led Millicent to think of it all as the reviving of an ancient feud. Using language that might seem overly dramatic but that reflected what she deeply felt, she described the disputes over Emily's papers as battles that perpetuated her own "lifetime of suffering because of the Dickinsons [and] what they did to my family, taking it on the chin always."[58]

The saga divided Emily's manuscripts between Harvard and Amherst, and left a fraught legacy whose resonances linger many

MILLICENT WITH L. QUINCY MUMFORD, DIRECTOR OF THE LIBRARY OF CONGRESS.
ALTHOUGH MOST OF HER COLLECTION ENDED UP ELSEWHERE, MILLICENT
DONATED THREE EMILY DICKINSON POEM MANUSCRIPTS TO THE LIBRARY OF
CONGRESS IN 1956.

decades later. But in the end, Millicent still firmly and uncompromis-
ingly held on to her principles. She had managed to keep her promise to
Mabel and publish all the Emily Dickinson materials in the camphorwood chest. She had done all she could to enable scholarship. She had
not taken a penny in exchange for the treasures she held. And finally,
she had delivered her Dickinson manuscripts back to Emily's home,
where she felt they truly belonged.

⌒

CHAPTER 15

SEEKING CLOSURE AND MEANING (1960–1968)

"To finish the unfinished work of others has been a sacred trust"

"Piles of papers, preliminary sorting on every chair in every room," Millicent wrote anxiously in November 1960. "I woke at 4 and tackled the first pile, which took me almost an hour . . . these residual piles and basketfuls of clippings, and mementoes, the thousands of books, the trunkfuls of materials saved by mamma and through the decades, honored by me." The task was overwhelming. "Yesterday my diaries were placed on the open shelves, opposite me, more than 70 years of them, and nearly 50 of mamma's." Fortunately, Millicent had the very able help of Gladys McKenzie, the archivist-cum-personal assistant whom she had hired to assist her with the complicated jobs before her.

Millicent had worked with Gladys since 1958, and she had quickly become reliant on her clear thinking and organizational skills. Gladys helped her sort through the mountains of papers and photos, recorded lists and notes, assisted in transcribing her journals and diaries and in turning scribbles into neatly typed pages. She aided Millicent in her ongoing negotiations about where the papers would ultimately be housed. Despite her dependence on Gladys, Millicent never made much effort to get to know her. Indeed, she continued to refer to her as "Mrs. Mackenzie" in her journals, seemingly not recognizing that she was consistently misspelling her name. But Millicent's lack of care about someone with whom she worked so closely did not go unnoticed; in a folder innocuously labeled "notes," McKenzie left behind a few thoughts about her boss for future researchers to contemplate: "She is neither tolerant nor very generous; interested only in herself and family and reading about the growth and development of her soul. Besides it didn't grow, just as petty and mean about certain things at end of life as earlier."[2]

Ever the list maker, Millicent typed up endless inventories of what she thought needed to be accomplished. There was emptying Walter's room and getting all of his papers a home and finding someone to write his biography; there was the need to catalog all of her parents' papers; there were the boxes of things being shipped to Amherst College for the "David and Mabel Todd Room"; there were thousands of books to be appraised and for which she had to find repositories. There was also the need to put her own papers in order and place them somewhere. She made innumerable registers of what was to go where, and since her arrangements changed with some frequency, made more lists. She placed paintings with the Mead Gallery at Amherst College and with the Concord Antiquarian Society; much of Mabel's original art went to the Botanical Museum at the Carnegie Institute of Technology. She gave artifacts to the Amherst Historical Society, to the Peabody Museum at Yale, and to the Peabody Essex Museum in Salem, Massachusetts. She sent books to many different libraries. But there were still the tens of thousands of papers—letters, articles, drafts of books and articles, drafts of drafts, medical documents, legal documents, scrapbooks, the diaries and journals of three generations of Wilder women and their men. Millicent wrote ruefully, "It is obvious that I shall not live to finish. The question is, how to manage so that I achieve the serenity to write at least some chapters in my own life story."[3]

Just as she had believed that Emily Dickinson's papers ultimately belonged all together and belonged in Amherst, Millicent also believed that her family's papers should reside there as well. This was part of the package deal she made with the Amherst College Board of Trustees. But by early 1960, President Cole "released" her from this agreement, should she wish to find another home for her extensive family papers and artifacts. Disappointed, Millicent felt Amherst's decision not to set up a "museum room" for her parents' expedition artifacts and allocate sufficient space for them was in some way a lack of validation of her father's "almost forty years" of service as a professor there. "So my mother's dream, and my goal, to carry out her dream, has disappeared," she wrote.[4] In her frustration, she began to realize that Amherst's library was not set up to receive or preserve her voluminous collection.

At the same time, Millicent was busily corresponding with Yale professor Richard Sewall, at work on his seminal biography of Emily Dickinson. Sewall was well aware of Millicent's dilemmas, and he knew what a large collection of papers she had. Unlike Amherst College, Yale *was* prepared to process and house large document collections. Sterling Library had been acquiring rare books and collections of personal papers since 1924; plans to open the Beinecke Rare Book and Manuscript Library were under way while Millicent was desperately trying to find a suitable repository. Sewall suggested to Millicent that Yale might be a better home for her papers than Amherst.

In consultation with librarians James Babb and Howard Gotlieb at Yale, Sewall met with Judith Schiff, a new librarian in the historical manuscripts division. After getting to know her, Sewall made a suggestion: "There is a woman in Washington D.C. named Mrs. Bingham. I think she'll like you. I would like you to go speak with her." Judy Schiff was dispatched to the nation's capital, where, on November 19, 1963, she spent three hours with Millicent. Sewall's intuition was correct: Millicent *did* like Schiff. She liked what Schiff said about the new state-of-the-art archival facilities at Yale. She liked Schiff's familiarity with the nineteenth-century families that had intersected with her own. She liked that Schiff seemed to understand her urge to keep all of her family papers together. She was also very taken with Schiff's understanding that even some odd documents, like canceled checks, might one day have relevance in telling the story of the Bingham/Todd families. "She must be an unusual administrator," Millicent mused. "At present, the impression she creates is one of quiet competence in doing what has to be done." For her part, Schiff felt she connected with Millicent because of their shared interests in the century past, and she thought Millicent, herself, "dressed and spoke like someone who came from another era."[5]

Because she trusted Judy Schiff and thought that Richard Sewall would be the only person to do justice to the story of Emily Dickinson and present a thoughtful portrait of Mabel that properly credited her work (while not delving too heavily into the story of Mabel and Austin), Millicent decided to leave her vast collection of family papers to Yale. Toward the very end of her life, she said, "Richard Sewall is my reason for having given to Yale the archives of my family on both sides dating back to the 18th century."[6]

Yale agreed to take over Amherst College's payments for rental of a separate space in Millicent's building in which the sorting of documents could continue, and also to pay Gladys McKenzie's salary for the duration of time it took to do this work. Gladys would also prepare a "scope note" for Yale, summarizing the approximately thirty-three thousand documents that had already been cataloged and shipped to Amherst, which would be transferred to Yale. Once the documents began arriving in New Haven, Gladys would be on site to assist the librarians with any questions and provide Millicent with regular updates (even writing her in 1968 about how progress on the Beinecke Library construction had been stalled by some environmentally oriented Yale students positioning themselves in front of a tree that was to be bulldozed). James Babb wrote to Millicent, "Be assured that . . . [Sewall] and I are thrilled that your wonderful archives will in time be the property of Yale University. May I also reassure you that we shall do our very best by and with them."[7] The remaining papers began to be shipped to Yale in 1964, and kept coming through June 1968.

In the early 1960s, Millicent noted in her journal that she had spoken with one of her oldest friends, Marta Milinowski. "When I told her that I had been sorting things in Amherst her only remark was, 'Still?'" Sorting things, and trying to sort things out, were the major preoccupations of most of Millicent's adult life, and continued to be in her final years.

In a 1959 interview, Millicent admitted that, approaching her ninth decade alone, she felt frightened and overwhelmed, "wallowing in unfinished business."

"The drive has taken on added pressure," she said, "a sense of urgency because there is not much time left."[8] Indeed, the last decade of Millicent's life became a race against a ticking clock, amplified, perhaps, by rapidly changing times.

As she watched the unrest of the 1960s unfold, Millicent regularly commented on her distrust of President John F. Kennedy ("an untested Democratic president at this time of the gravest danger that has threatened us in our lifetime, maybe ever," she wrote of the Cuban Missile Crisis). She fulminated about the building war in Vietnam ("the number of those killed . . . has the gruesome tone of a scoreboard for a game") and race riots across the country ("the anarchy in Chicago seems uncontrollable").[9] Despite her concerns about news of the day Millicent was more focused on the past. Even after finding permanent homes for her family's papers, Millicent felt that there was still unfinished business to resolve. Despite or maybe because of her unresolved feelings and what she referred to as the complication of her parents' "many faults and built-in tragedies," she was determined to find appropriate and lasting ways to pay tribute to each of her parents and to Walter. "To finish the unfinished work of others has been a sacred trust since my twenties when I tried to present the greatness of one of my teachers, Mrs. Stearns," she wrote in her eightieth year. "The editing of other people's writing as well as the care of other people's treasures is that to which I have given my life . . . it is the deposit left within."[10]

When Mabel died on her beloved Hog Island, Millicent knew that preserving the island permanently would be a meaningful tribute to her mother. However, it would take many decades to ensure the island's conservation. In 1936, Millicent had established the Audubon Nature Camp for Adult Leaders—quite prescient when viewed through the lens of twenty-first-century standards. The idea that teachers needed

MILLICENT (*RIGHT*) WITH RACHEL CARSON AT THE HOG ISLAND AUDUBON CAMP
DEDICATION CEREMONY, 1960.

an understanding of environmental issues to teach children about ecology was a radical notion in 1936. Teachers and "adult leaders" would
come to Hog Island in groups for two-week stays during the summer.
During that time, naturalists, ornithologists and other scientists would
instruct campers about the ecology of the island. "The main objective
was, if teachers of nature study to children can be sufficiently enthused
with the subject, then children's instinctive, inborn interest in birds and
beasts or flowers can be salvaged. That interest will not die but will be
fostered and encouraged . . . such camps will help to shield us from the
reproach of future generations."[11]

Millicent leased the camp to the Audubon Society for one dollar a
year, in return for their payment of taxes and her periodic occupancy of
one of the cabins. As Millicent entered the final period of her life, she was
keen to ensure that the camp and Audubon stewardship of Hog Island
would continue in perpetuity. Apart from her own mortality, Millicent

began to feel greater urgency about making permanent arrangements for Hog Island when she read the work of Rachel Carson.

Rachel Carson was a marine biologist by training and a writer by proclivity. She brought these passions together, along with her ardent belief in the need for conservation, in a series of books, essays and articles published in national periodicals such as *The New Yorker*, *Nature*, and *Collier's*. Her 1951 book, *The Sea around Us*, was on the *New York Times* best-seller list for more than eighty weeks and won the National Book Award for Nonfiction. Around this time, Carson became interested in the use of pesticides and what they might be doing to the environment. Millicent increasingly believed Carson's work was important; indeed, it came to define the American environmental movement after Carson's untimely death in 1964. Drawn together by their interests and by their common stories (each had mothers who had had strokes but "wouldn't admit it . . . the same old story"), the two women trained in science turned writers became friends. When Millicent arranged for the Audubon Society to take full ownership of Hog Island and held a dedication ceremony in August of 1960, Rachel Carson was one of the invited guests. Carson even mentioned the event in her seminal 1962 book *Silent Spring*: "In the summer of 1960 conservationists from many states converged on a peaceful Maine island to witness its presentation to the National Audubon Society by its owner, Millicent Todd Bingham. The focus that day was on the preservation of the natural landscape and of the intricate web of life whose inter-woven strands lead from microbes to men." To Millicent, Carson wrote, "Ever since I left you yesterday I have been thinking of how full your heart must be, and of the thoughts that must fill your mind—thoughts of the past, and of the future as your dreams for the Island are fulfilled. There should be for you a deep satisfaction in having been able to make such an abiding contribution to preserving not only the tangible beauty of the island, but the things that are 'eternal.' "[12]

Millicent paid tribute to her mother in her remarks at the dedication ceremony and with the placement of a large boulder in the middle of the island that bears the inscription:

The Todd Wildlife Sanctuary presented to the
National Audubon Society by Millicent Todd Bingham,
in memory of her mother, Mabel Loomis Todd,
who, fifty years ago, saved this island wilderness and
thus shaped its destiny as a perpetual preserve.

Privately, Millicent realized her efforts to pass along Hog Island to the Audubon Society were part of a complicated obligation she felt she owed Mabel. "As I felt responsible for [my parents'] conduct in my childhood, so now, in my old age, I am feeling responsible for the record they leave behind," she penned in notes for the autobiography she never wrote. Elsewhere in this file, she jotted down on a scrap of paper, "Hog Island Mamma's project, the camp for adults, mine."[13]

Similarly, Millicent worked to ensure that the tract of land Mabel had purchased in 1909 in Pelham, just outside of Amherst, would continue in a conservation trust. Millicent first suggested this to Amherst College's president Charles Cole in 1946 and her gifts to Amherst a decade later included the land. But the actual creation of a preserve didn't occur until 1961. Throughout that time, Millicent had been in close touch with Cole, and then his successor, Calvin Plimpton, about her intent for the land and what it should be called. On May 21, 1961, the Mabel Loomis Todd Forest was dedicated. The program commemorating the event noted, "Although both Mrs. Bingham and her mother are perhaps better known for their dedicated efforts as editors of the poems and letters of Emily Dickinson, their contributions to conservation have been extensive . . . with the presentation of the Mabel Loomis Todd Forest the long range hopes and plans of mother and daughter are now realized."[14]

Millicent's determination to preserve both Hog Island and Pelham Knob was ultimately an effort in land preservation and conservation, but it was also an effort to do what she thought Mabel would have wanted done. Amazingly, in an unpublished manuscript from 1936, Millicent wrote, "The problem of conservation has been brought to public attention very often of late, in books and articles, over the radio . . . but in spite of all the activity, however, the general public is not yet aware of what it is all about. . . . They are . . . results following causes which we, ourselves, have set in motion—destruction of forests, overgrazing, marsh drainage, and so on."[15] Years before anyone uttered the term "climate change," Millicent seemed aware of how human development can have far-ranging environmental consequences. Though she understood the ecological imperatives of conservation, she was also cognizant that her efforts to preserve the land were motivated by wanting to complete Mabel's unfinished task.

Millicent fulfilled her desire to find some way of ensuring Walter's contributions to the field of psychology were recognized and memorialized in less complicated ways. Walter's papers were divided between the Pentagon and Carnegie Mellon University. After his death, Millicent gave money to establish a yearly Bingham Lecture on an aspect of industrial psychology. She prepared a bibliography of his books and articles, and gave his library to the University of Oslo. She identified Lewis R. Frazier, an industrial psychologist who had worked with Walter at the Carnegie Institute of Technology, as the perfect person to write Walter's story, although he never did.

Memorializing her father was more difficult. Millicent was conscious of the many ways in which her father had been broken. "He did important work as a young man," she wrote, "and that has been overlooked because of the extravagances of his later years. A matter-of-fact account of his achievements is needed also as a back-drop for the tragedy which not only broke the back of his career, piled on top of a succession of cloudy eclipses, it broke his heart."[16] Millicent attempted to find someone to write a biography of David several times, unsuccessfully.

By the early 1960s, Millicent felt she had accomplished most of the things she had promised Mabel. She'd succeeded in getting the long-hidden Emily Dickinson materials published, and, through her own books, credited Mabel with the work she had done on Dickinson's poems while excoriating the Dickinson women—Vinnie, Sue and Mattie—for their behavior and for the "incorrect" versions of Emily they had promulgated. Millicent had managed to place most of Mabel's "curios," papers and paintings, and she had ensured the continued preservation of Hog Island and Pelham Knob. But there was one remaining task she knew Mabel had wished her to accomplish that Millicent was still loath to take on: publishing Austin's and Mabel's letters to each other. Throughout the battles with Harvard, Millicent feared someone would expose Mabel and Austin's illicit relationship; when Amherst professor George Whicher wrote a review of Millicent's books in 1945, she was alarmed at his elliptical allusion to the affair. Millicent knew that she would be mortified should the information in Mabel's journals and diaries go public; she was well aware of the power of the letters between Mabel and Austin, which she had held on to for years— even though she long denied reading them or fully understanding their import.

Millicent was also cognizant that the story of Mabel and Austin was "basic to an understanding of Emily Dickinson—who through the years suffered vicariously for Austin, and directly through Sue's 'ingenious cruelties.'" But the topic deeply unsettled her own conscience. "The day has gone when people think of a great passion, extra-curricular though it may be, as sin. But so it still seems to me. And it was my mother who sinned. . . . I knew that because it seemed to me so wrong, I could not touch it. I gave up the idea of a biography, acknowledged the fact that the relationship had existed, but, as throughout the previous half century, buried it, together with all recognition of the feud, deep within." And yet, she knew the story would somehow have to be told. She worried that if she didn't maintain some control over it, Mabel's story would be "besmirched" by so-called scholars and "others [who] will let loose in the same vein."[17]

"Other unfulfilled obligations still resting upon me include those to my mother's diaries covering nearly seventy years, and to her journals," Millicent wrote in her journal. Millicent knew she was not the right person to do anything other than preserve these documents: "How is it possible for me to present a great passion which ennobled two people which was to me sin? That is my limitation. I am not fit to write about it. But here are the documents, left in my charge, the journals and diaries and letters, and the authorization, implicit from my mother, explicit from Austin, to print them." She felt somewhat reassured, though, once she figured out where to safely place these documents. "By a provision of my will they are to be entrusted to the care of Richard [Sewall], and to his judgment. He will decide who is capable of writing her life, which will require the services of as 'multi-aptitude' a person (Walter's description of her), as herself. But that is a book the writing of which is inevitable, sooner or later. It will be safe in Richard's hands."[18]

Millicent's trust was not misplaced. Indeed, Sewall would not delve deeply into the Mabel/Austin letters in his 1974 biography of Emily Dickinson. However, in the preface he wrote for Polly Longsworth's book, published a decade later, which *did* recount the love letters in great detail, Sewall stated, "Veteran novel readers will rub their eyes to remind themselves that this really happened. And since it happened close to Emily Dickinson, it is important." Separately, in an unpublished tribute to Millicent, whom Sewall had gotten to know quite well, he wrote, "She was as fair-minded and just as it was possible for an intensely loyal daughter to be. She urged me constantly to 'get the other side of the story,' guided me to the sources, and, in turning over the family archive for my use, gave me a free hand to do with it as I would. What she wanted was to have all the truth told."[19]

Though she never quite allowed herself to dig into it very deeply, Millicent knew the obligations she felt to memorialize her parents and control how their stories were presented were duties she took on with a conflicted heart, with neither nostalgia nor joy. The weight of her filial debts hung on her heavily, for she was acutely, painfully aware of how flawed her parents had been. "In place of a sense of the joy of life I had a sense of responsibility, not only for my own conduct, but for the justification of that of my parents as well," she explained. More than that, Millicent came to believe that her duty to deal with her parents and their problems truly prevented her from having a fulfilling life with Walter:

For almost twenty years after I married him it was responsibility, and anxiety for their physical safety. For my father, whether to
keep him confined and endure his desperate unhappiness and his
reproaches to me as the cause of it or arrange for his comparative
freedom and agonize over what he might do next. For my mother,
partially paralyzed, but intrepid and gallant in her Florida home
which became a center of social life and musical life, I was always
anxious about the hangers on who benefitted from her susceptibility to art and beauty and feared lest her financial resources . . .
would not hold out.[20]

In her final years, Millicent spent significant time reading over her own
diaries and journals, as well as reading Mabel's. But for Millicent this
wasn't simply a passing indulgence; it was a painful and time-consuming
obsession.

"What are these drives, so compelling that they warp people's lives?"
she pondered in 1963. "To carry out my mother's wishes, to right her
wrongs, was mine, which took the place of the wish to comfort and
encourage Walter, which faded into second place in comparison." Millicent spent hour upon hour, day after day, rereading her own diaries, the
first volume of which she had begun in 1887—seventy-six years' worth
of the minutiae of her life. "I had thought that, being my daily companion, to which I turned each day before I went to sleep, they would
contain a record of my inner life. Certainly there was no one to talk
to about it." But what Millicent found were the listings of her life, and
not its meaning. Even her own companion journals, which offered more
insight into her thoughts and dreams, did not yield quite the road map
to her mind and heart, nor the level of self-awareness and analysis, that
Millicent sought in the last years of her life. She also spent enormous
amounts of time reading through Mabel's diaries and journals, and her
notebook "Millicent's Life," which she said, "gives me clues as to why, as
a child, I felt as I did."[21]

In a remarkable decade-by-decade recap written in 1959, Millicent elucidated what she believed to be the major events of her life, as gleaned from reading her diaries and journals, and reflected on their meanings. And yet even here, as she looked back from the perch of old age, Millicent's understanding of what drove her own life was still limited. She continued to point to "the Puritan point-of-view," as the polestar that guided her. It explained her reticence, her thriftiness and her morality. Millicent returned time and again to the "inheritance of my forebears," as a way of understanding herself and her place in the world. It was a convenient explanation that enabled Millicent to grasp her ideas and behaviors without delving more deeply into the other relational and personal issues that had shaped them.

In addition to her diaries and journals, Millicent was a lifelong, inveterate list maker. One of the many running lists she compiled was her "typed list of MTB's illnesses." Over the years she'd experienced many medical issues, the most serious of which were her bout with diphtheria and subsequent heart problems in 1908, and the type 3 pneumonia that nearly proved fatal in 1937. As an adult, she was excessively concerned with her health. There is a large file at Yale of her frequent letters to and responses from doctors about her real and imagined medical issues. As she reached her eighty-fifth year, Millicent was still well enough to travel to Hog Island and to Amherst one last time. But throughout her last years, while Millicent continued to read newspapers and comment on the news in her diaries ("the weight of the President's crookedness plus the hideous slaughter in Vietnam . . . leaves little hope that the man is not bent on self-destruction," she wrote of Lyndon Johnson), she did not delineate her own physical decline in the type of detail she had earlier devoted to both her actual and her psychosomatic infirmities.[22]

By 1965, Millicent finalized her will. She made clear not only where the remaining items in her possession would go but also how she wished her remaining funds to be dispersed. This included gifts to environmental and educational organizations, establishing the Walter Van Dyke Bingham Fellowship in Psychology, and, in a nod to her mother and an acknowledgment of the importance of their shared lineage, to the Mary Mattoon chapter of the DAR in Amherst. Her last effort to take care of her parents was to leave money to Wildwood Cemetery.

After Walter's death, Millicent had had some correspondence with the Green Mountain Marble Corporation in Vermont about his headstone. At the time, she let them know what she wanted on her own headstone, since she had no relatives to carry out her wishes. She queried about the possibility of making "a simple headstone of black slate" for a "marker at my family lot at Amherst, Mass. With a few lines indicating my place of burial in Arlington National Cemetery."[23] The company wrote back saying they didn't make any headstones out of slate, and apparently Millicent never followed up on finding anyone who did, for there is no such marker at Wildwood. Millicent's profound ambivalence carried on through the end, her intent to permanently connect and yet distance herself from her parents, signposted in slate, unrealized.

Millicent carefully listed the people she wished notified by telegram when she passed away (Walter's surviving brother and nephew), and the people she wanted notified by mail (the list included President Calvin Plimpton at Amherst College, the presidents of Vassar and Dickinson Colleges, and Richard Sewall at Yale). She meticulously specified the music she desired played at her funeral, to be held in the Washington Cathedral (including the adagio from Beethoven's first quartet, Bach's Suite #3 and the Kyrie of Mozart's unfinished Mass).

In 1964, Millicent observed, "it is curious how my life has been dedicated to the cause of the dead—Mrs. Stearns, Grandpa . . . my mother, even a brief memoir of Walter. But chiefly to carrying out the wishes of mother, to set the record straight about Emily Dickinson. . . . Tributes to the dead, in deference to the truth. Should not the final one be to myself—who have so short a time to wait? It would be in line with my life-order." Indeed, this is precisely what she did. Millicent carefully wrote her own obituary. Published in the *Washington Star*, it's not surprising that Millicent's abbreviated version of her life led with:

Mrs. Millicent Todd Bingham, a teacher, geographer, and author who compiled hundreds of previously unknown poems of Emily Dickinson, died Sunday after a long illness at her home. She was the daughter of David Todd, a member of the Amherst College faculty for almost 50 years, and Mabel Loomis Todd. Her mother was an author and the first editor of Emily Dickinson's works. During the 1890s, Mrs. Todd worked without compensation on the poetry, but she locked the manuscripts in a chest when a lawsuit estranged the Dickinson and Todd Families. In 1929 she gave her daughter the key and charged her to prepare the material for publication.

After situating herself squarely as her parents' daughter (and perhaps mistakenly giving her father credit for ten years more than he actually served as a faculty member at Amherst) and setting up her life's main work as a continuation of Mabel's, Millicent's obituary recounts her own educational, travel, geographic and literary accomplishments. It's also notable—and typical—in the obituary she prepared for herself, both that Millicent chose to emphasize Walter's achievements and that she was "a descendant of John Alden and of the New England clergyman Jonathan Edwards."[24]

Her obituary in the *New York Times* also included snippets of other things Millicent had written about her life. " 'I grew up with a feeling of wonder at the mysteries of nature, earth, sea and sky,' she said once. 'My father studied the stars on summer nights through a telescope, my mother studied flowers, mushrooms and trees, and I followed the birds.' " In the rest of this obituary, it's clear that Millicent also followed her parents in many other ways—on expeditions and with work on Emily Dickinson.[25]

It is typical and significant that the wording Millicent selected for her own tombstone, beside Walter's at Arlington National Cemetery, presents simply her name and dates, adding only "Wife of Lt. Col. W V Bingham, USA." It is only the back of the stone that contains the phrase, "Army Education Corps, France, 1918–1919," a phrase she didn't need as

MILLICENT MADE ARRANGEMENTS TO BE BURIED BESIDE WALTER IN ARLINGTON
NATIONAL CEMETERY, HUNDREDS OF MILES FROM HER PARENTS AND AMHERST.

a requirement for burial at Arlington, since she was a veteran's spouse.[26]
When she died on December 1, 1968, these final instructions were put
into place, memorializing her forever as she saw herself—in relation to
other people, a link in the chain of a Puritan tradition, last in the line
of Wilder women, someone who let other people's work and stories take
precedence over her own.

"I wish I had all day to write about the profound emotions that have
swept over me during the last twenty-four hours," wrote Millicent on a
cold spring day in March 1960. NASA had launched *Pioneer V*, a space
probe designed to investigate interplanetary space between Earth and
Venus. "With my mind full of these fairy tales, and what it would all
have meant to my father, I went out into the moonlit night, dazzlingly
bright reflected from the snow." The day of the launch coincided with an
eclipse. "It was almost uncanny that at 2:30, ten minutes before total-
ity began, I waked." Millicent went to a window and stared up at the
cloudless sky, noting the reddish-orange glow of the moon and the street

lamps' contrasting greenish beam, both of them throwing light on the snowy ground. It was a clear eclipse, unlike any she had seen.

The next morning, she took Mabel's *Total Eclipses of the Sun* from her bookshelf. This made her think of her parents—how David's eyes "were fixed on the heavens night after night, observing celestial events which he had predicted," and how Mabel's focus was always elsewhere—the next project, the next book, the next talk, Austin. "How small must have seemed the conflict of human emotions," she wrote. "The essential nobility of . . . character . . . is emerging, like the bright limb of the moon, from shadow, the shadow of the cloud that shrouded [them] and made me lose them . . . from view in misunderstanding."[27]

CHAPTER 16

UNPACKING THE
CAMPHORWOOD CHEST

When Mabel and Millicent opened the camphorwood chest in 1929, they released far more than just the last of Emily Dickinson's unpublished poems and letters. They also unsealed evidence of Mabel's passion for Austin and the betrayal and vindictiveness she believed perpetrated by the Dickinson women, as well as Millicent's often-repressed memories and conflicted feelings about her parents, and the consequent compromises in her own life.

All these ghosts haunted Emily's legacy. The love and the animosity between members of the Todd and Dickinson families affected the dispersal of Dickinson's poetry and letters; the legal battles over copyright and ownership lasted for years. Arguably, they've never quite disappeared. Since Millicent's death in 1968, opening the camphorwood chest has fueled debates over the editorial decisions she and Mabel made, and fired disputes about who has the right to define Emily Dickinson's persona and personal life.

Today, Emily Dickinson lives on in many modes—literary, biographical, visual and fictional. She's been brought to life on stage and screen. New elucidations of her life and work are born and grow in online communities worldwide. The appropriation of the so-called Belle of Amherst has taken on a life of its own.

But none of this would have happened without the contributions of Mabel Loomis Todd and Millicent Todd Bingham. The key to their influence on Emily Dickinson's legacy lies in the drama and tragedy of their own lives and their complicated relationship with each other.

———

How could Mabel feel she knew Emily well enough to be her interpreter when she never actually met her face-to-face? In contrast to the fictional confrontation depicted in the 2016 film *A Quiet Passion*, Dickinson biographers ranging from Polly Longsworth to Lyndall Gordon, websites including the Emily Dickinson Museum, Britannica.com and Wikipedia are all definitive: "Todd never met Emily Dickinson." As Longsworth points out, despite Mabel's early suggestion in an 1882 journal entry that "I know I shall see her. No one *has* seen her in all these years except her own family," in fact, Mabel never even laid eyes upon the poet until after her death, if then. Mabel even admitted under oath at the 1898 trial that she had never met nor spoken with Emily.

But clearly, Mabel believed that she did know Emily, and knew her fairly well. There are tantalizing, if secondary, suggestions that she did. Historian Sharon Nancy White suggests, "it would probably be a mistake to dismiss Mabel's respect and fondness for Emily Dickinson as mere posturing," pointing out the exchanges of notes and art in various forms as well as contemporaneous references in Mabel's diary to her "dear friend." Literary analyst James Guthrie references a note Emily wrote to Mabel on July 19, 1884, several months after the death of Judge Lord, which, he believes "assumed some knowledge on Todd's part of her [Emily's] involvement with the judge." On the evening of Emily's death Mabel noted in her diary she had spent "a sad, sad near hour" trying to comfort Austin, before going to bed, herself, "full of grief." Each of these instances might well suggest that despite never having met, Mabel and Emily did, indeed, form a bond.[1]

And Millicent? In 1965 she wrote to Charles Green at the Jones Library in Amherst, "How very thoughtful of you to send me the notices of the sale of Emily Dickinson's house! My early childhood was spent largely in that house, so I have a special affection for it."[2] But it is difficult to believe that Millicent actually spent much of her childhood at The Homestead. After all, the majority of Millicent's early years were spent living with her grandparents. Emily died when Millicent was only six, and, given the tensions that arose during the Mabel/Austin relationship, it seems unlikely she would have spent much time at the Dickinson family home. If she did spend time there, it is plausible she might have encountered Emily, either because her father—of whom Vinnie was quite fond—brought her there, or the same way other neighboring children did when the reclusive poet gave them baked treats lowered from her bedroom window in a basket.

But it is also possible that Millicent actually did encounter the poet. There is that famous line from one of Emily's letters to Mabel: "I trust that you are well, and the quaint little girl with the deep eyes, every day more fathomless," a letter that delighted Mabel so much she copied it over in her journal. Mabel certainly thought, and told Millicent, that Emily had been referring to *her* as the "quaint little girl." In 1907, Millicent received a letter from her friend Carol Fleming, in which Fleming wrote she had just read *The Letters of Emily Dickinson* and "I love the reference in one to you as the 'quaint child with the deep eyes.'" Years later Millicent repeated this story to Jean McClure Mudge, an author and teacher who in the 1960s lived in the Dickinson Homestead with her family and helped to rehabilitate the house when Amherst College purchased it. Mudge wrote in 2015, "She did confirm that she, Millicent, at age six, had seen her [Emily] at the Homestead. She did not say who had brought her there, but it could well have been Austin. . . . I remember thinking as I looked at Millicent that I was seeing the same eyes that ED had seen." And in a 2016 interview, Douglass Morse, who, as a young man had worked for Millicent on Hog Island, commented on her unusually "deep and intense dark eyes"—a description similar to the one Mabel reported as having come from Emily.[3]

But having met Emily or not, both Mabel and Millicent were firmly convinced that they knew her through what Austin and Lavinia had told them, and from their collective immersion into her letters and poetry. The two were indignant about what they saw as flawed images of Emily projected by others. In the preface to the 1931 edition of Emily Dickinson's *Letters* Mabel wrote, "the Emily legend has assumed a shape unrecognizable to one who knew her."[4]

Mabel and Millicent both pointed to Mattie Dickinson Bianchi as the source of "the Emily legend." This included portraying Emily as alternately otherworldly ("Taken from a distant sky . . . a creature as different as fallen meteor from pulsing star") or a flesh-and-blood woman so wounded by love early in life she had withdrawn from the world. Mabel and Millicent rejected the idea that Emily was some kind of "star-dust"; they saw Emily as a complicated human being, whose retreat from the world was slow and deliberate, and came about for complex reasons.

Millicent went a step further. In *Emily Dickinson: A Revelation* she posited, "Those who cherish the legend of a lifelong renunciation because of a broken heart in youth may prefer not to entertain the thought that her fidelity was not confined to one person"—that in fact, Emily experienced love not only as a young woman, but later in life, too. Many Dickinson biographers have speculated about the people who might have been objects of Emily's affection at different points in her life. The Emily Dickinson Museum website entry on "Emily Dickinson's Love Life" concludes, "Whatever the reality of Dickinson's personal experiences, her poetry explores the complexities and passions of human relationships with language that is as evocative and compelling as her writings on spirituality, death, and nature." Upon reading her book author Jay Leyda wrote to Millicent that he knew some would feel "wronged" by it because it countered the legend of the loss-sequestered Emily, and "a totally unhappy Emily is so much easier to examine!"[5]

So strongly did Millicent reject Mattie's image of Emily (and so indignant did she remain about it), that she even offered a posthumous rebuttal in her self-authored obituary: "She had little patience with the legends which made Emily Dickinson a recluse mooning in her chamber over her hopeless love. . . . Mrs. Bingham wrote that the poet's 'inch by inch withdrawal' was a gradual thing, natural in an artist who needed

ONE OF EMILY DICKINSON'S ICONIC WHITE DRESSES.

time to read and write, and for a woman upon whom heavy domestic demands were made."[6]

Millicent's refutations of Mattie's image of Emily were endless: "As the last of her family, Mrs. Bianchi's invention of the legend of a white-robed figure, 'a little white moth,' retiring from the world because of a broken heart, was accepted as authentic. It was a story she felt would take hold. And it did," she wrote in 1964. Of course what Mattie actually wrote in *Emily Dickinson Face to Face* offered a somewhat different explanation for Emily's proclivity for white dresses: "It puzzled women who wore sensible stuff dresses why Emily wore white the year round. Various fantastic tales were circulated about her . . . the only person who never thought of it as a mystery was Emily herself, as she moved about her father's house and garden. They could no more approach her than they could make the moon come down and sit on their parlor sofas!"[7]

And in truth, Mattie wasn't the only one to profit from discussing Emily's attire and the image it projected: Mabel, too, often included phrases such as "the recluse garbed in white" in her many talks about Emily, likely understanding that this vision and its symbolism would help to build intrigue—and to promote sales.

Some of the debate over Emily Dickinson's image focuses on what her relationship with Sue Dickinson truly was. If, as some have argued, Emily loved Sue as more than a friend or sister-in-law, it raises several issues. Were the "Master" love letters meant for Sue? Did Mabel (or Mabel and Austin) conceal any indications of Emily's love for Sue in the editing of her poems? Did the editing tone down or minimize the poet's true intent? Was this why Sue demurred or declined Lavinia's request that she edit Emily's poetry?

Dickinson scholars Ellen Louise Hart and Martha Nell Smith suggest that the relationship between Sue and Emily is "a story left untold." They point out that while much scholarship has been devoted to trying to understand and contextualize the Master letters, relatively little has focused on the extensive correspondence between Sue and Emily—correspondence which, they argue, is "passionately literary" and provides evidence of "romantic and erotic" expressions between the sisters-in-law. Hart and Smith posit that the relationship between the two women was suppressed by Mabel and Austin's desire to deter anyone from noting the intimate exchanges between Sue and Emily, and by Mabel's ambitions to market Emily's writing (including Mabel's role in crafting an image of Emily as a reclusive "spinster poetess" clad in virginal white, and the exclusion of Emily's letters to Sue in Mabel's original and subsequent edited volumes of letters). Hart and Smith conclude, "There was simply no place in the official Dickinson biography for the revelation of an immediate confidante and audience for her poetry—particularly not one who lived next door."[8]

Martha Nell Smith writes elsewhere that while Emily's expressions of love for Sue "might comfortably fit under the umbrella of [the] nineteenth-century female world," in fact "Dickinson's own words suggest that her participation in the female world of love and ritual is not so innocuous" and contained clear expressions of Emily's carnal desires and "powerful sexuality." Smith, along with several other scholars, suggests Mabel's Emily Dickinson was denuded because all references to Sue were scissored out, stripped or altered. "That the adulterous editor would want to deemphasize the importance of her lover's wife to the poet whom Loomis Todd commodified but never met face to face is not at all surprising." Smith also proposes "Austin" might be the culprit, but notes, "in referring to the mutilator as 'Austin,' all I have is Mabel Loomis Todd's word that Dickinson's brother, Austin, was indeed the perpetrator."9

While there is no doubt that Mabel had and harbored significant animosity toward Sue, there isn't any direct evidence in her correspondence, diaries or journals that she deliberately "mutilated" any of the Dickinson manuscripts. In fact, she took great pains to preserve them. While she did not print the letters between Sue and Emily (only a few of Sue's letters to Emily still exist), she probably did not have access to them, at least not in their entirety. And with regard to the development of "the Emily myth," while Mabel certainly did help to craft and popularize an image of the poet as someone removed from society, dressed in white, she did not think that Emily was someone who chose to remove herself from society entirely, or that Emily lived a life without love. Nor did Millicent, who spent years of her life trying to search for more direct evidence of a love relationship between Emily and Judge Lord.

Contemporaneous critics in the late nineteenth and early twentieth centuries largely praised both Mabel's and Millicent's editing of the poems, especially when contrasted with Martha Dickinson Bianchi's efforts. Though they credit Mabel with the considerable work she did to get the poems published, more recent analysts have failed to recognize Millicent's significant contributions. Millicent published *Bolts of Melody*, a volume that encompassed not only complete poems but also what she referred to as "scraps." Millicent believed these incomplete poems contained some of Emily's most powerful work, and also wanted to bring out the complete contents of the camphorwood chest so that "all possible data" would be available for interpretation and analysis. She probably would have been delighted to see Marta Werner and Jen Bervin's 2013 book *Emily Dickinson: The Gorgeous Nothings*, which artistically reproduces Emily's "scraps" and matches shapes, scale and types of paper on which these unfinished poems were written, and the 2017 exhibition of Emily's manuscripts and "scraps" at the Morgan Library in New York, depicting the poet's careful craft and creativity. Mabel and Millicent should be credited for their prescience in recognizing that Emily's "scraps" were well worth saving.

Mabel's and Millicent's work in bringing out four volumes of Emily's poems and two editions of her letters positioned them squarely in the debates over the intentionality in Emily's work and the explanations for what inspired it. Mabel's Emily Dickinson was largely influenced by Austin: she was the brilliant and loving sister who had a special relationship with her brother, a relationship that was compromised by Susan. Mabel's Emily was playful but her words could carry "sting"; she was "mysterious," her heart was "unfathomable." Like her own sensibility, Mabel's Emily was influenced and inspired by the beauty and mystery of nature. Mabel initially thought the poetry was "odd" but "full of power." She later came to believe that the poetry was "brilliant" and "opens the door into a wider universe."

With her ear for music, Mabel could appreciate the nontraditional tonalities and rhythms of Emily's verse. Though she acceded to Higginson's plan to normalize some of Emily's word choices to make the poems more palatable and marketable to the nineteenth-century audience, in doing so she was betraying her own ideas about Emily's intentions. In Richard Sewall's classic biography of Emily Dickinson he concludes Mabel's greatest distinction "was being among the first to 'hear' Emily Dickinson and far from being put off by her irregular form, to sense its creative power."[10]

Mabel probably thought Judge Lord had been the love of Emily's life (she had instructed Millicent to find out all she could about him), but also that he was a love her family sought to suppress. Mabel no doubt saw parallels between her own relationship with a much older married man and what she imagined Emily's situation had been. All of this would have strongly influenced how Mabel interpreted Emily's poetic intent.

Millicent's Emily was largely influenced by Mabel's. But she was convinced that Emily's poetic intent could be gleaned by the poet's word choice. So Millicent bent over backward to "discover Emily's own preference" for word choice and punctuation. Millicent thought that despite offering many alternatives, Emily left behind clear clues about her preference. Millicent's Emily was someone ensconced in the small universe of her own family and her own small town in ways that influenced her worldview and her art. But not surprisingly, given Millicent's own ambivalent feelings about Austin, her Emily was not as beholden to her brother as Mabel's Emily was; Millicent's Emily was capable of thinking and acting independently, despite what her austere older brother might have thought. Ultimately, wrote Millicent, "when all is said, explanations do not explain. Mystery remains, but it is the mystery of genius."[11]

But the debates go on. Among "ED" followers there are "the Mabel people" and "the anti-Mabel people." There's hardly anyone who feels neutral. In literary criticism, biography and fiction, Emily Dickinson's story is often filtered through the lens of those who believe Mabel Loomis Todd's role was central and inspired by her love for Austin, and those who feel Mabel's role was not as fundamental and *too* dominated by her love for Austin. Critics say this relationship negatively colored how she edited the poems, what she did and did not include in the letters and how she contextualized the story because of her jealousy and hatred for Sue and Mattie. Mabel is alternately portrayed as a hopeless romantic and martyr to her undying love for Austin, which led her to do what she did "for Emily," or an overly ambitious, manipulative, self-centered vamp, far more interested in what Mabel wanted than anything she would do "for Emily." Some texts are more neutral, but many, as Emily Dickinson once wrote, "tell it slant."

And the "war between the houses," as Richard Sewall so evocatively titled it, went on for decades. Quite apart from its dramatic effects on the lives of the people involved, it inspired the 1897 lawsuit Lavinia brought against the Todds, it set up the "battles against Harvard," as Millicent later termed them and it was ultimately responsible for Emily's papers ending up in two different repositories. Noting that "writing about Emily Dickinson, one cannot possibly hope to please every reader," Martha Nell Smith alludes to the contradictory images of the poet promulgated by divisive parties with deep-seated convictions based on issues emanating from long ago.[12] Millicent tended to refer to the rift in dramatic terms—"freeing the work of Emily Dickinson," "the ancient feud," "the Greek tragedy." Toward the end of her life Millicent wrote of "the expression of 'fiery indignation,' . . . the bubbling stream of venom generated eighty-two years ago and still active. In this connection, I have sometimes thought of the course of certain diseases which gain in virulence as they pass from host to host."[13]

Neither Mabel nor Millicent would be surprised to know this caldera established so long ago has uneasily continued to cover hidden primal heat. Occasionally it even erupts. In 2013, Harvard University announced the launch of its online Emily Dickinson Archive. The open-access website was designed, Harvard said, to bring together thousands of Dickinson manuscripts held not only at Harvard but also those held at Amherst College and six other institutions. Ostensibly, for the first time ever, researchers, fans and poetry aficionados would be able to turn to one place and find all of Emily Dickinson.

As Dickinson scholar and Mount Holyoke College professor Christopher Benfey said in a New York Times article: "With Dickinson, the truly bizarre thing is the quarrel has been handed to generation after generation." The old rivalries that caused the papers to end up in two main libraries seemed revived by this effort at digitization. A representative of Amherst College was quoted in the Boston Globe and the New York Times as being upset that Amherst had little input into decisions about the online archive, that the project didn't mention Amherst more prominently, that Harvard decided to limit the poetry it posted to those poems published in Ralph Franklin's three-volume version of Poems of Emily Dickinson—not coincidentally published by Harvard University Press. "What this site does is reaffirm that Franklin's text is the ultimate authority," said Amherst's Mike Kelly in the New York Times article. "It's a missed opportunity. I'm disappointed to be pulled back to a situation from the past, where ownership is the most important thing," countered Harvard's Leslie Morris in the same article.[14]

Undoubtedly, both Mabel and Millicent would have smiled wryly. The embers of the long-ago feud that caused Emily's papers to end up in archives across the Commonwealth of Massachusetts were still burning. Millicent would have approved of the Harvard Emily Dickinson Archive project in principle because digitization provides the access she believed was needed for true scholarship. But if she could, Millicent would also have been quick to point out that Amherst College, in fact, began its own Emily Dickinson digitization project years earlier—before Harvard. Their open-access website, which contained all of the Dickinson materials they owned, went live in August 2012. Amherst has also digitized all of the Todd/Bingham materials related to the Dickinson collection; the project to make them widely available is well under way. Millicent surely would have been delighted to know her desire to have all of Emily's papers freely available for researchers and poetry lovers around the world is becoming realized. Millicent's most ardent wish was to have "all the data" available to the public. As she wrote in *Ancestors' Brocades*, "The feuds are now dissolved in death. But the task remains unfinished."[15]

Another way of understanding the enduring legacies of Mabel and Millicent is to see them as women who were pushing up against the edges of conventional roles of their time. Each of them did so in both her professional and personal lives. These qualities made them unusual among women of their respective generations, but their activities and proclivities in many realms also influenced their interpretations of Emily's persona and poetry.

Mabel was a rare female public intellectual. Some contemporary historians see nineteenth-century ideas surrounding "modern intellectualism" as a progression from the evangelism emanating from the religious revivalist movements in the early part of the century to the advent of mass democracy and the ensuing growth of social movements like abolitionism, and the transcendentalist influence on literature, philosophy and social activism. Political theorist and author Jeremy Jennings points out that women, however, were "largely denied a public voice and scarcely existed as intellectuals."[16] But Mabel carved out a niche for herself as one of them, giving her some of the fame and credibility she so desired, and a platform for promoting not only herself but also the life and works of Emily Dickinson.

Through her dozen published books, hundreds of published articles and enormous number of talks given across the country on a vast array of topics, Mabel Loomis Todd was well-known in her own day as someone to read, someone to listen to and someone to watch. She knew it and was not modest about her accomplishments. She wrote of them frequently in her journals, seemingly oblivious to how phrases like "my life is positively the most brilliant one I know of" might be interpreted years later by those who read her musings. She kept scrapbooks of articles that sang her praises. Some articles tried to contextualize her achievements as outside of traditionally gendered frames: "How does she find the time? This is Mrs. Mabel Loomis Todd. Besides being the wife of an Amherst professor, she is an author, lecturer and society woman." Mabel was very much aware of her unusual role, summed up in one article that noted, "She is unquestionably the dean of American women lecturers."[17]

Similarly, Millicent's work as a geographer pushed up against the boundaries of what her generation of women did. It wasn't just being the first woman to receive a doctorate in geography and geology from Harvard, but her work with Raoul Blanchard and on the work of Paul Vidal de la Blache, translating cutting-edge ideas about geography and helping to build contemporary theories of regional geography that must be recognized as important and as pioneering. Millicent defined herself first as someone trained in science; she always strove to be thorough and methodical, she believed that good decisions or worthwhile analyses could be made only in the context of looking at "all the data," whether those data were about land use patterns, geological formations or Emily Dickinson's letters or poems.

Mabel's and Millicent's beliefs in the importance of conservation made them unusual among not only women of their day but among all people of their respective eras. They also pushed up against the edges of what historian Nancy Cott refers to as the "woman's sphere" of the eighteenth and early nineteenth century, through their travels and writings. Although by 1887, the year of the first eclipse expedition on which Mabel accompanied David, it was becoming more common for American women to travel abroad, it was still highly unusual to go to such places as Japan. Or Tripoli. Or the Dutch East Indies, Ceylon, Peru or China. Mabel made a name for herself writing about her unusual experiences and introducing American readers to the interesting cultures and people she observed. Though clearly no ethnographer and most certainly writing through the lens of her own ethnocentric and white middle-class perspective, Mabel's descriptive travel writing portraits can be seen as a series of fascinating—if biased—still lifes of places few Westerners had experienced, and still fewer women.

Finally, in evaluating the enduring legacies of Mabel's and Millicent's lives and the ways in which they pushed the professional envelope, we can look at some of the civic bequests they left behind, ranging from organizations they helped to found to land they helped to preserve. Neither Mabel nor Millicent was directly involved in any of the major progressive social movements of their respective eras. Mabel's tendencies were more liberal than Millicent's decidedly conservative politics, which only seemed to deepen in the last two decades of her life. Mabel was proud of her grandparents' involvement in the abolitionist movement and mentioned it frequently. Millicent consistently evinced more narrow views about anyone coming from a racial, ethnic or religious group different from her own. Mabel was the one who rejoiced in collecting "curios" from around the world and saw them as pieces of art, not oddities; Millicent viewed them as embarrassing "heathenish" clutter in her childhood home. Neither of them could be assessed as social reformers, despite their progressive views on women's professional roles and on civic and environmental issues.

It was not only in their professional lives that Mabel and Millicent defied the standards of late nineteenth- and early twentieth-century women; it was also in their personal ones.

To the extent to which she is remembered today, Mabel is likely either known as Emily Dickinson's first editor or as Austin's lover, some kind of nineteenth-century sexual free spirit. Historian Peter Gay wrote of Mabel in his classic book *Education of the Senses*, "Cheerful, talented, sociable, popular enough to arouse jealous gossip, she was capable of sustaining affectionate and amorous ties." Gay analyzed Mabel's male attachments as "unfinished oedipal business," since Eben was an astronomer by affinity and David one by training, and since Austin was, in fact, almost the same age as her own father. Mabel's continuous justifications of the affair as more vaunted, holier and entirely different from the love of mere mortals were, Gay believed, manifestations of "the very firmness of her snobbery that permitted her to be flexible about her morality."[18]

Mabel wasn't the only Victorian woman to be involved in a sexual relationship outside her marriage. Because divorce was so uncommon, writes historian Stephanie Coontz, relationships outside of American Victorian-era marriages actually were far more common than we might think. Mabel, herself, seemed to recognize that her relationship with Austin might have found more acceptance, if not other means for codifying it, in another era: "We should have been born later, that is all. One or two hundred years from now the world would rejoice with us." And Mabel certainly was unusual to have written so explicitly of her passions.[19]

Mabel also perhaps flouted the social conventions of nineteenth-century women in writing so openly about her ambivalent feelings on motherhood. As Nancy Cott has written, for "venturesome" women the traditionally female duties, such as being a mother, "had severe limits. For many women it utterly failed to 'resolve' the problem of inferiority, becoming instead a wellspring of strain." Mabel was one such "venturesome" woman who keenly felt the strain. While one can see her outsourcing of Millicent's care as a selfish gesture designed to free Mabel to paint, to write, to travel, to spend less-encumbered time with Austin, it's clear from her private writings that Mabel did so with at least some degree of ambivalence. When she wrote honestly, "I have not the quality of motherhood sufficiently developed," she was clearly articulating sentiments in a way that very few women of her era would have—even in their most private writings.[20]

Like mother, like daughter—at least in some ways. Millicent, too, pushed the boundaries for women of her time in her personal life. Millicent's decision to put off marriage until age forty was certainly unusual, regardless of whether the heartbreak over Joe Thomas or the overall ambivalence she might have had about relationships with men, in general, accounted for it. From the written record Millicent left behind it's not clear whether the relationships she had with several women were friendships that were emotionally intense and physically affectionate, or if they were romantic relationships with a sexual component. And her decision to seek private psychiatric help not once, but twice, in the late 1920s and then again in the late 1930s, was extremely rare, even among white and economically privileged women.

In an unpublished master's thesis Brooke Steinhauser writes that Mabel was

> relentlessly self-conscious of her own driving ambition. Throughout her lifetime, she privately referred to a "presentiment" that guided her actions—a sense of her deepest desires nearing their inevitable fulfillment. The candor of her private journals, diaries and correspondences, juxtaposed with her extraordinarily diverse public lifestyle and public works plainly illustrates a woman encountering and grappling with her own identity in an era of tremendous social change . . . simultaneously pushing the boundaries of accepted social mores.[21]

And yet, despite Mabel's prevailing optimism that she would fulfill her "deepest desires," ultimately the things she most wanted from life were the things she did not achieve. Mabel's fundamental professional aspiration was to be widely known as a great writer. Though she did enjoy some success, placed articles and essays in the leading newspapers and magazines of the time and published books with excellent presses, she regretted never having written the great American novel, as she once expressed to David, or anything that would endure and be recognized as classic. Mabel wrote a lot about writing; she often expressed frustration in her journal that her writing wasn't as "brilliant" as she thought it should be. Reflecting on her mother's life, Millicent wrote of how Mabel never succeeded "in doing the one thing she most wanted to do."[22] Millicent seemed to understand the irony implicit in Mabel being remembered more for her achievement of editing and promoting the writing of Emily Dickinson than for her own. Ultimately, Mabel's most important professional aspiration went unrealized.

Nor, of course, did Mabel ever realize her most salient personal goal, to live with Austin as his legal and societally sanctioned wife. Even though Mabel wrote after his death of her periodic certainty that she felt Austin's presence with her, in the end, she was buried in a plot of land next to David and near her parents, up the hill but out of sight from where Austin lies with Sue and their children at Wildwood Cemetery.

And Millicent, similarly, despite all of her many and considerable accomplishments, never achieved the things to which she most aspired. Her lifelong fears of being a dilettante were perhaps unfounded, and yet she knew that switching her academic focus from geography to Emily Dickinson in the middle of her professional life would ultimately mean she would not gain much recognition as a geographer or be fully accepted by the academy as a literary scholar, where even her possession of a Harvard PhD carried neither relevance nor cachet. She harbored resentment toward Mabel for having convinced her to turn her life's work to Emily Dickinson—even though Millicent, herself, found this work to be rewarding in many ways. Millicent never realized other professional goals she held: to be known as an inspirational teacher or to become a college president. Her anxiety about being "productive" never ceased; wrote Richard Sewall, "Like her mother before her she had the energy of six women, was never idle, and expected no one else to be . . . a day with her was a test."[23]

Millicent's personal life was similarly unfulfilled: she never had a satisfactory and joyful romantic relationship with anyone, and she never had a child.

The complex mixture of love, obligation, disappointment and disgust Millicent felt for both of her parents was something she tried to reconcile throughout her life. She never got over her unexpressed but keenly felt anger at Mabel for turning over the Emily Dickinson work to her, which "caused" her to be away from Walter when he died, and she was never able to resolve her guilt at institutionalizing her father. "So little did I understand because I never talked with him or with my mother, about anything that mattered," she admitted to herself in 1963.[24]

There's one more enduring story within the narratives of Mabel Loomis Todd and Millicent Todd Bingham, and that is the story of their relationship with each other. Anyone who is a mother or a daughter knows that even in the best of circumstances, mother/daughter relationships are complicated. And Mabel's and Millicent's circumstances were certainly not the best of circumstances.

To a certain extent the differences between Mabel and Millicent represented what historian Thomas Schlereth has described as the "paradoxes that abounded in Victorian American life." Mabel's interest and beliefs in the occult didn't necessarily square with her knowledge about science or astronomy, but it wasn't contradictory for Victorian Americans to believe in both the supernatural and the natural worlds. Yet Mabel's faith in things she couldn't see or easily explain sharply contrasted with Millicent's interest and beliefs in the rigor of science and her need to elucidate everything clearly and precisely. Millicent found her mother's beliefs in the occult inane and privately ridiculed them.

Another paradox of the era that exemplified the gulf between this mother and daughter was the contrasting idea that women should be "paragons of moral virtue" with the knowledge and reality that many Victorian women, in fact, were not. Millicent firmly believed the former and forever held the latter against Mabel, failing to see that both ideas coexisted during the era. Ironically, both women believed they had been born in the wrong time period. Millicent, who lived well into the twentieth century, believed she belonged in the past and thought herself to be more Victorian than her mother, and Mabel, whose life encompassed more of the nineteenth century than the twentieth, always believed she and Austin should have lived in a future time. The contrasts between their belief systems exemplified not only the time in which they lived but also the push and pull of this difficult mother/daughter relationship.

More recently, there has been further empirical work in child and human development, psychology and psychiatry studying mother/daughter relationships. Attachment theory may be particularly useful in examining the Mabel/Millicent relationship, because Millicent so clearly did not spend a significant amount of time as a very young child with her mother (social scientists suggest that this is the time when being with a parent is necessary for forming healthy bonds that will model mutually beneficial relationships), had in many ways a difficult if not dysfunctional relationship with Mabel, and as an adult, had a very difficult time forming primary attachments that were satisfying.[25] Her marriage to Walter started without love or physical attraction; in the thirty-two years they were married Millicent learned to love him, or at least to love his devotion to her and to her parents under very trying circumstances. But here, too, Millicent's reflections show that her attachment to Walter's memory was perhaps stronger than her attachment to Walter.

Mabel and Millicent's relationship was close in some ways, and, therefore, complex. This started from the very beginning, and lasted throughout their respective lifetimes. After Mabel died and Millicent read Mabel's thoughts in her diaries and journals, they alternately helped her to make sense of the world in which she'd grown up and left her feeling all the more ambivalent about it. Late in life, Millicent struggled with her antipathy, obsessed over her mother's "squandering her talents," "needless vanity" and "unwittingly pathetic soul."

An only child with two parents who were very needy in different ways, Millicent deeply felt the tug of her filial responsibility. In fact, she felt the weight of generations upon her. The Puritan inheritance of which she was so proud also limited her. She felt singularly responsible for dealing with the "accretions of the ages" that she had inherited.

But in the end it was Mabel's relationship with Austin Dickinson that weighed Millicent down the most. It was not only a defining feature of Mabel's life, but one that defined Millicent's, though she sought to suppress it for decades.

When Millicent opened the camphorwood chest in 1929 she found Mabel's and Austin's letters, along with the trove of Emily Dickinson

MABEL IN 1930 (*LEFT*) AND MILLICENT IN 1958 (*ABOVE*), TOWARD THE ENDS OF THEIR RESPECTIVE LIVES.

poems. She knew then what she had long suspected. But still, she chose to put aside this most personally painful part of the task. After Mabel died and Millicent inherited all of her private writings, she was forced to confront this relationship she had long known existed—and long repressed. But even then, she simply could not fully understand the long shadow that Mabel's relationship with Austin cast over all their lives. Even well into her eighties, Millicent struggled to reconcile her complicated feelings for the mother whom she dutifully loved with her feelings of true ambivalence.

"In writing about my parents I want to know the truth about them, with their many faults and built-in tragedies," mused Millicent in 1964. She cited a line from one of Emily's poems: "I like a look of agony, Because I know it's true." And then she concluded, "I cannot remember a time when I did not recognize, almost at a glance, fraud and pretense. I despised it. I felt it instinctively and turned from it with revulsion. Emily's remark, 'I never consciously touch a paint mixed by another person,' has been for me a life-long maxim."[26] Perhaps Millicent never encapsulated the essence of her relationship with Mabel better. It's not surprising that she did so with a line from Emily Dickinson.

Poet, feminist and essayist Adrienne Rich once wrote, "The cathexis between mother and daughter—essential, distorted, misused—is the great unwritten story."[27] Mabel and Millicent left behind a massive system of largely unmarked yet intertwined paper trails that reveal much about the directions of their complicated relationship. And it is certain that without the complex push and pull between this mother and this daughter—the love tempered by other emotions, the enduring sense of filial responsibility despite the knowledge of flawed relationships, the entangled web in which their own interactions were so thoroughly enmeshed—the world might never have known all of the poetry of America's greatest poet. Mabel Loomis Todd and Millicent Todd Bingham opened Emily's door.

⌒

$\mathcal{S}$ORTING THROUGH
THE CLUTTER

People often ask me how I first encountered Mabel Loomis Todd. Not surprisingly, it was through Emily Dickinson. Her life—what was known about it as well as what was not—and her poems' curious path to publication, always fascinated me. Fragments from some of her poetry stuck in my head ever since I first encountered them. I have a clear memory of a poster from my girlhood: fluttering birds and intertwining rainbows with the "Hope is the thing with feathers" line emblazoned across the top (from the poem Mabel titled "Hope" in the second volume of *Poems*).

During college my interest in Emily Dickinson intensified. I frequently walked by the two Dickinson homes in Amherst and wondered about the lives of those who had lived there. I did some research about Helen Hunt Jackson, poet, former Amherst resident and childhood Dickinson friend. I knew that she had encouraged Emily to share her poetic gift with the world, and yet Emily still demurred. I didn't know why, which only increased my curiosity. I wondered what had happened, after Emily. How was it that all of these iconic poems came to be published? I began to read biographies of her, which, in turn, introduced me to Mabel.

Fast-forward to the time, now a number of years ago, when my interest in nineteenth-century Amherst residents led me to read Polly Longsworth's *Austin and Mabel.* The more I investigated, the more there seemed to be to Mabel, beyond her work on Emily Dickinson's poems and aside from her relationship with Austin. I also learned a little about Millicent, whose work on Dickinson seemed largely undocumented and whose life story was virtually unknown. When I sought out Polly Longsworth she suggested to me that the best untold story was probably the one about several generations of "Wilder women." So in a sense, Emily Dickinson had led me to Mabel and Millicent.

Writing this book has meant learning to sift through the clutter of two intensively collected lives. Upon ascertaining that there were over seven hundred boxes of primary source material in Yale's Sterling Library, my first reaction was unmitigated joy: what a dream for a biographer to have two subjects who so meticulously—some would say, obsessively—documented their lives! My second reaction, upon starting to read through the well-crafted finding guide to this enormous collection, was panic: How do you start to wade through the hundreds of thousands of pages and try to make sense of someone's life? I had a span of almost a century's worth of both Mabel's and Millicent's reminiscences to go through. That Mabel wrote about her memories following Abraham Lincoln's assassination and Millicent, her thoughts following John F. Kennedy's, gives a sense of the breadth of the time period their lives covered.

Real history can often be found in the small details. Millicent had written in the preface to *Emily Dickinson's Home,* her contextualization of Emily's life, that she had been encouraged to realize that there "are no trivia." I came to agree with her.

I began by reading through all of Mabel's diaries and journals on microfilm. I did this because that was the only part of the collection I could get on interlibrary loan from Yale, but it turned out to be a very good strategy. I learned about Mabel through her own interpretations of her life, chronologically. Along the way, I needed to discover how to interpret the visual symbols she used (marking her sexual activity and menstrual cycle); how to understand her euphemisms ("a caller in the afternoon on the upstairs porch"); indeed, how to read her handwriting—penmanship that changed at different points in her life and altered radically after her 1913 stroke and paralysis required her to learn to write with her left hand. Historian Peter Gay once joked, "If you can't read it, it didn't happen," but I have worked to decipher writing that was compromised or illegible or faded from view, to try to understand what happened in Mabel's and Millicent's lives.

Reading Mabel's outlines of her talks and how they changed over time, or learning the differences between what she wrote in her diaries and her journal helped me understand this woman beyond the written record of her life. Seeing how Millicent laboriously thought through letters, wrote drafts and then wordsmithed them, how she wrote out pages of imaginary conversations she didn't dare to have in real life, or how she made list upon list upon list (and seemingly saved them all), gave me invaluable insights into an insecure, repressed and brilliant little girl who grew into an insecure, repressed and brilliant woman.

Once, I was sitting in the reading room of the Archives and Special Collections of Amherst College's Frost Library, reading Mabel's booklet *Witchcraft in New England*. Suddenly, with an epiphanal flash, I knew—knew for certain—why Mabel had become so obsessed with the witches of Salem. It was actually two chance phrases in the text that I thought I had read before that caught my eye: "The proceedings against 'witches' were instigated by all sorts of personal grudges and pique, and free rein was given to all maliciousness," and "the borderland of two worlds."[1]

Indeed, I *had* read these phrases before. They were in Mabel's journals. She'd written of "personal grudges, pique and maliciousness" in describing the ways she thought Sue Dickinson was treating her; "the borderland of two worlds" was a phrase she'd piloted when pondering where Austin had "gone" after he died. Suddenly, as I read what Mabel wrote in 1906 about the witches of New England, I knew that her interest in this topic was not merely academic—it was deeply and intensely personal. She had felt as persecuted and marginalized as the "witches" surely did; she had felt wronged by a judicial system meant to guarantee fairness; she, too, had wondered whether the dead are still in some way with us. I connected with her inner life through these words.

Getting to know Mabel and Millicent so intimately has also, inevitably, meant that I have had emotional moments along the way. When I came upon an envelope containing a lock of both Mabel's and Austin's hair, I held them in my hands and shivered, marveling at Mabel's impulse to preserve these bits of themselves, together. When I tracked down several tapes of interviews Millicent had recorded and heard her voice, almost a half century after she died, it was simultaneously eerie and yet oddly familiar, because I had long had the sense of hearing her whisper in my ear. Her voice sounded exactly as I'd imagined it would.

There was the time that I knew that Austin was going to die before Mabel did. He was becoming weaker daily, irreparably ill. Her pitiful diary and journal entries show that while in some ways she realized he would not recover, in others, she was in complete denial. And then came the day of August 16, 1895. Mabel wrote of her utter devastation; I sat there in the library, tears streaming down my face. A librarian came up to me and asked whether I was okay. "Austin died!" was all I managed to blurt out.

There was the moment I was sitting in the reading room at Yale, poring through Millicent's journals from France documenting her slow and painful realization that in fact, Joe Thomas was lying to her—and had been lying all along. Still, she continued to refute and justify what she saw. She didn't even wish to believe herself. "Millicent!" I wanted to shout right there in the library. "For someone so brilliant, you are so dense sometimes!"

And of course, there was the time that I read in Mabel's fall 1932 diary that she would write about the experience of seeing the last eclipse "tomorrow." But with the omniscience that comes from being a historical storyteller looking back, I already knew that there would be no more tomorrows for Mabel. When I walked out of the library, entranced, the snow on the ground was startling because I'd been lost in an October of long ago. Darkness had already fallen and it felt like I was in another world. I was.

I often found myself wondering about Mabel's and Millicent's acquisitiveness and their propensity for seemingly never throwing out a single scrap of paper. Mabel once explained her paper hoarding by saying, "My good friend Austin Dickinson asked me to save everything, all the papers and magazines entire, in which he was intensely interested. Of course being naturally a miser in personal reminiscences and relics I should have saved them anyway, but with the added incentive of his interest my collection became very valuable in time."[2] Millicent, more practical than her mother but perhaps no less sentimental, felt it was her duty to keep everyone's papers, books and artifacts, even though she increasingly realized—and even discussed with her psychiatrist— that holding on to all these materials was going to be a problem for her. But she never fully acknowledged the reasons she felt bound to her filial obligations or analyzed the enormous and long-standing conflicts that drove her to fulfill her parents' wishes, all the while resenting the impulse she so keenly felt.

Yet reading through their immense archives and paper trail enabled me to view Mabel and Millicent with the gift of a biographer's hindsight. And it's enabled me to see them as real and full human beings— damaged, flawed, complex. Millicent knew that it was difficult for her to leave behind an accurate record of her parents because she saw each of them as imperfect. But Millicent was imperfect, as well: she clearly eradicated certain documents so painful she wished to expunge them from the record of her life—the letter from Arthur Curtiss James in which he revealed the results of his investigation into Joe Thomas, alluded to in her journals but removed from her correspondence, for instance.

Yet there were some documents, anguishing to Millicent, which she chose to leave in plain sight. Despite her own complicated emotions on the subject, Millicent opted not to destroy the undeniable and lengthy record of Mabel and Austin's love. She just didn't want it to be published during her own lifetime.

As I slowly worked my way through their papers, I sometimes found that I had to alter theories I'd had about Mabel and Millicent. In particular, my understanding of their close but burdened relationship evolved. The convoluted push and pull between them, which changed over time, always contained elements of love and respect, disapproval and disappointment. And their relationship remained unresolved. The more I read, the better I could understand its nuances.

As I've researched and written this book, I have often found myself wondering what Mabel and Millicent would have thought of it. Of course, I cannot know for sure. Sometimes I've thought that Mabel would be delighted to be known as someone other than Emily's editor or Austin's lover. I've thought that Millicent, who believed she was simply "an intermediary" between the contents of the camphorwood chest and the world, would approve of the work I have done to present both her and her mother through a large number of their writings. Millicent believed that all of Emily Dickinson's poems and letters should be made public. I hope this philosophy would extend to her belief about her own and her mother's works. I also hope Millicent would realize that biographers are not simply intermediaries of lives; they are also interpreters of them.

Mabel would have wanted her papers and Austin's to be joined, to be in Amherst. They are not. Millicent would have wanted all her family's papers and artifacts to be together and to be on display in one place. They are not, either. Mabel's grave is perhaps 150 yards from Austin's; Mabel and Millicent are buried 396 miles apart. Emily Dickinson lies with her parents and sister in a different cemetery in Amherst, less than a mile away but forever separated from some of those whom she most loved and those who would be most responsible for bringing her work to the world. But their stories are inextricably linked.

Mabel's and David's gravesites can be found just off a dirt road in the woods; Austin and his family are in a clearing down the hill. Their graves are approximately the same distance apart as their homes were. Each time I go to Wildwood, I'm struck by the ways in which their families made statements in death about lives that were so interconnected, both through the symbolism of what is written and depicted on their stones (or in Austin's case, boulder), and through their spatial separation from one another.

More recently, I went to Arlington National Cemetery. Despite the excellent website directions, finding one tombstone amid more than a quarter of a million graves that all look essentially the same is no small task. Eventually, I found Millicent's grave, next to Walter's, within a seemingly unending grid of white stones on a green manicured hillside. So far from the parents with whom she had such difficult relationships, so distant from Amherst, scene of so much tumult that bound her to her past. Typical, I thought, that Millicent's ultimate choice was to situate herself in near anonymity, in such an orderly and predictable cemetery—and in so doing, to differentiate herself from Mabel. I placed the pebble I'd saved from the grounds of Wildwood on top of her grave. I'd like to think she appreciated the gesture.

I've also, of course, been to West Cemetery, to pay homage to Emily Dickinson. It's now become part of the routine I follow on many of my trips to Amherst. Because just as Emily first led me to Mabel and Millicent, Mabel and Millicent have led me back to Emily.

With this book, I've tried to add to the voluminous literature about Emily Dickinson through illuminating the lives of the two women who helped to bring her poetry to the world. Since I first conceptualized this project, I've believed that in understanding Mabel's and Millicent's lives, we come to understand more about how and why they were receptive to the vast undertaking of editing her poetry and letters, and how and why they edited her work as they did. In knowing more about Mabel and Millicent we can better interpret not only Emily Dickinson's poetry but also the image of the poet that they helped to create, curate and promote. It seems ironic that despite their own considerable efforts to make sure that the life and work of Emily Dickinson was not forgotten, their own lives and work have largely been overlooked.

Toward the end of her life, Millicent knew that she was running out of time to write her own biography. "Who will tell my story?" she lamented on a scrap of paper she left behind in the file labeled simply, "notes for autobiography." The moment I read that plaintive question, I knew the answer.

ACKNOWLEDGMENTS

Though I first found out about Mabel Loomis Todd and Millicent Todd Bingham many years ago, I had no thought of writing a book about them. When the idea began percolating I learned that their enormous archives resided at Yale, where my daughter was about to begin college. Kismet, it seemed. But deciding to take on a project like this was still daunting and it took something else.

I am grateful for the time I had leading an alumni event in California in August 2009. A continent away from the usual spaces in which I worked and lived, in a moment of suspended animation, almost, I crystallized the idea for this book, affirmed its importance and made the decision to start doing the writing that was most important to me. Mabel and Millicent have been present in my life ever since.

I've been the beneficiary of many important Dickinson scholars' research. My first debt of gratitude goes to Polly Longsworth, whose influential work on Mabel's and Austin's love letters initially interested me in this topic. Polly later brought me through The Homestead and The Evergreens and showed me things few people get to see. She also, importantly, suggested that the best way to understand this story was to look at multiple generations of Wilder women.

Marta Werner, a remarkably perceptive Dickinson scholar, has been so gracious with her thoughts, insights and collegiality; she is my "go-to" person on all Emily questions and she's welcomed me warmly into this world. Vivian Pollak asked questions that got me thinking in different directions, and her books helped me understand the context and substance of Emily's work.

The writing of many other Dickinson researchers has significantly informed my own. The seminal biography by Richard Sewall, along with the scholarship of Martha Ackmann, Christopher Benfey, Jen Bervin, Jane Eberwein, Judith Farr, Ralph Franklin, Lyndall Gordon, James Guthrie, Alfred Habegger, Ellen Louise Hart, Susan Howe, Virginia Jackson, Thomas Johnson, Jay Leyda, Marietta Messmer, Cristanne Miller, Martha Nell Smith, Barton Levi St. Armand, Helen Vendler, Brenda Wineapple and Cynthia Wolff have been particularly formative.

Historical biography is not possible without the very considerable resources provided by libraries. I've been fortunate to work in some of the finest ones, with some of the most innovative and able archivists and librarians. Special thanks to Jim Gerencser in the Archives and Special Collections at Dickinson College, Lugene Bruno and Angela Todd in the Hunt Institute of Botanical Documentation at Carnegie Mellon University, Kit Fluker of the Manuscripts and Archives division of the New York Public Library and Timothy Engels at the John Hay Library at Brown University. Leslie Morris, curator of Modern Books and Manuscripts at Harvard University's Houghton Library, kindly gave me an afternoon and a private tour of their Dickinson Room; her insights helped shape my understanding of how Harvard acquired its Dickinson holdings.

I spent a lot of time at libraries in Amherst, at Yale, and in my home library at Tufts University. I'm indebted to Susan Brady, Dianne Brown, Chao Chen, Connie Reik, Laurie Sabol and Chris Stauber of the Tisch Library at Tufts, who spent hours answering my questions and helping me locate sources. Ann Marie Ferraro, who bartered on my behalf with her interlibrary loan colleagues at Yale and enabled me to spend more time with the microfilms of Mabel's diaries and journals than was probably permissible by the customs governing such exchanges, deserves and has my special thanks.

Kate Boyle, Cyndi Harbeson and Tevis Kimball in Special Collections at the Jones Library in Amherst are very knowledgeable about all things Dickinson; they have been responsive, thoughtful and creative in their assistance. Mike Kelly, director of Amherst College's Archives and Special Collections, helped me with access and informed me with conversation and his own very astute blog. Jane Wald, executive director of the Emily Dickinson Museum, and Brooke Steinhauser, program director, have been extremely generous with their time and resources. They've brought me through Emily's house when no other people were there so I could close my eyes and imagine scenes that took place in those rooms, so many years ago.

The Manuscripts and Archives division of Yale's Sterling Library has often been my home away from home. I've gotten to know and depend on its incredibly able staff and sincerely thank all with whom I've worked for their interest, help and excellent support over several years: Jessica Becker, Brian Canning, Genevieve Coyle, Dika Goloweiko-Nussberg, Katherine Isham, William Massa, Kristin McDonald, Stephen Ross and Claryn Spies. Special thanks to Christine Weideman, director of Manuscripts and Archives, who arranged for me to speak at Yale; Bill Landis, who was very helpful in copyright sleuthing; Michael Frost, whose extra detective work helped to solve a mystery; Mark Bailey of the Yale Music Library, who converted Millicent's reel-to-reel tapes to digital copies I could listen to; and most especially Judith Schiff, who was responsible for the Bingham/Todd collection coming to Yale in the first place. Judy's memories and stories continue to serve as inspiration for this book. Half a century ago she understood and respected Millicent's sensibility to preserve her family's enormous trove of papers.

I have to put Mimi Dakin of Amherst College's Archives and Special Collections in a paragraph all her own. Mimi, who always apologizes for couching her observations in the phrase "I sense," in fact has more sense and better historical instincts than almost anyone I know. Her knowledge of nineteenth-century Amherst is astounding; her understanding of the Dickinson/Todd relations, profound. Time and again she has gone above and beyond what anyone could possibly expect or even hope for, tracking down sources, procuring permissions, reading drafts of chapters. I am "grateful beyond words," as Mabel would have said, for Mimi's thoughtful perusal of every page of this book.

Other colleagues in the world of Mabel and Millicent have lent both assistance and insight: Marianne Curling of the Amherst Historical Society and Museum, who gave me free rein to roam the museum and find Mabel's artifacts in storage, invited me to speak in Amherst multiple times, to lead "MLT tours of Amherst" and to co-curate an exhibit on "Mabel Loomis Todd in the World"; Dick Aronson of Amherst College, who's been a cheerful cheerleader along the way; Martha Umphrey of Amherst College's Center for Humanistic Inquiry, who invited me to speak there; Sharon Nancy White, who corresponded with me about her pioneering doctoral dissertation on Mabel; Elizabeth Horan of Arizona State University, who is always up for a talk about Mabel and Millicent even though her own work has migrated to other fascinating women; Candace Riddington, whose novel *Rubicon* helped me envision Mabel in new ways; Susan Snively, whose novel *The Heart Has Many Doors* opened up images of Emily Dickinson; and William Luce, whose classic play *The Belle of Amherst* was so inspirational, as was our lengthy conversation.

I spent a wonderful day with Steve Kress, Juanita Roushdy, Sue Schubel and Eric Snyder on Hog Island at the Audubon Camp in 2013. Their interest in and support of my project continued well past that lovely summer afternoon. Steve and Juanita invited me to come back and give the keynote address at the eightieth anniversary of the Hog Island camp in 2016. Staying on the island, tasting the salt on my skin, seeing the towering pine trees and hearing the early morning avian cacophony made me understand viscerally why Mabel and Millicent felt this was one of the most special spots on earth.

Friends and mentors from my days in the Valley remind me of another very special spot for the Todds, for the Dickinsons and for me. Many years ago they encouraged me to look beyond the twentieth-century Pioneer Valley and delve into its past. I especially thank Neal Salisbury, who started me on the historical journey I've continued.

Rick Sewall and Emily McDermott generously allowed me access to their attic and to the wonderful letters, files and unpublished papers of Richard Sewall. It was a biographer's dream come true to sit on the floor, sift through boxes and uncover treasures! Lincoln Brower, Doug Morse, Jean McClure Mudge and the late Hugh Hawkins, each of whom had met Millicent, kindly shared their recollections and offered insights that could only come from those who had looked into her deep and fathomless eyes.

Colleagues at Tufts University encouraged and reinforced me in numerous ways. I'm thankful for former vice-provost Mary Lee's belief in me and in this project and her financial support of it; Beth Knauss in her office made all the logistics work. The old "CMS team"—John Ciampa and Leslie Goldberg—were incredibly helpful in ways that kept my "day job" running smoothly. My former student, Menglan Chen, assisted with research at Harvard. David Brittan, past editor of *Tufts Magazine*, gave me the first opportunity to publish material on Mabel and Millicent. His sage advice and expert editorial instincts guided me well past that initial article.

Ralph Aarons, David Henry Feldman, Jonathan Garlick, Chip Gidney, Sonia Hofkosh, Paul Joseph, Peter Levine, Susan Napier, Diane O'Donoghue, Fernando Ona, Colin Orians, Martha Pott, Donna Qualters, George Scarlett, Annie Soisson and Alan Solomont have all been good friends and good colleagues, each in his or her own way helping me to believe in the importance of doing interdisciplinary work that gets us out of our academic silos. Tony Rudel, friend and colleague, has been quick to read a section of text, offer a contact or share experiences. Nina Gerassi-Navarro and Barbara Grossman have been especially inspirational and influential, as sister twenty-first-century biographers writing about the lives of nineteenth-century women. And very special thanks to Jennifer Burton, amazing colleague and dear friend, who also asked me to dress up and take on the role of Mabel in her film *Half the History*. My understanding of my subject took on new dimensions as I began to experience what it must have been like to wear long skirts and corsets in the summer's heat!

Mark Kramer, my most important writing teacher, offered good advice, good cheer and exceptional conversation over Chinese food in little hole-in-the-wall eateries. I'm also grateful to Gregory Maguire for tea at his kitchen table one day; he urged me not to be beholden to chronology and told me that I was ready to start writing this book.

Through a circuitous path, the extraordinary Gabrielle Burton helped me find the right agent. I'm sad that she didn't get to see this book but will forever be thankful she knew it would be published. My agent, Wendy Strothman, and her colleague Lauren MacLeod, have been founts of wisdom throughout this process. Wendy knew from the start how best to position this story and her impeccable instincts have been spot-on ever since. Anne Hulecki gave me valuable legal advice. John Netzer, general manager of the Concord Bookshop, helped me select W. W. Norton from the group of publishers who were interested in this project; his sterling knowledge of the world of books demonstrated anew why independent bookstores are so important.

My editor, Jill Bialosky, consistently helped steer this book's direction. Her deep interest in Emily Dickinson and her understanding of poetry's cultural roles undoubtedly helped to shape the narrative in significant ways. Drew Weitman cheerfully, competently and quickly assisted me with queries of all kinds and I am grateful for her organization, resourcefulness and responsiveness. The wonderful team at Norton designed, copyedited, checked and referenced this book from start to finish: thank you to Lauren Abbate, Michael Fodera, Jesse Fox, Nina Hnatov, Francine Kass, Sam Mitchell, Susan Sanfrey, Peter Tasca, Michelle Waters and Nancy Wolff. Janet Byrne helped to mold early chapters, and Gail Bambrick aided with intelligent and compassionate editing of later ones.

Other friends and family have been squarely there for me throughout the past several years of this project. Gretchen Dobson, Sandy Schultz Hessler, Elizabeth Henderson Norton, Deborah Robin and Roberta Oster Sachs have been stalwart friends who might not live close by anymore but who are forever close to me in different ways.

I almost don't have words to thank my brothers, Joe and Marty. Joe has been my web guru and marketer extraordinaire; our shared love of history, spending time in archives and the joy of discovering nineteenth-century sources reached new heights during this time in which each of us has been working on a book. Marty, my brother with the heart of a poet, and Missy-Marie Montgomery, my sister-in-law who actually is one, both understood the various layers of this project from its inception to its conclusion and consistently buoyed me with their interest and love.

From the time I was very young, my parents, Vicki and Alan Dobrow, nurtured my love of writing, of history and of books. To this day they delight in telling the story of how, as a newly mobile toddler, I would crawl over to bookshelves, pull myself upright and yank books off the shelf. I know I did this because they showed me from my earliest days that books open up worlds.

My love of books no doubt also came from my grandmother, Minna Levy Dobrow. Well into the final decade of her life, she and I enjoyed many talks about what we were reading and why it was important. I am indebted to her and to my parents for this legacy, as well as the many others they've given me.

And I'm deeply grateful to those with whom I live: my children Mira, Aaron, Jeremy and Jonathan, and my son-in-law Nick Allen, who have endured endless stories of Mabel and Millicent, asked good questions and sustained me with their interest, their teasing and their love. I also thank Nick for his work on this book's frontispiece and Aaron for additional website work. My husband, Larry Vale, read drafts promptly and offered expert editorial suggestions on everything from phrasing to sequencing. He went over and above what any editor would do to look up nineteenth-century word usages, explanations of astronomical phenomena and arcane bits of family history for some of the people who populate this book. He fortified and encouraged me in this endeavor more times and in more ways than I could recount, and for this, and for so much more, has my most profound gratitude and love.

Lincoln, Massachusetts, 2018

NOTES

ABBREVIATIONS

Archives

ACA: Amherst College Archives and Special Collections

BPL: Boston Public Library

DPTP: David Peck Todd Papers (MS 496B), Manuscripts and Archives, Yale University Library

HLHU: Dickinson Family Papers (MS Am 1118.95), Houghton Library, Harvard University

Jones: Emily Dickinson Collection, Jones Library Special Collections, Amherst

MDB: Martha Dickinson Bianchi Papers (MS 2010.046), Brown University Library Special Collections, John Hay Library

MLTP: Mabel Loomis Todd Papers (MS 496C). Manuscripts and Archives, Yale University Library

MTBP: Millicent Todd Bingham Papers (MS 496D), Manuscripts and Archives, Yale University Library

NYPL: Montague-Collier family papers, Manuscripts and Archives Division, The New York Public Library

TBPC: Todd-Bingham Picture Collection (MS 496E), Manuscripts and Archives, Yale University Library

Note: Wherever possible, the series, box and folder number are listed (for example, II, 11–22). Sometimes a range of folders is noted where appropriate (II, 11–22–25). Sometimes a page number is noted after the folder number, if appropriate (II, 11–22, 11). In the MLT collection, diaries and journals are on microfilm and the reel number is cited. Yale, Amherst, Harvard and Brown use different numbering systems for their boxes/folders; these are reflected in the notes. Dates are provided when they existed on the original source; if no date appeared, it is marked as such (n.d.). Some sources had only partial date information available, which is reflected in the notes. Nineteenth- and twentieth-century-style dating of sources are also reflected in the notes.

People

DPT: David Peck Todd
ED: Emily Dickinson
EJL: Eben Jenks Loomis
MAWL: Mary Alden Wilder Loomis
MLT: Mabel Loomis Todd
MT, MTB: Millicent Todd Bingham
WAD: William Austin Dickinson

Books

Ancestors' Brocades: Millicent Todd Bingham, *Ancestors' Brocades: The Literary Debut of Emily Dickinson* (New York: Harper and Brothers, 1945).

Austin and Mabel: Polly Longsworth, *Austin and Mabel: The Amherst Affair and Love Letters of Austin Dickinson and Mabel Loomis Todd* (New York: Farrar, Straus and Giroux, 1984).

Editing: Ralph W. Franklin, *The Editing of Emily Dickinson* (Madison: University of Wisconsin Press, 1967).

Home: Millicent Todd Bingham, *Emily Dickinson's Home* (New York: Harper and Brothers, 1955).

Letters: Mabel Loomis Todd, ed., *Letters of Emily Dickinson* (New York: Harper and Brothers, 1931).

Life: Richard Sewall, *The Life of Emily Dickinson* (Cambridge, MA: Harvard University Press, 1974).

Loaded Guns: Lyndall Gordon, *Lives Like Loaded Guns* (New York: Viking, 2010).

Revelation: Millicent Todd Bingham, *Emily Dickinson: A Revelation* (New York: Harper and Brothers, 1954).

PREFACE

1. Emily Dickinson, "In Vain," in *Poems by Emily Dickinson*, ed. Mabel Loomis Todd and T. W. Higginson (Boston: Roberts Brothers, 1890), 57. [Note: This is a later verse in the poem now known by its first line, "I cannot live with You" (poem 640 in the Thomas Johnson edition).]

2. *Life*, 19, 26.

3. Ibid., 66.

4. See, for example, Brenda Wineapple, *White Heat: The Friendship of Emily Dickinson and Thomas Wentworth Higginson* (New York: Alfred A. Knopf, 2008); Martha Nell Smith, *Rowing in Eden: Rereading Emily Dickinson* (Austin: University of Texas Press, 1992).

INTRODUCTION: ONE FINE DAY IN MAY

1. MLT, "Diary," 19 May 1896, MLTP, III, 41, reel 3.

2. ED to MLT, "Journal," 6 October 1882, MLTP, III, 46, reel 8.

3. MLT, "Journal," 6 October 1882, MLTP, III, 46, reel 8.

4. MLT, "Notes on Emily," 1889, MLTP, VII, 103–266.

5. MLT, "Diary," 2 August 1882, MLTP, III, 41, reel 3.

6. Thomas Wentworth Higginson, in Jay Leyda, *The Years and Hours of Emily Dickinson* (New Haven, CT: Yale University Press, 1960), 475. Note: Actually, Higginson's math was incorrect. Emily Dickinson was fifty-five at the time of her death, not fifty-four.

7. Mrs. John Jameson to Frank Jameson, 23 May 1886, in Leyda, *Years and Hours*, 475–76.

8. MLT to MAWL, 23 May 1886, MLTP, II, 34.

9. Mrs. John Jameson, May 1886, in *Austin and Mabel*, 121.

10. MLT, "Journal," 1 September 1886, MLTP, III, 46, reel 8.

11. MLT, "Diary," 17–18 May 1886, MLTP, III, 41, reel 3.

12. MLT to MAWL and EJL, 16 May 1886, MLTP, II, 30–916.

CHAPTER I: ARRIVING IN AMHERST

1. MAWL to MLT, 1 September 1884.

2. MAWL to MTB, 18 May 1897, MTBP, I, 17–256.

3. MLT, "The Thoreau Family: Two Generations Ago," 1930s, MLTP, V, 76–298.

4. MLT, "Early Memories," n.d., MLTP, VII, 116–452, 2.

5. Ibid., 5.

6. See, for example, Wendy Gamber, *The Boardinghouse in the Nineteenth Century* (Baltimore: Johns Hopkins University Press, 2007).

7. *Austin and Mabel*, 15.

8. MTB, "Reminiscences," 1933, MTBP, II, 46–8, 7.

9. Sharon Nancy White, "Mabel Loomis Todd: Gender, Power and Language in Victorian America" (PhD dissertation, Yale University, 1982).

10. MLT, "Journal," 1 May 1897, MLTP, III, 45, reel 7.

11. MLT, "Early Memories," n.d., MLTP, VII, 116–452, 11–12.

12. MLT to MAWL and EJL, 10 February 1875, MLTP, II, 30–916.

13. MLT to DPT, 1 August 1878, DPTP, I, 12–393.

14. *Austin and Mabel*, 23.

15. MLT, "Journal," 1879, MLTP, III, 46, reel 8.

16. Ibid., 23 March 1873, MLTP, III, 45, reel 7.

17. Ibid., 17 January 1878.

18. MLT to MAWL and EJL, n.d., MLTP, II, 30–916.

19. MLT, "Journal," 15 December 1876, MLTP, III, 45, reel 7.

20. Ibid., 30 November 1877.

21. Ibid., 21 July 1878; DPT to MLT, 9 October 1878; MLT, "Journal," 3 August 1879, MLTP, III, 46, reel 8.

22. MLT, "Journal," 5 March 1879, MLTP, III, 46, reel 8.

23. Stephanie Coontz, *Marriage: A History* (New York: Penguin, 2005).

24. MLT, "Diaries," 25 January 1879, III, 39, reel 1.

25. MLT, "Journal," 5 August 1879, MLTP, III, 45, reel 7.

26. DPT to MLT, 14 April 1927, MLTP, II, 37.

27. MLT, "Millicent's Life," n.d., MLTP, III, 46, reel 8.

28. Ibid.

29. MLT, "Journal," 5 August 1879, MLTP, III, 45, reel 7.

30. DPT to MLT, 31 August 1879, MLTP, II, 1043.

31. DPT, in White, "Mabel Loomis Todd," 106.

32. MLT, "Journal," September 1879, MLTP, III, 45, reel 7.

33. Ibid., 28 September 1879.

34. Ibid., 15 May 1879.

35. MLT, "Millicent's Life," n.d., MLTP, III, 46, reel 8.

36. Ibid., "Millicent's Life," n.d., Part II, 2.

37. MLT, "Diary," February 27, 1880, MLTP, III, 40, reel 2.

38. MLT, "Millicent's Life," n.d., MLTP, III, 46, reel 8.

39. Ibid.

40. MLT, "Journal," 3 March 1881, MLTP, III, 45, reel 7.

41. MLT, "Millicent's Life," n.d., MLTP, III, 46, reel 8.

42. MLT, "Journal," 31 December 1880, MLTP, III, 45, reel 7.

43. MLT, "Millicent's Life," n.d., MLTP, III, 46, reel 8.

44. MLT, "Journal," 12 September 1881, MLTP, III, 46, reel 8.

45. Ibid., 9 July 1881.

46. Ibid., 26 October 1881.

47. MLT, "Diary," 29 September 1881, MLTP, III, 39, reel 1.

48. MLT to MAWL, 2 October 1881; 4 October 1881, MLTP, II, 34.

49. MLT to MAWL, October, 1881.

CHAPTER 2: MEETING AND COURTING THE DICKINSONS

1. MLT, "Diary," 3 October 1881; 12 October 1881; 25 October 1881, MLTP, III, 39, reel 1.

2. See, for example, Vivian Pollak, *Dickinson: The Anxiety of Gender* (Ithaca, NY: Cornell University Press, 1984); Smith, *Rowing in Eden; Loaded Guns.*

3. See, for example, "Susan and Emily Dickinson," The Dickinson Electronic Archives Project, http://archive.emilydickinson.org/susanemilylivesinletters .html; Jean McClure Mudge, "Emily Dickinson and 'Sister Sue,'" *Prairie Schooner* 52, no. 1 (Spring 1978): 90–108.

4. Polly Longsworth, "The 'Latitude of Home': Life in the Homestead and the Evergreens," in *The Dickinsons of Amherst*, ed. Christopher Benfey et al. (Hanover, NH: University Press of New England, 2001), 37.

5. "Obituary of Susan Gilbert Dickinson," *Springfield Republican*, May 13, 1913.

6. MLT, "Journal," 26 October 1881, MLTP, III, 45, reel 7; MLT, "Scurrillous but True," MLTP, VII, 116–456.

7. MLT to MAWL, 2 October 1881; 4 October 1881, MLTP, II, 34.

8. MLT, "Journal," December 1881; 1 January 1882, MLTP, III, 45, reel 7.

9. Ibid., 20 January 1882.

10. Peter Gay, *Education of the Senses: The Bourgeois Experience: Victoria to Freud* (New York: W. W. Norton, 1984), 71–108.

11. White, "Mabel Loomis Todd," 150–62. Note: White and Longsworth interpret Mabel's symbols differently.

12. MLT, "Journal," 2 March 1882, MLTP, III, 45, reel 7.

13. MLT, "Diary," 8 February 1882, MLTP, III, 39, reel 1.

14. Ibid., 18 March 1882; several Dickinson scholars dispute the precise number of poems Emily shared with Sue during her lifetime—see, for example, discrepancies between Franklin (1967, 1998) and Smith (1992); Mike Kelly, "Emily Dickinson and the New York Press," https://consecratedeminence.wordpress .com/2013/07/15/emily-dickinson-and-the-new-york-press/.

15. "Emily Dickinson," http://www.poetryfoundation.org/bio/emily-dickinson.

16. MLT, "Diary," February–March 1882, 18, March 1882, MLTP, III, 39, reel 1.

17. Barton Levi St. Armand, *Emily Dickinson and Her Culture* (New York: Cambridge University Press, 1984), 358–80.

18. *Loaded Guns*; Polly Longsworth (September 2010) has written an extensive critique of Gordon's theory, held in the ACA. In this document, she disputes Gordon's assertion by pointing out that Emily Dickinson's prescription for glycerin was advised for suspected tuberculosis, not epilepsy; that Dickinson cousin Zebina Montague did not die from epilepsy; and that Emily's use of the word "fit" occurs at least thirty times in her writing, but only three times as a noun, and never to mean "a sudden attack."

19. MTB, "Notes on William Austin Dickinson's Diaries," n.d., MLTP, VII, 104–254.

20. Ned Dickinson to MLT, 14 February 1882, ACA (MS 79102), 10–16.

21. Ibid., 2 April 1882.

22. MLT, "Journal," April 1882, MLTP, III, 45, reel 7.

23. Ibid., 2 March 1882.

24. Ibid., 27 March 1882.

25. MLT, "Journal," 10 April 1882, MLTP, III, 45, reel 7.

26. Ibid., 2 March 1882.

27. MLT, "Diary," 28 May 1882, MLTP, III, 29, reel 1.

28. Ned Dickinson to MLT, n.d., ACA (MS 79102), 10–16.

29. MLT, "Diary," 14 June 1882, MLTP, III, 29, reel 1.

30. Ibid., 19 June 1882.

31. Ibid., 25 June 1882.

32. MLT, "Millicent's Life," 30 June 1882, MLTP, III, 46, reel 8.

33. MLT, "Journal," 10 April 1882, MLTP, III, 45, reel 7.

34. MLT, "Diary," 6 September 1882, MLTP, III, 29, reel 1.

35. MLT, "Journal," 15 September 1882, MLTP, III, 45, reel 7.

36. MTB, "Notes on William Austin Dickinson's Diaries," n.d., MLTP, VII, 104–254.

37. "Emily Dickinson," http://www.poetryfoundation.org/bio/emily-dickinson.

38. *Austin and Mabel*, 92.

39. Ibid., 71.

40. WAD, "Diary," 20 June 1882, MLTP, VII, 101–244.

41. MTB, "Notes on William Austin Dickinson's Diaries," n.d., MLTP, VII, 104–254; MLT, "MLT Speaks," n.d., MLTP, VII, 101–242.

42. *Letters*, xvii.

43. MTB, "Notes on William Austin Dickinson's Diaries," n.d., MLTP, VII, 104–254.

44. MLT, "Journal," 15 September 1882, MLTP, III, 45, reel 7.

45. Ibid., 6 October 1882.

46. See https://www.emilydickinsonmuseum.org/later_years; *Loaded Guns*.

47. MLT, "Journal," 6 October 1882, MLTP, III, 45, reel 7.

48. ED to MLT, in MLT, "Journal," 6 October 1882, MLTP, III, 45, reel 7.

49. MLT to WAD, 15 December 1882, MLTP, VII, 98–170.

CHAPTER 3: SOARING LOVE AND SEETHING TENSIONS

1. Joseph A. Conforti, *Imagining New England* (Chapel Hill: University of North Carolina Press, 2001), 3, 192, 220.

2. MTB, "The New England Way," 1949, MTBP, VIII, 157–58.

3. MLT to WAD, 15 October 1882, MLTP, VII, 98–170.

4. MLT, "Millicent's Life," 23 September 1882; 7 November 1882, MLTP, III, 46, reel 8.

5. MLT, "Diary," 7 November 1882; 14 November 1882, MLTP, III, 29, reel 1.

6. Note: In 2004, the next time a Transit of Venus occurred, astronomers at the Lick Observatory found David Todd's 1882 still photos and animated them, http://www.skyandtelescope.com/observing/reanimating-the-1882-transit-of-venus/.

7. MLT, "Journal," 4 November 1882, MLTP, III, 45, reel 7.

8. Ibid., 6 December 1882.

9. Ibid., 14 November 1882.

10. *Austin and Mabel*, 123.

11. WAD and MLT, notes/letters, November 1882, MLTP, VII, 98–170.

12. MLT to DPT, 12 November 1882, MLTP, II, 35–1042.

13. MLT, "Journal," 12 December 1882, MLTP, III, 45, reel 7.

14. WAD to MLT, MLT to WAD, December 1882, MLTP, VII, 98–170.

15. MLT to DPT, 19 December 1882, MLTP, II, 35–1042.

16. MLT to WAD, 6 December 1882; 15 December 1882, MLTP, VII, 98–170.

17. Ibid., 24–31 December 1882.

18. WAD to MLT, 28 December 1882, MLTP, VII, 98–170.

19. MLT to DPT, 19 December 1882, MLTP, II, 35–142.

20. DPT to MLT, 8 December 1882; 14 December 1882, MLTP, II, 35–42.

21. MLT, "Diary," 31 December 1882, MLTP, III, 29, reel 1.

22. MLT to WAD, 6–8 January 1883, MLTP VII, 98–171.

23. MLT, "Journal," 3 February 1883, MLTP, III, 45, reel 7.

24. MLT, "Diary," 8 January 1883, MLTP, III, 29, reel 1; MLT, "Journal," 30 March 1884, MLTP, III, 45, reel 7.

25. MLT, "Journal," 13 November 1883, MLTP, III, 45, reel 7.

26. MLT, "Diary," 11 January 1883, MLTP, III, 29, reel 1.

27. MLT, "Journal," February 1890, MLTP, III, 46, reel 8.

28. Ibid., 27 October 1884.

29. Ibid., 6 January 1885.

30. Ibid., 14 September 1886.

31. MLT to WAD, 20 November 1889, MLTP, VII, 99–203.

32. WAD to MLT, 11 April 1890, MLTP, VII, 96, 131; MLT to WAD, 20 April 1890, MLTP, VII, 99–216.

33. MLT, "Journal," 11 May 1885, MLTP, III, 45, reel 7.

34. Ibid., 3 August 1884.

35. WAD to MLT, n.d., MLTP, VII, 96–131.

36. Ibid., 24 March 1890.

37. MLT, "Journal," 14 September 1886, MLTP, III, 46, reel 8; MLT, "Famous Lovers," n.d., MLTP, VII, 103–270.

38. Coontz, *Marriage*, 187.

39. MLT to WAD, 27 March 1883; 12 May 1883, MLTP, VII, 98–173.

40. MLT, "Journal," 16 September 1883, MLTP, III, 45, reel 7.

41. *Austin and Mabel*, 5.

42. MLT, "Journal," 19 April 1883, MLTP, III, 45, reel 7.

43. Ibid., 16 November 1883.

44. *Ancestors' Brocades*, 219.

45. WAD to MLT, 1884, MLTP, VII, 94–81.

46. MLT, "Diary," 4–5 October 1883, MLTP, III, 29, reel 1; MLT, "Journal," 10 November 1883, MLTP, III, 45, reel 7.

47. *Austin and Mabel*, 121. Note: Longsworth's belief that Mabel and Austin consummated their relationship on December 13 is supported by the symbol in Austin's diary designating sexual intercourse on that date (=), and perhaps also by Mabel's diary entry that she had "a very happy evening" (often her euphemism for having sex) as well as by her mention that she went to "The Pines" that evening. In fact, there was no such named place in Amherst and she never mentioned it again; she might well have written this deliberately in an effort to be ambiguous about her actions that evening in her diary, the more public record of her life. There is no notation of Mabel's symbol for intercourse on the page of her December 13 diary entry. Longsworth's other suggestion, that the "AMUASBTEILN" neologism marked the consummation of Mabel and Austin's relationship, is less clear and perhaps not born out by the extant materials: the scrap with this word on it in Mabel's papers at Yale is dated December 9, not 13; the scrap of paper in the materials from Austin's wallet held at Harvard is not dated.

48. Ibid., 242.

49. MTB, "Reminiscences," 1927, MTBP, II, 46, reel 6.

50. MLT, "Journal," 1 September 1886, MLTP, III, 46, reel 8.

51. MLT to WAD, February 1884, MLTP, VII, 98–174.

52. MLT, "Journal," 5 March 1885, MLTP, III, 46, reel 8.

53. MLT to WAD, 8 October 1884, MLTP, VII 98–174; WAD to MLT, 10 October 1884, MLTP, VII, 94–88.

54. MLT, "Journal," January 1885, MLTP, III, 46, reel 8.

55. Ibid., 10 July 1885.

56. MAWL to MLT, 27 November 1884, MLTP, II, 38–111.

57. MLT, "Journal," 1 June 1885, MLTP, III, 46, reel 8.

58. Ibid., 25 May 1885.

59. WAD to MLT, 5 June 1885, MLTP, VII, 98–189.

60. MLT, "Journal," 9 June 1885, MLTP, III, 46, reel 8.

61. ED to MLT, 31 July 1885, in WAD to MLT, MLTP, VII, 94–96.

62. WAD to MLT, 6 July 1885, MLTP, VII, 94–91; MLT to WAD, 18 July 1885, MLTP, VII, 98–176.

63. MLT, "Journal," 15 December 1885, MLTP, III, 46, reel 8.

64. Ibid., 10 February 1890.

65. MLT to WAD, 28 November 1888, MLTP, VII, 99–197.

66. *Austin and Mabel*, 120.

67. ED, "Lost Joy," in *Poems by Emily Dickinson, Third Series*, ed. Mabel Loomis Todd (Boston: Roberts Brothers, 1896), 52. [Note: This poem is now known by its first line, "I had a daily Bliss" (poem 1057 in the Thomas Johnson edition).]

CHAPTER 4: DICKINSONIAN INSPIRATION: MABEL'S CREATIVE OUTPUT

1. MLT, "Journal," 11 November 1883, MLTP, III, 45, reel 7.

2. MLT, "Preface," in *Poems by Emily Dickinson, Second Series*, ed. Mabel Loomis Todd and Thomas Wentworth Higginson (Boston: Roberts Brothers, 1891), 54.

3. MLT, "Journal," 15 May 1879, MLTP, III, 45, reel 7.

4. MLT, "Diary," 25 January 1890, MLTP, III, 40, reel 2.

5. MLT, *Tripoli the Mysterious* (Cambridge, MA: Small, Maynard, 1912), 43–44.

6. Angela Todd, Carnegie Mellon University, e-mail message to author, October 2, 2012.

7. *Springfield Republican*, August 20, 1895.

8. MTB, "Reminiscences," n.d., MTBP, II, 46–10.

9. MLT "Notes," March 1886, MLTP, VII, 114-118.

10. MTB, "Mabel Loomis Todd's Contributions to the Town of Amherst," 1934, MTBP, VIII, 157–16, 23–24.

11. MLT, "Journal," 27 September 1883, MLTP, III, 45, reel 7.

12. MLT, "Footprints," *New York Independent*, September 27, 1883.

13. MLT, "Journal," 2 February 1886, MLTP, III, 46, reel 8.

14. Ibid., 11 May 1885; 2 February 1886.

15. Ibid., 22 October 1888.

16. Ibid., 13 March 1888

17. *Austin and Mabel*, 294, MLT, "Stars and Gardens," *Home Magazine*, January–September 1900, MLTP, V, 75–185. Note: Historian Polly Longsworth incorrectly suggests that while Mabel had labored on this story a long time, it was never published.

18. MLT, "Journal," 6 August 1900; 25 December 1900, MLTP, III, 47, reel 9.

19. Ibid., 1888.

20. MLT and DPT, "Ascent of Fuji the Peerless," *Century Magazine* XLIV, no. 4 (August 1892), 483–94.

21. MLT, "Diary," 19 August 1897, MLTP, III, 41, reel 3.

22. MLT, "The Eclipse Expedition to Japan," *Nation* 22 (September 1897), 229.

23. MLT to DPT, 22 April 1926; 18 January 1929, MLTP, II, 37–1075–1087.

24. MTB, interview with Sutherland, 1959, MTBP, II, 46, 11–12.

25. *Austin and Mabel*, 27.

CHAPTER 5: LINGERING PURITANISM AND MILLICENT'S SENSIBILITIES

1. MTB, interview with Sutherland, 1959, MTBP, II, 46–11–12, 15.
2. MTB, "Reminiscences," circa 1934, MTBP, II, 46–6; see also Thomas Schlereth, *Victorian America: Transformations in Everyday Life* (New York: HarperPerennial, 1991).
3. MTB, "Autobiographical Notes," n.d., MTBP, II, 476–18.
4. MTB, "Journal," 1896; 1911, MTBP, VII, 130–29.
5. MTB, interview with Sutherland, 1959, MTBP, II, 46–11–12, 143.
6. MTB, "Autobiographical Notes," n.d., MTBP, II, 476–18.
7. Ibid.
8. MTB, "Reminiscences," 1927, MTBP, II, 46–6.
9. Millicent Todd, *Eben Jenks Loomis, 1828–1912* (Amherst, MA: Self-published, 1913), 1.
10. MTB, "Reminiscences," 1927, MTBP, II, 46–6.
11. MT, *Eben Jenks Loomis*, 3.
12. Ibid. 18–20,
13. MTB, "Reminiscences," 1927, MTBP, II, 46–6.
14. MTB, interview with Sutherland, 1959, MTBP, II, 46–11–12.
15. Todd, *Eben Jenks Loomis*, 49.
16. MTB, "Reminiscences," 1963, MTBP, II, 46–6, 9.
17. MTB, interview with Sutherland, 1959, MTBP, II, 46–11–12, 3.
18. MAWL to MTB, 18 May 1897, MTBP, I, 17–256.
19. MTB, "Reminiscences," 1933, MTBP, II, 46–6, 6.
20. MTB, "The New England Way," 1949, MTBP, VIII, 157–58, 1.
21. MTB, "Reminiscences," 1905, MTBP, II, 46–6, 1–8.
22. Ibid.
23. MTB, interview with Sutherland, 1959, MTBP, II, 46–11–12, 4, 5, 12.
24. MTB, "Reminiscences," 1933, MTBP, II, 46–6, 2.
25. Ibid., 4.
26. MTB, "Journal," 12 July 1908, MTBP, VII, 133–46–50.
27. MTB, "Scrapbooks," 1882–1889, MTBP, VII, 147–116.
28. MTB, interview with Sutherland, 1959, MTBP, II, 46–11–12, 146.
29. Millicent Todd, *Mary E. Stearns* (Cambridge, MA: Riverside Press, 1909), v.
30. Heloise E. Hersey, *To Girls: A Budget of Letters* (Boston: Small, Maynard, 1901), 1.
31. MTB, interview with Sutherland, 1959, MTBP, II, 46–11–12, 17.
32. MTB, "Reminiscences," 1963, MTBP, II, 46–6, 8.
33. MTB, "Autobiographical Notes," n.d., MTBP, II, 47–18.
34. MTB, interview with Sutherland, 1959, MTB, II, 46–11–12, 147.
35. Ibid.
36. Ibid.
37. Ibid., 5, 6.

38. MTB, "Reminiscences," 1938, MTBP, II, 46–6, 5, 6.

39. MTB, "Ireland Journal," 1934, MTBP, VII, 130–22–23, 94.

40. MTB, interview with Sutherland, 1959, MTBP, II, 46–11–12, 13, 22.

41. MTB, "Reminiscences," 1938, MTBP, II, 46–6, 3.

42. Ibid., August 2, 1962, 6.

43. Ibid., 1927, 7–10.

44. MTB, interview with Sutherland, 1959, MTBP, II, 46–11–12, 11.

45. MTB, "Reminiscences," 1932, MTBP, II, 46–6, 69.

46. Ibid., 104.

47. Ibid., 1927, 9.

48. Ibid., 1932, 69.

49. Ibid., 1927, 5.

50. Ibid.

CHAPTER 6: EMBRACING EMILY'S POEMS

1. *Austin and Mabel*, 122.

2. Ibid., 117.

3. MLT, "Journal," 11 May 1885, MLTP, III, 46, reel 8.

4. Ibid., 13 March 1888.

5. Ibid., 2 February 1886.

6. Mrs. Sidney Turner, in *Life*, 273.

7. "Obituary of Emily Dickinson," *Springfield Republican*, 18 May 1886.

8. MLT, "Journal," 15 September 1882, MLTP, III, 46, reel 8; *Life*, 353–354, 405, 597; MLT to MAWL, 11 February 1885, MLTP, II; MLT, "Diary," 14 May 1886, MLTP, III, 39, reel 1.

9. MLT, "Emily Dickinson, Poet and Woman," n.d., MLTP, V, 77–306.

10. Virginia Jackson, *Dickinson's Misery: A Theory of Lyric Reading* (Princeton, NJ: Princeton University Press, 2005), 57–58.

11. Jen Bervin, in Marta Werner and Jen Bervin, *Emily Dickinson: The Gorgeous Nothings* (New York: Christine Burgin/New Directions, 2103), 9; Marta Werner, in Mike Kelly et al., *The Networked Recluse: The Connected World of Emily Dickinson* (Amherst, MA: Amherst College Press, 2017), 90.

12. MLT, "Notes on L. Dickinson's Remarks," n.d., MLTP, VII, 101–242.

13. *Life*, 129, 147.

14. MLT, in *Ancestors' Brocades*, 16–17.

15. Mary Lee Hall, in *Life*, 229–30.

16. https://www.emilydickinsonmuseum.org/susan_dickinson; Smith, *Rowing in Eden*.

17. *Ancestors' Brocades*, 18.

18. MLT, "Journal," 30 November 1890, MLTP, III, 46, reel 8.

19. *Life*, 220.

20. *Ancestors' Brocades*, 18.

21. Ibid., 21.

22. Ibid., 19.

23. White, "Mabel Loomis Todd"; MLT, "Journal," 30 November 1890, MLTP, III, 46, reel 8.

24. MLT, in *Ancestors' Brocades*, 18.

25. MLT, "Emily Dickinson's Literary Debut," *Harper's Magazine*, March 1930, 464.

26. *Editing*, 6.

27. MLT, in *Ancestors' Brocades*, 19.

28. *Austin and Mabel*, 296.

29. MLT, in *Ancestors' Brocades*, 31; MLT, "Lecture Notes," n.d., MLTP, IV, 53–15.

30. MLT to WAD, 27 March 1888, MLTP, VII, 98–195.

31. MLT, "Journal," 30 April 1889, MLTP, III, 46, reel 8.

32. Ibid., November 1890.

33. MLT, "Emily Dickinson's Literary Debut," 464.

34. *Ancestors' Brocades*, 19.

35. MLT, "Journal," November 1890, MLTP, III, 46, reel 8.

36. L. A. Dickinson to MLT, 11 September 1888, MLTP, VII, 101–235.

37. MLT, "Journal," November 1890, MLTP, III, 46, reel 8.

38. MLT, "Emily Dickinson's Literary Debut," 465.

39. *Editing*, 7; Ralph W. Franklin, "Editing Emily Dickinson" (PhD dissertation, Northwestern University, 1965).

40. *Ancestors' Brocades*, 18.

41. MLT, "Emily Dickinson's Literary Debut," 465.

42. MLT, in *Ancestors' Brocades*, 34.

43. MLT, "Emily Dickinson's Literary Debut," 465.

44. T. W. Higginson to MLT, 25 November 1889, BPL.

45. MLT, "Journal," November 1890, MLTP, III, 46, reel 8.

46. Ibid.

47. MLT, "Emily Dickinson's Literary Debut," 464.

48. Wineapple, *White Heat*, 13–14.

49. T. W. Higginson, "Emily Dickinson's Letters," *Atlantic Monthly*, October 1891.

50. MLT, "Journal," November 1890, MLTP, III, 46, reel 8.

51. Emily Dickinson, Poem XXXI ("Nature"), in Todd and Higginson, *Poems by Emily Dickinson*, 106. [Note: This poem is now known by its first line, "There's a certain slant of light" (poem 258 in the Thomas Johnson edition).]; *Editing*; see also Susan Howe, *My Emily Dickinson* (Berkeley, CA: North Atlantic Books, 1985); Smith, *Rowing in Eden*.

52. *Ancestors' Brocades*, 38.

53. *Editing*, 25.

54. *Ancestors' Brocades*, 40, http://www.poets.org/poetsorg/text/poetsorg-guide-emily-dickinsons-collected-poems.

55. Smith, *Rowing in Eden*; *Ancestors' Brocades*, 58; http://www.poets.org/poetsorg/text/poetsorg-guide-emily-dickinsons-collected-poems.

56. *Ancestors' Brocades*, 39.

57. *Editing*, 118.

58. *Ancestors' Brocades*, 40.

59. *Editing*, 125.

60. http://www.poets.org/poetsorg/text/poetsorg-guide-emily-dickinsons-collected-poems.

61. John Mulvihill, "Why Dickinson Didn't Title," http://www.english.illinois.edu/maps/poets/a_f/dickinson/mulvihill.htm.

62. MLT, "Journal," November 1890, MLTP, III, 46, reel 8.

63. *Ancestors' Brocades*, 33.

64. Elizabeth Horan, "Mabel Loomis Todd, Martha Dickinson Bianchi and the Spoils of the Dickinson Legacy," in *A Living of Words: American Women in Print Culture*, ed. Susan Albertine (Knoxville: University of Tennessee Press, 1995), 74.

65. Jackson, *Dickinson's Misery*, 17–20.

66. MLT, "Journal," November 1890, MLTP, III, 46, reel 8.

67. *Ancestors' Brocades*, 51.

68. Ibid.

69. Ibid., 53–54.

70. MLT, "Journal," November 1890, MLTP, III, 46, reel 8.

71. MLT, in *Ancestors' Brocades*, 57.

72. MLT, "Journal," November 1890, MLTP, III, 46, reel 8.

73. *Ancestors' Brocades*, 69. Note: It's also likely that in selecting the packaging she did for this volume Mabel was tapping into aesthetic changes of the era; historian Thomas Schlereth suggests that the new abundance of mass-produced goods and advertising about them "altered ideas regarding status and wealth in a society that aspired to be a people of plenty": Schlereth, *Victorian America*, xiii

74. *Ancestors' Brocades*, 61.

75. MLT, "Journal," November 1890, MLTP, III, 46, reel 8.

76. Ibid.

77. *Ancestors' Brocades*, 69.

78. *Editing*, 27.

79. MLT, "Emily Dickinson's Literary Debut," 467.

80. T. W. Higginson to MLT, 15 December 1890, BPL.

81. William Dean Howells, "Review of Emily Dickinson's Poems," *Harper's Monthly Magazine*, January 1891, 320.

82. MLT, "Journal," 30 November 1890, MLTP, III, 46, reel 8.

83. Horan, "Spoils of the Dickinson Legacy," 73.

84. MLT, "Diary," 26 March 1891, MLTP, III, 41, reel 3.

85. MLT, "Lecture Notes," n.d., MLTP, IV, 53–15.

86. Ibid.

87. MLT, "Journal," 9 May 1890, MLTP, III, 46, reel 8.

88. MLT, "Journal," 28 April 1896, MLTP, III, 46, reel 8; 2 May 1902, MLTP, III, 47, reel 9.

89. *Ancestors' Brocades*, 135.

90. Ibid., 127–37.

91. MLT, "Journal," November 1890, MLTP, III, 46, reel 8.

92. MLT to T. W. Higginson, 25 July 1891; T. W. Higginson to MLT, 28 July 1891, BPL.

93. *Ancestors' Brocades*, 177.

94. MLT, "Journal," 16 June 1891, MLTP, III, 46, reel 8.

95. S. G. Dickinson to T. W. Higginson, 23 December 1890, in *Ancestors' Brocades*, 86–87.

96. L. N. Dickinson to T. W. Higginson, 23 December 1890, in *Ancestors' Brocades*, 87–88.

97. MLT, "Journal," 16 June 1891, MLTP, III, 46, reel 8.

98. Horan, "Spoils of the Dickinson Legacy," 73.

99. MLT, "Diary," 1 December 1890, MLTP, III, 41, reel 3.

100. *Letters*, xiv.

101. Ibid., xv.

102. MLT, "Journal," 16 June 1891, MLTP, III, 46, reel 8; *New York Herald*, December 8, 1894.

103. *Ancestors' Brocades*, 193.

104. Ibid., 201.

105. Ibid.

106. MLT, "Diary," 24 May 1892, MLTP, III, 41, reel 3.

107. *Editing*, 85.

108. MLT to E. D. Hardy, 3 December 1894, ACA.

109. https://www.emilydickinsonmuseum.org/letters.

110. *Ancestors' Brocades*, 247.

111. *Revelation*, 1–2.

112. For a good summary of the discussion and theories about the Master letters, as well as their full text, see the Emily Dickinson Museum website: https://www.emilydickinsonmuseum.org/love_life.

113. MLT, "Diary," 1 November 1892, MLTP, III, 41, reel 3.

114. MLT, "The Evolution of Style: Reading Emily Dickinson," n.d., MLTP, V, 78–313. Note: While Mabel did realize that there were poems embedded in some of the letters Emily wrote to others, because she was not in possession of all of Emily's letters—most notably, her letters to Susan Dickinson—she probably did not realize that there might well be other poems that she, herself, had not yet seen.

115. WAD, n.d., ACA; Gardner Fuller, letter to the editor, *Nation*, 23 November 1891, ACA, 12–7.

116. WAD to E. D. Hardy, 26 September 1894; MLT to E. D. Hardy, 28 September 1894, in *Ancestors' Brocades*, 296–99.

117. *Ancestors' Brocades*, 303–304.

118. Ibid., 305.

119. "New Publications," *New York Times*, 25 November 1894, 3, 23; "New Publications," *Boston Herald*, 27 November 1894, 7.

120. *Ancestors' Brocades,*, 211–12.

121. Ibid., 211.

122. Marietta Messmer, *A Vice for Voices: Reading Emily Dickinson's Correspondence* (Amherst: University of Massachusetts Press, 2001), 5.

123. MLT to E. D. Hardy, 3 December 1894, ACA.

124. *Ancestors' Brocades*, 335.

125. Ibid.

126. *Editing*, 114; *Ancestors' Brocades*, 341.

127. "Recent Poetry," *New York Evening Post*, 10 October 1896, 14.

128. *Editing*, 114; *Ancestors' Brocades*, 341.

129. MLT to E. D. Hardy, 7 January 1896, ACA.

130. *Ancestors' Brocades*, 324.

CHAPTER 7: LOSING AUSTIN, FINDING MABEL

1. MLT, "Diary," 4 January 1895, MLTP, III, 39, reel 1.

2. MLT to WAD, 5 January 1895, MLTP, VII, 101–232.

3. MLT, "Diary," 7 January 1895, MLTP, III, 39, reel 1.

4. Ibid., 19 April 1895, MLTP, III, 41, reel 3.

5. Ibid., 1 June 1895.

6. Ibid., 14 July 1895.

7. Ibid., 17 July 1895.

8. Ibid., 19 July 1895.

9. Ibid., 28 July 1895.

10. Ibid., 3 August 1895.

11. MLT to WAD, 10 August 1895, MLTP, VII, 101–232.

12. MLT, "Diary," 11 August 1895, MLTP, III, 41, reel 3.

13. Ibid., 17 August 1895.

14. MTB, "Diary," 16–17 August 1895, MTBP, VII, 132, 42–43.

15. *Ancestors' Brocades*, 331.

16. Ibid., 331–32.

17. MTB, "Reminiscences," 25 August 1962, MTBP, II, 46–8, 9.

18. "Obituary of William Austin Dickinson," *Amherst Record*, cited in Theodore Green, ed., *Essays in Amherst History* (Amherst, MA: Vista Trust, 1978), 152.

19. *Springfield Republican*, 17 August, 1895.

20. MTB, "Diary," 19 August 1895, MTBP, VII, 132–42–43.
21. *Austin and Mabel*, 399–400.
22. MLT, "Journal," 19 August 1895, MLTP, III, 47, reel 9.
23. Ibid.
24. Ibid., 15 November 1895.
25. MTB, "Diary," 17 August 1895, MTBP, VII, 132–42–43.
26. MLT, "Journal," 19 August 1895; 15 November 1895, MLTP, III, 47, reel 9. Note: Perhaps giving further credibility to Mabel's belief that Austin had somehow arranged to have the bicycle sent to her is the fact that in the 1890s, Columbia bicycles were quite expensive, about ninety dollars, which is equivalent to $2,500.50 in 2018, http://www.in2013dollars.com/1895-dollars-in-2018?amount=90.
27. MLT, "Journal," 19 September 1895; MLT, "Diary," 3 December 1895, MLTP, III, 41, reel 3.
28. MLT, "Journal," 20 October 1895, MLTP, III, 47, reel 9.
29. Ibid., 13 March 1896.
30. Ibid., 16 September 1896.
31. Ibid., 13 December 1895.
32. Emily Dickinson, Poem II ("Time and Eternity"), in *Poems, Third Series*, ed. Mabel Loomis Todd (Boston: Roberts Brothers, 1896), 140. [Note: This poem is now known by its first line, "We learn in the Retreating" (poem 1083 in the Thomas Johnson edition).]; MLT, "Journal," 30 January 1896, MLTP, III, 47, reel 9.
33. MLT, "Journal," 28 April 1897, MLTP, III, 47, reel 9.
34. Ibid., 21 October 1895; 15 November 1895; 22 February 1896.
35. Ibid., 31 December 1899.
36. Ibid., 5 August 1903, MLTP, III, 48, reel 9.
37. Ibid., 14 May 1896, MLTP, III, 47, reel 9.
38. Mabel Loomis Todd, *Corona and Coronet* (Boston: Houghton Mifflin, 1898), 9–10.
39. MLT, "Journal," 8 April 1896, MLTP, III, 47, reel 9.
40. Ibid., 12 April 1896.
41. Ibid., 18 May 1896.
42. Ibid., 16 May 1896.
43. Todd, *Corona and Coronet*, 9, 324–25.
44. MLT, "Journal," 3 August 1896, MLTP, III, 47, reel 9.
45. Todd, *Corona and Coronet*, 9, 324–25.
46. MLT, "Journal," 3 October 1896; 12 October 1896, MLTP, III, 47, reel 9.
47. Ibid.
48. *Ancestors' Brocades*, 347.

CHAPTER 8: SUING THE "QUEEN OF AMHERST"

1. *Hartford Courant*, 2 March, 1898; *New York Times*, February 27, 1898.
2. *Hartford Courant*, 2 March, 1898.

3. WAD to MLT, November 1887, MLTP, VII, 102–249.

4. James R. Guthrie, *A Kiss from Thermopylae* (Amherst: University of Massachusetts Press, 2015), 89.

5. MLT, "Diary," 6 October 1896, MLTP, III, 41, reel 3.

6. *Austin and Mabel*, 403.

7. MLT, "Mabel Loomis Todd Speaks," n.d., MLTP, VII, 101–242.

8. MLT, "Diary," 7 February 1896, MLTP, III, 41, reel 3.

9. *Austin and Mabel*, 406.

10. Note: Interestingly, Maggie's testimony was so powerful in its insinuations about Mabel and Austin's relationship—and so upsetting to members of the Dickinson family—that Mattie apparently ripped it out of the materials she kept about the trial. The pages are clearly torn out and missing from the Martha Dickinson Bianchi collection; MDB, 220.

11. *Austin and Mabel*, 414. Note: Longsworth also suggests that Judge Bumpus had at one time evinced more than a professional interest in Mabel, and that his decision to remove himself from her legal team might have occurred for multiple reasons.

12. MLT, "Diary," 3 June 1897, MLTP, III, 41, reel 3.

13. *Ancestors' Brocades*, 351–52.

14. MLT, "Diary," 4 May 1897, MLTP, III, 41, reel 3.

15. Ibid., 23 February 1898.

16. L. N. Dickinson, "Deposition," *Lavinia N. Dickinson v. Mabel Loomis Todd et al.*, The Commonwealth of Massachusetts, Hampshire County Superior Court, 1897.

17. MLT, "Diary," 1 March 1898, MLTP, III, 41, reel 3.

18. *Ancestors' Brocades*, 353.

19. MLT, "Diary," 1 March 1898, MLTP, III, 41, reel 3.

20. MLT, "Cross-examination," *Lavinia N. Dickinson v. Mabel Loomis Todd et al.*, The Commonwealth of Massachusetts, Hampshire County Superior Court, 1897, 29.

21. DPT, "Deposition," *Lavinia N. Dickinson v. Mabel Loomis Todd et al.*, The Commonwealth of Massachusetts, Hampshire County Superior Court, 1897.

22. *Springfield Republican*, 1 March 1898.

23. T. G. Spaulding, "Deposition," *Lavinia N. Dickinson v. Mabel Loomis Todd et al.*, The Commonwealth of Massachusetts, Hampshire County Superior Court, 1897.

24. *Ancestors' Brocades*, 357.

25. MLT, "Diary," 3 March 1898, MLTP, III, 41, reel 3.

26. S. S. Taft, "Transcript," *Lavinia N. Dickinson v. Mabel Loomis Todd et al.*, The Commonwealth of Massachusetts, Hampshire County Superior Court, 1897.

27. *Springfield Republican*, 5 March 1898.

28. *Hartford Courant*, 2 March 1898.

29. Mary A. Jordan, in *Ancestors' Brocades*, 359.

30. *Life*, 150.

31. Horan, "Spoils of the Dickinson Legacy," 77.

32. MLT, "Diary," 15 April 1898, MLTP, III, 41, reel 3.

33. *Ancestors' Brocades*, 365.

34. Massachusetts Reports: Decisions of the Supreme Judicial Court, Volume 172, November 21, 1898.

35. MLT, "Diary," 21 November 1898, MLTP, III, 41, reel 3.

36. MLT, "Mabel Loomis Todd Speaks," n.d., MLTP, VII, 101-242.

37. MLT, "Journal," 31 December 1898, MLTP, III, 47, reel 9.

38. MLT, "MLT Speaks," October 10, 1931, MLTP, VII, 101-242.

39. *Ancestors' Brocades*, 347.

CHAPTER 9: TRAVELING AND TRAVAILS

1. MTB, "Diary," 1 January 1900, MTBP, VII, 133-46.

2. MLT, "Journal," 10 November 1899, MLTP, III, 47, reel 9.

3. MLT, *Tripoli*, 7.

4. MLT, "Journal," 31 December 1900, MLTP, III, 47, reel 9.

5. MTB, "Journal," March 1901, MTBP, VII, 129, 17.

6. MLT, "Diary," August 16, 1904, MLTP, III, 42, reel 4.

7. MLT, *Tripoli*, 7.

8. Millicent Todd Bingham, *Peru: A Land of Contrasts* (Boston: Little, Brown, 1918), 7-8.

9. MTB, "Diary," August 16, 1908, MTBP, VII, 128-11-12.

10. MLT, "Journal," July 22, 1910, MLTP, 43, reel 5.

11. MLT, "Diary," September 20, 1910, MLTP, III, 43, reel 5.

12. Ibid.; MLT, "Journal," November 30, 1912, MLTP, III, 48, reel 9.

13. MLT, "Journal," January 4, 1919, MLTP, III, 48, reel 9.

14. MTB, "The Story of Hog Island," n.d., MTBP, VI, 118, 71-72.

15. MLT, "Journal," November 26, 1911, MLTP, III, 48, reel 9.

16. MLT, "Scurrilous but True," n.d., MLTP, VII, 116-456.

17. MLT, "Diary," May 13, 1913, MLTP, III, 44, reel 6.

18. MTB, interview with Sutherland, 1959, MTBP, II, 46-11-12, 88.

19. MLT, "Scurrilous but True," n.d., MLTP, VII, 116-456.

20. MTB, interview with Sutherland, 1959, MTBP, II, 46-11-12, 42.

21. MTB, "Journal," November 11, 1961, MTBP, VII, 130-27.

22. Ibid., January 17, 1919, MLTP, III, 48, reel 9; MLT, "Scurillous but True," n.d., MLTP, VII, 116-456.

23. MLT, "Diary," April 7, 1913, MLTP, III, 44, reel 6.

24. MTB, "Journal," February 15, 1916, MTBP, VII, 129-15-16.

25. Ibid., February 15, 1914, MTBP, VII, 130-29, 10.

26. Ibid., 50.

27. MTB, interview with Sutherland, 1959, MTBP, II, 46-11-12, 46-47. For more information on this expedition, see Julie Dobrow, "The Star-Crossed Astronomer," *Amherst Magazine*, Summer 2017.

28. Charles J. Hudson, "Tribute to David Peck Todd," 1939, http://articles.adsabs
.harvard.edu//full/1939PA....47..472H/0000472.000.html.

29. MTB, "Journal," May 13, 1917, MTBP, VII, 129–15–16.

30. MTB, "Reminiscences," May 12, 1959, MTBP, II, 44–8.

CHAPTER 10: "SINCERELY, JOE THOMAS"

1. MTB, interview with Sutherland, 1959, MTBP, II, 46–11–12, 49.

2. MTB, "Journal," April 19, 1918, MTBP, VII, 129–17.

3. MT to MLT, April 15, 1918, MTB, VIII, 156–35.

4. Ibid., April 12, 1918.

5. Ibid., May 19, 1918.

6. MT, "World War I Notes," n.d., MTBP, VIII, 173–64.

7. MTB, interview with Sutherland, 1959, MTBP, II, 46–11–12, 149–150.

8. MT to MLT, June 26, 1918, MTBP, VIII, 156–35.

9. MTB, "Diary," July 1918, MTBP, 134, 51–54.

10. MT to MLT, August 5, 1918, MTBP, VIII, 156–35.

11. MTB, "Journal," September 28, 1918, MTBP, VII, 129–17.

12. http://www.census.gov/hhes/socdemo/marriage/data/acs/ElliottetalPAA2012
paper.pdf.

13. MTB, "Journal," September 8, 1918, MTBP, VII, 129–17.

14. MT, "World War I Notes," n.d., MTBP, VIII, 173–64.

15. MLT to MTB, April 24, 1918, MTBP, VIII, 156–35.

16. MTB, "Diary," October 17–18, 1918, MTBP, 134–51–54.

17. Note: Millicent's fear wasn't groundless. By some estimates, there were almost
half a million hospital admissions among British and Dominion troops because
of venereal disease during the First World War. In France, alone, in 1918 there
were over sixty thousand hospital admissions, http://wwicentenary.oucs.ox.ac
.uk/body-and-mind/the-british-army's-fight-against-venereal-disease-in-the
-'heroic-age-of-prostitution'/.

18. MTB, "Journal," October 19, 1918; November 21, 1918, MTBP, VII, 129–17.

19. Ibid., October 9, 1918.

20. Ibid., November 19, 1918, MTBP, VII, 134–51–54.

21. MT to MLT, January 8, 1919, MTBP, VIII, 156–35.

22. MTB, "Journal," December 19, 1918, MTBP, VII, 129–17.

23. U.S. Census, 1920.

24. MTB, "Journal," December 19, 1918, MTBP, VII, 12, 17.

25. MTB, "Diary," July 21, 1919, MTBP, 134–51–54.

26. Ibid.

27. Ibid., August 13, 1919.

28. Ibid.

29. MTB, interview with Sutherland, 1959, MTBP, II, 46–11–12, 56.

30. Ibid.

31. Emily Dickinson, "Bequest," in Todd and Higginson, *Poems by Emily Dickinson* 44. [Note: This poem is now known as "You left me—Sire—two Legacies" (poem 644 in the Thomas Johnson edition).]

32. MT to MLT, March 14, 1920, MTBP, VIII, 156–35.

33. MTB, "Diary," March 1, 1919, MTBP, VII.

34. MTB, "Journal," December 30, 1919, MTBP, VII, 129–17.

CHAPTER II: FIGHTING TO DEFINE EMILY DICKINSON

1. MTB, "Scrapbook," 1920, MTBP, VII, 152–126–127.

2. Ibid.

3. MTB, "Reminiscences," May 24, 1959, MTBP, II, 44–8.

4. MTB, interview with Sutherland, 1959, MTBP, II, 46, 11–12, 77.

5. MTB, "Reminiscences," May 24, 1959, MTBP, II, 44–8.

6. MTB, "Journal," January 11, 1921; February 22, 1921, MTBP, VII, 129–18.

7. MTB, "Reminiscences," 1963, MTBP, II, 44–8, 21.

8. MTB, "Journal," November 25, 1963, MTBP, VII, 130–28.

9. Ibid., March 26, 1924.

10. Ibid., December 31, 1938.

11. MTB, "Ireland Journal," n.d., MTBP, VII, 130–22–23.

12. *Kansas City Star*, September 3, 1921.

13. MTB, interview with Sutherland, 1959, MTBP, II, 4–11–12, 78.

14. Ibid.

15. MLT, "Journal," September 14, 1920, MLTP, III, 48, reel 9.

16. MTB, interview with Sutherland, 1959, MTBP, II, 46–11–12, 78.

17. G. D. Olds to MTB, June 25, 1925, MTBP, VIII, 167–241–242; MTB, interview with Sutherland, 1959, MTBP, II, 46–11–1, 79.

18. MTB, interview with Sutherland, 1959, MTBP, II, 46–11–1, 80.

19. MTB, "Key West in the Summer of 1864," *Florida Historical Quarterly* 43, no. 3 (1965): 262.

20. *Miami Herald*, February 28, 1922.

21. Howard Hilder to MLT, November 16, 1924, MLTP, II, 14–303–313; MLT, "Diary," November 30, 1930, MLTP, III, 48, reel 9.

22. MTB, "Journal," 1919, MTBP, VII, 129–18.

23. Ibid.

24. Elizabeth Horan, "To Market: The Dickinson Copyright Wars," *The Emily Dickinson Journal* (1996): 93.

25. http://www.edickinson.org/resources#selected-posthumous-editions.

26. *Ancestors' Brocades*, 378.

27. Ibid.

28. Ibid.

29. Martha Dickinson Bianchi papers, MDB.

30. Elizabeth Shepley Sergeant, "Review of *The Single Hound*," *New Republic*, August 14, 1915.

31. Harriet Monroe, "Review of *The Single Hound*," *Poetry* V, no. 3 (December 1914).

32. Martha Dickinson Bianchi, *The Life and Letters of Emily Dickinson* (Boston: Houghton Mifflin, 1924).

33. Martha Dickinson Bianchi, *The Single Hound* (Boston: Little, Brown, 1914), vi.

34. *Ancestors' Brocades*, 383.

35. Ibid., 384.

36. Ibid.

37. MTB to Amy Lowell, November 13, 1924, MTBP, II, 3–48.

38. MTB, interview with Sutherland, 1959, MTBP, II, 46–11–12, 103.

39. MLT, "Journal," October 1929, MLTP, III, 48, reel 9.

40. MTB, "Journal," April 5, 1929, MTBP, VII, 131–30–38.

41. *Life*, 234.

42. Bianchi, *Single Hound*.

43. Genevieve Taggard to MLT, June 24, 1929, MLTP, II, 23–671.

44. Mary Woolley to Anne Crowell, November 7, 1929, HI HU.

45. Horan, "Dickinson Copyright Wars," 101.

46. MLT, "Emily Dickinson's Literary Debut," 471.

47. MLT, "Journal," October 1, 1930, MLTP, III, 48, reel 9.

48. *Home*, xii.

CHAPTER 12: BRINGING LOST POEMS TO LIGHT

1. *Home*, xii.

2. MTB, interview with Sutherland, 1959, MTBP, II, 46–11–12, 86.

3. Ibid., 104, 87; MTB, "Reminiscences," 1963, MTBP, II, 44–8, 33.

4. *Home*, xiii.

5. See Helen Vendler, *Dickinson: Selected Poems and Commentaries* (Cambridge, MA: Harvard University Press, 2010).

6. *Home*, xiii–xiv.

7. MTB, interview with Sutherland, 1959, MTBP, II, 46–11–12, 153–154.

8. Ibid.; MTB, "Journal," July 10, 1951, MTBP, VII, 131–30–38.

9. MTB, "Journal," July 10, 1951, MTBP, VII, 131–30–38.

10. *Home*, xv.

11. Louis Untermeyer, "Thoughts after a Centenary," *Saturday Review of Literature*, June 30, 1931.

12. MLT, "Journal," n.d., MLTP, III, 48, reel 9.

13. *Letters*, xxii.

14. MTB, interview with Sutherland, 1959, MTBP, II, 46–11–12, 105.

15. *Letters*, x.

16. MTBP, V, 87–307, version 3. Note: Mabel wrote several versions of the preface. These versions are actually housed with Millicent's papers, within the series on her Emily Dickinson work.

17. Horan, "Dickinson Copyright Wars."

18. MLT, "Journal," November 1, 1930, MLTP, III, 48, reel 9.

19. MLT, "The Story of Emily Dickinson's Letters," 1930, MLTP, V, 82–390.

20. MLT, "Journal," 1930, MLTP, III, 48, reel 9; "Scrapbook, 1926–1930, VI, 89–12.

21. MLT, "Journal," 1931, MLTP, III, 48, reel 9.

22. Martha Dickinson Bianchi to Theodore Frothingham, April 19, 1932, HLHU, 1996, 1.

23. MTB, interview with Sutherland, 1959, MTBP, II, 46–11–12, 105–106.

24. Horan, "Spoils of the Dickinson Legacy," 68.

25. Edna Lou Walton, "Review of *Letters of Emily Dickinson*," *New York Times*, November 22, 1931.

26. Marianne Moore, "Review of *Letters of Emily Dickinson*," *Poetry* 41 (1934): 62–63; Ruth Corrigan, "Emily Dickinson: The Growth of Her Reputation in Periodical Criticism, 1890–1934" (MA thesis, Loyola University, 1934).

27. Morris Schappes, "Errors in Mrs. Bianchi's Edition of Emily Dickinson's Letters," *American Literature* 4, no. 4 (January 1933): 369–84.

28. George Whicher, "Review of *The Letters of Emily Dickinson*," *American Literature* 4, no. 3 (November 1932), 318–22.

29. MLT, "Journal," May 27, 1932, MLTP, III, 48, reel 9.

30. Ibid., October 1, 1932; MLT, "Diary," August 31, 1932, MLTP, III, 45, reel 7.

31. MTB, "Journal," October 17, 1932, MTBP, VII, 131–30–38.

32. Howard Hilder to Arthur Curtiss James, October 1932, MLTP, VII, 112–392.

33. MTB, "Journal," October 17, 1932, MTBP, VII, 131–30–38.

34. ED, Poem VIII in "Time and Eternity" in Todd and Higginson, *Poems by Emily Dickinson, Third Series*, 146. [Note: This poem is now known by its first line, "That Such have died enable Us" (poem 1030 in the Thomas Johnson edition).]

35. MTB, "Scrapbook," 1932, MLTP, VII, 112A–393.

36. Nathan Haskell Dole, November 19, 1932, MLTP, VII, 111–388.

37. MTB, "A Friend of Amherst," *Amherst Record*, November 9, 1932, MLTP, VII, 111–390.

38. MTB, interview with Sutherland, 1959, MTBP, II, 46–11–12, 154.

39. MTB, "Diary," October 17, 1932, MTBP, VII, 137–62–64; MTB, "Reminiscences," May 25, 1959, MTBP, II, 44–8.

40. MTB, "Diary," October 23, 1932, MTBP, VII, 137–62–64.

41. MTB, "Psychiatric Notes," 1942, MTBP, II, 48–36–37; MTB, interview with Sutherland, 1959, MTBP, II, 46–11–12, 135.

42. MTB, "Psychiatric Notes," 1942, MTBP, II, 48–36–37; MTB, interview with Sutherland, 1959, MTBP, II, 46–11–12, 135; MLT to Charles Green, n.d., Jones.

43. MTB, "Reminiscences," July 21, 1933, MTBP, II, 44–8.

44. MTB, interview with Sutherland, 1959, MTBP, II, 46–11–12, 90.

45. MTB, "Journal," October 2, 1933, MTBP, VII, 131–30–38.

46. Ibid.

47. MTB to Arthur Curtiss James, May 13, 1934, MTBP, I, 3–45–46.

48. William Sheehan and Anthony Misch, "Ménage a Trois: David Peck Todd, Mabel Loomis Todd, Austin Dickinson, and the 1882 Transit of Venus," *Journal for the History of Astronomy* 35, no. 2 (2004): 130–31.

49. MTB, "Notes," n.d, MTBP, VII, 167–245.

50. MTB, "Psychiatric Notes," 1943, MTBP, II, 48–36–37; MTB, interview with Sutherland, 1959, MTBP, II, 46–11–12, 93.

51. MTB, interview with Sutherland, 1959, MTBP, II, 46–11–12, 94.

52. MTB, "Psychiatric Notes," October 18, 1938, MTBP, II, 4–36–37.

53. MTB, "Notes," September 10, 1937, MTBP, VII, 167–245.

54. MTB, "Psychiatric Notes," 1938–1952, MTBP, II, 48–36–37.

55. *Home*, xiii.

CHAPTER 13: DEALING WITH "DICKINSONIANA"

1. MTB, "Journal," August 20, 1934, MTBP, VII, 131, 30–38, 109–110.

2. MTB, interview with Sutherland, 1959, MTBP, II, 46–11–12, 100.

3. Ibid., 153–54.

4. MTB, "Journal," August 20, 1934, MTBP, VII, 131–30–38, 110.

5. Ibid., 111.

6. Emily Dickinson, "Love," Poem VII, *Poems, Second Series*, ed. Mabel Loomis Todd and Thomas Wentworth Higginson (Boston: Roberts Brothers, 1891), 97. [Note: This poem is now known as "Wild nights—wild nights!" (poem 249 in the Thomas Johnson edition).]

7. MTB, "Journal," 1934, MTBP, VII, 131–30–38, 110.

8. MTB, interview with Richard Sewall, June 17, 1963, MTBP, II, 46–13, 22.

9. *Ancestors' Brocades*, ii.

10. Sydney McLean, "Review of *Bolts of Melody* and *Ancestors' Brocades*," *American Literature* 17, no. 4 (1946), 363–64; Babette Deutsch, "Miracle and Mystery," *Poetry* 66 no. 5 (1945), 275.

11. MTB, "Journal," February 16, 1945, MTBP, VII, 131–30–38; Robert Hillyer, *New York Times*, February 5, 1945.

12. MTB, interview with Sutherland, 1959, MTBP, II, 46–11–12, 128, 160.

13. MTB, "Reminiscences," May 25, 1959, MTBP, II, 44–8. Note: Millicent's publisher's name changed over the years. Known as Harper & Brothers during most of her life, it became Harper & Row in 1962. She referred to it in different ways in her writings.

14. Horan, "Spoils of the Dickinson Legacy," 88.

15. Ibid., 7; Charles Green, "An Emily Dickinson Bibliography," 1930, 3–5, Jones; Dickinson Bianchi to Herbert Jenkins, May 11, 1930; MDB to Theodore Frothingham, April 19, 1932, HLHU, 1996, 1.

16. Theodore Frothingham to Martha Dickinson Bianchi, May 5, 1933; Horan, "Dickinson Copyright Wars," 7.

17. Theodore Frothingham to Martha Dickinson Bianchi, May 5, 1933; Horan, "Dickinson Copyright Wars," 7.

18. Bingham, Bolts of Melody (New York: Harper and Brothers, 1945), xii, xv.

19. Ibid., xii.

20. Ibid., 301. [Note: This poem is now known as "The sun in reining to the west" (poem 1636 in the Thomas Johnson edition).]

21. Emily Dickinson, Poem 623, Bolts, 317. [Note: This poem is now known as "Soft as the massacre of Suns" (poem 1127 in the Thomas Johnson edition).]

22. Ibid., 317.

23. Ibid., xvii.

24. Ibid., xi.

25. Ibid.

26. Ad for Bolts of Melody, n.d., MTBP, V, 95–418–420.

27. Robert Hillyer, New York Times Book Review, April 15, 1945; Richard Sewall, "Review of Bolts of Melody," New England Quarterly 18, no. 3 (1945): 409; Sydney McLean, "Review of Bolts of Melody and Ancestors' Brocades," American Literature 17, no. 4 (1946): 363; Babette Deutsch, "Miracle and Mystery," Poetry 66, no. 5 (1945): 278.

28. George Whicher, "Review of Bolts of Melody and Ancestors' Brocades," New York Herald Tribune, April 21, 1945.

29. Ibid.

30. MTB, "Journal," April 8, 1945, MTBP, VII, 131, 30 38.

31. "Books," The New Yorker, April 21, 1945.

32. MTB, "Reminiscences," July 28, 1964, MTBP, II, 44–8.

33. Ibid., May 25, 1959.

34. MTB, interview with Sutherland, 1959, MTBP, II, 4–11–12, 118.

35. Ibid., 108.

36. Ibid., 106.

37. Revelation, 2.

38. Christopher Benfey, "Emily Dickinson's Secret Lover," Slate.com, October 9, 2008, http://www.slate.com/articles/arts/culturebox/2008/10/emily_dickinsons _secret_lover.html.

39. T. W. Higginson, in *Revelation*, 12.

40. Ralph W. Franklin, ed., *The Master Letters of Emily Dickinson* (Amherst, MA: Amherst College Press, 1986), 6.

41. Ibid., 15, 22, 32.

42. *Revelation*, 3.

43. Ibid., 10.

44. Ibid., 33–34; This poem appeared in a letter to Judge Lord, Amherst manuscript 755—Emily Dickinson letter to Otis Phillips Lord—asc: 461, 1, ACA. [Note: This poem is now known as "How fleet, how indiscreet an one" (poem 1771 in the Thomas Johnson edition).]

45. See, for example, Howe, *My Emily Dickinson*; Judith Farr, ed., *Emily Dickinson: A Collection of Critical Essays* (Upper Saddle River, NJ: Pearson, 1995)

46. Hillary Kelly, "Review of *Emily Dickinson in Love*, John Evangelist Walsh, *Los Angeles Review of Books*, July 22, 2012.

47. Susan Snively, *The Heart Has Many Doors* (Amherst, MA: White River Press, 2014), x.

48. https://www.emilydickinsonmuseum.org/love_life.

49. Walter M. Merrill, "Review of *Emily Dickinson: A Revelation*," *New England Quarterly* 28, no. 2 (1955): 283.

50. Jay Leyda, "Review of *Emily Dickinson: A Revelation*," *American Literature* 27, no. 3 (1955): 436–37.

51. Founder's Day citation, Dickinson College, May 1, 1952, Dickinson College Manuscripts and Archives; MTB, "Diary," May 1, 1952, MTBP, VII–140, 72.

52. MTB, interview with Sutherland, 1959, MTBP, II, 46–11–12, 164.

53. Ibid., 124.

54. Ibid., 10.

55. MTB, "Diary," July 9, 1952; July 27, 1952; August 2, 1952; September 7, 1952; June 10, 1962, MTBP, VII, 131–38, 140, 72, 141–76

CHAPTER 14: BATTLING OVER EMILY'S PAPERS

1. *Loaded Guns*, 323.

2. Horan, "Dickinson Copyright Wars," 95.

3. *Loaded Guns*, 347.

4. MTB, interview with Sutherland, 1959, MTBP, II, 46–11–12, 108.

5. *Loaded Guns*, 371.

6. R. M. Smith to George Whicher, April 27, 1944; George Whicher to MTB, May 1, 1944, MTBP, V, 83–303.

7. MTB to Gilbert Montague, n.d., NYPL, b1.

8. MTB, interview with Sutherland, 1959, MTBP, II, 46–11–12, 110.

9. Ibid., 109.

10. Confidential memo by Charles W. Cole, February 2, 1947, president's office papers: Charles Cole, 1946–1961, Box 3, ACA.

11. MTB, interview with Sutherland, 1959, MTBP, II, 46–11–12, 109.

12. Archibald MacLeish to MTB, August 3, 1945, MTBP, I–3, 49; MTB, "Journal," November 11, 1961, MTBP, VII, 132–39–40.

13. MTB, interview with Sutherland, 1959, MTBP, II, 46–11–12, 109.

14. *Loaded Guns*, 379.

15. MTB, "Diary," March 19, 1950, MTBP, VII, 131–30–38.

16. MTB, interview with Sutherland, 1959, MTBP, II, 46–11–12, 9.

17. William Jackson to Charles Cole, April 28, 1953, Cole papers, ACA.

18. Charles Cole to MTB, September 14, 1953; Charles Cole to Polly Longsworth, July 17, 1977, Cole papers, ACA.

19. MTB, interview with Sutherland, 1959, MTBP, II, 46–11–12, 112.

20. Ibid., 114.

21. Ibid., 116.

22. MTB, "Diary," October 7, 1950, MTBP, VII, 139–68–71.

23. Ibid.; MTB, interview with Sutherland 1959, MTBP, II, 46–11–12, 116.

24. MTB, "Diary," November 10, 1950, MTBP, VII, 139–68–71.

25. Ibid., December 31, 1950; MTB, interview with Sutherland, 1959, MTBP, II, 46–11–12, 117.

26. MTB, interview with Sutherland, 1959, MTBP, II, 46–11–12, 118, 162.

27. MTB, "Diary," January 20, 1952, MTBP, VII, 140–72–75; MTB, interview with Sutherland, 1959, MTBP, II, 4–11–12, 118, 162; Gilbert Montague to MTB, December 14, 1955; MTB to Gilbert Montague, December 17, 1955, NYPL, b1.

28. MTB, "Diary," October 2, 1952; October 2, 1953, MTBP, VII, 140–72–75.

29. Ibid., January 23, 1952; MTB to Charles Cole, April 22, 1953, ACA; MTB, notes on conversation with Robert Frost, January 18, 1954, MTBP, I, 2–31.

30. MTB, "Diary," January 23, 1953, MTB, VII, 140–72–75.

31. Ibid., November 29, 1952; MTB, interview with Sutherland, 1959, MTBP, II, 46–11–12, 122.

32. MTB, "Notes, 1954–55," n.d., MTBP, V, 93–373.

33. MTB, "Diary," April 2, 1953, MTBP, VII, 140–72–75; MTB interview with Sutherland, 1959, MTBP, II, 46–11–12, 122.

34. MTB, "Diary," October 2, 1953, MTBP, VII, 140–72–75.

35. Charles Cole to MTB, April 28, 1953; MTB to Charles Cole, September 30, 1953, Cole papers, ACA.

36. Charles Cole to MTB, October 9, 1953, ACA.

37. Ibid.; MTB, interview with Sutherland, 1959, MTBP, II, 46–11–12, 124; Agreement between MTB, Harvard University and Harper and Brothers, June 25, 1954, ACA.

38. *Revelation; Home.*

39. Jay Leyda to MTB, September 20,1954, MTBP, V, 84–236–242.

40. John Ciardi to MTB, May 13, 1955, MTBP, I, 2–24; Jay Leyda to MTB, September 20, 1954, MTBP, V, 8, 236–242.

41. MTB, interview with Sutherland, 1959, MTBP, II, 46–11–12, 155.

42. Ibid., 126, 130.

43. MTB to Charles Cole, March 9, 1956, ACA.

44. Charles Cole to MTB, April 18, 1960, ACA.

45. Gilbert Montague to MTB, May 16, 1956, ACA.

46. MTB, interview with Sutherland, 1959, MTBP, II, 46–11–12, 156–57.

47. MTB to Charles Cole, 1957; Charles Cole to MTB, 1957, MTB to Charles Cole, November 12, 1959, ACA; MTB to Archibald MacLeish, December 21, 1959; Archibald MacLeish to MTB, October 30, 1959, MTBP, I, 3–49.

48. Charles Cole to Polly Longsworth, July 17, 1977, Cole papers, ACA.

49. Charles Cole to MTB, May 1959, ACA.

50. Charles Cole to Polly Longsworth, July 17, 1977, Cole papers, ACA.

51. Cole papers, ACA, "Bingham 1960."

52. Author interview with Leslie Morris, Harvard University, February 23, 2015.

53. Calvin Plimpton to Nathan Pusey, December 15, 1966; Nathan Pusey to Calvin Plimpton, January 11, 1967, president's office papers: Calvin Plimpton, 1960–1971, Box 44, ACA; Calvin Plimpton to MTB, April 21, 1967, MTB, I, 7–110–111.

54. MTB to Charles Cole, February 4, 1957, ACA.

55. MTB citation, Amherst College, May 1957, ACA.

56. MTB, "Journal," November 13, 1960, MTBP, VII, 130–77

57. Ibid.

58. MTB, "Diary," November 10, 1950, MTBP, VII, 140–72–75.

CHAPTER 15: SEEKING CLOSURE AND MEANING

1. MTB, "Journal," November 11, 1960, MTBP, VII, 130–27.

2. Gladys McKenzie, "Notes," MTBP, VIII, 175–393.

3. MTB, "Reminiscences," March 8, 1960, MTBP, II, 46–6–101, 3.

4. MTB, "Journal," November 11, 1960, MTBP, VII, 130–27.

5. Author interview with Judith Schiff, 2013; August 13, 2015; MTB, "Journal," November 20, 1963, MTBP, VII, 130 28.

6. MTB, "Notes," April 20, 1967, MTBP, VIII, 174–371.

7. Gladys McKenzie to MTB, June 1968, MTBP, VII, 174–392; James Babb to MTB, October 14, 1960, MTBP, VII, 173–370.

8. MTB, interview with Sutherland, 1959, MTB, II, 46–11–12, 164–65.

9. MTB, "Diary," June 13, 1963, MTBP, VII, 141, 79; July 14, 1966, MTBP, VII, 140–77.

10. MTB, "Reminiscences," May 11, 1959, MTBP, II, 46–6–10.

11. MTB, "The Story of Hog Island," MTBP, VI, 118–71–72.

12. Rachel Carson, *Silent Spring* (New York: Houghton Mifflin, 1962), 69; Rachel Carson to MTB, August 14, 1960, MTBP, I, 2, 23. For additional information about Mabel's and Millicent's environmental impulses and quest to save Hog Island, see Julie Dobrow, "Mabel Loomis Todd: The Civic Impulses and Civic Engagement of an Accidental Activist," *Historical Journal of Massachusetts* 45, no. 2 (June 2017); Julie Dobrow, "Early 20th Century 'Tree Huggers': Mabel Loomis Todd, Millicent Todd Bingham and the Development of Their Conservation Impulses," http://www.juliedobrow.com/hog-island-booklet/.

13. MTB, "Autobiographical Notes," MTBP, II, 47–18.

14. Mabel Loomis Todd, Forest ceremony dedication pamphlet, May 21, 1961, MTBP, VI, 124–153.

15. MTB, "Toward Conservation: An Island Leads the Way," 1937, MTBP, VI, 118–75.

16. MTB, "Reminiscences," May 11, 1959, MTBP, II, 46–6–10.

17. Ibid., March 5, 1960.

18. Ibid., July 28, 1962; August 24, 1962.

19. Richard Sewall, "Preface," in *Austin and Mabel*, xi; Richard Sewall, "Appreciation of Millicent Todd Bingham," n.d,, Newton, MA.

20. MTB, "Reminiscences," May 18, 1959, MTBP, II, 46–6–10.

21. MTB, "Journal," March 24, 1963; MTB, "Reminiscences," August 2, 1962; August 24, 1962, MTBP, II, 46–6–10.

22. MTB, "Diary," December 31, 1966, MTBP, VII, 141–79.

23. MTB to Green Mountain Marble Corporation, June 1953, MTBP, VIII, 159–88.

24. MTB, "Journal," January 1, 1964, MTBP, VII, 130, 28; "Millicent T. Bingham, Dickinson Editor, Dies," *Washington Star*, December 3, 1968.

25. "Millicent Todd Bingham Dies; Authority on Emily Dickinson," *New York Times*, December 3, 1968.

26. MTB will, 1967, Jones.

27. MTB, "Reminiscences," March 13, 1960, MTBP, II, 46–6–10.

CHAPTER 16: UNPACKING THE CAMPHORWOOD CHEST

1. White, "Mabel Loomis Todd," 274; MLT, "Diary," 15 May 1886, MLTP, III, 41, reel 3; Guthrie, *Thermopylae*, 181.

2. MTB to Charles Green, January 28, 1965, Jones.

3. ED to MLT, in MLT, "Journal," 6 October 1882, MLTP, III, 45, reel 7; Carol Fleming to MT, January 26, 1907, MTBP, III, 65–168; Jean Mudge, e-mail to author, May 22, 2015; author interview with Douglass Morse, August 8, 2016.

4. MLT, "Preface" to *Letters*, x.

5. Bianchi, *Single Hound*, xviii; *Revelation*, 9, https://www.emilydickinsonmuseum.org/love_life; Jay Leyda to MTB, September 20, 1954, MTBP, V, 84, 236–242.

6. *Washington Star*, December 3, 1968.

7. MTB, "Journal," July 28, 1964, MTBP, VII, 130–28; Martha Dickinson Bianchi, *Emily Dickinson Face to Face* (Boston: Houghton Mifflin, 1932), 37.

8. Ellen Louise Hart and Martha Nell Smith, eds., *Open Me Carefully: Emily Dickinson's Intimate Letters to Susan Huntington Dickinson* (Ashfield, MA: Paris Press, 1998), xv.

9. Smith, *Rowing to Eden*, 6, 13, 25, 40.

10. *Life*, 228.

11. *Revelation*, 10.

12. Smith, *Rowing to Eden*, 1.

13. MTB, "Journal," July 28, 1964, MTBP, VII, 130–28.

14. Jennifer Schuessler, "Enigmatic Emily Dickinson Revealed Online," *New York Times*, October 23, 2013.

15. *Ancestors' Brocades*, 399.

16. Jeremy Jennings, "Intellectuals and the Myth of Public Decline," in *The Changing Role of the Public Intellectual*, ed. Dolan Cummings (New York: Routledge, 2005), 17.

17. MLT, "Scrapbook," MLTP, VI, 84–19.

18. Gay, *Education of the Senses*, 71, 74, 101.

19. Coontz, *Marriage*; Gay, *Education of the Senses*, 110.

20. Nancy Cott, *The Bonds of Womanhood* (New Haven, CT: Yale University Press, 1977), 204; MLT, "Millicent's Life," 30 June 1882, MLTP, III, 46, reel 8.

21. Brooke Steinhauser, "Public Spirit, Private Ambition: Mabel Loomis Todd and the Women's Era in Amherst MA 1881–1917" (MA thesis, SUNY Onconta, 2011), 4.

22. MTB, interview with Sutherland, 1959, MTBP, II, 46–11–12.

23. Richard Sewall, "Appreciation of Millicent Todd Bingham," n.d., Newton, MA.

24. MTB, "Journal," July 24, 1963, MTBP, VII, 130–28.

25. See, for example, Shea Dunham, Shannon Dermer and Jon Carslon, eds., *Poisonous Parenting: Toxic Relationships between Parents and Their Adult Children* (New York: Routledge, 2011); K. N. Levy et al., "Change in Attachment Patterns and Reflective Function in a Randomized Control Trial of Transference-Focused Psychotherapy for Borderline Personality Disorder," *Journal of Consulting and Clinical Psychology* 74, no. 6 (2006): 1027–40.

26. MTB, "Journal," July 28, 1964, MTBP, VII, 130–28.

27. Adrienne Rich, *Of Woman Born* (New York: W. W. Norton, 1986), 3.

AFTERWORD

1. MLT, *Witchcraft in New England*, Connecticut River Historical Society (Springfield, MA: F. A. Bassette, January 1906), 15.

2. MLT to Charles Green, n.d., Jones.

TEXT CREDITS

ILLUSTRATION CREDITS

Frontispiece
Map of Amherst 1886. Library of Congress, Geography and Map Division, Digital Map Collections. Annotations by Nick Allen.

Page 3
Main Street, Amherst. Amherst College Archives and Special Collections.

Page 10
The "Wilder women." Todd-Bingham Picture Collection (MS 496E). Manuscripts and Archives, Yale University Library.

Page 17
(*Left*) Mabel Loomis Todd. Todd-Bingham Picture Collection (MS 496E). Manuscripts and Archives, Yale University Library.
(*Right*) David Peck Todd. Amherst College Archives and Special Collections.

Page 23
Mabel with baby Millicent. Todd-Bingham Picture Collection (MS 496E). Manuscripts and Archives, Yale University Library.

Page 30

(*Left*) Austin Dickinson. Todd-Bingham Picture Collection (MS 496E). Manuscripts and Archives, Yale University Library.
(*Right*) Susan Huntington Gilbert Dickinson. Courtesy of The Emily Dickinson Museum.

Page 32

(*Top*) The Homestead. Todd-Bingham Picture Collection (MS 496E). Manuscripts and Archives, Yale University Library.
(*Bottom*) The Evergreens. Courtesy of The Jones Library, Inc., Amherst, MA.

Page 39

Ned Dickinson. Amherst College Archives and Special Collections.

Page 54

(*Left*) Mabel Loomis Todd diary. Mabel Loomis Todd Papers (MS496C). Manuscripts and Archives, Yale University Library.
(*Right*) Austin Dickinson diary. Mabel Loomis Todd Papers (MS496C). Manuscripts and Archives, Yale University Library.

Page 71

Neologism. Mabel Loomis Todd Papers (MS496C). Manuscripts and Archives, Yale University Library.

Page 79

"Mabel Loomis Dickinson" signature. Yale University Manuscripts and Archives Digital Images Database.

Page 91

(*Left*) "I had a daily bliss." Amherst College Archives and Special Collections.
(*Right*) "Lost Joy." Amherst College Archives and Special Collections.

Page 95

(*Left*) Eben Jenks Loomis. Todd-Bingham Picture Collection (MS 496E). Manuscripts and Archives, Yale University Library.
(*Right*) Mary Alden Wilder Loomis. Todd-Bingham Picture Collection (MS 496E). Manuscripts and Archives, Yale University Library.

Page 100

Millicent with violin. Todd-Bingham Picture Collection (MS 496E). Manuscripts and Archives, Yale University Library.

Page 112
Daguerreotype of Emily Dickinson. Amherst College Archives and Special Collections.

Page 119
Thomas Wentworth Higginson. Courtesy of the Boston Public Library.

Page 125
Ad for World Typewriter. http://type-writer.org/wp-content/uploads/2014/02/Lippincotts-ephemera003.jpg.

Page 136
Cover of first edition of Poems. Amherst College Archives and Special Collections.

Page 152
(*Left*) Portrait of Dickinson children. Houghton Library, Harvard University.
(*Right*) "Doctored" image of Emily Dickinson. Amherst College Archives and Special Collections.

Page 165
Mabel with bicycle. Amherst College Archives and Special Collections.

Page 174
Portrait of William Austin Dickinson. Mead Art Museum, Amherst College, Bequest of Mrs. Millicent Todd Bingham.

Page 177
The Dell. Todd-Bingham Picture Collection (MS 496E). Manuscripts and Archives, Yale University Library.

Page 182
Lavinia Dickinson. Courtesy of The Jones Library, Inc., Amherst, MA.

Page 194
Mabel at midlife. Todd-Bingham Picture Collection (MS 496E). Manuscripts and Archives, Yale University Library.

Page 195
Millicent at midlife. Yale University Manuscripts and Archives Digital Images Database.

Page 198

(*Top*) Millicent, Mabel and David in Peru, 1907. Todd-Bingham Picture Collection (MS 496E). Manuscripts and Archives, Yale University Library.
(*Bottom*) Ticket to Mabel's talks. Courtesy of the Amherst Historical Society and Museum, Amherst, MA.

Page 203

David and Mabel, 1907. Todd-Bingham Picture Collection (MS 496E). Manuscripts and Archives, Yale University Library.

Page 207

Walter Van Dyke Bingham. Todd-Bingham Picture Collection (MS 496E). Manuscripts and Archives, Yale University Library.

Page 212

Millicent in France, 1918. Todd-Bingham Picture Collection (MS 496E). Manuscripts and Archives, Yale University Library.

Page 214

Possibly Joe C. Thomas. Todd-Bingham Picture Collection (MS 496E). Manuscripts and Archives, Yale University Library.

Page 219

Arthur Curtiss James. Amherst College Archives and Special Collections.

Page 225

Mabel and Millicent at Millicent's wedding. Yale University Manuscripts and Archives Digital Images Database.

Page 227

Walter and Millicent. Todd-Bingham Picture Collection (MS 496E). Manuscripts and Archives, Yale University Library.

Page 231

Balloon launch. Todd-Bingham Picture Collection (MS 496E). Manuscripts and Archives, Yale University Library.

Page 251

Mabel and Millicent on Hog Island. Yale University Manuscripts and Archives Digital Images Database.

Page 253

Martha Dickinson Bianchi. Courtesy of The Emily Dickinson Museum.

Page 259

Mabel Loomis Todd's gravestone. Photo by Lawrence J. Vale.

Page 282

One of Emily's "scraps." Amherst College Archives and Special Collections.

Page 288

(*Left*) Judge Otis Phillips Lord. Amherst College Archives and Special Collections.
(*Right*) A "Master" letter. Amherst College Archives and Special Collections.

Page 324

L. Quincy Mumford and Millicent at the Library of Congress. Todd-Bingham Picture Collection (MS 496E). Manuscripts and Archives, Yale University Library.

Page 330

Rachel Carson and Millicent on Hog Island. Photo courtesy of Friends of Hog Island.

Page 340

Walter and Millicent's gravestones, Arlington National Cemetery. Photo by Lawrence J Vale

Page 346

Emily Dickinson's dress. Photo by Basya Kasinitz, Amherst Historical Society and Museum, Amherst, MA.

Page 360

Mabel toward the end of her life. Yale University Manuscripts and Archives Digital Images Database.

Page 361

Millicent toward the end of her life. Todd-Bingham Picture Collection (MS 496E). Manuscripts and Archives, Yale University Library.

INDEX

Note: Page numbers in *italics* refer to illustrations.